3D Web Development with Three.js and Next.js

Creating end-to-end web applications that contain 3D objects

Andrei Tazetdinov

bpb

www.bpbonline.com

First Edition 2025

Copyright © BPB Publications, India

ISBN: 978-93-65895-063

To View Complete
BPB Publications Catalogue
Scan the QR Code:

www.bpbonline.com

Dedicated to

My beloved daughters:
Alisa
and
Aelita

About the Author

Andrei Tazetdinov is a senior engineer with 19 years of cross-platform development experience, blending applied mathematics with modern web technologies. His journey spans from low-level algorithmic optimization to architecting high-performance React applications, currently shaping mobile monitoring solutions at Dynatrace's Mobile Agent team.

A self-proclaimed React geek, Andrei specializes in bridging mathematical rigor with practical engineering—whether optimizing React Native performance, troubleshooting rendering pipelines, or teaching developers how to measure what matters. His career reflects a constant tension between precision and pragmatism: mathematical foundations applied to real-world systems, theoretical concepts hardened in production environments.

When not instrumenting mobile agents or dissecting virtual DOM implementations, he contributes to open-source projects and mentors developers in performance-conscious UI architecture. This book distills his two decades of lessons into actionable insights for building dimensional web experiences that perform as brilliantly as they impress.

About the Reviewers

❖ **Raunak Burrows** is a full-stack software engineer with 4+ years of experience building performant web applications using React, Next.js, Node.js, and Spring Boot. He has contributed to multiple high-scale products across startups and enterprises, and actively maintains open-source projects including 3D visualizations with Three.js. His technical reviews draw from real-world expertise in modern JavaScript ecosystems and microservice architectures.

❖ **Denny N J** has been actively working in web development since November 2023. He specializes in creating responsive, secure, and user-friendly applications, with a strong focus on API integration and efficient database management using MongoDB and MySQL. Denny is skilled in modern web technologies including React.js, Next.js, Redux, and TypeScript.

Currently, he is a full stack developer at Ametzo Technologies, where he develops and maintains scalable web applications using Next.js with TypeScript on the frontend and Laravel on the backend.

He holds a B.Sc. in mathematics with physics and a certificate in full stack web development. Denny is passionate about solving complex problems through clean, maintainable code and thrives in collaborative, team-oriented environments.

❖ **William Muganwa** is a passionate software developer with a strong background in building scalable and efficient systems. With experience across full-stack development, cloud platforms, and emerging technologies, he enjoys solving complex problems and contributing to impactful projects. Outside of work, he is an active learner, always exploring new tools and frameworks in the tech ecosystem.

Acknowledgement

This book would not have been possible without the love, patience, and relentless inspiration from a few incredible people.

First, my tiny but mighty cheerleaders—my daughters. Alisa, my fearless 3-year-old, reminded me every day what true strength looks like, and Aelita, my speedy 6-month-old, taught me the art of efficiency (because when you have a baby, quick becomes your default speed).

To BPB Publications—thank you for believing in this project and giving me the space to explore such a vast field without rushing. Your support made all the difference.

And finally, to every reader who picks up this book, thank you for trusting me to guide you through this journey. Let us keep learning, one page at a time.

Preface

This book unlocks the full potential of modern web development by combining stunning 3D graphics with high-performance rendering. This book is for developers ready to transform ordinary websites into extraordinary, interactive 3D experiences, whether you're creating games, data visualizations, product showcases, or experimental web art.

Three.js brings the power of WebGL to the web browser, while Next.js provides a robust framework for fast, scalable applications. Together, they open up a world where 3D is no longer confined to native apps or game engines, it is accessible right in the browser, with all the flexibility of the web.

What you hold is not just a technical manual. It is a bridge between two paradigms: the document-centric web we know and the experiential web we are building. The examples within aren't mere tutorials, but provocations, each demonstrating how 3D, when used thoughtfully, solves real problems rather than creating flashy distractions.

By the end, you will have the skills to build captivating 3D web applications that engage users in new ways. Whether you're a front-end developer expanding into 3D or a creative coder experimenting with the web as a canvas, this book will help you bring your ideas to life, one vertex at a time.

This book unfolds across 24 chapters as a complete odyssey through modern 3D web development. We begin by establishing the conceptual foundations of spatial interfaces, examining how depth, light, and motion fundamentally alter user engagement. The journey then progresses through the technical architecture of Three.js, revealing how abstract mathematical concepts transform into living digital environments.

We will construct bridges between 3D visualization and production-grade web development. Here we explore the nuanced marriage of Three.js with Next.js rendering pipeline, demonstrating how to maintain immersive experiences while satisfying real-world requirements like performance and maintainability.

Chapter 1: Industrial Application Evolution - We will explore the evolution and future prospects of industrial and multipurpose applications powered by the combination of Three.js and Next.js. Explore the transformative impact these technologies have had on various industries and uncover the potential for further innovation. Discover how the integration of Three.js and Next.js has paved the way for immersive visualization, interactive dashboards, and cutting-edge solutions that revolutionize industrial processes.

Chapter 2: Capabilities of Web Development for Industrial and Multi-purpose - We will explore the vast capabilities of web development for industrial and multi-purpose applications. Discover how web technologies, combined with the power of Three.js and Next.js, can enable transformative solutions for industries. Explore the potential for creating immersive experiences, real-time data visualization, seamless integrations, and scalable applications that drive efficiency and innovation across various sectors.

Chapter 3: Introduction to Tools - We will get acquainted with the essential tools that will be used throughout the book to build powerful industrial and multi-purpose applications. Explore the capabilities and features of tools such as Three.js, Next.js, AWS Amplify, Storybook, and Tailwind, and learn how they synergistically contribute to the development process. Gain a solid foundation in using these tools effectively and understand their role in creating robust and scalable web applications.

Chapter 4: Setting up All Tools for Quickstart of Development - In this chapter, we will learn how to set up all the necessary tools required for a quick and efficient start to your development process. We will guide you through the installation and configuration of the essential tools, including Three.js, Next.js, AWS Amplify, Storybook, and Tailwind.

Chapter 5: Introduction to 3D Development - In this chapter, we will be introduced to the exciting world of 3D web development. Discover the fundamentals of creating immersive and interactive 3D experiences using technologies like Three.js, WebGL, and other essential tools. Gain insights into the concepts, techniques, and best practices that form the foundation of 3D web development.

Chapter 6: Getting Started with Three.js - In this chapter, we will embark on our journey into the world of Three.js, a powerful JavaScript library for creating interactive 3D graphics in the browser. Gain a solid foundation in using Three.js and learn the essential concepts and techniques required to kickstart your development process. From setting up a basic Three.js project to rendering objects, applying transformations, and handling user interactions, this chapter will equip you with the fundamental knowledge needed to start building captivating 3D web applications.

Chapter 7: Geometries and Materials - In this chapter, we will delve into the fascinating world of geometries and materials in 3D web development. Explore the various types of geometries available in Three.js and learn how to create and manipulate 3D objects using these geometries. Discover the power of materials to define the appearance, textures, and properties of objects in your 3D scenes.

Chapter 8: Lights and Shadows - In this chapter, we will delve into the fascinating world of lighting and shadows in Three.js. Lighting plays a crucial role in creating realistic and visually captivating 3D scenes, while shadows add depth and dimension to objects. You will learn about various lighting techniques, light source types, and shadow generation methods available in Three.js.

Chapter 9: Camera and Perspective - In this chapter, you will explore the crucial concepts of camera and perspective in Three.js, which play a vital role in defining the viewpoint and rendering of 3D scenes. You will learn about different types of cameras available in Three.js, including perspective and orthographic cameras, and understand how to position and manipulate them within your scenes. Gain insights into the perspective projection, field of view, aspect ratio, and other camera-related properties that influence the visual perception of your 3D web applications.

Chapter 10: Textures and Mapping - In this chapter, we will dive into the world of textures and mapping in Three.js, discovering how to add depth, realism, and visual details to your 3D objects. Textures play a crucial role in enhancing the appearance of materials and adding surface details, while mapping techniques allow you to precisely position and wrap textures onto your geometries. You will explore various types of textures, such as color maps, normal maps, and specular maps, and learn how to apply them to your objects using different mapping methods.

Chapter 11: Interaction and User Input - In this chapter, we will explore the exciting realm of interaction and user input in Three.js, enabling users to engage with and manipulate 3D scenes in their web applications. You will learn how to handle mouse and touch events, implement object picking and selection, and enable user-driven interactions such as rotation, scaling, and translation of objects. Discover how to create interactive controls, implement custom user interfaces, and incorporate user input for enhanced user experiences.

Chapter 12: Animation and Particle Systems - In this chapter, we will dive into the dynamic world of animation and particle systems in Three.js, bringing your 3D scenes to life with movement, motion, and visual effects. Animation allows you to create captivating and fluid motions for objects, while particle systems enable the generation and simulation of dynamic particles such as smoke, fire, and rain. You will learn how to animate objects, control their transformations over time, and implement particle systems with various behaviors and properties.

Chapter 13: Introduction to Next.js and Three.js Integration - In this chapter, we will embark on a journey into integrating Next.js and Three.js, harnessing the power of both frameworks to create seamless and interactive web applications. You will explore the fundamental concepts of Next.js, a popular React framework for server-side rendering and building modern web applications, and learn how to combine it with Three.js, a powerful JavaScript library for creating 3D graphics in the browser. Gain insights into the benefits of integrating Next.js and Three.js, and discover techniques for setting up a development environment, handling routing, and managing state transitions.

Chapter 14: Next.js Fundamentals - In this chapter, we will delve into the fundamental concepts and features of Next.js, a powerful React framework for building modern web applications. You will gain a solid understanding of Next.js architecture, routing mechanisms, data fetching capabilities, and server-side rendering. Discover how Next.js simplifies the development process by providing built-in tools and conventions, allowing you to focus on creating robust and scalable applications.

Chapter 15: Data Management and State in Next.js - In this chapter, we will explore the crucial aspects of data management and state in NextJS applications that integrate ThreeJS. You will learn how to efficiently handle and organize data within your NextJS projects, including fetching and manipulating data from various sources. Additionally, you will discover effective strategies for managing application state, enabling seamless communication and synchronization between NextJS and ThreeJS components

Chapter 16: User Interactions and Controls - In this chapter, we will explore the exciting realm of user interactions and controls within NextJS applications integrated with ThreeJS. We will learn how to create immersive and interactive user experiences by implementing various input mechanisms and control methods. Discover techniques for capturing user input, handling events, and integrating user controls, such as mouse, keyboard, touch, or even device motion. Gain insights into incorporating user interactions seamlessly between NextJS and ThreeJS components, enabling users to navigate, manipulate objects, and interact with the 3D environment. By the end of this chapter, you will be equipped with the knowledge and skills to create engaging and responsive user interactions within your NextJS and ThreeJS applications.

Chapter 17: Optimization and Performance Considerations - In this chapter, we will explore essential techniques and strategies for optimizing and improving the performance of ThreeJS integration within NextJS applications. We will learn how to address common challenges related to rendering efficiency, memory management, and overall performance optimization. Discover best practices for optimizing loading times, reducing unnecessary computations, and enhancing the overall user experience.

Chapter 18: Introduction to AWS Amplify - In this chapter, we will be introduced to AWS Amplify, a powerful cloud development platform that provides a seamless experience for hosting, authentication, and data storage in your NextJS and ThreeJS applications. We will learn about the key features and benefits of AWS Amplify and how it can accelerate your development workflow. Explore the setup and configuration process of Amplify within your project and understand the core concepts, including authentication, storage, and serverless functions.

Chapter 19: Host Web Applications with AWS Amplify - In this chapter, we will delve into the world of hosting web applications using AWS Amplify, a comprehensive cloud development platform. We will learn how to leverage the hosting capabilities of AWS Amplify to deploy and manage your NextJS and ThreeJS applications with ease. Explore different deployment options and configurations, including static site hosting, serverless functions, and **content delivery network (CDN)** integration. Gain insights into managing custom domains, SSL certificates, and configuring advanced routing and redirects.

Chapter 20: User Authentication with AWS Amplify - In this chapter, we will explore the powerful authentication and authorization capabilities offered by AWS Amplify. We will learn how to implement user authentication and manage user access within your NextJS and ThreeJS applications using AWS Amplify's authentication services. Discover different authentication methods, including username/password, social sign-in, and federated identity providers. Dive into user management features, such as user registration, password reset, and user profile customization. Gain insights into implementing fine-grained authorization controls to secure your application's resources.

Chapter 21: Data Storage and Management with AWS Amplify - In this chapter, we will explore the robust data storage and management capabilities offered by AWS Amplify. We will learn how to leverage AWS Amplify to store, manage, and access data in your NextJS and ThreeJS applications. Discover different data storage options, including NoSQL databases and object storage. Dive into the setup and configuration of data storage services using AWS Amplify, such as Amazon DynamoDB and Amazon S3. Explore how to perform (create, read, update, delete) CRUD operations on data, implement data relationships, and handle complex queries.

Chapter 22: Real-time Functionality with AWS Amplify - In this chapter, we will explore the powerful real-time functionality offered by AWS Amplify. We will learn how to leverage real-time updates and subscriptions to create dynamic and interactive experiences in your NextJS and ThreeJS applications. Dive into AWS Amplify's real-time features, including AWS AppSync and GraphQL subscriptions, and understand how they enable real-time data synchronization and bidirectional communication. Discover how to implement real-time functionality for collaborative applications and real-time notifications.

Chapter 23: Create the UI Design System with Storybook - In this chapter, we will learn how to create a robust UI design system using Storybook in your NextJS and ThreeJS applications. Storybook is a powerful tool that enables you to develop, document, and test UI components in isolation. Discover the benefits of using a design system and how Storybook can streamline your UI development process. Learn how to set up Storybook in your project, configure various add-ons, and organize your UI components. Dive into creating reusable and modular UI components, documenting their usage, and visually testing their behavior.

Chapter 24: Final Requirement and Recommendations - In this final chapter, we will bring together all the tools and concepts covered throughout the book to create a comprehensive industrial and multipurpose application using ThreeJS and NextJS. We will conclude the topic of how to integrate ThreeJS scenes seamlessly into your NextJS application, leverage AWS Amplify for hosting, authentication, and data storage, and incorporate the UI design system developed with Storybook

Code Bundle and Coloured Images

Please follow the link to download the
Code Bundle and the *Coloured Images* of the book:

https://rebrand.ly/8c572e

The code bundle for the book is also hosted on GitHub at
https://github.com/bpbpublications/3D-Web-Development-with-Three.js-and-Next.js.
In case there's an update to the code, it will be updated on the existing GitHub repository.

We have code bundles from our rich catalogue of books and videos available at
https://github.com/bpbpublications. Check them out!

Errata

We take immense pride in our work at BPB Publications and follow best practices to ensure the accuracy of our content to provide with an indulging reading experience to our subscribers. Our readers are our mirrors, and we use their inputs to reflect and improve upon human errors, if any, that may have occurred during the publishing processes involved. To let us maintain the quality and help us reach out to any readers who might be having difficulties due to any unforeseen errors, please write to us at:

errata@bpbonline.com

Your support, suggestions and feedbacks are highly appreciated by the BPB Publications' Family.

Did you know that BPB offers eBook versions of every book published, with PDF and ePub files available? You can upgrade to the eBook version at www.bpbonline. com and as a print book customer, you are entitled to a discount on the eBook copy. Get in touch with us at :

business@bpbonline.com for more details.

At www.bpbonline.com, you can also read a collection of free technical articles, sign up for a range of free newsletters, and receive exclusive discounts and offers on BPB books and eBooks.

Piracy

If you come across any illegal copies of our works in any form on the internet, we would be grateful if you would provide us with the location address or website name. Please contact us at business@bpbonline.com with a link to the material.

If you are interested in becoming an author

If there is a topic that you have expertise in, and you are interested in either writing or contributing to a book, please visit www.bpbonline.com. We have worked with thousands of developers and tech professionals, just like you, to help them share their insights with the global tech community. You can make a general application, apply for a specific hot topic that we are recruiting an author for, or submit your own idea.

Reviews

Please leave a review. Once you have read and used this book, why not leave a review on the site that you purchased it from? Potential readers can then see and use your unbiased opinion to make purchase decisions. We at BPB can understand what you think about our products, and our authors can see your feedback on their book. Thank you!

For more information about BPB, please visit www.bpbonline.com.

Join our Discord space

Join our Discord workspace for latest updates, offers, tech happenings around the world, new releases, and sessions with the authors:

https://discord.bpbonline.com

Table of Contents

CHAPTER 1
Industrial Application Evolution

Introduction

In this chapter, we embark on a journey into the world of industrial applications and explore their significance in diverse sectors. We will explore the challenges industries face and how technology plays a crucial role in overcoming them. We will provide a comprehensive overview of industrial applications, focusing on their definition, scope, and relevance in various sectors. We will emphasize how the combination of Three.js and Next.js opens up new possibilities for creating immersive 3D visualizations, enabling advanced simulations and efficient prototyping. Throughout this chapter, we aim to ignite curiosity and inspire creativity by utilizing these powerful frameworks to address industrial needs and drive innovation.

Structure

The chapter covers the following topics:

- Introduction to industrial applications
- Evolution of Three.js and Next.js
- Industrial visualization
- Real-world use cases with Three.js

Objectives

After reading this chapter, you will learn the critical role of industrial applications and the challenges they address in various sectors, explore the historical development of Three.js and Next.js, and get into real-world examples that showcase the practicality of Three.js in industrial contexts.

Introduction to industrial applications

Industrial applications encompass various solutions and techniques specifically designed to revolutionize and streamline operations within diverse industrial sectors. By harnessing the power of technology, software, and advanced systems, these applications aim to bring about substantial improvements in productivity, efficiency, safety, and decision-making processes.

One of the primary objectives of industrial applications is to optimize various industrial processes. This involves the integration of cutting-edge technologies, such as **virtual reality (VR)** (as seen in *Figure 1.1)*, energy management systems, the **Internet of Things (IoT)**, environmental monitoring, and many other fields, to create smart and interconnected systems. These interconnected systems enable seamless communication and data exchange between different components, leading to enhanced coordination and synchronized workflows.

Figure 1.1: Features of virtual reality

Similarly, the energy sector has witnessed significant advancements through industrial applications. Using smart grids, energy management systems, and predictive analytics has led to more efficient energy distribution, reduced wastage, and better utilization of resources. As a result, energy-intensive industries can optimize their consumption patterns and become more environmentally sustainable.

Moreover, industrial applications play a vital role in revolutionizing the healthcare sector. Medical imaging technologies (*Figure 1.2*), such as **magnetic resonance imaging (MRI)** and **computed tomography (CT)** scanners, provide accurate and detailed visualizations, enabling precise diagnoses and better treatment planning. Additionally, VR and **augmented reality** (**AR**) are transforming medical training by offering realistic simulations and enhancing the skills of healthcare professionals.

Figure 1.2: Medical imaging technologies

Beyond these examples, industrial applications extend their influence to various other domains, including transportation, construction, and logistics. For instance, smart transportation systems leverage real-time data and connectivity to optimize traffic flow, enhance public transportation, and reduce congestion. In construction, **Building Information Modeling** (**BIM**) enables efficient planning, design, and construction of complex structures.

Overall, the adoption of industrial applications continues to proliferate, driven by the pursuit of enhanced performance, safety, and sustainability. By leveraging technological advancements, industries can overcome complex challenges, make data-driven decisions, and navigate a rapidly evolving business landscape successfully. As industrial applications continue to evolve, they hold the potential to reshape industries and contribute to a more efficient, interconnected, and innovative world.

Evolution of Three.js and Next.js

In the ever-evolving landscape of web development and 3D graphics, certain technologies stand as a testament to the remarkable journey of innovation. This section embarks on a captivating exploration of the evolutionary trajectories of Thee.js and Next.js, two frameworks that have played instrumental roles in shaping the present-day fusion of interactive web experiences and immersive 3D visuals.

3D graphics web development origins

Three.js is a popular and powerful JavaScript library used for creating 3D graphics and animations in web applications. It was first released in April 2010 by *Ricardo Cabello,* also known as *Mr. Doob,* and has since become one of the leading frameworks for 3D web development. Let us delve into the evolution of Three.js and explore its journey from its inception to its current state.

Three.js was conceived as a lightweight and intuitive library for developers to work with **Web Graphics Library** (**WebGL**) (*Figure 1.3*), a web standard for rendering 3D graphics in browsers. WebGL, itself, was relatively new at the time, and its raw API was complex and difficult to use directly. Three.js aimed to abstract away the complexity of WebGL and provide developers with a higher-level, more user-friendly interface for working with 3D graphics.

Figure 1.3: WebGL logo

WebGL is a low-level API based on the **Open Graphics Library** (**OpenGL**) Embedded Systems, specifically designed for rendering 2D and 3D graphics within web browsers. While WebGL provided the capability to create impressive 3D graphics on the web, it was challenging to use directly due to its low-level nature. WebGL requires developers to manage low-level graphics primitives, shaders, and other intricacies, making it difficult for newcomers and web developers without extensive 3D graphics experience.

The origins of WebGL can be traced to an experimental project called *Canvas 3D* initiated by *Vladimir Vukicevic* at Mozilla Corporation in 2006. The project aimed to bring hardware-accelerated 3D graphics to web browsers using the HTML5 canvas element. In 2009, the *Khronos Group*, an industry consortium responsible for developing open standards for graphics and multimedia, formed the WebGL Working Group. Major technology companies like Mozilla, Google, Apple, and Opera were actively involved in this effort. On March 3rd, 2010, the WebGL Working Group released the first public WebGL specifications. This allowed web developers to access low-level graphics capabilities directly from JavaScript, enabling them to create hardware-accelerated 3D graphics in web browsers without plugins. In 2011, several browsers started to implement WebGL support. Mozilla Firefox and Google Chrome were among the first to offer stable API implementations. Other browsers, including Safari and Internet Explorer, followed with their implementations over time. WebGL quickly gained popularity and widespread adoption within the web development community. Developers started using it to create impressive 3D visualizations, interactive games, and virtual experiences directly within web browsers.

WebGL quickly gained popularity and widespread adoption within the web development community. Developers started using it to create impressive 3D visualizations, interactive games, and virtual experiences directly within web browsers. While WebGL offered powerful capabilities, it also introduced some security concerns. Due to its direct access to hardware, potential vulnerabilities could be exploited for malicious purposes. As a result, browser vendors worked on addressing these issues to ensure safe and secure implementation.

Recognizing the need to abstract away the complexities of WebGL and make 3D graphics more accessible to web developers, *Ricardo Cabello* (*Mr. Doob*) started the development of Three.js (*Figure 1.4*) in April 2010. The primary objective was to create a higher-level, intuitive library that could serve as a bridge between WebGL and developers, enabling them to work with 3D graphics without getting lost in the intricacies of the raw API.

Figure 1.4: *Three.js logo*

In its early days, Three.js aimed to provide a simple API for creating 3D scenes, managing geometries, materials, lights, cameras, and rendering. The library's design principles emphasized ease of use and quick prototyping. Developers could focus on creating compelling 3D content without worrying about the underlying WebGL code. As Three.js evolved, multiple versions were released, each introducing new features, improvements, and bug fixes. The development team and the active community of contributors constantly refined the library based on user feedback and emerging web technologies.

Rise of the frontend engineering

As web technologies advanced, web applications began to emerge, allowing users to interact with web-based software and services directly through their browsers. This marked a shift towards more dynamic and interactive web experiences. The capabilities of web browsers improved significantly, leading to the introduction of **Cascading Style Sheets (CSS)** for styling and JavaScript for interactivity, enabling developers to create more dynamic and sophisticated user interfaces.

In 1995, *Brendan Eich* developed JavaScript (originally named LiveScript) for the Netscape Navigator (*Figure 1.5*) web browser. JavaScript provided a way to add interactivity and dynamic content to web pages, significantly enhancing the user experience. To capitalize on the popularity of Java at that time, Netscape renamed the language LiveScript to JavaScript. Despite the name, JavaScript and Java are two different programming languages with distinct purposes.

In November 1996, Netscape submitted JavaScript to the **European Computer Manufacturers Association** (**ECMA**) International, a standards organization, to create a standardized version of the language. This led to the development of **ECMAScript**, with the first edition (ECMAScript 1) published in June 1997.

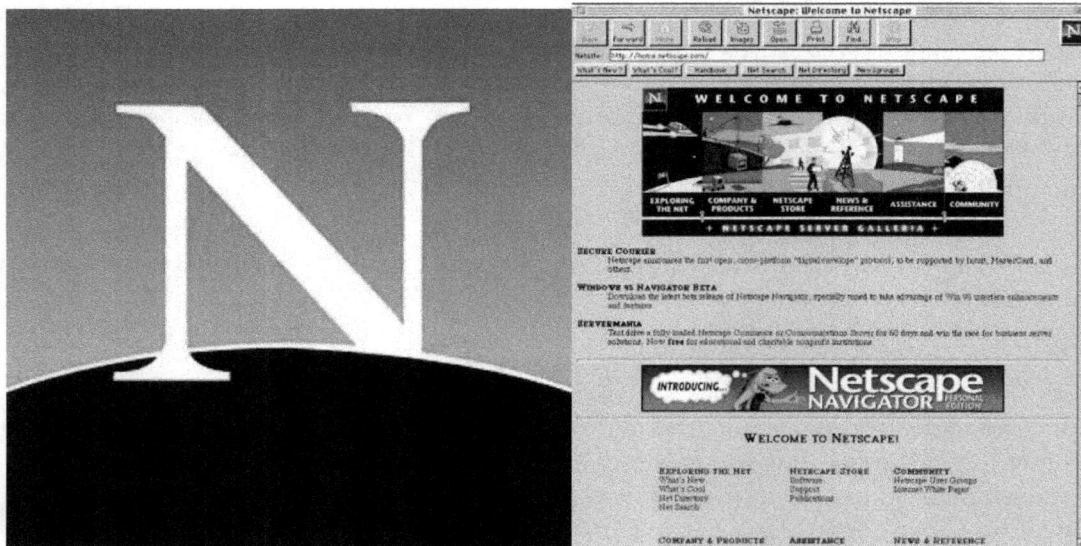

Figure 1.5: Netscape Navigator and logo from 1995

JavaScript's capabilities and popularity grew rapidly, especially during the browser wars of the late 1990s and early 2000s, when Netscape Navigator and Microsoft's Internet Explorer were competing for dominance in the browser market.

Most modern features started in ECMAScript from version 5, several years later. It was released in December 2009, bringing significant improvements to the language, including strict mode, JSON support, and new methods for arrays and objects.

ECMAScript 6, also known as ECMAScript 2015 (ES2015), was a major update to the language, introducing features like classes, arrow functions, template literals, and more. After ES6, ECMAScript started following a yearly release cycle, regularly introducing new features and improvements. JavaScript's popularity soared with frontend frameworks, libraries like React and Angular (*Figure 1.6*), and many others. These frameworks gave developers powerful tools for building complex and interactive user interfaces.

Figure 1.6: React and Angular

In October 2016, *Guillermo Rauch* made his first release of Next.js. It is a React-based framework that provides the possibility to build **server-side rendered (SSR)** pages using a file base router out of the box. Next.js quickly gained popularity among developers due to its simplicity, performance, and support for various rendering methods. Next.js 2.0 was released in January 2017, bringing improved performance, better error handling, and support for custom server routes. This version further solidified Next.js as a reliable and efficient framework for building React applications.

One of the most popular versions of Next.js in modern projects is 12. Before the official release of Next.js 12, there was an experimental version of Next.js 11, which introduced many significant improvements and features, such as faster startup times, optimized image loading, and built-in ESLint support. This experimental version laid the groundwork for some of the enhancements that would be further refined in Next.js 12. One of the most significant changes in Next.js 12 was the upgrade to Webpack 5. Webpack is a popular bundler that helps optimize and package JavaScript, CSS, and other assets for the web. Webpack 5 brought several performance improvements and optimizations, resulting in faster build times and better overall performance for Next.js applications.

The latest version for today is Next.js 15. It is the most powerful front-end framework in web development. It has support for the latest React 19. Also, it has an updated routing system that includes not only page files but also special pages, like errors and layouts, that can be used as reusable components for the nested files.

Industrial visualization

Visualization in industrial applications refers to the use of graphical representations, such as 3D models, charts, graphs, and animations, to present complex data and information more intuitively and understandably. This approach allows stakeholders, including engineers, operators, and decision-makers, to gain insights and make informed decisions about industrial processes, systems, and operations.

3D visualization stands for design and prototyping. It allows engineers and designers to create virtual prototypes of industrial products, machines, and equipment. This enables them to visualize and evaluate designs, identify potential issues, and make necessary improvements before the physical manufacturing process, reducing development time and costs. Moreover, 3D can be used for process visualization. It provides a realistic representation of complex industrial processes. It allows operators and engineers to monitor and analyze visually. Immersive 3D simulations are used for training industrial personnel. They provide a safe and cost-effective way to familiarize operators with equipment and procedures, improving their skills and responsiveness to various scenarios. In maintenance and repairs, it can be used for detailed visual representations of complex machinery and equipment. Technicians can use these visualizations to understand the internal workings of machines, identify faulty components, and plan maintenance tasks more effectively. In the context of the **Industrial IoT**, 3D visualization is combined with real-time data from sensors to create digital twins of physical assets. These virtual replicas help monitor and analyze the performance of the actual assets, enabling predictive maintenance and optimization. 3D visualizations are valuable for marketing products and solutions. They allow companies to showcase their offerings engagingly and interactively, helping clients and stakeholders understand the features and benefits of the products.

We will also mention the most meta-capable technologies, AR and VR technologies, that are increasingly used in industrial applications to enhance visualization.

Overall, 3D visualization enables a deeper understanding of complex systems and processes, promotes better decision-making, and accelerates the development and deployment of industrial solutions. As technology continues to advance, 3D visualization will likely become even more sophisticated and integral to various industrial sectors.

While web applications have embarked on their journey to assert dominance in the software development market, we have the opportunity to draw a comparison between the potential of Three.js + Next.js over native development. Throughout this book, we will delve into several crucial aspects to uncover the advantages of Three.js + Next.js and explore how they stack up against traditional native development.

Cross-platform

Cross-platform compatibility means that 3D content created with Three.js can be accessed and experienced on various devices and operating systems without the need for platform-specific installations or updates. This ease of accessibility makes it more convenient for users to interact with 3D content. This can be achieved because Three.js is a web-based library, and to run the application, you will need a browser and any operating system that can run a browser. It also leads to the opportunity that we will not need any installation or download any software to run the application.

Real-time interaction

As we use web applications, we can easily render 3D visualization using real-time data obtained from various sources. In this book, we will use Pub/Sub from AWS. AWS Pub/Sub is **Amazon Simple Notification Service (SNS)** and **Amazon Simple Queue Service (SQS)** working together to implement a **publish-subscribe messaging pattern**, where publishers send messages to a topic, and multiple subscribers (queues, applications, or endpoints) can receive those messages simultaneously or selectively. This allows us to have collaborative functionality in our 3D application. This possibility, with the fact that the application does not require any installation, makes a 3D web app with Three.js an overkill solution for industrial purposes.

Low cost of development and maintenance

Developing web-based 3D applications typically involves lower development and maintenance costs than traditional desktop applications. The web environment offers a standardized platform, reducing the need for custom configurations for different operating systems and devices. Moreover, the number of front-end engineers with JavaScript knowledge is growing yearly. With web-based applications, updates can be deployed seamlessly, ensuring that users can always access the latest features and improvements. This continuous update process eliminates the need for users to manually download and install updates, leading to a better user experience, which will lead to lower maintenance costs.

Mobile compatibility

Three.js applications can be optimized for mobile devices, providing a consistent and interactive 3D experience on smartphones and tablets. This mobile compatibility extends the reach of 3D applications to users on the go.

Visualization of 3D objects is not the only possibility that we would require to complete the application. We will also need a wrapper that will have the possibility to store the data for the screen render and also have the UI interfaces that will contain forms, tables, and elements that will allow users to manipulate, change, and use 3D models.

Let us imagine any application that provides us the possibility to manipulate the 3D object; it will contain a lot of elements, except the model itself. For example, take a look at the Blender3D interface (*Figure 1.7*). Blender is a free-to-use tool to create 3D models, animations, and even interactive applications for desktops.

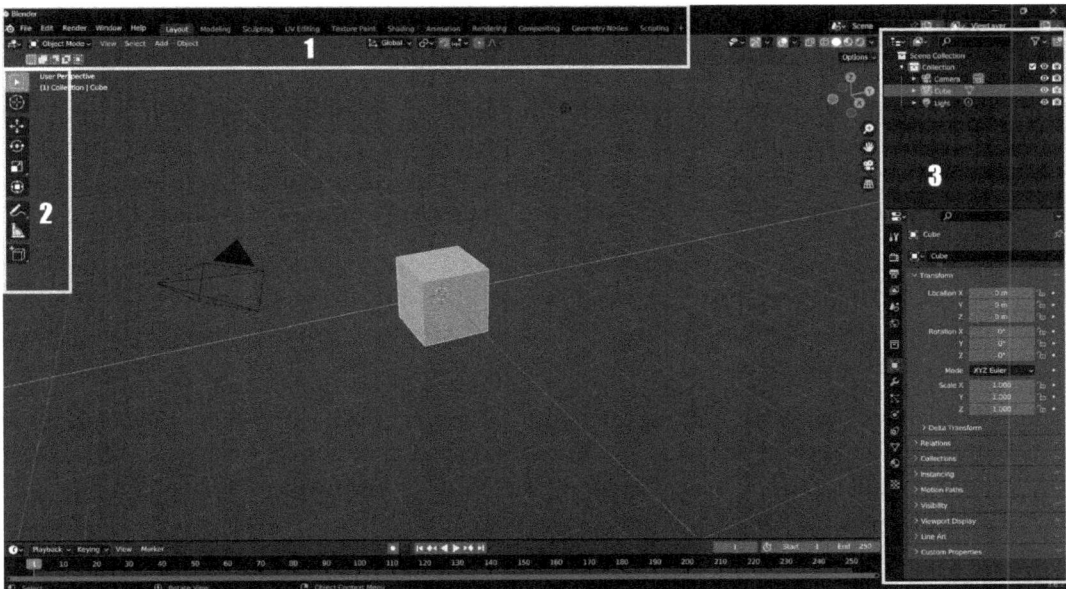

Figure 1.7: Blender 3D interface

Here you can see several sections:

1. This is the menu that can be used to change the main view and all interfaces around.

2. This is a submenu for the top menu selection.

3. When the user selects an object (in this case, it is a box) in the right panel, we can see the properties of the selected object and possible actions.

Some limitations of the application are as follows:

- The application is offline and requires installation for each computer working with the model.

- The models created by the application are not interactive.

- A special script needs to be created to create a model based on the data or to incorporate the changes.

Here on the stage will step Next.js as a perfect solution for the interfaces in web applications. As it is based on React, it will allow us to create an easily maintainable system that could be used for manipulating any object on the screen.

Here are the key features of Next.js that will be used to create an application for 3D visualization:

- **Streamlined routing for organized interfaces**: Next.js simplifies routing within applications, providing an intuitive structure for navigating various sections. This feature aids in creating well-organized user interfaces, enabling users to seamlessly access distinct components of industrial applications.

- **API Routes for real-time data handling:** Industrial applications thrive on real-time data communication. With Next.js's built-in API routes, developers can seamlessly integrate backend services and databases. This real-time data exchange enhances the application's ability to deliver accurate and up-to-date information.

- **Comprehensive styling support:** Styling is a cornerstone of user interface design. Next.js offers versatile styling options, including CSS modules and CSS-in-JS libraries, ensuring consistent branding and aesthetics across different segments of industrial applications.

- **Real-time data visualization with Next.js and libraries like Three.js.**: Collaboration with libraries like Three.js empowers developers to create real-time data visualizations. This capability aids in decision-making, process optimization, and data-driven insights within industrial applications.

Real-world use cases with Three.js

The use cases for the Three.js are the most exciting part of any presentation of the library's possibilities or any mention of it. Even if WebGL is a mature technology, rendering 3D objects and animations in the browser is an eye-catching feature. We will start with simple examples from the library itself, and then we will check the more complex realizations of applications with this library.

We will start with basic examples. These examples show the basics of Three.js usage in web development and show how to insert and see the 3D object into the web page. We will then take on more complex examples.

Low-poly pink flamingo with light setup

This example can be found at **https://Three.js.org/examples/#webgl_lights_hemisphere**. In this example, (*Figure 1.8*), we can observe animated 3D objects on the web page. You also can play around with light objects on the scene, we will talk about that in the upcoming chapters. For now, let us just check the possibilities of the library itself.

Figure 1.8: Animated 3D object from Three.js examples

Voxel 3D picture on page

There are many applications to create 3D images, like 3D Max, Maya, Cinema 4D, or Blender. But there is a low-poly application that allows you to create 3D images using boxes like in Minecraft. This application is called MagicaVoxel. It is free and open-sourced and can be found at: **https://ephtracy.github.io/**. Using this application, we have made a low-poly dog, inspired by one of the developers from YouTube, and inserted it into the web page (*Figure 1.9*). The trick is that it does not use the usual file extensions. Three.js supports it out of the box and easily inserts Vox files.

Figure 1.9: Voxel file insertion into page example

3D Force-directed graph

This application is located at **https://vasturiano.github.io/3d-force-graph/,** and it represents a visualization of graph data in 3D (*Figure 1.10*). It can represent any graph-oriented data on the screen. You can turn around the rendered graph, and each node is clickable and can contain text data or a link.

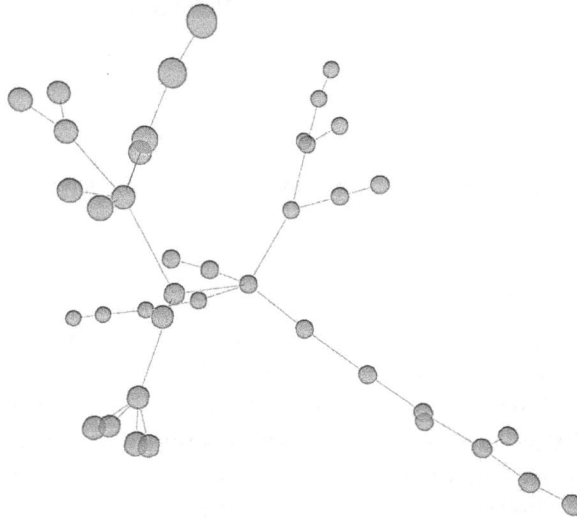

Figure 1.10: *Graph-data representation with Three.js*

3D background for website

Inserting objects into the page can also be used for the background of the page. The next example is a customizable 3D background for the web page library (*Figure 1.11*). You can collect it at **https://www.vantajs.com/**. You can also play around with different templates and customization.

Figure 1.11: 3D background library

WebVR framework

As Three.js is a library, the next stage of the tooling is a framework. Each framework is limited to solving problems around which it was created; it can be a good solution in some cases. We will use pure Three.js in our book to use all the advantages of freedom. But if we need to solve the exact task with WebVR, we can look at the A-Frame framework (*Figure 1.12*), which can be found at: **https://aframe.io/**

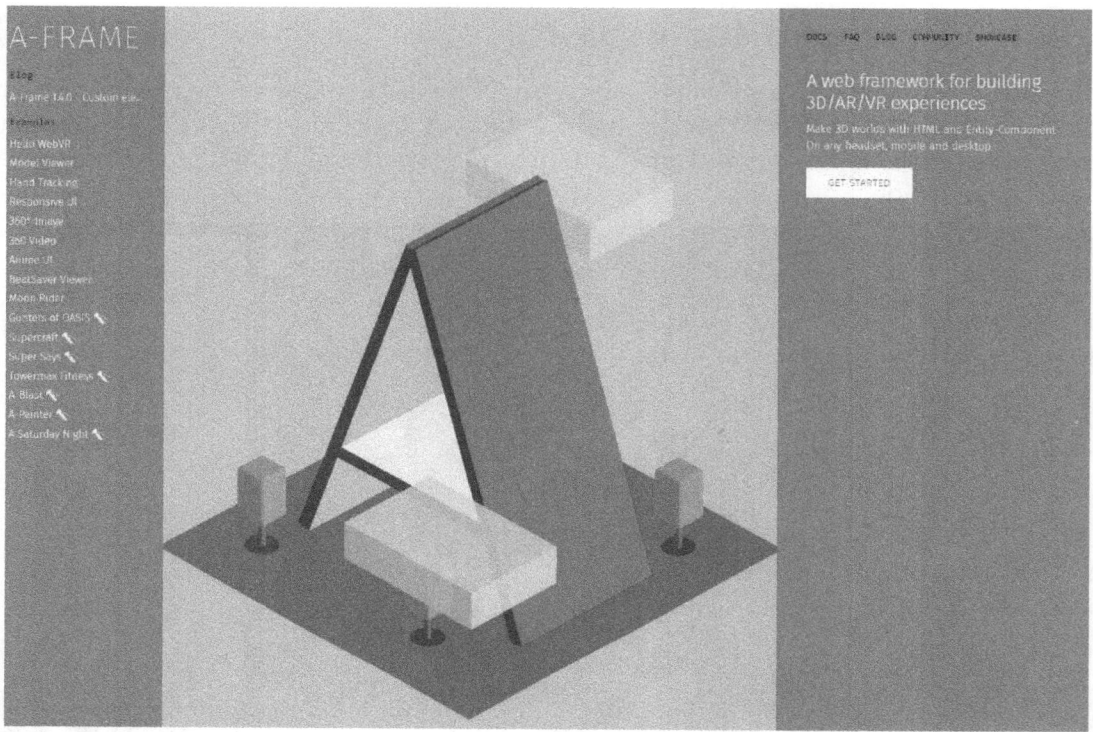

Figure 1.12: A-Frame framework for WebVR solutions

The next two examples represent web applications for the 3D animation and gaming industries.

Motion design tool

As we know already, there are a lot of ways to insert an object on the page. But what if we needed to create the animation? Using Three.js, we will need to code the movements and a camera. But what if there is a tool to make it visually like any desktop application, like Blender? There is a solution to it. The library is called TheatreJS (*Figure 1.13*), and it allows you to create magnificent animations with imported 3D objects. You can grab it here: **https://www.theatrejs.com/**

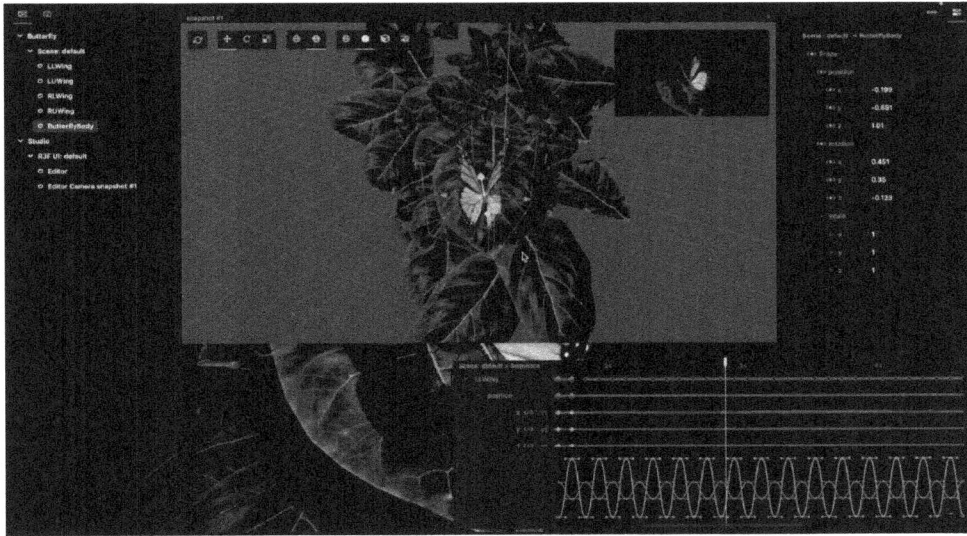

Figure 1.13: TheatreJS interface for the animation of 3D objects in web

The 3D web-based visual game engine

As the last example, we will talk about the web 3D engine to create games, visual presentations, and industrial apps (*Figure 1.14*). We will rely on the possibilities of this engine in this book when we create our interfaces. While this engine could be ideal for industrial use cases, its primary focus is game development. As a result, many of its features may go unused, especially when constrained by the application's specific scene requirements. This situation often leads to an abundance of 3D objects that could be created using pure JavaScript, similarly utilizing your PC's resources. The engine can be collected at **https://playcanvas.com/** and is called PlayCanvas.

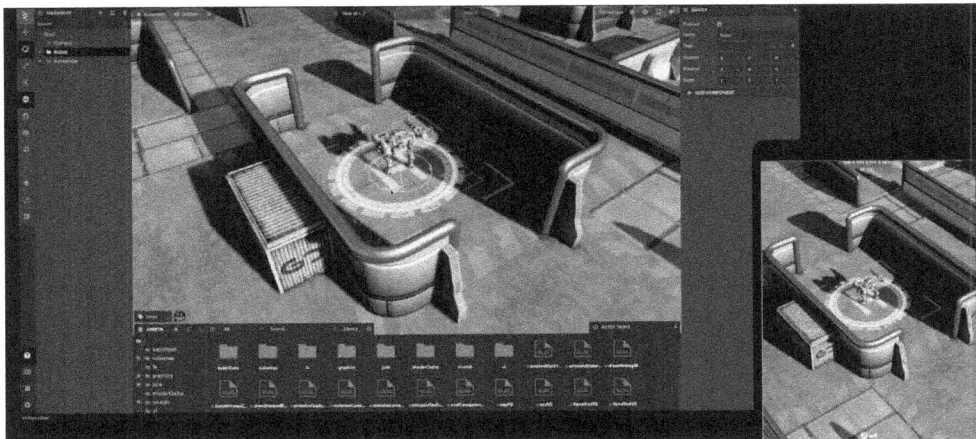

Figure 1.14: Playcanvas interface to create 3D web games

Conclusion

This chapter embarks on a comprehensive journey through the world of industrial applications, shedding light on their critical significance and the intricate challenges they grapple with across various sectors. It then navigates through the evolutionary landscape of Three.js and Next.js, charting their transformative contributions to the realms of web development and 3D graphics.

As the narrative unfolds, the focus seamlessly shifts towards industrial visualization, a realm where the combined prowess of Three.js and Next.js takes center stage. The chapter underscores how this dynamic synergy empowers the creation of immersive 3D visualizations, offering invaluable insights for industrial processes, simulations, and prototyping.

Real-world use cases provide tangible illustrations of Three.js' prowess within industrial contexts, showcasing its versatility and practical applicability. These examples span industries ranging from manufacturing to healthcare, showcasing Three.js' potential to redefine conventional paradigms.

In conclusion, this chapter showcases the seamless fusion of Three.js as a potent catalyst for reshaping industrial applications. As industries seek to optimize processes and enhance decision-making, the amalgamation of web technologies and 3D graphics emerges as a transformative force, poised to revolutionize the future of industrial landscapes.

In the next chapter, we will deep dive into the web development tools. We will talk about topics related to integration, security, and the possibility of using web apps offline with **Progressive Web Apps (PWA)** technology.

Points to remember

- Three.js is the perfect solution to integrate 3D graphics into a web application.
- Modern web development can work offline and can be rendered into a desktop or mobile application. Three.js can be one of the tools that render 3D objects.
- Even if there are many tools to wrap Three.js as a renderer into an application, there is always a space to create a new one.

Exercises

1. To get into the library possibilities, please check all examples at this link **https://threejs.org/examples/**. This will help you to get into the 3D rendering possibilities.

CHAPTER 2

Capabilities of Web Development for Industrial and Multi-purpose

Introduction

Within this chapter, we plunge into the dynamic domain of web development, probing its substantial potential across industrial and versatile applications. We reveal how web technologies confer advantages that reshape processes and decision-making paradigms. Embracing responsive design, we ensure seamless encounters spanning diverse devices and platforms. Also, we will get into the abilities of **Progressive Web Applications (PWAs),** which provide offline capabilities and app-like engagements. Take a seat as we unveil the layers of web development, reshaping industrial landscapes through its capabilities.

Structure

The chapter will cover the following topics:

- Introduction to web development capabilities
- Responsive design and cross-platform compatibility
- Data visualization and analytics
- Real-time communication and collaboration
- Integration with external systems and APIs
- Scalability and performance optimization

- Security and privacy considerations
- Accessibility and inclusive design
- Progressive Web Applications

Objectives

After reading this chapter, you will learn what capabilities exist in modern web development that will help you to understand how we could use Three.js and Next.js to create the most progressive applications.

Introduction to web development capabilities

Web development offers a wide range of tools and technologies that can be used for many different purposes, including in various industries. The flexibility of these web technologies lets us create things quickly, make changes easily, and adjust to new needs as they come up.

Imagine web development like building with versatile Lego blocks. These blocks can be combined in various ways to make all sorts of things. Similarly, web technologies give us these building blocks to create websites and applications for different needs, including industries.

The cool thing is that because these web technologies are so flexible, we can build and change things faster. It is like being able to change the design of a building without having to tear it down and start from scratch.

Plus, these web tools make it easier to connect different parts of a system. Like how roads connect different places, web technologies connect different parts of a website or application. This makes everything work together smoothly, like gears in a machine.

So, web development is not just about making websites look good; it is about using these tools to build things quickly, make changes easily, and connect different parts seamlessly. This is super useful in industries where things can change a lot and need to work together smoothly.

Web technologies can completely change how old-fashioned industrial processes work. Imagine it like upgrading from a basic phone to a smartphone; it is a huge leap forward. These technologies can bring in automation, which means tasks can happen on their own without needing constant human input. Think of machines in a factory running automatically.

Real-time monitoring is another cool thing. It is like having a live camera feed of what is happening in the factory. This allows us to identify problems as they occur and fix them more quickly.

Also, web technologies let us make decisions based on data. It is like having a super-smart assistant who tells us what is best to do next. This helps in making smarter choices for the business.

And you know how apps on a smartphone make things easy? Well, digital interfaces, which are like screens on your phone, make things easy in industries, too. They help workers interact smoothly with machines, making tasks faster and smoother.

So, just like smartphones changed how we communicate, web technologies can change how industries work by making things automated, helping us see what is happening in real time, and guiding us with smart decisions.

Key advantages of web development

The realm of web development brings forth a spectrum of advantages that distinguish it from traditional desktop development approaches. These advantages stem from the inherent nature of web applications, which leverage the internet to offer unique features and capabilities. As we delve into comparing web development and desktop development, let us explore the key strengths that position web development as a pivotal choice for modern software creation. From broad accessibility to dynamic user experiences, each advantage showcases the prowess of web development in shaping the digital landscape. The following are the advantages of web development:

- **Accessibility**: Web applications can be accessed from anywhere with an internet connection. This universal availability ensures users can interact with the application using a variety of devices, whether it is a desktop computer, laptop, tablet, or smartphone.

- **Easy updates**: Web apps can be updated seamlessly without requiring users to install new versions manually. This ensures that users always have access to the latest features and improvements.

- **Low installation barrier**: Users can access web apps instantly without the need for installation. This eliminates the friction associated with downloading and installing software, making it easier for users to start using the application.

- **Cost efficiency**: Developing and maintaining web apps often requires fewer resources compared to traditional desktop software. The ability to deploy a single version accessible to all users reduces complexity and costs.

- **Real-time collaboration**: Web apps enable real-time collaboration among users regardless of their location. Multiple users can work on the same document or project simultaneously, enhancing teamwork and productivity.

- **Scalability**: Web apps can easily scale to accommodate increasing user demands. Cloud-based infrastructure allows applications to allocate resources dynamically, ensuring optimal performance even during peak usage.

- **Enhanced user experience**: Modern web technologies enable the creation of interactive and dynamic user interfaces. This enhances user engagement and satisfaction by providing a more visually appealing and intuitive experience.

Responsive design and cross-platform compatibility

In the not-so-distant past, the internet was a simpler place, predominantly accessed through desktop computers. Websites were designed with fixed dimensions and optimized for the standardized screens of the era. However, as technology advanced, new devices with varying screen sizes emerged, disrupting the seamless browsing experience. This marked the birth of a transformative concept: responsive design.

Origin of responsive design

Around 2010, responsive design emerged as a solution to the burgeoning challenge of adapting websites to a diverse array of devices. This innovative approach aimed to craft websites that could seamlessly adjust and present content optimally across different screen sizes, be it a desktop, tablet, or smartphone.

The history of responsive design is marked by pivotal milestones. *Ethan Marcotte*'s groundbreaking article, *Responsive Web Design*, published on *A List Apart* in 2010, laid the conceptual foundation. It introduced fluid grids, flexible images, and media queries as the pillars of responsive design. This approach enabled websites to fluidly resize and restructure content based on the user's device.

The adoption of **Cascading Style Sheets (CSS)** media queries played a crucial role in this evolution. These queries allowed developers to apply different styles based on screen characteristics like width, height, and orientation. This meant that a single website could elegantly adjust its layout, fonts, and images to suit devices ranging from oversized desktop monitors to pocket-sized smartphones.

As responsive design (*Figure 2.1*) gained traction, frameworks like Bootstrap and Foundation emerged, streamlining the development process. These frameworks provided pre-designed responsive components, empowering developers to create adaptable layouts without reinventing the wheel.

Figure 2.1: *Design that adapts to the screen resolution*

The evolution of responsive design dovetailed with the mobile revolution. The rise in mobile device usage propelled the need for a seamless, consistent user experience. Google's emphasis on mobile-friendly websites in its search rankings further catalyzed the shift towards responsive design.

Fast forward to today, and responsive design has become an industry standard. Web designers and developers consider adaptability across devices as an essential aspect of the design process. Responsive design is not merely about fitting content into different screens; it is about crafting user-centric experiences that remain engaging and intuitive, regardless of the device.

The history of responsive design is a journey of adaptation and innovation. From fixed layouts to fluid grids and media queries, responsive design has shaped the modern web landscape. Its evolution reflects the dynamic interplay between technological advancements and the ever-changing ways users engage with digital content.

In the dynamic realm of web development, catering to a diverse audience is paramount. Users access websites and applications on an array of devices, operating systems, and browsers. Meeting these multifaceted demands gave rise to the concept of cross-platform development, a pivotal approach that bridges the digital divide. The digital landscape has transformed, with users relying on smartphones, tablets, laptops, and even smart TVs to access online content. Each device comes with its unique screen size, resolution, and user interface considerations, making it a complex puzzle for developers.

Cross-platform development, often dubbed *write once, run anywhere*, offers an elegant solution. It enables developers to create web applications that function seamlessly across a spectrum of devices and platforms without the need for extensive platform-specific coding.

Responsive web design is the cornerstone of cross-platform development. It involves crafting websites that fluidly adapt to different screen sizes and orientations. This ensures content remains readable and usable, regardless of the device used.

Traditionally, cross-platform development meant wrestling with various programming languages, tools, and frameworks to create separate versions of an application for each target platform. This approach was time-consuming, resource-intensive, and often resulted in inconsistent user experiences.

However, the emergence of JavaScript frameworks and libraries has revolutionized cross-platform development. JavaScript, a language once primarily confined to web browsers, has now become a formidable force in building cross-platform mobile and desktop applications.

Advantages of cross-platform development

The advantages of the cross-platform development are discussed as follows:

- **Code reusability**: Developers can write code once and use it across different platforms, saving time and effort.

- **Faster development**: JavaScript's large developer community, along with the availability of libraries and frameworks, speeds up development cycles.

- **Consistency**: Users enjoy a consistent experience, regardless of the platform they use, enhancing user satisfaction.

- **Wider reach**: Applications can target a broader audience, reaching users on various devices and operating systems.

Future of cross-platform development

Modern cross-platform development with JavaScript has democratized application development, making it accessible to a broader audience of developers. As technology evolves, the distinction between native and cross-platform applications becomes increasingly blurred. With ever-improving tools and frameworks, the future holds the promise of even more efficient and powerful cross-platform development solutions.

In a world where versatility, cost-efficiency, and a consistent user experience are paramount, JavaScript-based cross-platform development has become a cornerstone of modern software engineering, bridging the app divide and reshaping the way we build applications for an interconnected world.

Data visualization and analytics

In the modern era of data-driven decision-making, the art and science of data visualization play a pivotal role in conveying complex information concisely and comprehensibly. As we delve into the origins of data visualization in web development, we embark on a journey that unveils its humble beginnings and evolution into an indispensable tool for understanding, interpreting, and communicating data.

History

Before the digital age, data visualization had its origins in various forms, demonstrating humanity's innate drive to represent information visually. Here is a deeper look into the historical antecedents.

In the late 18th century, Scottish economist and engineer *William Playfair* pioneered the use of graphical methods to represent economic data. His work included the invention of line graphs, bar charts, and pie charts, which are still fundamental to data visualization today.

In 1854, physician *John Snow* (not from *Game of Thrones*) created a map showing the locations of cholera cases in London. By plotting cases on the map, he identified a contaminated water pump as the source of the outbreak, demonstrating the power of geographic data visualization in epidemiology.

During the Crimean War, *Florence Nightingale* used rose diagrams to illustrate the causes of mortality among soldiers. Her innovative use of visualization not only conveyed information effectively but also drove improvements in healthcare practices.

In 1869, *Charles Joseph M*inard produced a famous flow map depicting *Napoleon's Russian* campaign. This map elegantly combined multiple dimensions of data, including troop size, temperature, and geographic location, in a single visualization.

These historical examples highlight the early attempts to use visual representations to convey complex information. While these methods were manual and labor-intensive, they laid the foundation for the digital data visualization techniques we use today.

Art of storytelling through data

Human beings are inherently drawn to stories. From ancient cave paintings to contemporary cinema, narratives have been our preferred mode of conveying information, emotions, and wisdom. Stories captivate our attention, engage our emotions, and make complex ideas more accessible. It is no surprise that storytelling has found a natural home in the realm of data visualization.

Data storytelling (*Figure 2.2*) begins with a clear objective: to guide the audience through a specific story or message. Whether it is uncovering trends in financial data or presenting the impact of climate change, the narrative provides context and direction.

Figure 2.2: Data storytelling

Effective data storytelling requires placing the data within its broader context. This includes providing background information, explaining the significance of the data, and highlighting its real-world implications.

Data storytelling is not a one-way street. Interactive elements, such as clickable charts or maps, allow the audience to actively engage with the data. Users can explore data points, filter information, and draw their conclusions.

Effective data storytelling aims to do more than convey information; it seeks to evoke emotions and foster empathy. By connecting data to real-life scenarios or human stories, visualizations can make data personally relevant. For example, data on hunger becomes more impactful when accompanied by the story of a struggling family.

Three.js in storytelling

Integrating Three.js into data storytelling adds a layer of emotional impact. 3D visualizations have the potential to create a visceral connection with data. For instance, environmental data on deforestation becomes more poignant when users can witness virtual forests dwindling before their eyes.

What advantages can three.js provide for the storytelling approach? Let us explore this aspect:

- Three.js allows us to transform data into dynamic 3D scenes. Instead of static charts, we can craft immersive environments where data points become tangible elements, inviting users to explore and engage.

- Interactive 3D models enable users to navigate through data narratives intuitively. They can zoom in on specific data points, rotate visualizations for different perspectives, and interact with elements to uncover insights independently.

- The power of Three.js lies not only in visualizing data but also in contextualizing it within rich environments. Imagine exploring geological data within a 3D representation of the Earth's surface or financial trends amidst a virtual cityscape.

What industries can be aligned in using Three.js for storytelling? Look at this list of examples to have inspiration and generate more ideas for the usage of 3D in web development:

- **Immersive journalism**: News organizations can use Three.js to create immersive data-driven experiences. Visual narratives on climate change, for example, can transport readers to virtual worlds where they witness the consequences of environmental shifts.

- **Business insights**: In the realm of business intelligence, Three.js can bring complex data to life. Instead of static dashboards, executives can explore 3D representations of market dynamics, gaining a deeper understanding of trends.

- **Scientific communication**: Researchers can leverage Three.js to illustrate complex scientific concepts. Whether explaining molecular structures or astronomical phenomena, immersive 3D models help make scientific data accessible.

- **Educational engagement**: In education, Three.js-driven data storytelling captivates students. History lessons can be enriched with 3D reconstructions of ancient civilizations, while biology classes can explore cellular processes in 3D.

- **Data-driven art and advocacy**: Creative artists can harness Three.js to fuse data with art. Interactive installations and exhibits turn abstract data points into tangible experiences that provoke thought and dialogue.

Real-time communication and collaboration

In the fast-paced world of digital collaboration and communication (*Figure* 2.3), Three. js emerges as a transformative force, revolutionizing how we interact and work together in real time. This dynamic JavaScript library takes the concept of collaboration to new heights, opening up a world of possibilities for industries, education, entertainment, and beyond.

Figure 2.3: *Communication*

While Three.js is renowned for its 3D graphics capabilities, its potential extends far beyond creating immersive visualizations. It serves as a bridge that connects individuals across the globe, enabling real-time collaboration in 3D environments.

Key features in real-time collaboration with Three.js

Three.js allows multiple users to access and interact within the same 3D environment simultaneously. Whether it is a virtual classroom, a design studio, or a shared gaming world, users can collaborate as if they were physically present.

Users can interact with 3D objects and elements in real-time. This means they can jointly manipulate objects, draw on virtual whiteboards, or conduct experiments in a shared laboratory.

Real-time communication is facilitated through integrated voice and text chat systems. Users can converse, share ideas, and provide feedback while immersed in the 3D environment.

Applications in various industries

Three.js-powered real-time collaboration is redefining remote education and training. Students can attend virtual lectures, collaborate on assignments, and conduct experiments together, regardless of their physical location.

Architects and designers can collaborate in real-time on 3D models and prototypes. They can discuss changes, iterate designs, and make decisions collectively, enhancing creativity and productivity.

Multiplayer online games and virtual reality experiences are leaping forward with Three.js. Gamers can engage in shared adventures, competitions, and social interactions within richly detailed 3D worlds.

Researchers and engineers can use Three.js to create collaborative simulations and experiments. They can jointly analyze data, simulate complex phenomena, and share insights in real-time.

As technology advances and user demand grows, the future of real-time collaboration powered by Three.js holds limitless possibilities. From shared virtual workspaces to collaborative scientific exploration, the Three.js revolution is reshaping how we work, learn, and connect in the digital age. It is an exciting frontier that brings people together across screens and borders, igniting innovation and camaraderie in the virtual realm.

Integration with external systems and APIs

In the dynamic world of web development, the ability to seamlessly integrate with external systems and **Application Programming Interfaces (APIs)** has become a linchpin for creating robust and feature-rich applications. This integration empowers developers to leverage a vast ecosystem of services and data sources, opening doors to unparalleled functionality and interoperability.

Integration is connecting different software systems and allowing them to work together as a cohesive unit. In web development, this often involves interfacing with external systems, such as databases, third-party applications, or cloud services, through APIs.

APIs (*Figure 2.4*) act as intermediaries that enable communication between various software components. They provide a standardized way for developers to request and exchange data or perform specific actions within external systems. APIs come in various forms, including **Representational State Transfer Application Programming Interfaces (RESTful APIs), SOAP APIs, Simple Object Access Protocol (SOAP), Graph Query Language (GraphQL),** and more.

Figure 2.4: Application Programming Interface

Integration with external systems and APIs broadens the capabilities of web applications. Developers can tap into a multitude of services, from payment gateways to machine learning algorithms, to enhance their applications.

Access to external data sources allows web applications to enrich their content with real-time or up-to-date information. For example, an e-commerce site can display current product prices or availability from an external inventory system.

Integration simplifies complex workflows by automating tasks that would otherwise require manual intervention. This not only saves time but also reduces the risk of errors.

Web applications can scale more effectively by offloading certain functionalities to specialized external services. This ensures that the application remains responsive even under heavy user loads.

While integration with external systems and APIs is transformative in its own right, the introduction of Three.js opens up new dimensions of possibility:

- Three.js empowers developers to create immersive 3D worlds within web applications. This means users can collaborate, interact, and engage with 3D content in real-time, whether it is exploring virtual landscapes, visualizing complex data, or even gaming together.

- Users can manipulate 3D objects and elements collaboratively, enhancing the potential for data visualization, design collaboration, and interactive simulations.

- Three.js can be integrated with real-time communication tools, such as voice and text chat, allowing users to interact within 3D environments seamlessly.

Challenges and considerations

While the benefits of integration with Three.js are vast, there are important considerations:

- **Security**: Security measures are paramount when integrating external systems, ensuring data protection, and preventing unauthorized access to 3D environments.

- **Data consistency**: Maintaining data consistency when integrating with external sources is crucial to avoid discrepancies and errors in 3D models.

- **Learning curve**: Users may require some orientation to navigate 3D environments effectively, emphasizing the importance of intuitive design.

Emerging trends like microservices architecture, serverless computing, and containerization will further streamline integration processes, making them even more accessible and scalable. In a world where connectivity knows no bounds, the fusion of integration and Three.js promises a future filled with innovative, immersive, and collaborative web experiences that meet the ever-evolving needs of users and businesses.

Scalability and performance optimization

In the ever-evolving landscape of web development, two critical pillars stand tall: Scalability and performance optimization. These twin pillars have played a pivotal role in shaping the digital world, and their journey through history highlights both the remarkable progress made so far and the promising future ahead.

Interesting facts from history

The early days (1990s-2000s): The web, in its infancy, was a realm of static HTML pages and modest interactivity. Scalability and performance were less pressing concerns as the web served primarily as an information repository.

The rise of dynamic web (2000s-2010s): The emergence of dynamic web applications, driven by technologies like PHP, **ASP.NET (Active Server Pages)**, and Java, brought forth the need for scalability. Scalable architectures, including load balancers and **Content Delivery Networks (CDNs)**, entered the scene to handle increased traffic.

The mobile revolution (2010s): With the proliferation of smartphones, optimizing performance for diverse devices and screen sizes became paramount. Responsive web design techniques emerged to adapt layouts seamlessly, ensuring a consistent user experience.

Present day

Scalability has been redefined with the advent of cloud computing. Services like **Amazon Web Services (AWS)**, Google Cloud, and Microsoft Azure offer elastic scaling, enabling applications to handle fluctuating loads effortlessly.

CDNs have evolved to deliver content efficiently worldwide. They cache and distribute static assets, reducing latency and enhancing performance for global audiences.

Modern web development focuses on front-end performance optimization (*Figure 2.5*). Techniques like code splitting, lazy loading, and Progressive Web Apps (PWAs, we will open a topic about it later in this chapter) enhance user experiences by minimizing load times.

Figure 2.5: Performance optimization

Mobile-first development strategies ensure that web applications perform seamlessly on smartphones and tablets, catering to the mobile-driven user base.

Possible challenges in the future

As web applications scale and improve performance, security remains a paramount concern. Protecting against evolving threats and vulnerabilities is an ongoing challenge.

Balancing performance optimization with user privacy, especially in a post-**General Data Protection Regulation (GDPR)** era, requires careful consideration of data handling practices.

The energy consumption of data centers powering scalable web applications is a growing concern. Sustainable computing solutions will play a vital role in the future.

Security and privacy considerations

In the vast realm of web development, security and privacy have transformed from mere considerations into indispensable foundations. Their historical evolution reflects the determined commitment to safeguard user data and digital assets in the ever-expanding digital frontier.

The technical landscape of web development is marked by continuous innovation and evolving threats. This journey is fueled by the recognition that security and privacy are not merely optional but indispensable.

In the early days of the web, security and privacy were often treated as afterthoughts. Basic authentication mechanisms and minimal data encryption were commonplace. This allow-anything attitude left web applications vulnerable to attacks.

In contrast, modern web development embraces a security-first approach (*Figure 2.6*). Developers are armed with a myriad of tools, protocols, and best practices to thwart cyber threats.

Figure 2.6: Security-first

Here are some key technical considerations:

Data encryption

Data encryption is the bedrock of securing data in transit. The adoption of **Hypertext Transfer Protocol Secure (HTTPS)** using **Secure Sockets Layer/Transport Layer Security (SSL/TLS)** encryption ensures that data transmitted between the user and the server remains confidential and integral. This encryption mechanism scrambles data into an unreadable format during transmission, rendering it useless to malicious actors even if intercepted. The utilization of SSL/TLS certificates validates the identity of the server, assuring users of the authenticity of the website they are interacting with. This technology is vital for protecting sensitive information like login credentials, financial transactions, and personal data, thereby maintaining the confidentiality and integrity of user data.

Authentication protocols

Authentication protocols are the first line of defense against unauthorized access. Robust authentication mechanisms like **Multi-Factor Authentication (MFA)** and **OAuth** provide multiple layers of user verification. MFA requires users to provide two or more authentication factors (for example, passwords, biometrics, or smart cards) to access their accounts, making it significantly harder for malicious actors to breach accounts. OAuth, on the other hand, enables third-party applications to access user data without exposing login credentials. These protocols serve as digital bouncers, allowing only authorized users through the virtual door while deterring unauthorized access.

Authorization models

Authorization models are the gatekeepers of data access within an application. **Role-Based Access Control (RBAC)** and **Attribute-Based Access Control (ABAC)** are two fundamental paradigms that enable precise control over user permissions. RBAC assigns roles to users, each with specific permissions. For instance, an **admin** role might have access to all areas of an application, while a **user** role has limited access. ABAC, on the other hand, considers various attributes of a user, the requested action, and the resource in question to determine access. These models ensure that only authorized parties can access specific data or perform certain actions within an application, guarding against data breaches and unauthorized activities.

Input validation

Input validation is the shield against injection attacks, including the notorious SQL injection. This technique ensures that data from untrusted sources, such as user input, is thoroughly validated and sanitized before being processed by the application. Data sanitization scrubs user inputs of potentially malicious code, while parameterized queries ensure that SQL statements are immune to injection attacks. By effectively filtering and validating input data, developers prevent attackers from inserting malicious SQL queries, JavaScript, or other harmful code into the application, thereby averting security breaches and data leaks.

Technical security and privacy considerations in web development have evolved from being reactive to proactive. Developers now have a vast toolbox of measures to protect against an ever-expanding array of threats. As technology continues to advance, the resilience of web applications against cyberattacks and the preservation of user privacy will remain paramount. Developers are the sentinels of the digital realm, charged with not only creating feature-rich web applications but also ensuring they are secure and respectful of user privacy.

Accessibility and inclusive design

Within the dynamic sphere of web development, accessibility and inclusive design stand as the most important tenets. This discourse delves deep into the technical facets underpinning the imperative of rendering web applications accessible to all, irrespective of disabilities or constraints.

Web accessibility, in its essence, embodies the art and science of creating web content and applications that can be comprehended, navigated, and interacted with by a broad spectrum of individuals. These individuals encompass those with diverse abilities and disabilities, spanning visual, auditory, motor, cognitive, and even situational limitations. Within this intricate tapestry, technical ingenuity plays a paramount role in enabling universal access.

Laws and regulations around the world mandate web accessibility. Non-compliance can result in legal consequences and hefty fines. For example, the **Americans with Disabilities Act (ADA)** in the United States and the **Web Content Accessibility Guidelines (WCAG)** are legal frameworks that enforce accessibility standards. Ensuring compliance is not just a matter of ethics but also risk mitigation.

By making web applications accessible, businesses and organizations tap into a larger audience. The World Health Organization estimates that over a billion people worldwide live with some form of disability. Creating accessible digital experiences opens doors to a vast market segment that might otherwise be excluded.

The principles and practices of web accessibility go beyond just accommodating those with disabilities. They often lead to better user experiences for everyone. Clear navigation, well-structured content, and adaptable interfaces benefit all users, making accessibility a universal enhancement.

Fostering a culture of accessibility is not just about legal compliance; it is about ethical responsibility. It reflects an organization's commitment to social responsibility, emphasizing a dedication to inclusivity, diversity, and respect for all individuals.

As technology continues to evolve, accessibility will remain a central consideration. Ensuring accessibility now future-proofs web applications, making them adaptable to emerging technologies and the changing needs of users.

Compliance with established accessibility standards, such as WCAG, aligns web development with internationally recognized guidelines. This not only ensures accessibility but also facilitates interoperability across different platforms and technologies.

In essence, web accessibility is not just about compliance; it is about recognizing and respecting the diversity of users and their needs. It is about building a digital world where everyone has the opportunity to participate fully, ensuring that technology serves as an enabler rather than a barrier. Web accessibility matters not only for the present but for shaping a more inclusive and equitable future in the digital landscape.

Following WCAG in Three.js applications

Implementing WCAG principles in Three.js applications involves a combination of design, development, and testing. Here are the key steps to get you started:

1. **Make a semantic structure:**

    a. **Use semantic HTML**: Even within a 3D environment, use semantic HTML elements to provide structure and context to content that might be accessible to screen readers.

    b. **ARIA Roles**: Apply **Accessible Rich Internet Applications (ARIA)** roles and attributes to Three.js elements to convey their roles and states to assistive technologies.

2. **Keyboard navigation:**

    a. **Focus management**: Ensure that interactive elements can be reached and activated using keyboard navigation. Elements should receive keyboard focus and provide clear visual indicators.

    b. **Keyboard controls**: Allow users to navigate and interact with the 3D environment using keyboard controls, such as arrow keys or custom keybindings.

3. **Text alternatives:**

    a. **Provide descriptive text**: For non-text content like images or 3D models, provide descriptive text alternatives to convey their purpose and content to screen reader users.

4. **Contrast and readability:**

    a. **Contrast ratio**: Ensure that text and interactive elements have sufficient contrast with their background, making them readable for users with visual impairments.

    b. **Text resizability**: This allows users to resize text within the 3D environment, accommodating those who need larger text for readability.

5. **User controls:**

    a. **Pause and reset**: Implement controls to pause or reset animations or interactions, allowing users to navigate content at their own pace.

    b. **Customizable settings**: Provide users with the ability to adjust settings such as animation speed, brightness, or audio volume.

Implementing WCAG principles in Three.js applications is not only feasible but also essential for making immersive 3D worlds accessible to everyone. By prioritizing accessibility, you ensure that your 3D creations can be enjoyed by a diverse audience, including individuals with disabilities. In doing so, you contribute to a more inclusive and equitable web, where captivating 3D experiences are accessible to all.

Progressive Web Applications

In the ever-evolving landscape of web development, PWA have emerged as a game-changer. These applications combine the best of web and mobile apps, offering offline capabilities, faster loading times, and an app-like user experience. PWAs are web applications that provide users an experience akin to traditional native mobile apps. They represent a transformative approach to web development, aiming to combine the best of both web and native mobile applications.

The story of PWA is one of innovation, evolution, and a quest to bridge the gap between web and native mobile applications.

In 2015, Google engineer *Alex Russell* and designer *Frances Berriman* coined the term "Progressive Web App" to describe web apps that take advantage of modern browser capabilities. Chrome for Android was one of the first browsers to support PWAs.

In 2017, PWA (*Figure 2.7*) gained momentum as more major browsers, including Firefox and Edge, began supporting the technologies and standards that made **PWA** possible.

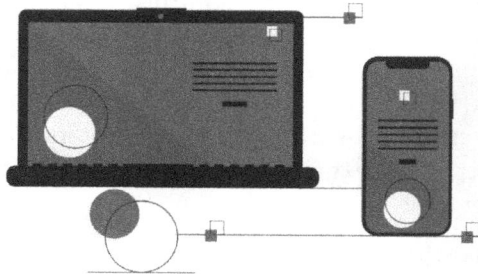

Figure 2.7: Progressive Web Apps

In 2018, *Twitter Lite*, a PWA by Twitter, and the Starbucks PWA garnered attention for their exceptional user experiences and performance. These successes demonstrated the potential of PWAs for businesses.

Key advantages of Progressive Web Apps

Some advantages of PWAs are as follows:

- Cross-platform compatibility. **PWA** are designed to be platform-agnostic, meaning they work seamlessly across a variety of platforms and devices, including:

- o **Desktop**: PWA function on desktop computers, providing a consistent user experience regardless of the operating system, whether Windows, macOS, or Linux.

- o **Mobile**: PWAs are mobile-friendly and responsive, adapting to various screen sizes and orientations on smartphones and tablets.

- o **Offline**: One of the remarkable features of **PWA** is their ability to function offline or in low-network conditions, ensuring users can access content and services even when an internet connection is unreliable or non-existent.

- o **Multi-browser**: PWAs are compatible with multiple web browsers, including Chrome, Firefox, Safari, Edge, and more, ensuring users can access them regardless of their preferred browser.

- **App-like experience**: PWAs aim to replicate the immersive and interactive experiences traditionally associated with native mobile apps.

- **Improved performance**: PWAs prioritize performance to deliver snappy and responsive user experiences. Key aspects of their improved performance include:

  - o **Faster load times**: PWAs are optimized for quick loading, reducing the time users spend waiting for content to appear. This is particularly crucial on mobile devices with limited bandwidth.

  - o **Efficient resource handling**: They use techniques like lazy loading to minimize the initial load and only fetch resources when needed, conserving bandwidth and speeding up rendering.

  - o **Caching**: Service workers cache assets and data, allowing **PWAs** to retrieve content from the local cache, which is significantly faster than fetching it from a server.

- **Offline functionality**: Offline functionality is a hallmark feature of **PWA**, made possible by service workers that are used in modern browsers.

- **No app store hassle**: One of the significant advantages of **PWA** is the simplified distribution process:

  - o **Direct installation**: Users can install **PWA** directly from the web, typically with a single click or tap. There is no need to go through the app store approval process or deal with app store limitations.

  - o **Automatic updates**: PWA can update automatically, ensuring that users always have access to the latest version without the need for manual updates through an app store.

  - o **Reduced friction**: The elimination of app store downloads and updates reduces friction for both users and developers, streamlining the distribution process.

Using PWA with Three.js

Integrating Three.js, a powerful 3D graphics library, with PWAs opens up exciting possibilities for creating immersive and interactive 3D web experiences.

Three.js allows developers to create stunning 3D content, from 3D models and animations to entire 3D scenes. This content can be seamlessly integrated into a PWA, offering users immersive and visually engaging experiences.

PWAs inherently support responsive design, and when combined with Three.js, this ensures that your 3D content adapts to different screen sizes and orientations. Whether users access your PWA on a desktop, tablet, or smartphone, they will enjoy a consistent and visually appealing experience.

Three.js is optimized for performance, making it well-suited for PWAs. It can efficiently render complex 3D scenes, animations, and interactions while ensuring fast load times and smooth user experiences. This enhanced performance contributes to the overall responsiveness of your PWA.

PWAs leverage service workers to enable offline functionality. When it comes to Three.js, this means you can cache 3D assets, models, and scenes so that users can still interact with your 3D content, even when they are offline or in low-network conditions.

Three.js enables you to create app-like interactions within your PWA. Users can manipulate 3D objects, explore virtual environments, and engage with interactive elements, all while enjoying smooth animations and gestures that mimic native app behavior.

Conclusion

In this chapter, we have initiated an exploration into the expansive realm of web development's capabilities for industrial and multi-purpose applications. We have uncovered the vast potential that this dynamic field holds, offering solutions that transcend traditional boundaries and redefine the way we approach digital landscapes.

From responsive design, ensuring seamless experiences across diverse devices and platforms, to data visualization and analytics powering industrial insights, we have explored the fundamental building blocks that empower us to create transformative web applications. Real-time communication and collaboration have been unveiled as catalysts for teamwork and efficiency, while integration with external systems and APIs has demonstrated the limitless expansion of functionality and data exchange.

As we conclude this chapter, we have only scratched the surface of what is possible in the world of web development. Our exploration has set the stage for exploring the tools and technologies that will empower us to bring these capabilities to life. In the chapters to come, we will unravel the intricacies of Three.js and Next.js, unveiling their strengths, applications, and the creative possibilities they offer to developers in the ever-evolving landscape of web development.

Points to remember

- Web development encompasses a broad range of technologies and practices that enable building dynamic, interactive, and user-friendly applications.

- Responsive design ensures that websites and applications look and function well across various devices and screen sizes, improving user experience and accessibility.

- Cross-platform compatibility involves designing systems that perform consistently across different browsers, operating systems, and devices.

- Data visualization helps users interpret complex data through charts, graphs, and dashboards, making insights more accessible and actionable.

- Real-time communication technologies, like WebSockets and WebRTC, enable live data updates and collaborative features within web applications.

- External system and API integration allows web apps to extend functionality, pull data, or connect to services like payment gateways, social platforms, and databases.

- Scalability and performance optimization are critical for handling increasing traffic and ensuring fast load times, which enhance user satisfaction and system reliability.

- Security and privacy must be built into the design, including protection against threats like XSS, CSRF, and data breaches, while complying with regulations like GDPR.

- Accessibility means designing for users with diverse needs, including those with disabilities, by following standards like WCAG and using semantic HTML.

- Progressive Web Applications (PWAs) blend the best of web and mobile apps, offering offline access, push notifications, and installation capabilities on devices.

Exercise

1. Investigate a popular Progressive Web App (e.g., Twitter Lite or Spotify Web). Identify at least three PWA features it uses.

2. Discuss the trade-offs between performance optimization and feature richness in web applications.

Join our Discord space

Join our Discord workspace for latest updates, offers, tech happenings around the world, new releases, and sessions with the authors:

https://discord.bpbonline.com

CHAPTER 3
Introduction to Tools

Introduction

This book chapter sets out on a journey through a curated selection of powerful tools and frameworks that are redefining the way we design, develop, and deploy web applications. Our adventure begins with an exploration of Three.js. We will delve into the world of 3D web development and discover how Three.js can unlock new dimensions in user experiences. After that, we will shift our focus to Next.js. We will provide an overview of its key features and showcase how it streamlines the development process, enabling faster, more efficient, and SEO-friendly web applications.

AWS Amplify, our next stop, is a cloud-powered suite of tools and services that simplifies the deployment and scaling of web applications. The journey continues with a deep dive into Storybook and discovers how Storybook enhances collaboration and promotes design system consistency, all while making it a breeze to showcase your UI components in isolation. Finally, we will introduce you to Tailwind CSS, a utility-first CSS framework designed to streamline your styling workflow.

Structure

The chapter will cover the following topics:

- Introduction to the Three.js library
- Overview of Next.js and its features

- Understanding AWS Amplify
- Exploring the benefits of Storybook
- Introduction to Tailwind CSS

Objectives

By the end of this chapter, you will have gained valuable insights into powerful tools and frameworks that are instrumental in modern web development. These insights will not only broaden your understanding of these technologies but also empower you with the practical knowledge needed to elevate your web development projects to new heights. You will be well-equipped to harness the capabilities of Three.js, Next.js, AWS Amplify, and Storybook effectively. Whether you are a newcomer to web development or an experienced developer, this chapter aims to provide you with a solid foundation to explore the full potential of these tools and frameworks in your projects.

Introduction to Three.js library

Three.js is an open-source JavaScript library that empowers developers to bring 3D magic to the web browser. It simplifies the often-complex world of 3D graphics, making it accessible to a broader audience. Three.js abstracts away the complexities of WebGL, the standard for rendering 3D graphics in browsers.

With Three.js, developers can create stunning 3D content without becoming 3D graphics experts (*Figure 3.1*). This accessibility opens up new creative possibilities for web projects. Three.js can handle simple 3D models to complex simulations and games. Its versatility is why it is used in various industries, from entertainment and education to e-commerce and data visualization. It ensures your 3D creations work seamlessly across different browsers and devices. It takes care of browser-specific quirks, making cross-browser development a breeze. Whether you are a beginner or a seasoned pro, you will find resources to help you learn and troubleshoot.

Figure 3.1: Low-poly 3D object

Possibilities of Three.js

Exploring Three.js is like embarking on an exciting adventure in web development. It allows you to create interactive websites that stand out from regular ones. In simple terms, learning Three.js opens up a world of possibilities for your web development journey. The official website for the library is presented in *Figure 3.2*.

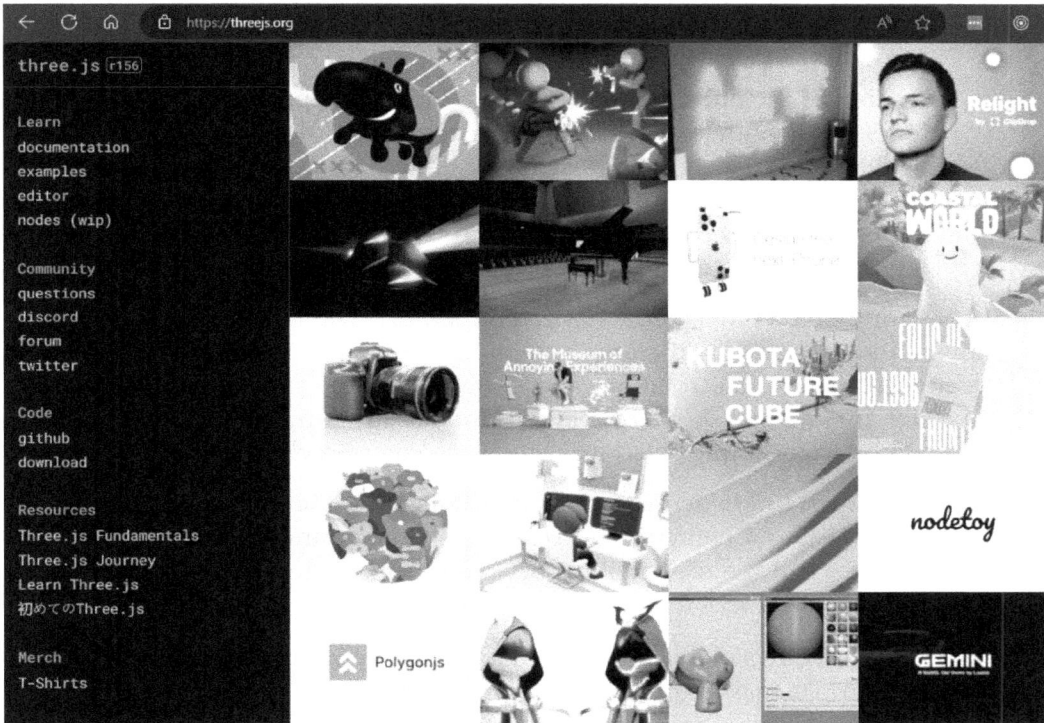

Figure 3.2: Three.js main page

Let us delve deeper into the base possibilities that the Three.js library brings to the table:

- First of all, it is a rendering of 3D objects in a web browser. These objects can be created using library tools or can be taken from the objects that were created using 3D modeling software (Blender, 3D Max, Maya, and others). That is the main idea of the library, and it is mostly used for this purpose. To render the object, we will need to create the scene, and after that, we will need to create a camera that will focus on the object.

- Three.js provides a robust camera system, including perspective and orthographic cameras. This control allows for dynamic camera movement and perspective changes, enabling users to explore 3D scenes from any angle. Coupled with user input (for example, mouse or touch events), developers can create immersive camera interactions that enhance the user experience.

- Three.js gives access to managing and object transformation. This means that after we place the object into the scene and the camera is focused on it, we can manage and transform the object. Depending on the object itself, we can operate with object properties. Using it, we can perform the following actions:

    o   Move the object in XYZ dimensions.

    o   Resize the object.

    o   Rotate the object.

- **Quaternion of the object**: This is the most interesting part of object modification. Quaternion is a mathematically correct rotation for a 3D object. Quaternions help avoid the problem of gimbal lock, a limitation of Euler angles, where certain orientations can cause a loss of one degree of freedom in rotation. Quaternions can represent any 3D rotation without encountering a gimbal lock. We will speak about gimbal lock in the next chapter, as it is an important part of 3D graphics.

- Animating objects in Three.js is straightforward. The library provides keyframe animation, skeletal animation, and morph target animation. Developers can animate the position, rotation, and scale of objects, as well as create complex skeletal animations for characters and models. This makes it ideal for creating everything from simple object movements to complex character animations.

- Geometries are fundamental components that define the shape and structure of 3D objects or meshes. Geometries describe the spatial arrangement of vertices (points in 3D space) and the relationships between them, such as edges and faces. They are the building blocks for creating 3D models.

- Light and shadows play a crucial role in creating realistic and visually appealing 3D scenes in Three.js. Understanding how to work with light sources and shadows is essential for achieving depth, dimensionality, and a sense of realism in your 3D renderings.

- Materials determine how light interacts with surfaces, leading to various visual effects and realism. Three.js provides a wide range of material types to choose from, each with its own set of properties and use cases.

With these capabilities, Three.js empowers developers to explore a wide range of possibilities, from creating 3D data visualizations and games to interactive educational content and architectural simulations. Whether you are a seasoned 3D developer or just starting with web-based 3D graphics, Three.js is a valuable tool that unlocks the potential for crafting engaging and visually captivating web experiences. Its active community, extensive documentation, and continuous development make it a valuable asset for anyone venturing into the world of 3D web development.

Overview of Next.js and its features

Next.js is an open-source JavaScript framework that extends React's capabilities to enable **Server-Side Rendering (SSR)**, **Static Site Generation (SSG)**, and efficient **Client-Side Rendering (CSR)**. Additionally, Next.js supports **Incremental Static Regeneration (ISR)** for on-demand updates to static content, Middleware for advanced request handling and personalization, and API routes for seamless backend functionality. It also offers built-in features like Image Optimization, Internationalization (**i18n**), and enhanced SEO capabilities. It seamlessly combines these rendering strategies, offering developers a flexible toolset for building dynamic and performant web applications. The official website for the library is presented in *Figure 3.3*

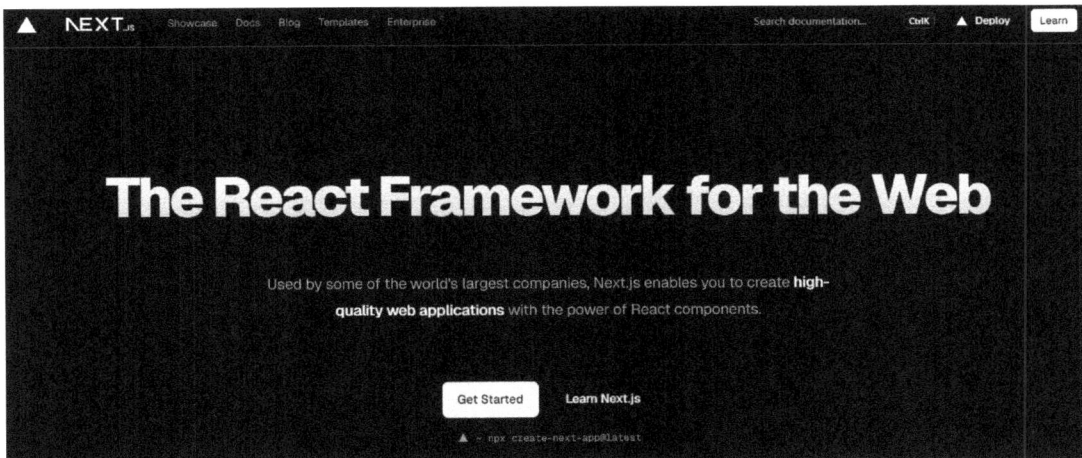

Figure 3.3: *Next.js main page*

Possibilities of Next.js

Some possibilities for Next.js are as follows:

- **Server-Side Rendering**: Next.js's SSR capability allows you to render React components on the server instead of the client, resulting in faster initial page loads and improved SEO. SSR is particularly advantageous for content-rich websites and web applications that require rapid first-time rendering.

- **Seamless routing**: Routing in Next.js is straightforward and intuitive. The framework offers both file-system-based routing and dynamic routing for defining routes and handling dynamic data. This simplicity streamlines the development process and ensures clean, organized code.

- **CSS support**: Whether you prefer CSS modules, CSS-in-JS, or traditional global CSS, Next.js provides robust support for styling your applications, giving you the flexibility to choose the approach that suits your project best.

- **Error handling**: With built-in error handling and customizable error pages, Next. js simplifies the process of identifying and resolving issues, ensuring a smoother user experience.

- **Extensive deployment options**: Next.js applications can be deployed effortlessly to a variety of hosting platforms, including Vercel, Netlify, AWS, and others, thanks to its versatile deployment options.

- **Static Site Generation (SSG) with Incremental Static Regeneration (ISR)**: Next. js enables you to pre-render pages at build time for optimal performance and SEO. With ISR, you can update static pages incrementally, ensuring content stays fresh without rebuilding the entire application. These features are ideal for projects like blogs, marketing sites, and e-commerce platforms.

Additional tools

As we will work with Next.js, we will need additional tools to work with React using Three.js. We will need a wrapper around Three.js called React-fiber and also a library to provide the web accessibility options for the Three.js object called React-three-a11y. Let's delve deeper into the libraries.

React Three Fiber

React Three Fiber (R3F) is a JavaScript library that bridges the gap between React and Three. js. It allows developers to create and manipulate 3D scenes and objects using a declarative, component-based approach similar to React. R3F (*Figure 3.4*), often abbreviated as R3F, simplifies the integration of Three.js into React applications and provides a more intuitive way to work with 3D graphics. The official website for the library is presented in *Figure 3.4*.

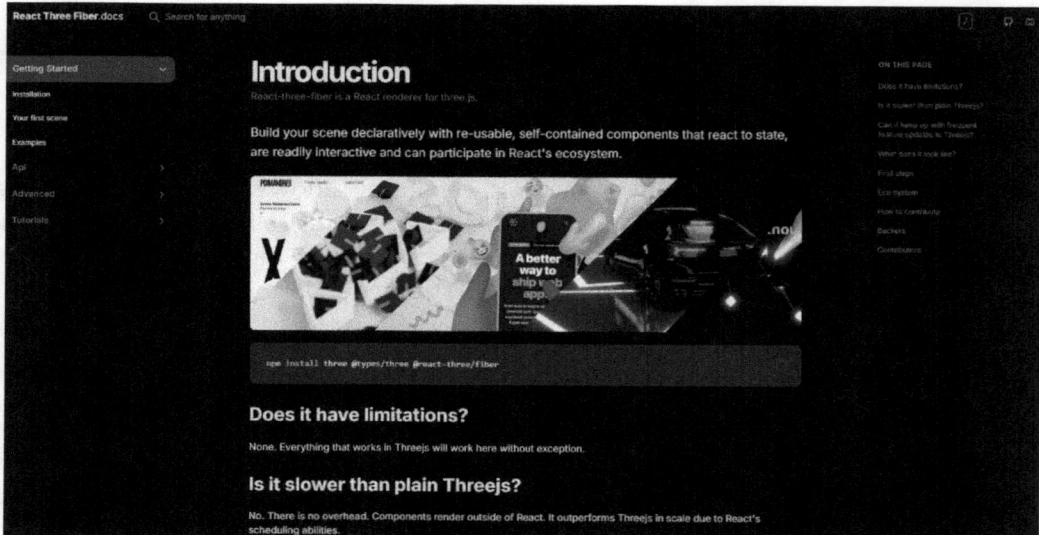

Figure 3.4: React Three Fiber main page

Here are some key points to understand about R3F:

- **Component-based 3D development**: R3F brings the component-based development paradigm of React to 3D graphics. It allows you to define 3D scenes, objects, cameras, and lights as components, making it easier to manage and structure complex 3D applications.

- **Declarative API**: Like React, R3F provides a declarative API, where you describe what your 3D scene should look like based on the current state of your application. This declarative approach simplifies 3D development by focusing on the desired outcome rather than the step-by-step imperative process.

- **Hooks-based**: R3F utilizes React hooks, such as useEffect and useState, to handle lifecycle events and state changes within your 3D components. This allows for dynamic and interactive 3D scenes that respond to user interactions and data changes.

- **Performance optimization**: R3F optimizes performance by automatically handling updates and re-renders efficiently. It uses a reconciliation mechanism to update only the parts of the 3D scene that have changed, similar to React's virtual DOM.

- **Shader material**: R3F supports custom shaders and materials, allowing you to create visually stunning and highly customized 3D objects. You can write shaders using **OpenGL Shading Language** (**GLSL**) and apply them to your components.

- **Physics integration**: R3F can be used in conjunction with physics libraries like Cannon.js or Ammo.js to simulate realistic physics interactions in your 3D scenes.

- **VR and AR support**: R3F provides support for building **virtual reality** (**VR**) and **augmented reality** (**AR**) experiences, making it suitable for immersive 3D applications.

- **Cross-platform compatibility**: R3F works across different platforms and devices, ensuring that your 3D applications are accessible to a broad audience.

- **Camera and viewport control**: R3F provides components like `<Canvas>` and hooks like `useThree` for configuring and managing camera settings (position, rotation, and zoom). Additionally, the `OrbitControls` component allows users to interactively navigate 3D scenes, adjusting the camera through rotation, zoom, and panning.

- **Lighting and shadows**: R3F enables realistic lighting using components like `<ambientLight>`, `<directionalLight>`, `<spotLight>`, and `<pointLight>`. Shadows are easily implemented with the `<shadowMap>` prop on `<Canvas>`, and meshes can be configured to cast or receive shadows using properties like `castShadow` and `receiveShadow`, enhancing the 3D scene's realism.

React-three-a11y

React-three-a11y is a library that brings accessibility to WebGL by adding **Web Content Accessibility Guidelines** (**WCAG**) standards to the R3F components. This library will open to developers these possibilities:

- Focus and focus indication
- Tab index and keyboard navigation
- Screen reader support and alt-text
- Roles and cursor shapes
- Descriptive links

Using these tools will allow us to create not only magnificent WebGL applications but also make them accessible to various users.

Understanding AWS Amplify

AWS Amplify is a comprehensive platform for building modern web and mobile applications, offering a robust set of features that make it an attractive choice compared to other services. If you anticipate growth or need advanced customization, Amplify's flexibility is ideal. Amplify's reliance on AWS infrastructure ensures better scalability and performance for growing apps. Also, Amplify offers more flexibility and avoids vendor lock-in, providing easier migration options.

Here is a short comparison with other services:

Criteria	AWS Amplify	Firebase	Supabase	Appwrite	Netlify + FaunaDB
CI/CD Integration	Full CI/CD with Git support	Limited CI/CD with Firebase Hosting	No built-in, external tools needed	No native CI/CD, requires external setup	Full CI/CD with Git support
Git Integration	GitHub, GitLab, Bitbucket, AWS CodeCommit	GitHub only	GitHub, GitLab (via external setup)	No direct Git integration	GitHub, GitLab, Bitbucket
Automatic Deployment	Yes	Yes	No, requires external setup	No, needs an external setup	Yes
Pre/Post Build Configurations	Customizable via buildspec.yml	Limited customization via CLI	Requires external setup	Needs external CI/CD config	Customizable build scripts
Preview Deployments	Yes, for PRs	Limited	Via external CI/CD tools	No native support	Yes, for PRs

Criteria	AWS Amplify	Firebase	Supabase	Appwrite	Netlify + FaunaDB
Rollback Capability	Easy via Amplify Console	Firebase CLI/Console	Manual via external CI/CD tools	Requires manual setup	Easy via Netlify Console
Pricing	Free tier, pay-as-you-go	Free tier, pay-as-you-go	Free tier, external tools may incur costs	Free tier, external hosting may cost	Free tier, pricing based on usage
Ease of Use	Easy setup with Git-based workflows	Easy for Firebase projects	Moderate (external setup required)	Requires external CI/CD setup	Easy setup, Git-focused workflows

Table 3.1: Comparison with other services

AWS Amplify is a development platform that simplifies the process of building web and mobile applications on AWS cloud services. It provides a set of tools and services that cover a wide range of tasks, from front-end development to back-end infrastructure management, authentication, and more. AWS Amplify aims to accelerate the development process, making it faster and more efficient while ensuring best practices and scalability.

Industrial applications have long relied on legacy systems and on-premises solutions. However, the demands of modern industry, including real-time data processing, scalability, and remote monitoring, have spurred the adoption of cloud-based technologies. AWS Amplify seamlessly integrates with the AWS ecosystem to meet these demands and drive innovation in industrial settings.

Industrial processes can be highly dynamic and may require rapid scalability to handle fluctuations in demand. AWS Amplify's cloud-native architecture allows applications to scale effortlessly, ensuring that industrial operations can adapt to changing requirements in real-time. The official website for the service is presented in *Figure 3.5*:

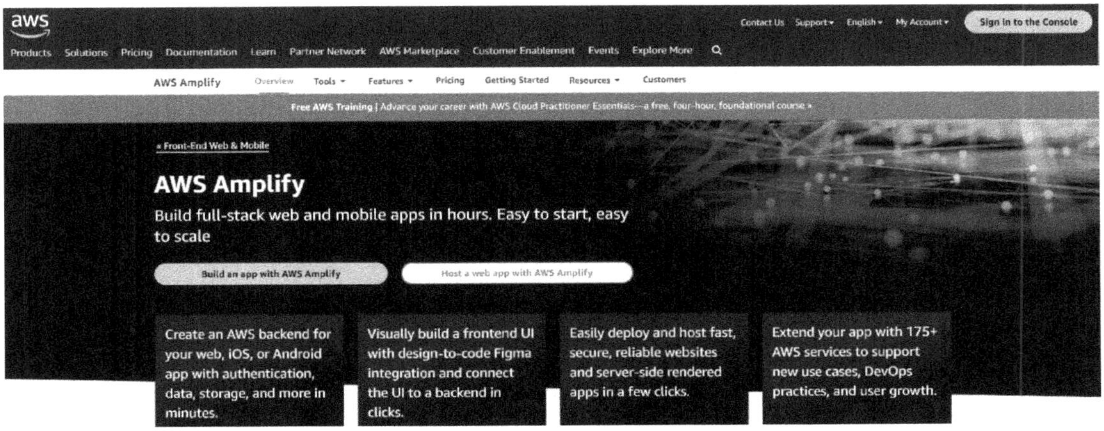

Figure 3.5: AWS Amplify main page

AWS Amplify is a huge SAAS software, and we will not deep dive into every aspect as it is out of the scope of this book topic, but let us look at some features that we will use:

- **Authentication and authorization**: AWS Amplify offers robust authentication and authorization mechanisms out of the box. Developers can easily set up user sign-up, sign-in, and **multi-factor authentication (MFA)** flows. Amplify also integrates with popular identity providers like Amazon Cognito, social logins, and custom authentication methods.

- **Data storage**: Managing data is made effortless with Amplify. You can create and configure data models and databases using Amplify's DataStore, which supports real-time data synchronization, offline access, and conflict resolution. It integrates seamlessly with Amazon DynamoDB and other AWS storage services.

- **Real-time and offline support**: Building real-time and offline-capable applications is simplified with Amplify. It handles data synchronization and conflict resolution, allowing users to work seamlessly even when offline.

- **Hosting and continuous deployment**: Amplify offers hosting and continuous deployment capabilities, making it easy to deploy your application to AWS Amplify Console or other hosting platforms. It automates the build and deployment process, ensuring that your app is always up to date.

By leveraging AWS Amplify, developers can focus on building innovative features and delivering exceptional user experiences while AWS takes care of the underlying infrastructure and operations. Whether you're a seasoned AWS user or new to cloud development, AWS Amplify is a valuable tool that empowers you to bring your application ideas to life with ease.

Exploring the benefits of Storybook

User interface (UI) development can be a complex and time-consuming process. Ensuring that components look and behave as intended across various scenarios and edge cases is a daunting task. This is where Storybook comes to the rescue. Storybook is an essential tool in modern front-end development, empowering developers to build, test, and showcase UI components in isolation. In this part, we will take a deep dive into Storybook, exploring its features, benefits, and how it simplifies UI development. The official website for the library is presented in *Figure 3.6*:

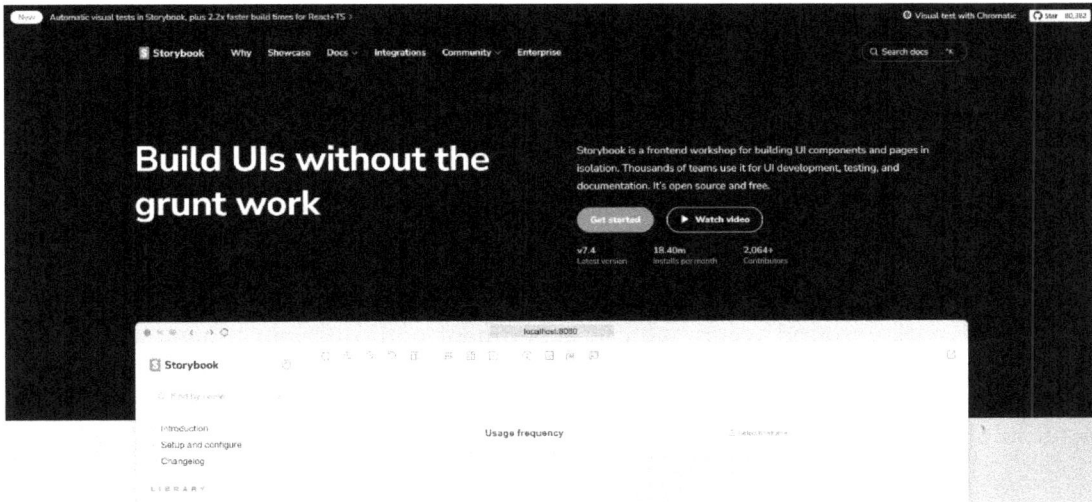

Figure 3.6: Storybook main page

Storybook is an open-source tool for developing UI components in isolation. It provides a development environment where developers can design, build, and test UI components in isolation from the rest of the application. Each UI component is presented as a *Storybook*, which is a self-contained unit showcasing the component's various states and variations.

Let us explore the fundamental characteristics that establish Storybook as an indispensable asset for UI development:

- Storybook allows developers to work on individual UI components in isolation. This isolation prevents unintended side effects from affecting other parts of the application.

- Storybook enables visual testing, making it easy to identify visual regressions and inconsistencies as components evolve. Developers can spot issues early and maintain a consistent UI.

- Storybook serves as a centralized showcase for UI components, making it easy for designers, developers, and stakeholders to see how components look and behave under different conditions.

- Developers can interact with and test UI components by adjusting their props and states directly in Storybook, providing instant feedback and reducing the need for context switches.

- Storybook automatically generates component documentation, including usage examples and prop descriptions. This documentation is valuable for onboarding new team members and maintaining a consistent coding style.

- Storybook supports a wide range of add-ons that extend its functionality. Developers can add custom add-ons or use community-contributed ones to enhance their workflow.

- Storybook provides tools and add-ons for accessibility testing, helping developers ensure that UI components are usable by individuals with disabilities.

As we will work with a component-based framework for the UI, using Storybook for the component creation will be very convenient. Also, this will allow us to test our Three.js implementations independently before using them in the page component. We will also use Storybook for generating documentation for our 3D components. As Storybook provides an interactive playground where we can experiment with different things, we will use this possibility too. This accelerates the development and fine-tuning process. Ultimately, we will create the UI system for our application to wrap the 3D-based application with beautiful designs.

Introduction to Tailwind CSS

As we plan to wrap our 3D application with a robust UI, we will need a **Cascade Style Sheets** (**CSS**) framework.

Tailwind CSS is a utility-first CSS framework that provides developers with a powerful set of tools for designing and building responsive and efficient web applications. In this article, we will explore what Tailwind CSS is, its core principles, key features, and how it can streamline your web development workflow. The official website for the library is presented in *Figure 3.7*:

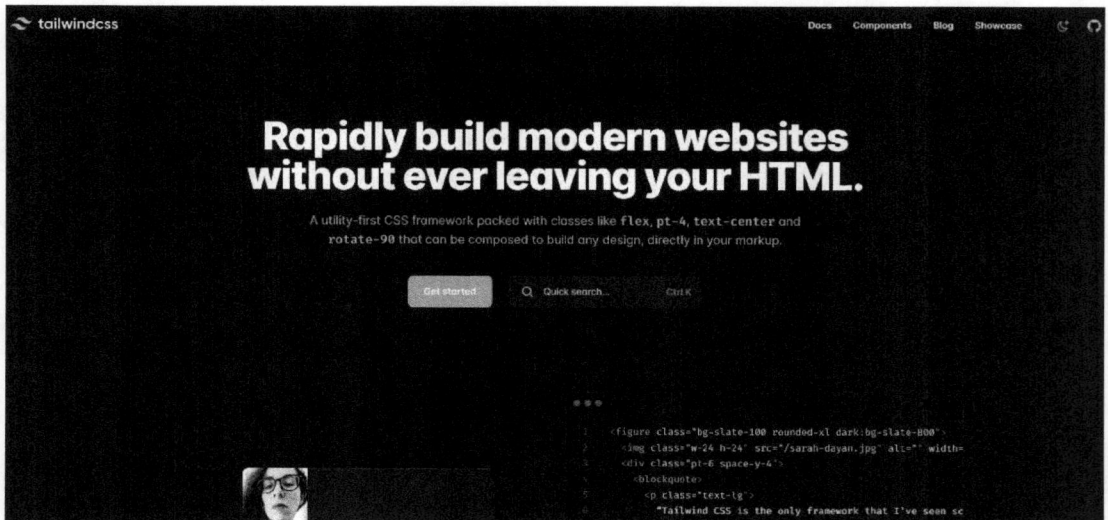

Figure 3.7: Tailwind CSS main page

Tailwind CSS is not just another CSS framework; it is a paradigm shift in how developers approach styling web applications. It is designed to help developers rapidly build UIs by providing a set of pre-defined utility classes that can be easily applied directly to HTML elements. Here are the core principles that define Tailwind CSS:

- Tailwind CSS follows a utility-first approach, meaning that it provides a comprehensive set of utility classes that you can use to apply styling directly to your HTML elements. This approach promotes a declarative and intuitive way of writing CSS.

- While Tailwind CSS comes with an extensive set of default utility classes, it is highly customizable. Developers can extend, modify, or even create their utility classes to suit their specific project requirements.

- While Tailwind CSS comes with an extensive set of default utility classes, it is highly customizable. Developers can extend, modify, or even create their utility classes to suit their specific project requirements.

- Tailwind CSS is designed with performance in mind. By composing styles from utility classes, you can eliminate unused CSS, resulting in smaller file sizes and faster load times.

- Tailwind CSS makes it easy to create responsive layouts with classes like `sm: flex` and `md:px-4`. This ensures your application looks great on all devices.

- Tailwind CSS works well with component-based libraries like React and in our case it's Next.js based on top of React.

- Tailwind CSS supports dark mode out of the box, making it easy to create interfaces that adapt to users' preferences.

Conclusion

In this chapter, we have explored the world of modern web development, exploring a diverse set of tools and technologies that have revolutionized the way we create web applications.

As we conclude this chapter, we have gained valuable insights into these tools and technologies that are shaping the landscape of web development. These tools have not only expanded our creative horizons but also empowered us to build web applications that are visually captivating, performant, and efficient. In the ever-evolving world of web development, embracing these tools opens up exciting possibilities for innovation, collaboration, and user-centric design.

In the next chapter, we will make a setup for these tools to have a soft start in our 3D web development journey.

Points to remember

About Three.js

1. Three.js is a powerful 3D graphics library for web development.

2. It enables the creation of interactive 3D web experiences.

3. Its versatility spans various industries and projects.

About Next.js

1. Next.js is a popular framework for building React applications.

2. It simplifies rendering and routing.

3. It offers great features like automatic code splitting and hot module replacement.

About AWS Amplify

1. AWS Amplify is a set of tools and services for web and mobile app development.

2. It simplifies backend development, authentication, and data storage.

3. It's known for its ease of use and scalability.

About Storybook

1. Storybook is a development environment for UI components.

2. It helps with component documentation, testing, and collaboration.

3. It streamlines UI development and promotes reusability.

About TailwindCSS

1. Tailwind CSS is a utility-first CSS framework.

2. It allows for rapid and flexible styling of web components.

3. It's a popular choice for efficient and responsive web design.

Join our Discord space

Join our Discord workspace for latest updates, offers, tech happenings around the world, new releases, and sessions with the authors:

https://discord.bpbonline.com

Chapter 4

Setting up All Tools for Quickstart of Development

Introduction

In this chapter, we will demonstrate how to set up both **Three.js** and **Next.js** projects, ensuring that you have a solid foundation to build upon. Additionally, you will learn how to harness the power of **Amazon Web Services** (**AWS**) **Amplify Command Line Interface** (**CLI**) tools to streamline your workflow development and make deployment easier. We will not stop there, you will understand the importance of **user interface** (**UI**) design and development in modern applications. Therefore, we will also cover the integration of **Tailwind CSS**, a utility-first CSS framework, to effortlessly style your components and create a visually appealing user experience. Furthermore, you will also be introduced to **Storybook**, a tool for developing UI components in isolation, allowing you to build and test your UI elements efficiently.

Structure

This chapter covers the following topics:

- Setting up a Three.js project
- Setting up a Next.js project
- Setting up AWS Amplify CLI tools

Objectives

By the end of this chapter, you will be equipped with the knowledge and tools needed to start your Three.js and Next.js project with confidence. Whether you are an experienced developer or just beginning your journey, this chapter will serve as your roadmap to creating stunning 3D web applications that can captivate users and elevate your online experiences. So, let us dive in and get started on this exciting adventure in web development.

Setting up Three.js project

As we mentioned in the previous chapter, for the web application producing Three.js objects in **React**, we will use a special library that will wrap our objects into components. But before that, we need to learn the generic usage of the Three.js library. For this, we will need to set up Three.js independently and learn the basics. Then, we will switch to React Fiber in *Chapter 13, Introduction to Next.js and Three.js Integration,* knowledge of the basics will allow us to get into the usage of the React library faster.

To start the project, we will need to install **Node.js** (at the current time, version 20. You can use any version, but avoid using a version lower than 16, as the **Minimal NPM (Node Package Manager)** version is 8. Also, we will require a build tool, you can use Webpack or Vite. In the current example, we will take Vite as the build tool. There are numerous ways to install Three.js with other tools, including a direct insertion of the library into the page, including the **Content Delivery Network (CDN)**.

To start working with Three.js, please create the project folder and follow these steps:

1. Create the **index.html** file and add code from *Code Listing 4.1* inside:

```
2.  <!DOCTYPE html>
3.  <html lang="en">
4.  <head>
5.    <meta charset="utf-8">
6.    <title>My first three.js app</title>
7.    <style> body { margin: 0; } </style>
8.  </head>
9.  <body>
10.   <script type="module" src="/main.js"></script>
11. </body>
12. </html>
```

Code Listing 4.1: Source code for index.html

2. Create a file **main.js** with the code from *Code Listing 4.2:*

```
1.  import * as THREE from 'three';
2.  console.log('Let`s start 3D adventure');
```

Code Listing 4.2: Source code for main.js

3. After that, we will need to install dependencies. To install them, run these commands in your project folder: `npm install-- save three vite`

4. Now, we can start the project by typing this command in the CLI from the project root: `npx vite`

5. Now, in the console, you will see the port application that gets started, like in *Figure 4.1*:

VITE v4.4.9 ready in 195 ms

➜ **Local: http://localhost:5173/**

➜ **Network: use --host to expose**

➜ **press h to show help**

Figure 4.1: *Vite response in the console*

Your page will look like *Figure 4.2*:

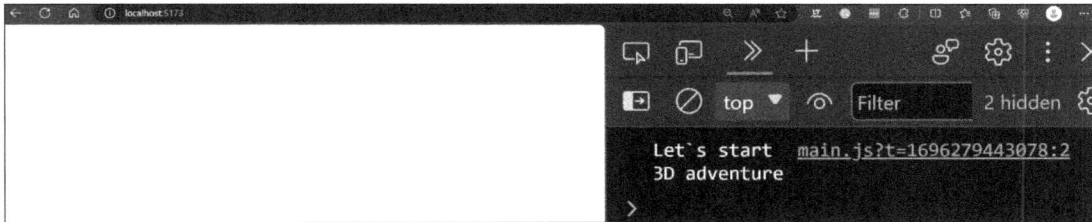

Figure 4.2: *Browser screen after Vite start*

Setting up the Next.js project

To start with Next.js, create a separate folder for it and open the command line tool. Be sure that your local setup fits these requirements: Node.js **version 18.17** or the later version.

In this book, we will use Next.js version **14.1.4**, which is the latest version. When you read this book, make sure that there are no major updates to the framework so that no additional setup is required.

1. Enter the following command to initiate the project in your folder:
   `npx create-next-app@latest`

2. Enter selections from *Figure 4.3* in the CLI dialogue:

√ What is your project named? ... **industrial-app**

√ Would you like to use TypeScript? ... **No** / Yes

√ Would you like to use ESLint? ... No / **Yes**

√ Would you like to use Tailwind CSS? ... No / **Yes**

√ Would you like to use `src/` directory? ... No / **Yes**

√ Would you like to use App Router? (recommended) ... No / **Yes**

√ Would you like to customize the default import alias (@/*)? ... No / **Yes**

√ What import alias would you like configured? ... **@/***

Figure 4.3: CLI dialogue selections. Use marked bold as selected

3. To simplify the learning path, we will not use **TypeScript** in this book to avoid diverting the focus from 3D development. However, you can choose TypeScript if you have the experience and prefer strict typing in your daily coding.

Adding SASS support to the project

As we will use Tailwind CSS for styling our project, we will also require **Syntactically Awesome Stylesheet** (**SASS**). And yes, it is awesome support. This will allow us to create nested styles and stick to the **Block Element Modifier** (**BEM**) topology if it will be required. To do that, enter the following command in your project root:

1. **npm install sass (or yarn add sass)**

2. **npm run dev (or yarn dev)**

Setting up Tailwind

As you remember from the installation stage, we already added the Tailwind CSS library to the project. At the current stage, we only need to check that everything is set up correctly. To do that, open the file from your Next.js project directory with the name **tailwind. config.js** and add the code from *Code Listing 4.3* inside.

```
1.  # Code source of the Tailwind CSS configuration file
2.  @type {import('tailwindcss').Config} */
3.  module.exports = {
4.    content: [
5.      './src/pages/**/*.{js,ts,jsx,tsx,mdx}',
6.      './src/components/**/*.{js,ts,jsx,tsx,mdx}',
7.      './src/app/**/*.{js,ts,jsx,tsx,mdx}',
8.    ],
9.    theme: {
10.     extend: {
```

```
11.      backgroundImage: {
12.         'gradient-radial': 'radial-gradient(var(--tw-gradient-
    stops))',
13.         'gradient-conic':
14.            'conic-gradient(from 180deg at 50% 50%, var(--tw-gradient-
    stops))',
15.      },
16.    },
17.  },
18.  plugins: [],
19. }
```

Code Listing 4.3: Tailwind CSS configuration file

Adding Storybook

Storybook is an open-source development tool that is used for building and testing isolated UI components in web applications. It provides a development environment that allows you to create, preview, and interact with individual components outside of your main application. Storybook is primarily designed to be used with React (although it supports other JavaScript frameworks as well), making it a great choice when working with Next.js, which is built on React.

In this book, we will create various components in React; for this, a tool is required to visually test components and keep everything well documented. To keep on plan, we will add Storybook to our Next.js project. To add it to the project, open your Next.js project root and enter the following command in the CLI: **npx storybook@latest init.**

The installation procedure will automatically detect the project and its configuration. The software will be installed in the **src** folder as stories, and you will also find the configuration files in the **.storybook** folder in your project root.

After the successful installation, we need to make several changes to configure the Storybook to work correctly with Next.js. The first issue that we need to resolve is including global styles in the project. Open the file from the Storybook configuration **storybook/ preview.js** and add the code from *Code Listing 4.4* inside:

```
1.  # Add Global styles into the preview.js file
2.  import "../src/app/globals.scss";
```

Code Listing 4.4: Adding global styles to the configuration

As we use the **.scss** file, we will also be required to add this package to the project. To do that, enter the following command in the CLI in your root folder:

```
npm i -D style-loader css-loader sass-loader
```

After this, we can update the **.storybook/main.js** with code from *Code Listing 4.5*.

```
1.  # Add support for the SCSS files in the configuration
2.  import { join, dirname, resolve } from "path";
3.
4.  // old code here
5.
6.  const config = {
7.    // old code here
8.    rules: [
9.      {
10.        test: /\\.s(a|c)ss$/,
11.        include: resolve(__dirname, '../'),
12.        use: [
13.          'style-loader',
14.          {
15.            loader: 'css-loader',
16.            options: {
17.              modules: {
18.                auto: true,
19.                localIdentName: '[name]__[local]--[hash:base64:5]',
20.              },
21.            },
22.          },
23.          'sass-loader'
24.        ],
25.      }
26.    ]
27. // old code here
28. };
29.
30. export default config;
```

Code Listing 4.5: Update for main.js in Storybook

Finally, we can start the Storybook from the command in your project root: **npm run storybook.**

Setting up AWS Amplify CLI tools

AWS Amplify is a set of tools and services provided by AWS that simplifies the development of full-stack web and mobile applications. Amplify offers a wide range of features and services that cover various aspects of application development, including authentication, API management, storage, and hosting. When used with Next.js, a popular React framework for building web applications, Amplify can enhance the development process in several ways.

Let us add the latest AWS Amplify tools to the project. First of all, open your browser and click on this link: **https://aws.amazon.com/amplify** (you will see the same page as on *Figure 4.4*)

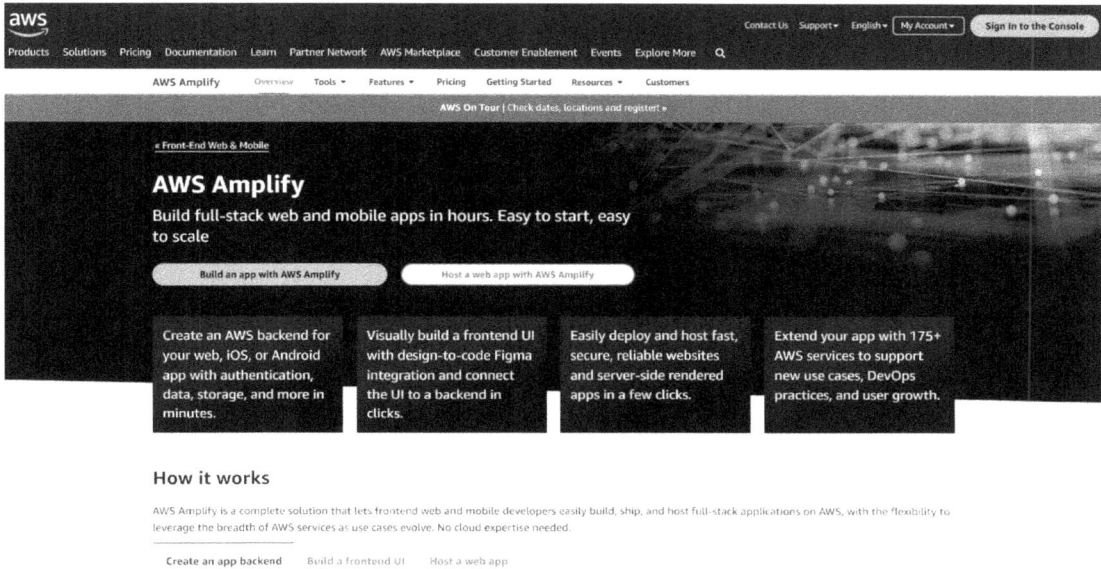

Figure 4.4: *AWS Amplify main page*

Sign up to create an account in AWS. After that, enter the console, and you will find the search component in the header line. Use the search to find the Amplify section. You will see the layout as shown in *Figure 4.5*:

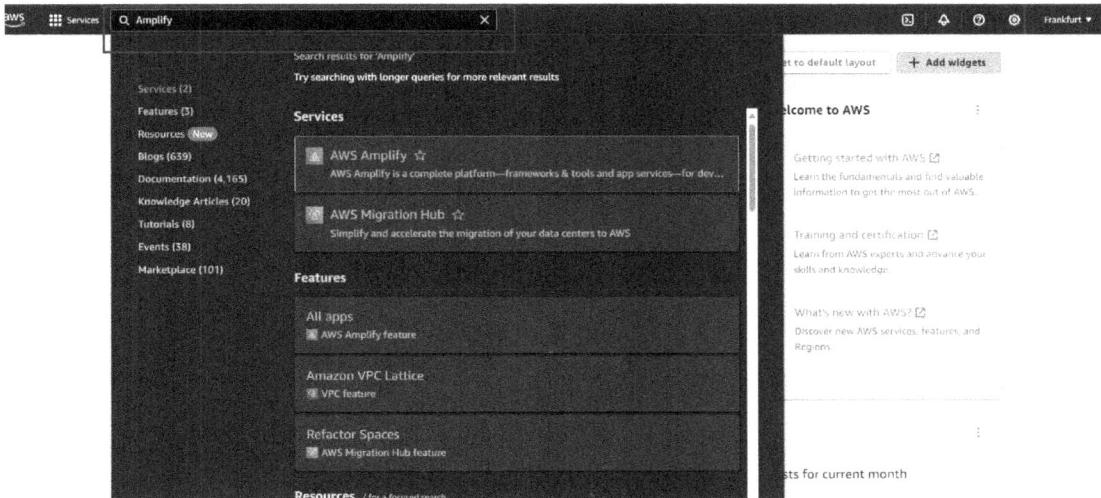

Figure 4.5: *Using search to find Amplify*

On the Amplify page, you will find the button with the menu to create your first project, as shown in *Figure 4.6*. Use it to build your first project.

Figure 4.6: Create and build your first app

Enter the name for your application and confirm the deployment by using the button with the label shown in *Figure 4.7*:

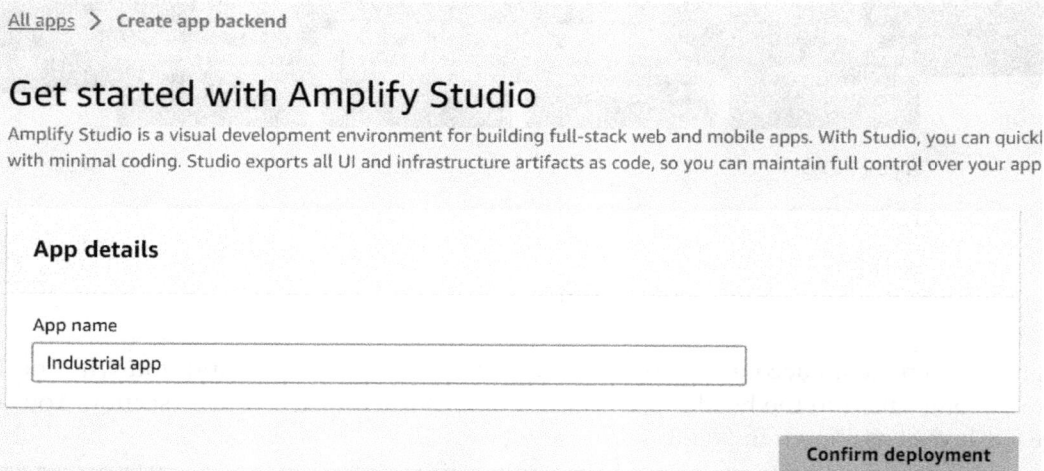

Figure 4.7: Entering the name and confirming the deployment

Configuration on the AWS side takes some time. While it is creating the configuration, you will see the status information similar to *Figure 4.8*:

Figure 4.8: Status of the deployment

Finally, you can enter the Amplify studio by pressing the **Launch Studio** button as shown in *Figure 4.9*:

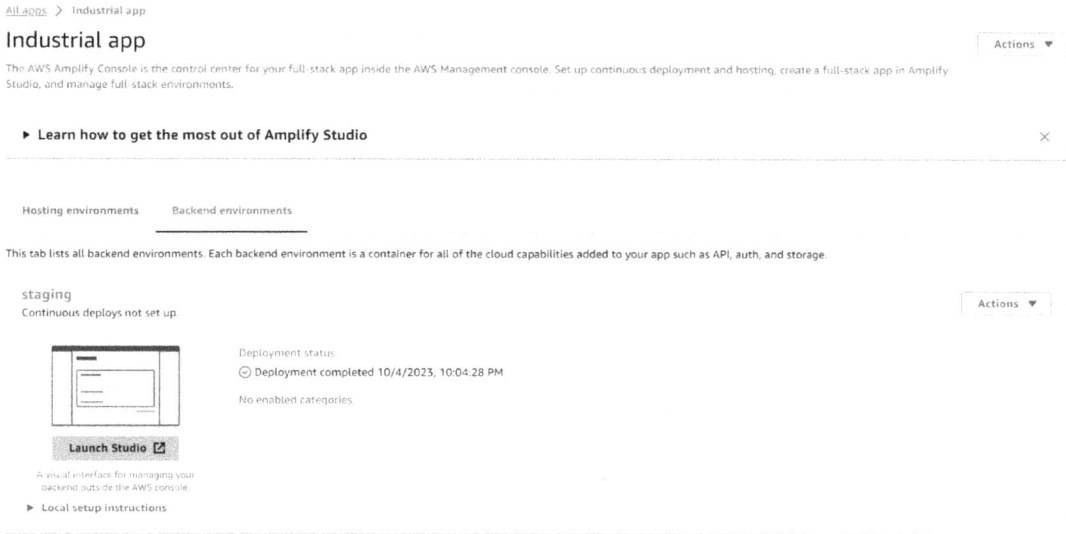

Figure 4.9: Complete deployment screen

On the project page, find the link with the caption *Local setup instruction* and you will see the screen from *Figure 4.10*:

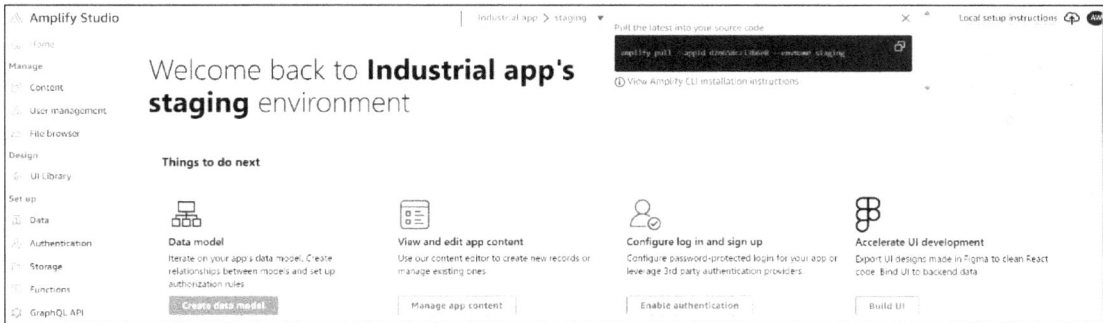

Figure 4.10: Local instruction modal window

Enter the following command to install the CLI tools on your machine: **npm I -g @aws/ amplify/cli**

Then, use the command given below in the project root to add Amplify:

amplify pull --appId <YOUR-ID> --envName staging

Finally, we have the AWS Amplify project linked with Next.js. We will come back to it in the upcoming chapters.

Conclusion

In this chapter, we have laid the foundation for our journey into web development, focusing on integrating cutting-edge technologies. We have also learned how to set up projects using Three.js and Next.js, two powerful tools enabling us to create immersive and interactive web applications.

We began by exploring the setup process for both Three.js and Next.js, ensuring that our development environments are ready to support our endeavors. We delved into the specifics of setting up a Next.js project and learned how to add essential features like SASS support for improved styling, and the integration of the popular utility-first CSS framework, Tailwind, to streamline your workflow styling.

Additionally, we introduced Storybook, a tool that will help us to develop and document components more efficiently, enhancing the overall development process.

To further expand our capabilities and simplify backend development, we discussed the setup of AWS Amplify CLI tools, which will enable us to manage backend services seamlessly.

As we conclude this chapter, we have a solid foundation in place and are ready to embark on the exciting journey of 3D development using Three.js. In the next chapter, we will discuss Three.js, exploring its capabilities and gradually building interactive 3D applications.

Points to remember

- Learning the basics of Three.js is important.
- Knowing both ways of using will give you the possibility to increase performance and optimize maintainability with the combination of using React Fiber and vanilla Three.js.

Exercises

1. Follow the chapter blocks and set up your development environment.

CHAPTER 5

Introduction to 3D Development

Introduction

In the evolving landscape of web development, the integration of **three-dimensional** (**3D**) elements has emerged as a transformative force. This chapter marks the beginning of an exciting journey into the world of 3D web development. We will explore the fundamental principles and techniques that underpin this dynamic field. Whether you are a seasoned web developer looking to expand your skill set or an aspiring creator eager to craft immersive online experiences, this chapter will provide the solid foundation you need to venture into the captivating world of 3D web development.

Structure

The chapter covers the following topics:

- Introduction to world of 3D development
- Basic concepts of 3D graphics

Objectives

By the end of this chapter, you will learn the fundamental 3D concepts. So, get ready to apply them in your web development endeavors. Whether you aspire to build stunning 3D games, interactive product showcases, virtual environments, or simply enhance your web applications with 3D elements, the insights gained here will be the building blocks of your journey.

Introduction to world of 3D development

When you delve into the world of graphics, you will soon discover that crafting the sophisticated programs you had admired was far more challenging than anticipated. Your attempt to navigate this complex terrain involved hacking through a plethora of resources, such as the **Open Graphics Library (OpenGL)** pipeline specifications, various books, and articles. We will try to deliver this knowledge to you in a more basic way.

Let us commence with an illustration. Imagine an idyllic coastal scene with sandy shores, an endless expanse of the sea, and a clear sky, reminiscent of the serene coastal paintings by the renowned artist, refer to *Figure 5.1*:

Figure 5.1: Idyllic coastal scene

Now, the challenge is to visually represent this intricate 3D scene. We can start by painting an image that encapsulates all the elements.

This artistic 3D scene involves several key steps:

1. **Choosing the right perspective**: We must decide on the viewing angle that best captures the essence of the scene. This means highlighting only the elements visible from our chosen perspective and disregarding those that are hidden from view.

2. **Managing occlusion**: Next, we need to determine which parts of the various objects are concealed by others. For instance, while the meadow is in plain sight, it partially obscures the river. The distant mountains, although breathtaking, obstruct everything positioned behind them, allowing us to disregard these hidden elements.

3. **Scaling to fit**: Given that the physical expanse of the actual scene exceeds the dimensions of our canvas, we must figure out how to scale the visible components to fit within the confines of the canvas.

4. **Rendering with precision**: With these considerations in mind, we can now proceed to paint the objects. This process considers factors like lighting, shadows, the atmospheric effects of distant mountains, and more. It closely mirrors the techniques employed in computer graphics to bring the scene to life.

In the realm of computer graphics, the following steps align with this artistic analogy:

1. **Determining object appearance**: We define the visual characteristics of objects within the virtual world.

2. **Spatial arrangement**: We establish the spatial positions of these objects in the 3D world.

3. **Setting the camera view**: We position the virtual camera within the scene and select a portion of the scene to render.

4. **Camera-object relations**: We calculate the relative positions of objects with respect to the camera's viewpoint.

5. **Scene rendering**: Objects are then drawn and rendered within the scene.

6. **Viewport scaling**: Finally, the scene is proportionally scaled to fit the dimensions of the viewing window or canvas.

However, we paint the image on paper, and 3D rendering works in the same direction. Our eyes do not recognize the difference if it is 2D and 3D before this image starts to show the information that makes this image 3D. But how is the magic happening? Let us look into some key concepts.

Perspective

Perspective is the technique used to create the illusion of depth and three-dimensionality in a two-dimensional space. In 3D development, this concept is essential for achieving realism. In 3D development, **perspective** is a fundamental concept that closely mirrors the techniques used in real painting to create a sense of depth, distance, and realism. Just as painters manipulate **perspective** to make their artwork appear 3D, 3D developers use similar principles to render a life-like scene.

In traditional painting, artists use foreshortening to depict objects or scenes in a way that mimics how they appear to the human eye. For example, when painting a road or a river, objects closer to the viewer are rendered larger, while distant elements are smaller.

Let us take a look at *Figure 5.1* that we had before and add some helpful information to it. We will put lines of perspective to understand how the human eye recognizes distance and depth, refer to the figure given below:

Figure 5.2: *The point of horizon representation*

In *Figure 5.2*, we can see how the human eye detects depth. We look into the point of the horizon and see how far each object in the picture is located. The picture gets into the human brain, where we utilize the information and understand the position of everything.

Lights

Lighting is a fundamental aspect of 3D development that profoundly impacts the visual quality, realism, and mood of a scene or environment. It involves the simulation and manipulation of light sources and how they interact with objects in a 3D space. Understanding lighting principles is critical for creating immersive and visually appealing 3D experiences.

As an explanation for the perspective, lights are also a part of the process of how the human eye sees the world. The way they collide with the objects is important as it makes them visually 3D. Lights are also used by the artists to show you that the object in a painting is not flat. Let us look at *Figure 5.3*:

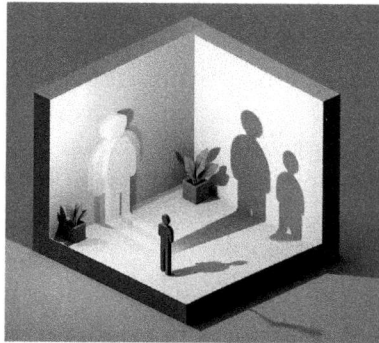

Figure 5.3: *Lights example in 3D image*

In 3D development, light sources can include directional lights (for example, sunlight), point lights (for example, lamps), spotlights (for example, car headlights), and ambient light (for example, natural sunlight). Each type of light source has distinct characteristics that affect the objects differently. Directional light, for example, simulates the parallel rays of the sun, while point lights emit light in all directions from a single point.

Shadows are crucial for creating depth and realism in 3D scenes. Shadows can be hard (sharp) or soft (blurred), and they depend on the type of light source, the distance from the object, and the objects in the scene. Implementing shadow maps and shadow algorithms is common in 3D development.

Lighting is a powerful tool for conveying emotion and atmosphere. For example, a horror game may use dim lighting and dramatic shadows to create a suspenseful mood. A sunny outdoor scene in a 3D simulation might use bright and warm lighting to evoke a sense of serenity.

This leads us to another important part of the 3D: volume.

Volume

In the context of 3D development, volume refers to the 3D space occupied by an object within a virtual environment. It is a critical aspect of 3D graphics, as it gives objects substance, mass, and a sense of occupying physical space. Understanding and effectively representing volume is essential for creating realistic and immersive 3D worlds.

In 3D modeling, volume is determined by the geometry and shape of an object. When modeling an object, such as a car or a character, it is crucial to define the volume accurately to ensure it appears life-like. This involves creating a 3D mesh with precise dimensions, proportions, and contours. It affects how light interacts with objects in a 3D scene. The way light is absorbed, reflected, or refracted by objects is influenced by their volume. Properly representing it is essential for realistic shading and rendering in 3D graphics. Refer to *Figure 5.4*:

Figure 5.4: Creating a 3D effect with volume

Simulating physical properties, such as the behavior of fluids, gases, or deformable objects, relies on accurate representations of volume. Realistic physics simulations require precise volume calculations to ensure that the objects respond naturally to external forces.

In 3D development, it is about accurately representing the 3D space occupied by objects in a virtual world. It is crucial for creating realism, whether you are designing characters, architecture, or entire 3D environments.

Basic concepts in 3D graphics

Before we start exploring by using Three.js, we need to land on the fundamental building blocks of 3D computer graphics. This will help us better understand the tools and possibilities of the library. These basics are the cornerstone of creating immersive and visually stunning 3D environments. Let us dive in and uncover the foundational knowledge that will empower you in the exciting realm of 3D graphics.

3D coordinate systems and space

In 3D graphics, we use Cartesian coordinates to represent points in 3D space. The most common system is the right-handed coordinate system, where the X-axis points right, the Y-axis points up, and the Z-axis points forward (towards the viewer). The intersection of these axes, called the origin, is (0,0,0). Refer to the following figure:

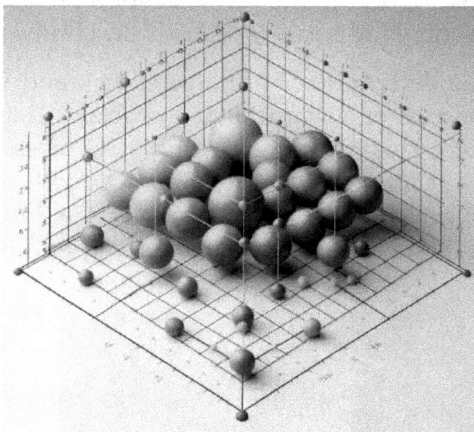

Figure 5.5: Cartesian coordinate system view

In Cartesian coordinates, positive values extend along the positive direction of each axis, while negative values extend along the negative direction. For example, moving in the positive X direction increases the X-coordinate, and moving in the negative Y direction decreases the Y-coordinate. It also allows precise measurement of distances, angles, and positions in 3D space. This is essential for accurately defining the geometry and location of 3D objects.

Cartesian coordinates are crucial for applying transformations in the 3D space. Translations, rotations, and scaling operations are typically represented using matrices and vectors in these coordinates.

And in the end, it affects the rendering process. Cartesian coordinates of the objects are projected onto a 2D plane, such as a computer screen, to create a 2D image. This projection is usually done through perspective, as we have mentioned before.

3D space in the context of graphics refers to the virtual, 3D environment where objects and scenes are represented, manipulated, and rendered. Understanding 3D space is fundamental for creating immersive, realistic, and visually appealing graphics.

3D Models and objects

In 3D space, objects are represented as 3D models. These models can be simple geometric primitives like cubes, spheres, and cones. It also includes highly complex structures, such as characters, vehicles, architectural buildings, and natural landscapes. 3D models are defined by their geometry, which includes vertices, edges, and faces, and may be textured to give them color and detail.

3D models and objects are the fundamental building blocks of 3D graphics, serving as the representation of entities, characters, environments, and props in 3D virtual spaces. Understanding these models and objects is essential for creating visually engaging and immersive experiences.

Let us look into the basic types of 3D objects:

- **Geometry**: 3D models are defined by their geometric properties. Geometry includes vertices (points in 3D space), edges (lines connecting vertices), and faces (planar surfaces defined by edges). The arrangement and connectivity of these elements determine the shape and structure of the 3D model.

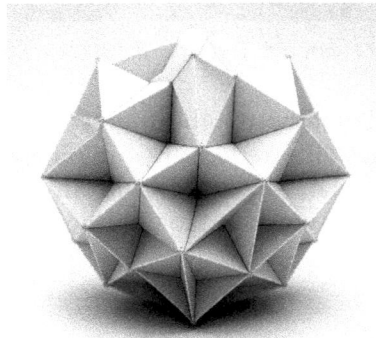

Figure 5.6: Geometry 3D model

- **Meshes**: 3D models are often constructed as meshes consisting of vertices, edges, and faces. They come in various types, including polygonal meshes (triangles, quads), parametric surfaces, **Non-Uniform Rational B-Splines (NURBS)**, and voxel grids (3D pixels). Polygonal meshes are the most common structures in 3D graphics.

Figure 5.7: Meshes in a 3D object

- **Texturing**: Textures are applied to 3D models to add color, patterns, and surface details. Texture mapping involves wrapping a 2D image onto the surface of a 3D model to enhance its appearance. Diffuse maps provide color information, normal maps influence surface normals for better lighting, and other maps can represent specularity, reflectivity, and more.

Figure 5.8: Texturing the 3D object

- **Materials**: Materials define how light interacts with the surface of a 3D model. They control properties like reflectivity, shininess, and transparency. Shading models, such as **Lambertian** (diffuse) and **Blinn-Phong** (specular), are often used to determine how materials respond to lighting.

Figure 5.9: Materials in 3D objects

Cameras and views in 3D

Cameras and views are essential components of 3D graphics that provide the perspective through which we observe and interact with the scenes and objects. Understanding cameras and views is crucial for creating immersive and visually compelling experiences.

If we take a painting as an example of a camera view, in this case, the eyes of artist will be a camera view. For a better example, let us get a camera and talk about photography. But speaking of 3D graphics, the ability of the camera is not limited by the model, lenses, or the possibility of where to stand. For the 3D graphics, we will have limitless camera possibilities that we can put at any point of the scene with any lens that we prefer. How good does it sound? It is great.

Figure 5.10: Camera representation in the 3D scene

Cameras have various parameters that define their properties, including position, orientation, **field of view** (**FOV**), near and far clipping planes, and aspect ratio. These parameters influence what the camera can see and how the scene is projected.

The camera's FOV is often represented as a pyramid called the **view frustum**. This frustum defines what is visible to the camera, including objects within its boundaries. Refer to *Figure 5.11*:

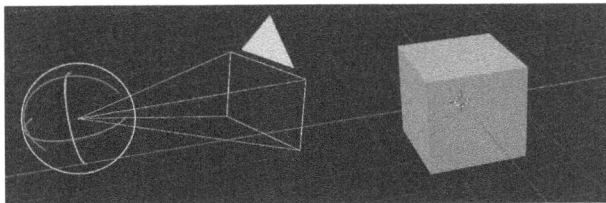

Figure 5.11: Camera View Frustum in Blender

In interactive 3D applications, camera controls are often provided to allow users to change the camera's position and orientation. This may include features like panning, zooming, orbiting, and transitioning between cameras.

Some 3D applications use multiple cameras to provide different viewpoints or to achieve specific effects. For instance, a game might use a separate camera for a rearview mirror, and a security camera system might use multiple cameras to monitor different areas.

Conclusion

In this introductory chapter, we have delved into the fascinating world of 3D development, exploring fundamental concepts and building blocks that are essential for creating immersive and visually captivating 3D experiences. We began by discussing the key concepts in 3-D development, including **perspective**, which allows us to create the illusion of depth and realism. **Lights** play a pivotal role in shaping the mood and atmosphere of 3D scenes. **Volume** defines the 3D space occupied by objects and is crucial for representing mass and depth. Then we smoothly transitioned into a deeper exploration of *Basic concepts in 3D graphics*, where we delved into the importance of *3D Coordinate systems and space*. It provides the framework for positioning and navigating objects. *3D Models and Objects* are the building blocks that define the geometry, appearance, and structure of the virtual world. We also discussed *Cameras and views in 3D*, which serve as our eyes in the virtual world, defining our perspective and how we interact with 3D scenes.

In the next chapter, we will embark on a hands-on journey into 3D development with Three.js, a powerful JavaScript library for creating 3D experiences in web applications.

Points to remember

- We live in a 3-dimensional world. Each time you get stuck in scene creation with issues like light, camera view, or materials, you can easily find solutions in the real world.

- The coding part is the easiest one in 3D application development. Please invest time in prototyping your scene before you get into coding. Blender can be a good solution for it.

Exercise

1. Make several pictures of your room, house, street, or anything that can act as your scene around you. Use *Figure 5.2* of this chapter and find the point of the horizon on the picture and the light direction.

CHAPTER 6

Getting Started with Three.js

Introduction

As with any art, 3D development requires practice. It means that it is not enough just to know the theory of three-dimensional development. We will start this chapter by setting up a fundamental Three.js environment. We will learn how to create a canvas for our 3D world, giving a hands-on experience with the essential building blocks of a 3D environment. The 3D development adventure may encounter hurdles and hitches, which we will tackle through effective debugging techniques and best practices for addressing common challenges that may arise during the Three.js projects.

Structure

This chapter will cover the following topics:

- Creating a basic Three.js scene
- Understanding core components of Three.js
- Debugging and troubleshooting

Objectives

By the end of this chapter, the readers will be equipped with the knowledge and skills needed to create a basic Three.js scene, manipulate core components, and troubleshoot common issues. These skills will lay the foundation for more advanced 3D development concepts, which we will explore in the following chapters.

Creating a basic Three.js scene

In Three.js, a **scene** is a fundamental concept that represents the 3D world or environment where objects, lights, cameras, and other elements are placed and interact. It is a container that holds all the visible and interactive components of your 3D application.

To draw a parallel with a real movie scene, think of a movie scene as the fundamental unit that represents a specific location or moment in a film storyline. Similarly, a Three.js scene serves as the stage for the 3D world. Just as a movie scene holds actors, props, and lighting, a Three.js scene contains 3D objects, lights, cameras, and more.

Each scene in Three.js corresponds to a particular part of the 3D world, just like a movie scene represents a specific part of the film plot. These scenes are environments where the action takes place, objects interact, and the story unfolds.

Whether in a movie or a 3D web application, scenes are vital containers that encapsulate the key elements needed to convey a story or create an immersive experience, providing the context and stage for the action to happen.

We already made an initial setup for the Three.js project in *Chapter 4, Setting up all tools for the QuickStart of the development*. It is suggested to make a project setup before proceeding with this chapter.

The following are the steps to set up a scene:

1. Ensure that the library is initiated in the browser. To do that, open the **main.js** file and insert this code:

```
1.  // Importing the Three.js module into the application
2.  import * as THREE from 'three';
3.  // Getting the Three.js object into the console of the browser
4.  console.log(THREE);
```

Code Listing 6.1: Initial code

2. As a result, we will see the object in the browser console or the **IDE**, if we use an extension for it, as in *Figure 6.1* and *Figure 6.2*:

```
16:56:01.586
  {
    ACESFilmicToneMapping: 4,
    AddEquation: 100,
    AddOperation: 2,
    AdditiveAnimationBlendMode: 2501,
    AdditiveBlending: 2,
    AgXToneMapping: 6,
    AlphaFormat: 1021,
    AlwaysCompare: 519,
    AlwaysDepth: 1,
    AlwaysStencilFunc: 519,
    AnimationUtils: {},
    AttachedBindMode: 'attached',
    BackSide: 1,
    BasicDepthPacking: 3200,
    BasicShadowMap: 0,
    ByteType: 1010,
    Cache: { enabled: false, files: {} },
    CineonToneMapping: 3,
    ClampToEdgeWrapping: 1001,
    ColorManagement: {
      enabled: true,
      _workingColorSpace: 'srgb-linear',
      workingColorSpace: 'srgb-linear'
    },
    ConstantAlphaFactor: 213,
    ConstantColorFactor: 211,
    CubeReflectionMapping: 301,
    CubeRefractionMapping: 302,
    CubeUVReflectionMapping: 306,
    CullFaceBack: 1,
    CullFaceFront: 2,
    CullFaceFrontBack: 3,
    CullFaceNone: 0,
    CustomBlending: 5,
    CustomToneMapping: 5,
    DataUtils: {},
    DecrementStencilOp: 7683,
    DecrementWrapStencilOp: 34056,
    DefaultLoadingManager: LoadingManager {
      onStart: undefined,
      onLoad: undefined,
      onProgress: undefined,
      onError: undefined
```

***Figure 6.1**: Console output in VS Code using the Console Ninja extension*

In the browser, it will look like *Figure 6.2*:

```
▼ Module {…} ⓘ                                          main.js:90
    ACESFilmicToneMapping: (...)
    AddEquation: (...)
    AddOperation: (...)
    AdditiveAnimationBlendMode: (...)
    AdditiveBlending: (...)
    AgXToneMapping: (...)
    AlphaFormat: (...)
    AlwaysCompare: (...)
    AlwaysDepth: (...)
    AlwaysStencilFunc: (...)
    AmbientLight: (...)
    AnimationAction: (...)
    AnimationClip: (...)
    AnimationLoader: (...)
    AnimationMixer: (...)
    AnimationObjectGroup: (...)
    AnimationUtils: (...)
    ArcCurve: (...)
    ArrayCamera: (...)
    ArrowHelper: (...)
    AttachedBindMode: (...)
    Audio: (...)
    AudioAnalyser: (...)
    AudioContext: (...)
    AudioListener: (...)
    AudioLoader: (...)
    AxesHelper: (...)
    BackSide: (...)
    BasicDepthPacking: (...)
    BasicShadowMap: (...)
    BatchedMesh: (...)
    Bone: (...)
    BooleanKeyframeTrack: (...)
    Box2: (...)
    Box3: (...)
    Box3Helper: (...)
    BoxGeometry: (...)
    BoxHelper: (...)
    BufferAttribute: (...)
```

Figure 6.2: Console output in the browser

3. To add the **Scene** to the project, add one line to the code as follows:

```
4.  // Importing the Three.js module into the application
5.  import * as THREE from 'three';
6.  // Getting the Three.js object into the console of the browser
7.  console.log(THREE);
8.  const scene = new THREE.Scene();
9.  console.log(scene);
```

Code Listing 6.2: Adding a scene to the code

10. We will see the scene object in the console, like in *Figure 6.3:*

```
Scene {isObject3D: true, uuid: 'e36debc7-6fd5-40ca-a7c9-ead9bbd5b9cd', nam
e: '', type: 'Scene', parent: null, …} i
  ▶ animations: []
    background: null
    backgroundBlurriness: 0
    backgroundIntensity: 1
  ▶ backgroundRotation: _Euler {isEuler: true, _x: 0, _y: 0, _z: 0, _order:
    castShadow: false
  ▶ children: (2) [PerspectiveCamera, Mesh]
    environment: null
    environmentIntensity: 1
  ▶ environmentRotation: _Euler {isEuler: true, _x: 0, _y: 0, _z: 0, _order:
    fog: null
    frustumCulled: true
    isObject3D: true
    isScene: true
  ▶ layers: Layers {mask: 1}
  ▶ matrix: _Matrix4 {elements: Array(16)}
    matrixAutoUpdate: true
  ▶ matrixWorld: _Matrix4 {elements: Array(16)}
    matrixWorldAutoUpdate: true
    matrixWorldNeedsUpdate: false
    name: ""
    overrideMaterial: null
    parent: null
  ▶ position: _Vector3 {x: 0, y: 0, z: 0}
  ▶ quaternion: Quaternion {isQuaternion: true, _x: 0, _y: 0, _z: 0, _w: 1,
    receiveShadow: false
    renderOrder: 0
  ▶ rotation: _Euler {isEuler: true, _x: 0, _y: 0, _z: 0, _order: 'XYZ', …}
  ▶ scale: _Vector3 {x: 1, y: 1, z: 1}
    type: "Scene"
  ▶ up: _Vector3 {x: 0, y: 1, z: 0}
  ▶ userData: {}
    uuid: "e36debc7-6fd5-40ca-a7c9-ead9bbd5b9cd"
    visible: true
    id: 5
  ▶ modelViewMatrix: _Matrix4 {elements: Array(16)}
  ▶ normalMatrix: Matrix3 {elements: Array(9)}
```

Figure 6.3: *Scene object in the browser console output*

It is the only place where we can see the scene. While we use Three.js, we also need to render the scene after initialization. It will not work if not done at this stage. A render needs eyes to see the scene. These eyes are presented by the camera object that we need to add to the scene. We will speak more concretely about cameras in the next chapters. In the present context, we will just take the camera object and align it to the scene. To align the camera to the scene, we will need to add some code to the **main.js** file, like in *Code Listing 6.3:*

```
1.  // Importing the Three.js module into the application
2.  import * as THREE from 'three';
3.  // Getting the Three.js object into the console of the browser
4.  console.log(THREE);
5.  const props = {
6.  width: 800,
7.  height: 600
8.  };
9.  const scene = new THREE.Scene();
10. const camera =
11. new THREE.PerspectiveCamera(75, props.width / props.height);
12. scene.add(camera);
```

Code Listing 6.3: Adding a camera to the scene

We have also added the **props** object, which will be required at the next step when we will render the scene. To render the scene, we will need to align the size of the renderer and reuse data, we aligned the size of the view field with the object.

To render the scene, we need to add these updates to our code:

- We need to align the HTML object where we will render the scene. It should be a Canvas tag with some identificatory to call it from the JS. We will call it a **container**.

- We need to align the container with the renderer and call the render function.

11. Now, open your **index.html** file and update it with code from *Code Listing 6.4*:

```
1.  <!DOCTYPE html>
2.  <html lang="en">
3.   <head>
4.    <meta charset="utf-8">
5.    <title>My first three.js app</title>
6.    <style>
7.     body { margin: 0; }
8.    </style>
9.   </head>
10.  <body>
11.   <canvas id="container"></canvas>
12.   <script type="module" src="/main.js"></script>
13.  </body>
14. </html>
```

Code Listing 6.4: updated HTML file

Your **main.js** file should contain the code with the renderer in *Code Listing 6.5*:

```
1.  // Importing the Three.js module into the application
2.  import * as THREE from 'three';
3.
4.  // Getting the Three.js object into the console of the browser
5.  console.log(THREE);
6.
7.  const props = {
8.    width: 800,
9.    height: 600
10. };
11.
12. const scene = new THREE.Scene();
13.
14. const camera = new THREE.PerspectiveCamera(75,
    props.width / props.height);
15. scene.add(camera);
16.
17. // Create the connection with the Canvas object in the HTML file
18. const canvas = document.querySelector('#container');
19. // Create the renderer. There are different types of them,
    but it's part of another chapter
20. const renderer = new THREE.WebGLRenderer({
21.   canvas: canvas
22. });
23.
24. // Setup the renderer
25. renderer.setSize(props.width, props.height);
26.
27. // Render the scene using scene and camera objects
28. renderer.render(scene, camera);
29.
```

Code Listing 6.5: Basic empty scene in the code

We will see a black rectangle on the screen with 800px width and 600px height. These sizes are aligned by the **setSize** method, we used in the code. We have a black rectangle and nothing more because our scene is empty and does not contain anything right now.

Understanding core components of Three.js

The core components of Three.js are Scene, Camera, Renderer, Geometry, Material, Mesh, and Light. These concepts will be discussed in detail in the following chapters. Let us see what these components mean:

- **Renderer**: The renderer takes the 3D scene and renders it into a 2D representation on the web page. Three.js supports multiple renderers, including **WebGLRenderer** for hardware-accelerated 3D graphics.

- **Scene:** The scene is the 3D environment where objects, lights, and cameras are placed. It acts as the stage for your 3D world.

- **Camera**: The camera determines the perspective through which you view the 3D scene. Three.js offers various types of cameras, such as **PerspectiveCamera** and **OrthographicCamera**, each with its unique way of projecting the scene.

- **Geometry**: Geometry defines the shape and structure of 3D objects. Three.js provides various built-in geometries like **CubeGeometry**, **SphereGeometry,** and custom geometry creation options.

- **Materials**: Materials define the appearance and surface properties of 3D objects. You can apply materials to geometries for different textures, colors, or visual effects.

- **Mesh**: A **mesh** is created by combining geometry and a material. It is a 3D object with a specific shape and appearance. Meshes are what is seen in the 3D scenes.

- **Light**: Lights illuminate the scene and affect the way objects are shaded. Three.js supports various lights, including ambient, directional, point, and spotlights.

Adding objects to the scene

If a scene does not contain any objects and there is only a black screen on the page. We need to fix it. We will need to add something simple to the page. The simplest object in 3D is a box. Thus, we will add it to the scene.

To add this or any object, we need to create a container for this object. For example, we will see how it looks in a 3D model editor like **Blender** *(Figure 6.4)*. We can see in the picture that each object has two instances: the object and the object mesh. This is how we can create a 3D image on the screen. The same logic is used in Three.js.

As a container, we use the object called **Geometry**. The cool part of this object is that it is also used for collisions so we do not need to create another wrapper around the object.

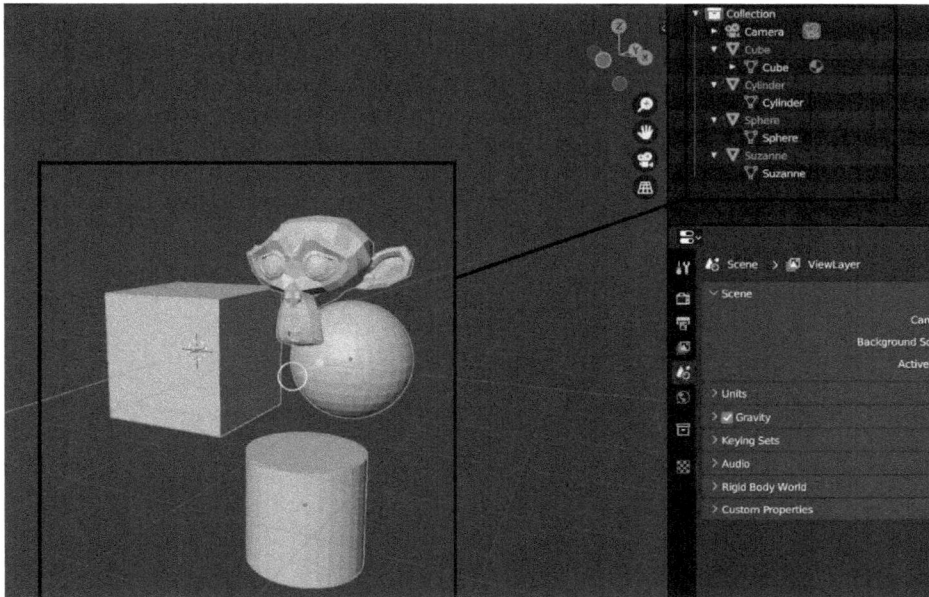

Figure 6.4: Blender interface that shows objects and meshes

At the same time, we also need a **mesh** object that will represent the real shape of the object. This object will consume the material to represent the **skin** of the object.

When all these objects are created, we can align them to the scene and see it on the screen. Let us add the box to our scene. To do that, add the following code from *Code Listing 6.6* to your **main.js** file:

```
1.  // Put new code before renderer.setSize
2.
3.  // Creating the box container for our object
4.  const geometry = new THREE.BoxGeometry(1, 1, 1);
5.  // Assign the color of the object
6.  const material = new THREE.MeshBasicMaterial({ color: 0xff0000 });
7.  // Create the shape object using the container and material combined
8.  const mesh = new THREE.Mesh(geometry, material);
9.  scene.add(mesh);
10.
11. // Setup the renderer
12. renderer.setSize(props.width, props.height);
13.
14. // Render the scene using scene and camera objects
15. renderer.render(scene, camera);
```

Code Listing 6.6: Adding the first object into the scene code

We will not be seeing the object after that. We cannot see the object because our camera does not look at the object in the current setup. By default, the camera is created in point with coordinates (0,0,0) and is the same as the newly created object. We will discuss the special setup of the cameras later. For now, we will just move the camera a little, for it is possible to see something. To fix that, add one line as shown in *Code Listing 6.7* into your code:

```
1.  // Put new code after scene.add(mesh);
2.  scene.add(mesh);
3.
4.  // Moving the camera by the Z-axis to see the object
5.  camera.position.z = 5;
6.
7.  // Setup the renderer
8.  renderer.setSize(props.width, props.height);
9.
10. // Render the scene using scene and camera objects
11. renderer.render(scene, camera);
12.
```

Code Listing 6.7: Fix camera position

Now, if we look at our browser, we will see the red rectangle with the black background. This is our first scene with an object like that shown in *Figure 6.5*.

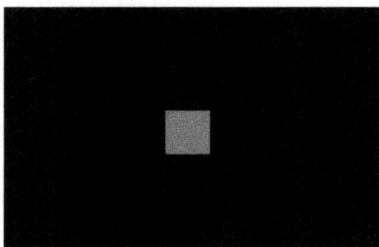

Figure 6.5: Our first scene with the box object

Debugging and troubleshooting

As web developers, we require some debugging tools in our daily jobs. We need it with Three.js as objects render on each browser separately, which means that to bring changes into production, we have to go through a long path of creating pull requests, approvals, builds, etc. In some cases, we are required to make changes immediately and see the result without waiting for the CI/CD process. Here are several tools that can save time:

- **Tweakpane: (https://cocopon.github.io/tweakpane/)** It is a cool and robust solution for the creative developer. It has a lot of input types and configurations (*Figure 6.6*)

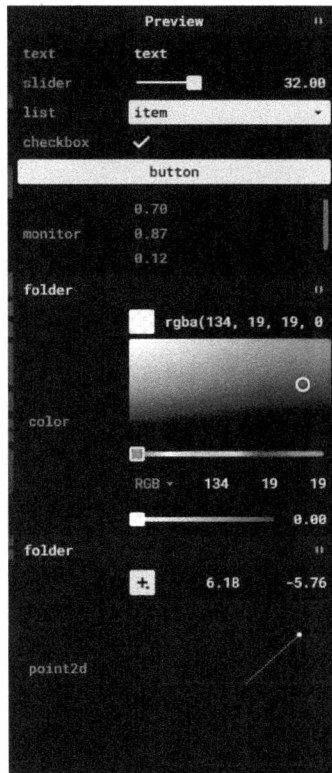

Figure 6.6: Tweakpane interface

- **Control-panel:** (**https://github.com/freeman-lab/control-panel**). It is a powerful solution for UI debugging, and contains a lot of controls and configurations, as shown in *Figure 6.7:*

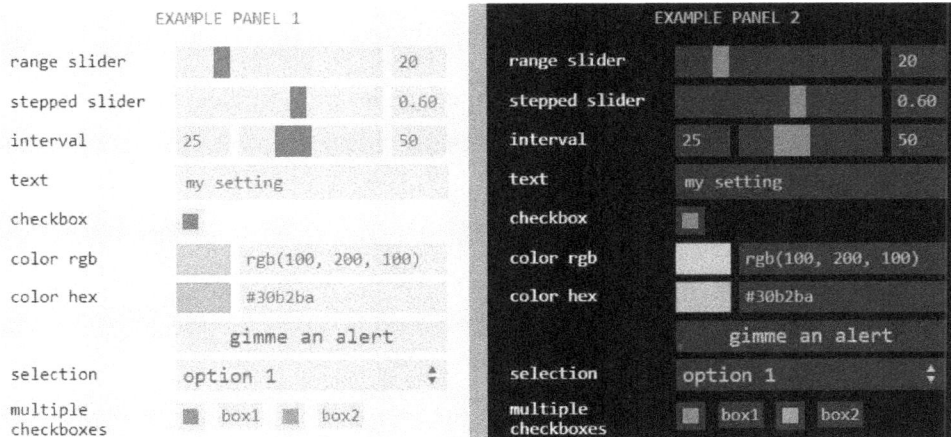

Figure 6.7: Control-panel interface

- **Lil-gui(https://lil-gui.georgealways.com/**). The most popular debug UI interface that we will use in this book (*Figure 6.8*). It is tiny and simple to use. It does not need complex inputs.

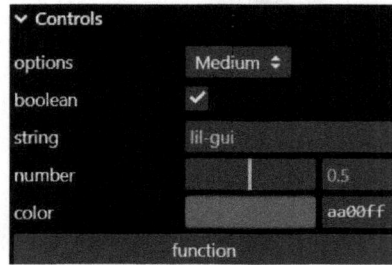

Figure 6.8: Lil-gui interface

Install and implement Lil-gui.

The following are the steps to install Lil-gui:

1. As we use a module type of library usage combined with Vite, to add a library to the project, type this command in the folder CI:

```
1. // Installing the library
2. npm install lil-gui
3.
```

2. .In the **main.js** file, add an import after the line where Three.js is imported:

```
1. // Importing the Three.js module into the application
2. import * as THREE from 'three';
3. // Adding Debug UI to project
4. import GUI from 'lil-gui';
5. const gui = new GUI();
```

Code Listing 6.8: Adding the debug GUI

There is a list of controls that we can use to make changes in the scene:

- **Numbers and sliders**: They help to smoothly change the numerical data, like coordinates or depth

- **Dropdowns**: These are used to implement some pattern or object into properties

- **Colors**: Color controls can help us change the material or light color in the scene

- **Folders**: They are made to group the controls. For example, we have different types of controls like camera positions, object positions, and colors. We can group them in folders, and it makes using them more convenient

- **Functions**: They create the button with some action inside. We can put their animation start or add some properties and patterns

Let us check the code for the Debug UI that we can create. Look into *Code Listing 6.9* with explanations:

Slider

At this block, we will add the slider UI element that will help us to change number values using the mouse:

```
1.  // Object with default parameters
2.  const obj = { number1: 1, number2: 50 };
3.
4.  // Creating the slider with a range from 0 to 1,
5.  // that takes obj.number1 value as default
6.  gui.add( obj, 'number1', 0, 1 ); // min, max
7.
8.  // // Creating the slider with a range from 0 to 100,
9.  // that takes obj.number2 value as default and
10. // Each slider change will have a step that equals 10
11. gui.add( obj, 'number2', 0, 100, 10 ); // min, max, step
12.
```

Code Listing 6.9: Adding the slider GUI

The result is shown in *Figure 6.9:*

Figure 6.9: Number sliders

If we need a regular text field for a number or even string value, then we can remove range data from the code to have a pure text field.

Button

To add a button that will trigger some function, we need to create the function and assign it to the GUI. It takes the value type and uses the button as the view.

Check *Code Listing 6.10* to create the button:

```
1.  // Object with actions inside
2.  const buttons = { triggerOnClick: () => console.log('click') };
3.
4.  // Assign a function to the GUI to create the button
5.  gui.add( buttons, 'triggerOnClick' );
```

Code Listing 6.10: Adding the button GUI

The result is shown in *Figure 6.10:*

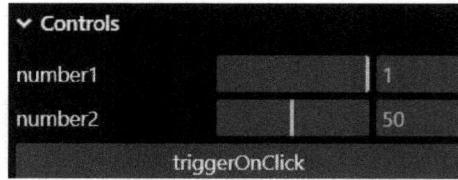

Figure 6.10: Button added to the GUI

Dropdowns

The following is the code to add a dropdown:

```
1. // Object with list data and default values
2. // For  better readability , we recommend using a flat object
3. // to store configurations
4. const lists = {
5.   numberList: [ 0, 1, 2 ],
6.   labeledObject: { Label1: 0, Label2: 1, Label3: 2 },
7.   numbers: 1,
8.   labels: 1
9. };
10.
11. // Adding numbers dropdown that represents data array as is
12. gui.add( lists, 'numbers', lists.numberList );
13.
14. // Adding objects dropdown that will show keys in the list
15. gui.add( lists, 'labels', lists.labeledObject );
```

Code Listing 6.11: Adding the dropdown GUI

The result is shown in *Figure 6.11:*

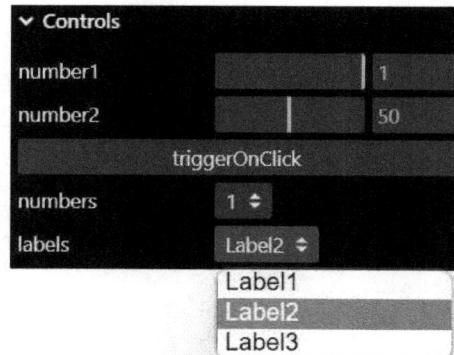

Figure 6.11: Dropdowns in the Debug UI

Colors

The color input is a helpful tool for 3D development, and it contains two ways of inserting data:

- Regular text field
- Color palette with RGB inputs

The following is the code to add color input to the console:

```
1.  // Object with colors configuration for the objects
2.  const colors = {
3.      // The format of the color can be one of these:
4.      // '#ffffff'
5.      // 0xffffff
6.      // { r: 1, g: 1, b: 1 }
7.      // [ 1, 1, 1 ]
8.    meshColor: '#ffffff',
9.  };
10. gui.addColor( colors, 'meshColor' );
```

Code Listing 6.12: *Adding the colors GUI*

The result is shown in *Figure 6.12*:

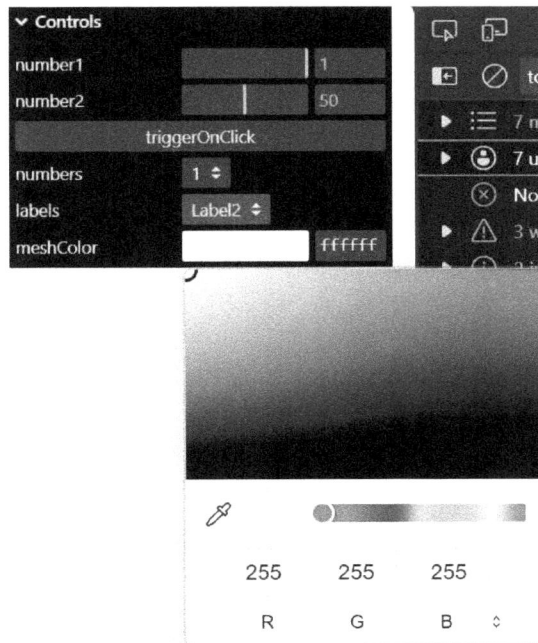

Figure 6.12: *Color picker in Debug UI*

None of them will work in the current state. To solve this problem, we need to add a function that will re-render the scene and react to changes. Update your code with this function from *Code Listing 6.13* to make the scene interactive:

```
1.  // Render the scene using scene and camera objects
2.  // remove the renderer below and add the function to animate
3.  // the scene
4.  // renderer.render(scene, camera);
5.  function animate() {
6.
7.    requestAnimationFrame( animate );
8.    renderer.render( scene, camera );
9.
10. }
11. animate();
```

Code Listing 6.13: Update for Animate function

We can try to connect our debug tools to the scene parameters. For example, if we have to change the material color, we need to use a chain function possibility from the Debug UI library. Check *Code Listing 6.14* for the solution:

```
1.  const material = new THREE.MeshBasicMaterial({ color: props.color });
2.  const mesh = new THREE.Mesh(geometry, material);
3.
4.  // Place this code after you have created the material as
5.  // We will change the parameter of it
6.  Gui
7.     // At the beginning, we created the props object with parameters
8.     .addColor(props, 'color')
9.     .onChange(() =>
10.    {
11.        material.color.set(props.color)
12.    });
```

Code Listing 6.14: Update for colors with callback

Now, if we change the color in the color picker, the material color will also change, as in *Figure 6.13*:

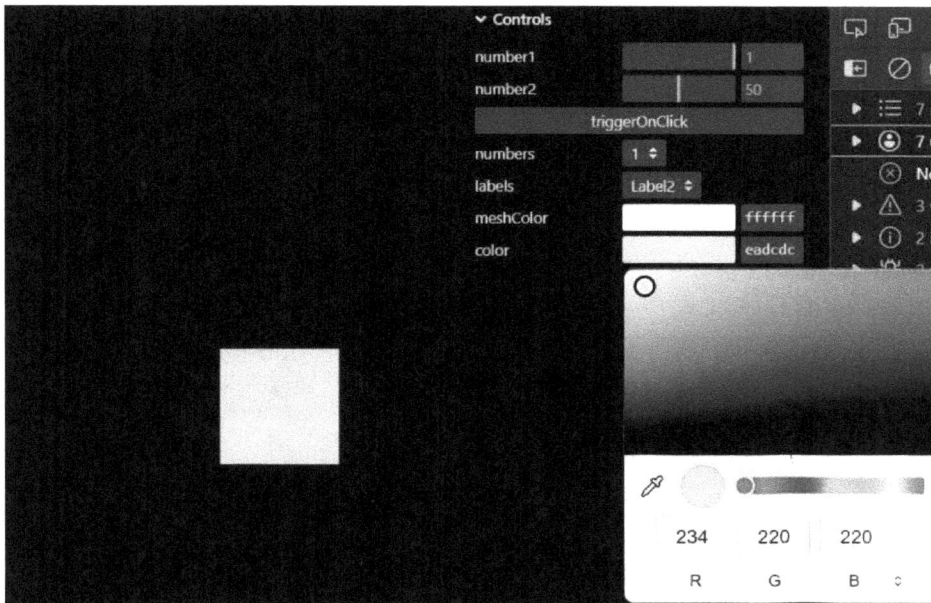

Figure 6.13: *Color changing in GUI*

Orbit controls

One more useful addition is an orbit control. Everything that we see on the scene comes from the camera. If we need to turn around the scene but keep the camera in place where it was created for debugging, we can create an orbit control object and connect it to the camera. It will allow us to operate the camera using mouse movements. Please update your code with *Code Listing 6.15* to add the orbit controls:

```
1.  import { OrbitControls } from 'three/examples/jsm/controls/
    OrbitControls.js';
2.  …
3.  // Render the scene using scene and camera objects
4.  // Add orbit controls object here and link it to the
    camera object
5.  const controls = new OrbitControls( camera, renderer.domElement );
6.  // Update controls on the start
7.  controls.update();
8.  function animate() {
9.
10. requestAnimationFrame( animate );
11.  // required if controls.enableDamping or controls.
    autoRotate are set to true
12. controls.update();
```

```
13. renderer.render( scene, camera );
14.
15. }
16. animate();
17.
```

Code Listing 6.15: *Adding OrbitControls*

Now, we can rotate the scene to look at the object from different angles and zoom in or out, as shown in *Figure 6.14*:

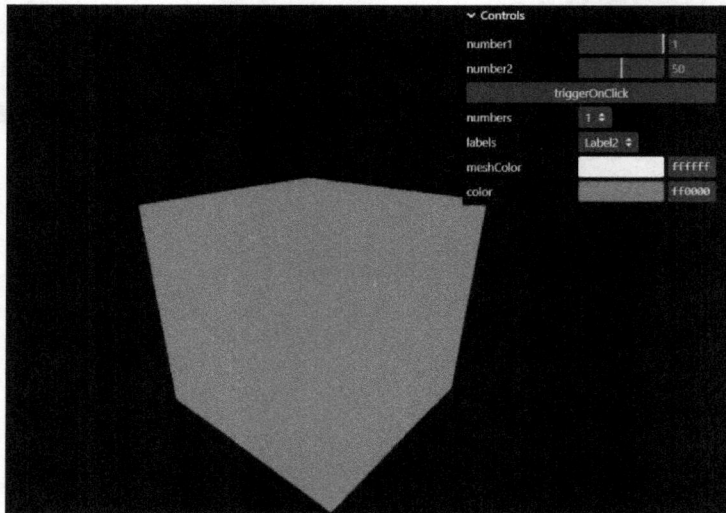

Figure 6.14: *Changing the camera view in real-time to look at the scene from a different angle*

Conclusion

This chapter has laid the foundation for the journey into the captivating world of 3D web development using Three.js. We have learned about the core components that make up a Three.js scene, gaining insights into scenes, renderers, cameras, geometries, materials, meshes, and controls. These components enable us to build 3D environments on the web.

With this knowledge, we can create 3D scenes, add and manipulate objects, apply materials and textures, and even animate our creations. As we move forward in this book, we will discuss every topic in detail, mastering the art of 3D web development.

In the following chapters, we will explore each core component in more detail, providing practical examples and hands-on experience. Whether an aspiring 3D developer or an experienced web programmer, this will harness the full potential of Three.js and bring creative 3D visions to life on the web.

CHAPTER 7

Geometries and Materials

Introduction

In the previous chapter, we introduced BoxGeometry as a means to render objects on the screen. This chapter will provide a comprehensive discussion on the various geometry objects available in Three.js. Geometries serve as the foundational blueprints for 3D objects, defining the positions of vertices, the edges connecting these points, and the faces that form surfaces. For example, a sphere geometry specifies the sphere's radius and level of detail, establishing the essential framework for rendering objects such as celestial bodies or spherical items in a 3D scene.

In 3D web development, geometries play a crucial role in shaping objects, constructing structures, and bringing visual elements to life within a 3D environment. A thorough understanding of geometry is vital for creating dynamic and interactive 3D web experiences. In the expansive realm of Three.js, geometries are indispensable for the development of innovative web applications.

Structure

This chapter will look into the following topics:

- Types of geometry
- Types of materials

Objectives

By the end of this chapter, you will be able to create various types of objects using Three.js. Additionally, we will learn how to create custom geometries by specifying the positions of vertices, enabling us to craft unique shapes for your 3D web applications. Also, you will learn how to manage materials to color your objects or make them more realistic.

Types of geometry

In Three.js, geometries are the fundamental building blocks for constructing 3D objects. They consist of two essential components:

- **Vertices:** They are essentially the cornerstones of the 3D world. Each vertex represents a specific point in the 3D space. Imagine them as coordinates in a vast, virtual universe. They define the positions of various points within this space, essentially acting as the framework on which the 3D objects will be built.

- **Faces:** These are the bridges that connect these vertices. They are typically composed of triangles, which efficiently join the vertices to form surfaces. Think of faces as the structural elements that shape the outer appearance of your 3D objects. They transform the scattered points (vertices) into coherent surfaces.

It is important to note that geometries are not limited to just storing position data in vertices. While vertex positions are crucial, additional information can also be included within geometries. Two prominent examples are UV coordinates and normals. These two topics will be discussed in the section, *Materials*. The following are the types of Geometries:

BoxGeometry

BoxGeometry is used to create rectangular cuboids with defined **width**, **height**, and **depth**. When we create a cuboid using this geometry, it is automatically centered at the origin point, and each of its edges aligns perfectly with one of the coordinate axes.

To create geometry, we need to stick to the pattern from *Code Listing 7.1*. Every 3D object on the scene has three elements: **geometry**, **material**, and **mesh**. **Geometry** is the container that holds information about the shape and borders of a 3D object. **Material** is the element that creates the skin of the object; it can be color or complex texture. Finally, we need a **Mesh** object that uses both and generates a 3D object on the screen. This object should be added to the scene to be visible on the screen:

```
1. const geometry = new THREE.<YOUR-TYPE-OF-GEOMETRY>(<PARAMETERS>);
2. const material = new THREE.<YOUR-TYPE-OF-MATERIAL> (<PARAMETERS>);
3. const mesh = new THREE.Mesh(geometry, material);
4. scene.add(mesh);
```

Code Listing 7.1: *Adding geometry pattern*

We already created BoxGeometry in the previous chapter, but we will do it here in detail. For this chapter, we will create a new file for the project. We will also create the debug GUI, which is specific to each object. Please take a starter code to use in the exercises from *Code Listing 7.2*:

```
1.  import * as THREE from 'three';
2.  import { OrbitControls } from 'three/examples/jsm/controls/
    OrbitControls.js';
3.  import GUI from 'lil-gui';
4.
5.  // Init Debug UI
6.  const gui = new GUI();
7.
8.  // Object with default parameters
9.  const obj = { width: 1, height: 1, depth: 1, widthSegments: 1,
    heightSegments: 1, depthSegments: 1};
10.
11. // Init Scene
12. const props = {
13.   width: 800,
14.   height: 600,
15.   color: 0xff0000
16. };
17. const scene = new THREE.Scene();
18. const camera = new THREE.PerspectiveCamera(75, props.width / props.
    height);
19. scene.add(camera);
20.
21. // Object creation with special Geometry type
22. const initBoxGeometry = () => {
23.   return new THREE.BoxGeometry(
24.     obj. width,
25.     obj.height,
26.     obj. depth,
27.     obj.widthSegments,
28.     obj.heightSegments,
29.     obj.depthSegments );
30. };
31.
32. // Initiate Wireframe to see the Geometry parameters
33. let wireframe, geo, mat = null;
```

```
34. const initWireframe = (mesh) => {
35.   geo = new THREE.WireframeGeometry( mesh.geometry );
36.   mat = new THREE.LineBasicMaterial( { color: 0xffffff } );
37.   wireframe = new THREE.LineSegments( geo, mat );
38. };
39.
40. // Geometry regeneration for Debug UI updates
41. const regenerateGeometry = (mesh, currWireframe) => {
42.   const newGeometry = initBoxGeometry();
43.   mesh.remove(currWireframe);
44.   mesh.geometry = newGeometry;
45.
46.   initWireframe(mesh);
47.   mesh.add( wireframe );
48.
49. }
50. const geometry = initBoxGeometry();
51. const material = new THREE.MeshBasicMaterial({ color: props.
     color });
52. const mesh = new THREE.Mesh(geometry, material);
53.
54. // This is the object wrapper that we will need to see the wireframe in
55. // real-time
56. initWireframe(mesh);
57. mesh.add( wireframe );
58.
59. gui.add( obj, 'width', 1, 20)
60.   .onChange(() => regenerateGeometry(mesh, wireframe));
61. gui.add( obj, 'height', 1, 20)
62.   .onChange(() => regenerateGeometry(mesh, wireframe));
63. gui.add( obj, 'depth', 1, 20)
64. ..onChange(() => regenerateGeometry(mesh, wireframe));
65. gui.add( obj, 'widthSegments', 1, 20)
66.   .onChange(() => regenerateGeometry(mesh, wireframe));
67. gui.add( obj, 'heightSegments', 1, 20)
68.   .onChange(() => regenerateGeometry(mesh, wireframe));
69. gui.add( obj, 'depthSegments', 1, 20,)
70.   .onChange(() => regenerateGeometry(mesh, wireframe));
71.
72. scene.add(mesh);
```

```
73. camera.position.z = 6;
74.
75. // Setup the renderer
76. const canvas = document.querySelector('#container');
77. const renderer = new THREE.WebGLRenderer({
78.   canvas: canvas
79. });
80.
81. renderer.setSize(props.width, props.height);
82.
83. // Render the scene using scene and camera objects
84. // Remove the renderer below and add the function to animate
85. // the scene
86. // renderer.render(scene, camera);
87. const controls = new OrbitControls( camera, renderer.domElement );
88. controls.update();
89. function animate() {
90.
91.   requestAnimationFrame( animate );
92.       // required if controls.enableDamping or controls.
    autoRotate are set
93.       // to true
94.   controls.update();
95.   renderer.render( scene, camera );
96.
97. }
98. animate();
```

Code Example 7.2: Initial code

We will also add explanations to the code that we will use further. This will also apply to the new parts required for educational purposes. First, let us align the part of the code that will be new for every Geometry type (do not change code around this part without a reason):

```
1. let wireframe, geo, mat = null;
2. const initWireframe = (mesh) => {
3.   geo = new THREE.WireframeGeometry( mesh.geometry );
4.   mat = new THREE.LineBasicMaterial( { color: 0xffffff } );
5.   wireframe = new THREE.LineSegments( geo, mat );
6. };
```

Code Listing 7.3: Wireframe creation

The code from *Code Listing 7.3* is new, and we have never created it before. It is a special wrapper that will create a visible wireframe around the object. We will need it as we will add parameter changes for each Geometry type, and we need to see these changes visually:

```
1. const initGeometry = () => {
2.    return new THREE.BoxGeometry(
3.       obj. width,
4.       obj. height,
5.       obj. depth,
6.       obj.widthSegments,
7.       obj.heightSegments,
8.       obj.depthSegments );
9. }
```

Code Listing 7.4: Geometry creation

Code listing 7.4 is used to create new Geometry types, and in further parts of the chapter, we will provide only this part of the code for each type. Only this needs to be changed as an exercise at the end of the chapter.

And finally, this code from *Code Listing 7.5* will represent the Debug UI. We will provide both updates in named sections: Geometry code and GUI.

```
1.  gui.add( obj, 'width', 1, 20)
2.    .onChange(() => regenerateGeometry(mesh, wireframe));
3.  gui.add( obj, 'height', 1, 20)
4.    .onChange(() => regenerateGeometry(mesh, wireframe));
5.  gui.add( obj, 'depth', 1, 20)
6.  .onChange(() => regenerateGeometry(mesh, wireframe));
7.  gui.add( obj, 'widthSegments', 1, 20)
8.    .onChange(() => regenerateGeometry(mesh, wireframe));
9.  gui.add( obj, 'heightSegments', 1, 20)
10.   .onChange(() => regenerateGeometry(mesh, wireframe));
11. gui.add( obj, 'depthSegments', 1, 20,)
12.   .onChange(() => regenerateGeometry(mesh, wireframe));
```

Code Listing 7.5: Debug UI for the geometry

Now, if we run the project, we will see the result as in *Figure 7.1*, with the possibility to see all changes on the object using the Debug UI:

Figure 7.1: BoxGeometry implementation

CapsuleGeometry

CapsuleGeometry is a geometric class that defines a capsule shape characterized by specified radii and height. This shape is created using a lathe-based construction method. To create it, we need to make updates provided in *Code Listing 7.6* as shown:

```
1.  // Object with default parameters
2.  const obj = { radius: 1, length: 1, capSegments: 1,
    radialSegments: 1};
3.
4.  // Object creation with special Geometry type
5.  const initGeometry = () => {
6.    return new THREE.CapsuleGeometry(
7.      obj. radius,
8.      obj. length,
9.      obj.capSegments,
10.     obj.radialSegments);
11. }
12.
13. // GUI elements to update parameters
14. gui.add( obj, 'radius', 1, 20)
15.   .onChange(() => regenerateGeometry(mesh, wireframe));
16. gui.add( obj, 'length', 1, 20)
17.   .onChange(() => regenerateGeometry(mesh, wireframe));
```

```
18. gui.add( obj, 'capSegments', 1, 20)
19. .onChange(() => regenerateGeometry(mesh, wireframe));
20. gui.add( obj, 'radialSegments', 1, 20)
21.  .onChange(() => regenerateGeometry(mesh, wireframe));
```

Code Listing 7.6: CapsuleGeometry parameters code and GUI

After the code update, we will see the result, as shown in *Figure 7.2:*

Figure 7.2: Capsule object example

CircleGeometry

Circle geometry is a basic shape derived from Euclidean geometry. It is formed by arranging triangular segments around a central point, extending outward up to a specified radius. This arrangement is typically counterclockwise, beginning from a defined starting angle and expanding to a designated central angle. Additionally, it is versatile and can be employed to construct regular polygons, with the number of segments dictating the polygon's sides. To create it, we need to make the updates provided in *Code Listing 7.7:*

```
1.  // Object with default parameters
2.  const obj = { radius: 5, segments: 32, thetaStart: 1, thetaLength: 7};
3.
4.  // Object creation with special Geometry type
5.  const initGeometry = () => {
6.    return new THREE.CircleGeometry(
7.      obj. radius,
8.      obj. segments,
9.      obj.thetaStart,
10.     obj.thetaLength);
```

```
11. }
12.
13. // As Circle is a 2D object, to color it from both sides, we need to add
14. // parameter 'side' to have color for each side
15. const material = new THREE.MeshBasicMaterial(
16.    { color: props.color, side: THREE.DoubleSide }
17. );
```

Code Listing 7.7: Circle object code updates

After the code update, we will see the result, as shown in *Figure 7.3:*

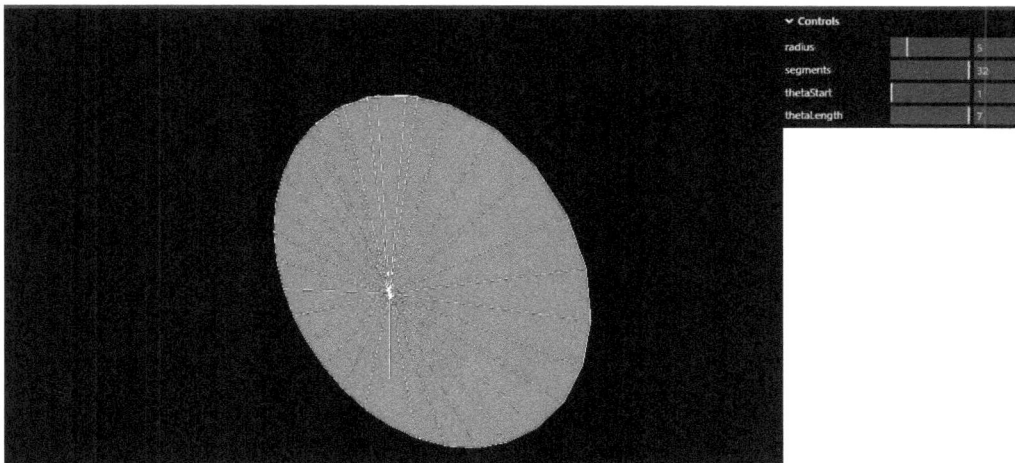

Figure 7.3: Circle object rendering

ConeGeometry

ConeGeometry in Three.js represents the geometric shape of a cone. It's defined by specifying its **radius** at the base, **height**, and various parameters like the number of **radial segments** for the base and **height segments** for the height. The cone is typically centered on the origin, with its central axis along the positive y-axis. To create it, we need to make the updates provided in *Code Listing 7.8:*

```
1. // Object with default parameters
2. const obj = {
3.     radius: 5,
4.     height: 15,
5.     heightSegments: 10,
6.     radialSegments: 30,
7.     openEnded: true,
```

```
8.      thetaStart: 20,
9.      thetaLength: 7
10. };
11. const currentGeometry = 'ConeGeometry';
12.
13. // Object creation with special Geometry type
14. // To optimize future code, we will use the spread operator.
15. // Form current state, to create new Geometry we will need
16. // to update only object parameters. But keep order as is and do not
    // remove parameters from object in this case
17. const initGeometry = () => {
18.   return new THREE[currentGeometry](...Object.values(obj));
19. }
20.
21. // GUI elements to update parameters
22. // We will also optimize GUI to not make changes each time
23. const objKeysAsArray = Object.keys(obj);
24. objKeysAsArray.forEach(key => {
25.    gui.add( obj, key, 10, 50)
26.       .onChange(() => regenerateGeometry(mesh, wireframe));
27. });
```

Code Listing 7.8: Cone object code and future improvements

In the *Code listing 7.8,* we made an improvement. Now, to create a new geometry type, we only need to change the initial object and current type variable. After the code update, we will see the result, as shown in *Figure 7.4:*

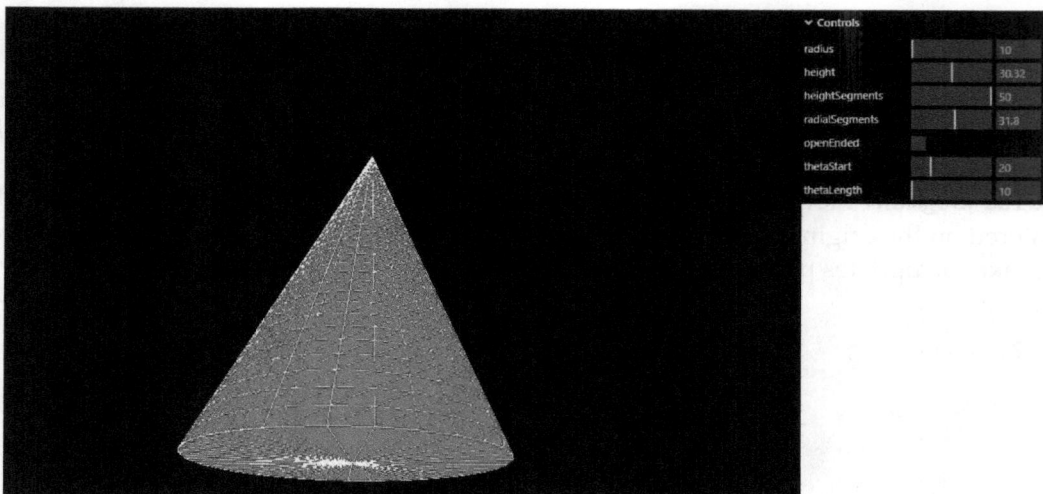

Figure 7.4: Cone object rendering

CylinderGeometry

CylinderGeometry in Three.js represents the geometric shape of a cylinder. It is defined by specifying its **radiusTop** and **radiusBottom** for the top and bottom faces, **height** for the height of the cylinder, and parameters such as the number of **radialSegments** for the circular faces and **heightSegments** for the height. The cylinder is typically centered on the origin, with its central axis along the positive *y-axis*. To create it, we need to make the updates provided in *Code Listing 7.9:*

```
1.  // Object with default parameters
2.  const obj = {
3.      radiusTop: 5,
4.      radiusBottom: 5,
5.      height: 10,
6.      radialSegments: 8,
7.      heightSegments: 1,
8.      openEnded: false,
9.      thetaStart: 0,
10.     thetaLength: 6.283185307179586
11. };
12. const currentGeometry = 'CylinderGeometry';
```

Code Listing 7.9: *Cylinder geometry object configuration*

After the code update, we will see the result as shown in *Figure 7.5:*

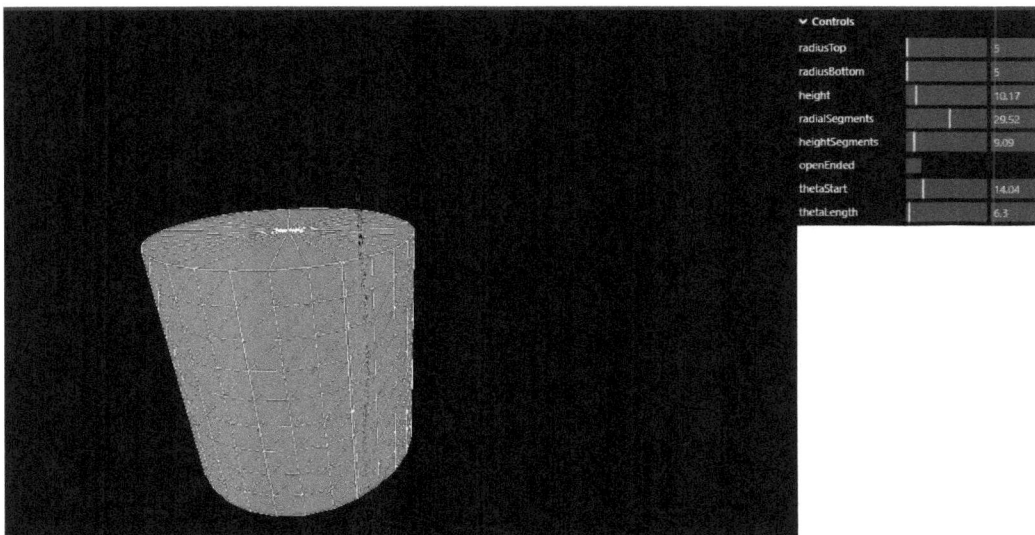

Figure 7.5: *Cylinder geometry render*

DodecahedronGeometry

DodecahedronGeometry in Three.js is a geometry class representing a dodecahedron, one of the five Platonic solids. A dodecahedron is a polyhedron with 12 regular pentagonal faces, 20 vertices, and 30 edges. In Three.js, we can create a dodecahedron by specifying a radius, which determines the size of the dodecahedron. It is a geometric shape often used in 3D modeling and graphics applications. The interesting part is that it changes the shape on one parameter change. Several Geometry objects are the same, but the only difference is in the default minimal detail parameter. The following is a list of them:

- IcosahedronGeometry

- OctahedronGeometry

- TetrahedronGeometry

This parameter is a detail. To create it, we need to make the updates provided in *Code Listing 7.10*:

```
1.  // Object with default parameters
2.  const obj = {
3.      radius: 10,
4.      detail: 5
5.  };
6.  const currentGeometry = 'DodecahedronGeometry';
7.  // Please also add the step parameter to the GUI,
    as detailed value can // only be an integer like this
    `gui.add( obj, key, 0, 5, 1)`
```

Code listing 7.10: Dodecahedron geometry object configuration

After the code update, we will see the result as shown in *Figure 7.6:*

Figure 7.6: Dodecahedron render result

EdgesGeometry

EdgesGeometry in Three.js is a utility class used to create a new geometry that represents the edges of an existing geometry. When we create a 3D object using Three.js, it is typically composed of *vertices* (points in 3D space) and *faces* (triangular or polygonal surfaces). EdgesGeometry allows us to extract the edges of this object's geometry and represent them separately.

As an example, let us take the first geometry file and add edges. We will make changes in the file as per *Code Listing 7.11*:

```
1.  // Find the line where you initialize your geometry and place the
    new code there
2.  const geometry = initGeometry();
3.  const edges = new THREE.
    EdgesGeometry( geometry ); const line = new THREE.LineSegments(
4.  edges,
5.  new THREE.LineBasicMaterial( { color: 0xffffff } )
6.  );
7.  scene.add( line );
8.  // comment wireframe adding as it also creates the edges around
9.  // The code for it looks like this - mesh.add( wireframe );
```

Code Listing 7.11: *Inserting Box into Edges wrapper*

This is useful for various purposes, such as creating wireframe renderings of 3D objects or highlighting the edges of objects in the 3D scenes. We can use EdgesGeometry to create a new geometry that only contains the edges of The existing object's geometry, making it easy to manipulate or style the edges as needed in 3D application.

After the code update, we will see the result as shown in *Figure 7.7*:

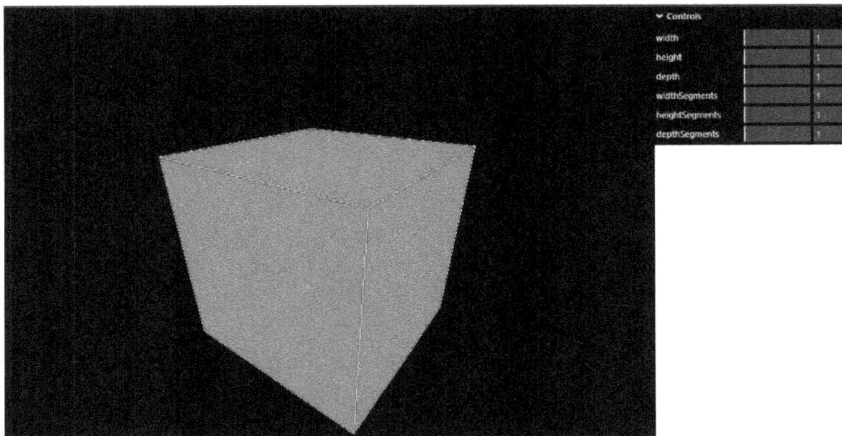

Figure 7.7: *Edges wrap around the box object*

ExtrudeGeometry

ExtrudeGeometry in Three.js is a class used for creating three-dimensional geometries by extruding a shape along a path. It takes a 2D shape (such as a closed path or polygon) and extends it in the third dimension, creating a three-dimensional object with depth.

This extrusion process can be used to create a variety of 3D shapes and objects. For example, we can create 3D text by extruding the shapes of letters, or you can generate complex 3D structures by extruding intricate 2D outlines along a path. ExtrudeGeometry is a versatile tool for creating 3D geometry from 2D shapes, and it is commonly used in 3D graphics and modeling applications.

To create extruded geometry, there are some points we need to keep in mind. **First**, to create some shape to wrap it with extruded objects. **Second**, for the GUI, each change should be an integer. **Third**, the geometry should contain the shape within the parameters. So, to create the extrude, we need to stick to the code from *Code Listing 7.12*:

```
1.  // Object with default parameters
2.  const obj = {
3.       steps: 2,
4.    depth: 16,
5.    bevelEnabled: true,
6.    bevelThickness: 1,
7.    bevelSize: 1,
8.    bevelOffset: 0,
9.    bevelSegments: 1
10. };
11. const currentGeometry = 'ExtrudeGeometry';
12.
13. // Do not forget to create the shape. For  example, we will take a
14. // plain rectangle and make it  a box with rounded bevels
15. const length = 12, width = 8;
16. const shape = new THREE.Shape();
17. shape.moveTo( 0,0 );
18. shape.lineTo( 0, width );
19. shape.lineTo( length, width );
20. shape.lineTo( length, 0 );
21. shape.lineTo( 0, 0 );
22.
23. // Object creation with special Geometry type
24. const initGeometry = () => {
25.     return new THREE[currentGeometry](shape, obj);
26.     // Do not forget to add shape to the object
27. }
```

Code Listing 7.12: Extrude geometry code update

For the exercise, we can create any shape using the **lineTo function**. This function works as a regular Canvas drawing. Canvas drawing works using this algorithm:

1. We move the cursor to the initial point
2. We draw a line at the new point
3. We draw lines until we get to the starting point
4. As lines, we can also use Bezier lines to create curves

After the code update, we will see the result as shown in *Figure 7.8:*

Figure 7.8: Extruding box with rounded edges from the plane object

LatheGeometry

LatheGeometry in Three.js is a class for generating 3D geometry by lathe-shaping a 2D shape around an axis. In other words, it creates a 3D object by rotating a 2D profile around a specified axis.

We define the 2D shape as a path or a set of points, and then the **LatheGeometry** class rotates and connects those points to create the desired 3D object. This can be used to generate a wide range of objects, from vases and cups to more complex 3D structures, and it is a useful tool for 3D modeling and computer graphics.

For the creation of the object, we will need to create an array of curves. This is possible using an object from Three.js, called **Vector2**. Using it, we can create the curve by mathematical elements like *sine, cosine,* or *tangent*. After that, we can collect these vectors in one array and create a mesh around it. We can make changes in the file as shown in *Code Listing 7.13:*

```
1.  // Object with default parameters
2.  const points = [];
```

```
3.  for ( let i = 0; i < 10; i ++ ) {
4.    points.push(
5.  new THREE.Vector2( Math.sin( i * 0.3 ) * 10 + 5,
6.        ( i-5 ) * 3 ) );
7.  }
8.  const obj = {
9.        points: points,
10.       segments: 5,
11.       phiStart : 0,
12.       phiLength : 1
13. };
14. const currentGeometry = 'LatheGeometry';
15. // Do not forget to exclude points from GUI as we can't operate objects // in there.
16. // Example: key !== 'points' && gui.add( obj, key, 5, 50)
17. // If you want to change points dynamically, you need to create
18. // custom GUI for it
```

Code Listing 7.13: LatheGeometry object configuration code

After the code update, we will see the result as shown in *Figure 7.9*:

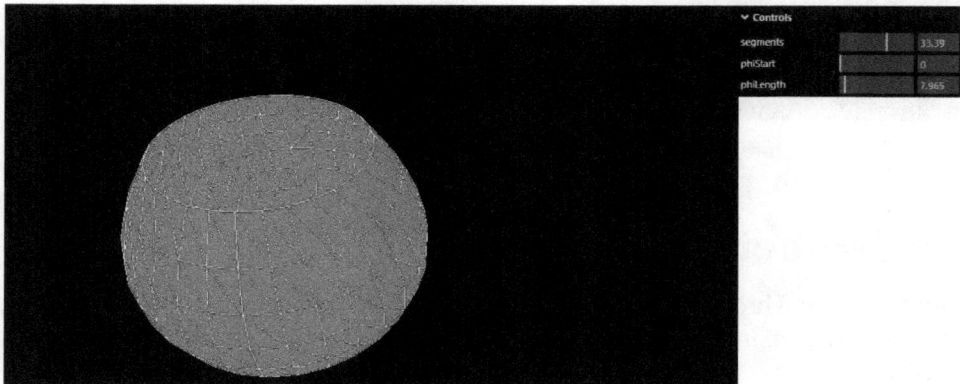

Figure 7.9: Lathe object rendering

There are several more geometries to mention, like the following:

- PlaneGeometry
- RingGeometry
- SphereGeometry
- TorusGeometry
- TorusKnotGeometry
- TubeGeometry

None of them has a special configuration, which is not there in our code examples. We will work with them in the exercise section of the chapter.

Types of materials

In Three.js, materials are a fundamental concept defining the visual properties of 3D objects or geometries. Materials determine how an object's surface interacts with light, influencing its color, shininess, texture, and other visual characteristics. We will need a light source in our scene. It can be something simple, like directional light. To add light to the scene, we will take our first example with box geometry and add code from *Code Listing 7.14*:

```
1.  scene.add(mesh);
2.  // Find this line and put the light configuration after
3.  camera.position.z = 6;
4.
5.  // Simple light creation for the scene
6.  const ambientLight = new THREE.AmbientLight(0xffffff, 0.5)
7.  scene.add(ambientLight)
8.  const color = 0xFFFFFF;
9.  const intensity = 15;
10. const light = new THREE.DirectionalLight(color, intensity);
11. light.position.set(2, 3, 4);
12. scene.add(light);
```

Code Listing 7.14: Adding light to the scene

Now, we are ready to introduce the material types, as there will be differences for each type in context to the light management used in rendering. To see the difference, we will create the GUI element that will change the material type for us. We will make changes to the code to implement material type changes like in *Code Listing 7.15:*

```
1.  // Object with default parameters
2.  const obj = {
3.      width: 1,
4.      height: 1,
5.      depth: 1,
6.      widthSegments: 1,
7.      heightSegments: 1,
8.      depthSegments: 1
9.  };
10. const materialProps = {
11.     color: '#ebebeb',
12.     shininess: 20,
```

```
13.    flatShading: false,
14.    roughness: 1,
15.    metalness: 1,
16.    clearcoat: 0,
17.    clearCoatRoughness: 0,
18.    wireframe: false
19. };
20. const materialTypeProps = {
21.    type: 'MeshBasicMaterial'
22. };
23. const currentGeometry = 'BoxGeometry';
```

Code Listing 7.15: Adding material parameters to the code

Now we have parameters object for any kind of material. Not all of them exist in each material type. For example, we will not make GUI dynamic, but we can play around with this while practicing. To add Material type switching we add code from *Code Listing 7.16* to the file.

```
1.  // GUI elements to update parameters
2.  const materialPropsArray = Object.keys(materialProps);
3.  materialPropsArray.forEach(key => {
4.      key !== 'color' && gui.add( materialProps, key, 0, 10)
5.          .onChange(() => regenerateGeometry(mesh));
6.      key === 'color' && gui.addColor( materialProps, 'color')
7.          .onChange(() => regenerateGeometry(mesh));
8.  });
9.
10. gui.add( materialTypeProps, 'type', [
11.             'MeshBasicMaterial',
12.             'MeshStandardMaterial',
13.             'MeshPhysicalMaterial',
14.             'MeshDepthMaterial',
15.             'MeshNormalMaterial',
16.             'ShaderMaterial',
17.             'MeshLambertMaterial',
18.             'MeshPhongMaterial',
19.             'MeshToonMaterial' ] )
20.     .onChange(() => regenerateGeometry(mesh));
```

Code Listing 7.16: GUI parameters to change the Material type

Finally, we need to change the rendering of the material to dynamically implement different types of material, like in *Code Listing 7.17:*

```
1.  const regenerateGeometry = (mesh) => {
2.    const newGeometry = initGeometry();
3.    mesh.material = new THREE[materialTypeProps.type](materialProps);
4.    mesh.geometry = newGeometry;
5.
6.  }
7.  const geometry = initGeometry();
8.
9.  const material = new THREE[materialTypeProps.type](materialProps);
10. const mesh = new THREE.Mesh(geometry, material);
```

Code Listing 7.17: *Dynamic material render implementation*

After the code update, we will see the result as same as shown in *Figure 7.10*:

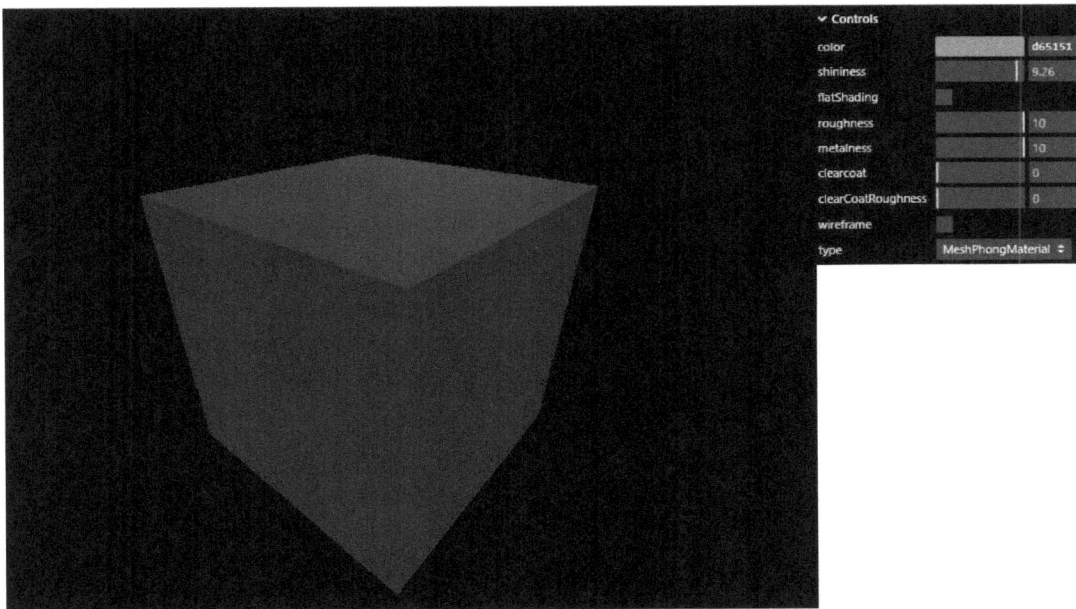

Figure 7.10: *The shininess parameter increases will show reflection on the side of the box*

Each material type is roughly dependent on light and textures. We will discuss each one in detail in the next chapters.

For now, we can check the difference using different kinds of geometries. By choosing types in the control area, you will see the required selector in the list.

The following are key differences between material types that will help choose the one to use in the next 3D model:

- **MeshBasicMaterial**: This material provides a simple, unlit surface with a solid color. It does not respond to lighting conditions. It is often used for objects that should have a consistent color without shading effects, like GUI elements or wireframes.

- **MeshLambertMaterial**: Lambert materials provide diffuse reflection with soft, even shading. They respond to ambient light and are commonly used for matte or non-shiny surfaces. These materials do not have specular highlights, making them suitable for objects like clay sculptures or fabrics.

- **MeshPhongMaterial**: Phong materials offer specular highlights and can simulate shinier surfaces. They respond to direct light sources and produce more complex shading effects. This material is ideal for surfaces with pronounced reflections, like plastic or metal.

- **MeshStandardMaterial**: Standard materials are designed for **physically based rendering (PBR)**. They offer a wide range of properties, including diffuse, specular, normal, and emissive maps. They can represent a variety of real-world materials, from metals to plastics, by adjusting their properties.

- **MeshPhysicalMaterial**: Physical materials extend the capabilities of standard materials by introducing more advanced features. They can handle complex interactions between light and surfaces, such as energy conservation. This material type is suitable for photorealistic rendering and highly detailed scenes.

- **MeshToonMaterial**: Toon materials are designed to create a cell-shaded or cartoon-like appearance. They do not produce smooth gradients and instead use a limited number of shading levels. These materials are often used in applications with a stylized, non-realistic visual style.

- **MeshDepthMaterial and MeshNormalMaterial**: These materials are used for specific purposes. `MeshDepthMaterial` renders objects based on their depth, which is useful for post-processing effects like depth of field. `MeshNormalMaterial` visualizes the surface normals of objects to help with debugging and visual analysis.

- **Shader Material**: Shader materials allow us to write custom GLSL shaders for complete control over an object's appearance. We can create unique and complex visual effects with this material type.

- **MultiMaterial**: This material type is used when an object is composed of multiple materials applied to different parts or facets. It is often employed for complex models with varied surfaces.

- **RawShaderMaterial**: `RawShaderMaterials` are used for low-level shader programming, giving us complete control over the rendering process.

Conclusion

In this chapter, we explored the fundamental aspects of Three.js, one of the most powerful and versatile 3D graphics libraries for web development. We learned about the key concepts such as geometries and materials, laying the foundation for creating captivating 3D web applications.

Geometries provided us with a deeper understanding of how to define the structure of 3D objects, while materials introduced us to the art of rendering and shading, enabling us to craft visually stunning and realistic surfaces.

With an understanding of these core components we can proceed to advanced techniques and concepts. In the next chapter, we will explore how to manipulate these elements, animate scenes, and bring interactivity to our 3D creations.

Points to remember

- All materials mostly depend on the light that exists in the scene (except basic ones).
- Geometries contain the segments to render that can allow us to achieve better performance or better details for the application.
- Dynamic change of parameters is easy, and that is what we will use in more complex examples.

Exercises

1. Create a scene with 3 objects in it. Sphere, Tor, and Ring. Create object parameters for each one (you can create separate variables or an array of objects). Create the Debug UI for each one using folders
2. Add the dynamic position parameters for each object and add the Debuig UI elements to move the objects

Join our Discord space

Join our Discord workspace for latest updates, offers, tech happenings around the world, new releases, and sessions with the authors:

https://discord.bpbonline.com

CHAPTER 8
Lights and Shadows

Introduction

Lighting is a crucial element in the world of 3D scenes. It can enhance realism, set the mood, and add depth to creations. In this chapter, we will study lighting in 3D scenes, exploring its significance and understanding how to implement various lighting models. We will discuss the intricacies of different light sources, the nuances of shadow creation, and the concept of shadow mapping. This chapter will teach us how to illuminate 3D scenes effectively and create visually captivating environments.

Structure

In this chapter, we will discuss the following topics:

- Understanding the role of lights in 3D scenes
- Implementing different types of lights

Objectives

By the end of this chapter, we will understand the pivotal role of lighting in 3D scenes and its impact on visual quality and realism. This chapter explores different types of lighting models and their practical applications in 3D development. This chapter also helps discover techniques for creating realistic shadows, which enhance the visual quality of 3D scenes.

Understanding role of lights in 3D scenes

Imagine you are in a dim room. You can make out some shapes, but nothing is clear. Now, turn on a lamp. The objects will become visible, shadows appear, and the whole space has depth. This is the magic of light.

In 3D graphics, lighting does exactly this: it illuminates the virtual world, transforming how we see objects, their textures, and their positions. Proper lighting can differentiate between a flat, dull scene and one that feels alive and immersive.

There are several lighting models in 3D graphics, each defining how light interacts with surfaces:

- **Lambertian reflection**: This model is like a matte surface; light scatters in all directions, which gives it a soft, non-reflective look.

- **Phong reflection**: This adds specular highlights, making objects appear shinier, like a polished surface.

- **Blinn-Phong reflection**: A twist on Phong that is easier on performance but still realistic.

- **Cook-Torrance model**: A more advanced option for simulating complex materials like metals and glass.

Shadows are key to making a 3D scene look real. Without them, scenes can feel fake and flat. They add the depth that makes everything feel anchored.

So, mastering light in 3D graphics? It is both an art and a science. Knowing lighting models, shadow techniques, and the types of light sources helps create amazing virtual worlds. Also, an artistic eye can turn that technical knowledge into something that really hits home with the viewer.

Implementing different types of lights

Light is the brushstroke of the virtual world, shaping our perception of 3D scenes and breathing life into digital environments. In 3D graphics, understanding how to implement different types of lights is essential for creating compelling, realistic, and visually engaging experiences. This article delves into the world of lighting in 3D graphics, exploring various types of light sources, lighting models, and their impact on the visual quality of virtual scenes.

Creating the light on the scene uses a pattern like that in *Code Listing 8.1*. To initiate the light object, we need to create it with parameters and then add it to the scene:

```
1. const light = new THREE.<YOUR-TYPE-OF-LIGHT> (<LIGHT-PARAMETERS>);
2. scene.add(light);
```

Code Listing 8.1: Light initiation pattern

Before we start, take the code from *Code Example 8.1*. We will use it as a template for the light's implementation:

```
1.  import * as THREE from 'three';
2.  import { OrbitControls } from
    'three/examples/jsm/controls/OrbitControls.js';
3.  import GUI from 'lil-gui';
4.
5.  // Init Debug UI
6.  const gui = new GUI();
7.
8.  // Objects with default parameters
9.  const objectsOnScene = [
10.     {
11.         name: 'SphereGeometry', // This is the name of the geometry
        used
12.         params: { // this is the default params that will be
        used to create it
13.             radius: 10,
14.             detail: 30
15.         },
16.         position: [-20, 5, 0], // this is XYZ position of the object
17.         color: '#7DAA92' // This is a color of the object
18.     },
19.     {
20.         name: 'TorusGeometry',
21.         params: {
22.             radius: 10,
23.             tube : 3,
24.             radialSegments: 16,
25.             tubularSegments: 100
26.         },
27.         position: [10, 10, 0],
28.         color: '#8E4A49'
29.     }
30. ];
31.
32. // Init Scene
33. const props = {
34.   width: 800,
35.   height: 600
36. };
```

```
37. const scene = new THREE.Scene();
38. const camera =
    new THREE.PerspectiveCamera(75, props.width / props.height);
39. scene.add(camera);
40.
41. // Object creation with special Geometry type
42. const initGeometry = (object) => {
43.   return new THREE[object.name](...Object.values(object.params));
44. }
45.
46. // Here we use an array of objects and create them using parameters
47. objectsOnScene.forEach(object => {
48.     const geometry = initGeometry(object);
49.     // Remember this part of the code about material,
    we will change it
50.     const material =
    new THREE.MeshBasicMaterial({ color: object.color });
51.     const mesh = new THREE.Mesh(geometry, material);
52.     mesh.position.set(...object.position);
53.     scene.add(mesh);
54. });
55.
56. // We make a ground object to see shadows
57. const loader = new THREE.TextureLoader();
58. //In this chapter, we will not deep dive into textures, but we need
    this one to
59. // see shadows reactions
60. // This code is to create a flat plane that will be used as ground
61. // The callback for the loader is required, as in the other case,
    you will // not see the texture
62. // The texture will be loaded after the renderer because of how
    JS works by itself
63. loader.load(
64. // We will take a texture from the three.js manual
65. 'https://threejs.org/manual/examples/resources/images/checker.png',
    (texture) => {
66.     // This part will be more detailed in the chapter about Texture
67.     texture.wrapS = THREE.RepeatWrapping;
68.     texture.wrapT = THREE.RepeatWrapping;
69.     texture.magFilter = THREE.NearestFilter;
70.     texture.colorSpace = THREE.SRGBColorSpace;
71.     const planeSize = 80;
```

```
72.     const repeats = planeSize / 2;
73.     texture. repeat.set( repeats, repeats );
74.
75.     // This is an important part of the code. We will change
    the material
76.     // of the plane
77.     // to see how it reacts to light changes
78.     const planeMaterial = new THREE.MeshBasicMaterial(
79. { map: texture, side: THREE.DoubleSide  });
80.     const planeGeometry = new THREE.PlaneGeometry( planeSize,
    planeSize );
81.     const planeMesh = new THREE.Mesh(planeGeometry, planeMaterial);
82.     planeMesh.position.set(0, -5, 0);
83.     planeMesh.rotation.set(Math.PI / -2, 0, 0);
84.
85.     scene.add(planeMesh);
86. });
87.
88. camera.position.z = 50;
89. camera.position.y = 10;
90. camera.position.x = -30;
91.
92. // Setup the renderer
93. const canvas = document.querySelector('#container');
94. const renderer = new THREE.WebGLRenderer({
95.   canvas: canvas
96. });
97.
98.     // Here we will place our code with light creation
99.
100.     renderer.setSize(props.width, props.height);
101.
102.     // Render the scene using scene and camera objects
103.     const controls = new OrbitControls( camera,
    renderer.domElement );
104.     controls.update();
105.     function animate() {
106.
107.      requestAnimationFrame( animate );
108.     // required if controls.enableDamping or controls.autoRotate
    are set
```

```
109.        // to true
110.        controls.update();
111.        renderer.render( scene, camera );
112.
113.    }
114.    animate();
```

Code Example 8.1*: Initial code*

This is a basic scene with 2 objects and a plane representing the ground. On this ground, we will need to show several important points regarding the light:

- The shadows from the objects
- The reaction of the ground to light
- The reflections from the ground

Types of light sources

Light sources are important for the visual world, in real life, or the digital realm of 3D graphics. To harness the power of light in 3D scenes, it is crucial to comprehend the types of light sources and their real-world counterparts. To make it more understandable, let us take an example from the real world and relate it with types of light in Three.js.

- **Directional lights**: This type of light is analogous to sunlight. Just as the sun shines in uniform, parallel rays of light, directional light replicates this effect in virtual environments. It creates long shadows and shapes outdoor scenes. It gives the same visual effect of a serene sunrise, where the sun casts distinct shadows and sets the mood for the day.

- **Point lights:** In 3D scenes, they simulate local light sources like lamps or light bulbs in the real world. Just as a table lamp illuminates the corner of a room or a string of fairy lights and adds a warm glow to an outdoor terrace, point lights create localized, uniform illumination.

- **Spotlights:** They focus their beams within a cone-shaped area, drawing attention to specific objects or creating dramatic effects. The perfect example is a flashlight guiding the way through a dark forest or a spotlight on a grand stage, highlighting a performer. In 3D, spotlights are instrumental in guiding the viewer's gaze.

- **Hemisphere lighting**: It replicates the dynamic of changing colors and brightness of the sky, from the zenith to the horizon. This type of light source is perfect for crafting realistic outdoor scenes. Just as the sky transitions from a bright blue during the day to warm hues during sunset, hemisphere lighting captures these variations.

- **Ambient light:** In 3D, it provides uniform illumination throughout a scene, ensuring even the darkest corners receive some level of light. It is akin to the soft, indirect light that fills a room, making it feel inviting.

Post a comparison with real-world examples, we are ready to step into the practice of Three.js lights. We need to revise the content of the material before we proceed several types of material react to light changes. It is: **MeshLambertMaterial**, **MeshPhongMaterial**, **MeshToonMaterial** or **MeshStandardMaterial**. As the best learning material for rendering and practice, we will use **MeshStandardMaterial**. For this, we need to change all materials in the code to the same as in *Code Listing 8.2:*

```
1. // In the part where we render objects for the scene,
   please use this // code
2. const material = new THREE.MeshStandardMaterial(
3. { color: object.color }
4.   );
5.
6. // For the ground plane initiation, please also change the
   material to // standard
7. const planeMaterial = new THREE.MeshBasicMaterial(
8. { map: texture, side: THREE.DoubleSide  }
9.         );
```

Code Listing 8.2: Material changes for the light implementation

After this change, we will see a black scene that contains nothing. It happened because there was no light on it, which we will fix.

Ambient light

In **Three.js**, ambient light functions as a gentle, uniform illumination that fills the entire 3D scene. Unlike other light types, such as directional or point lights, which have specific positions and directions, ambient light does not originate from a defined source. Instead, it provides soft, even lighting throughout the scene, ensuring no area is left completely dark.

Here are several contexts in which ambient light proves especially useful:

- **Indoor Scenes**: In interior spaces within 3D models, ambient light can simulate soft, natural illumination, similar to light entering through windows and diffusing across surfaces, creating a warm and inviting atmosphere.

- **Setting Different Times of Day**: Ambient light can be adjusted to represent various times of the day. Warmer tones can evoke the soft hues of sunset, while cooler tones may replicate the bluish atmosphere of early morning, adding realism and depth to the 3D environment.

- **Outdoor Scenes**: For outdoor environments, ambient light helps prevent shadowed areas from appearing overly dark. This subtle illumination maintains visibility across the scene, even in areas not directly lit by other light sources.

To add ambient light, refer to the reusable code snippet provided in *Code Listing 8.3*, which is designed to support different types of light within a scene. For a visual example, see *Figure 8.1*.

Figure 8.1: Ambient light at the scene

```
1.  // Put this code before the renderer.setSize call
2.  // Create light with a parameter
3.  const lightParams = {
4.      color: 0x404040,
5.      intensivity: 2
6.  };
7.  let light = null;
8.  // Initiation of the light type. You can follow examples from other
9.  // chapters and optimise this code using light type as a parameter
10. const initLight = () => {
11.     light = new THREE.AmbientLight(...Object.values(lightParams));
12.     scene.add(light);
13. };
14. // Here we will destroy the current light and re-implement
    it with new parameters
15. // For more optimization, you can directly change the parameters
16. // but we will speak about it in the next chapters
17. const regenerateLight = () => {
18.     scene.remove(light);
19.     initLight();
```

```
20. };
21. initLight();
22. // GUI elements to update parameters
23. const lightKeysAsArray = Object.keys(lightParams);
24. lightKeysAsArray.forEach(key => {
25.     if (!key.toLowerCase().includes('color')) {
26.         gui.add( lightParams, key, 0, 50)
27.             .onChange(() => regenerateLight());
28.     } else {
29.         gui.addColor( lightParams, key)
30.             .onChange(() => regenerateLight());
31.     }
32. });
```

Code Listing 8.3: Implementing Ambient Light

Hemisphere light

Hemisphere light is a light source in Three.js that provides ambient and indirect lighting. It imitates the way light scatters in the real world. Typically, the sky acts as a source of illumination, and the ground reflects the light. Hemisphere light consists of two components:

- **Sky Color**: This represents the color of the sky, often a light blue or other daytime hues.

- **Ground Color**: This corresponds to the color of the ground or any surfaces that receive indirect lighting.

The sky color contributes to the ambient light in the scene, while the ground color enhances the indirect or bounced light. Hemisphere light plays a significant role in adding depth and realism to 3D scenes, providing softer shadows and more complex lighting interactions.

To integrate the Hemisphere light, change the code as in *Code Listing 8.4:*

```
1. // Create light with a parameter
2. const lightParams = {
3.     skyColor: 0x404040,
4.     groundColor: 0xB1E1FF,
5.     intensivity: 2
6. };
7.
8. // Change the light type in the initLight function
9. light = new THREE.HemisphereLight(...Object.values(lightParams));
```

Code Listing 8.4: Changes to initiate Hemisphere light

The result will be as shown in *Figure 8.2:*

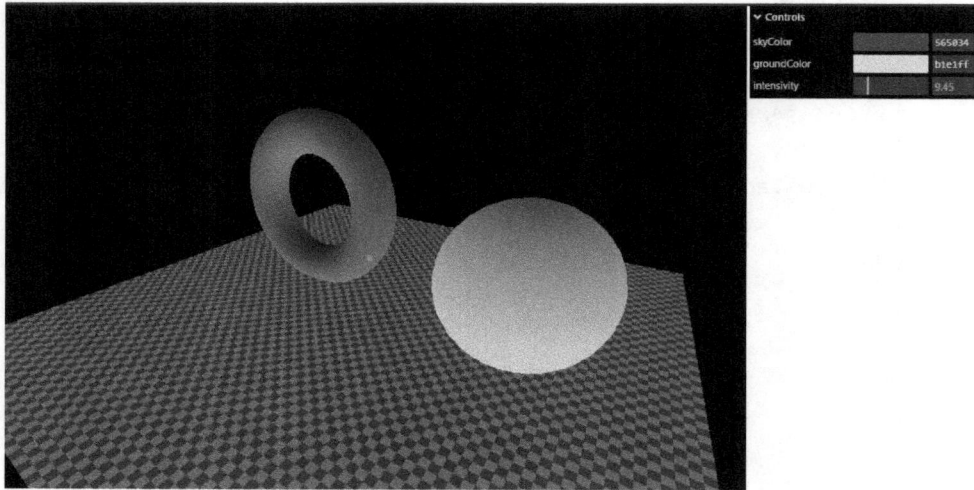

Figure 8.2: Hemisphere light rendering

In the result, you will see that the objects now look three-dimensional with reflections and shadows. You can play with parameters to see how the scene will react to changes.

Directional light

A directional light source in Three.js is like the sun in the real world. It emits parallel rays of light illuminating the entire scene from a specific direction. Since the rays are parallel, there are no diminishing intensity or fall-off effects, making directional light ideal for simulating distant light sources like the sun or moon. A directional light in Three.js has various properties, including:

- **Color**: We can specify the color of the light.

- **Intensity**: This controls the brightness of the light source.

- **Position**: A directional light does not have a physical position; we set its direction using the **target** property.

- **Shadow**: Directional lights are often used to create shadows, making them a key component in rendering realistic scenes.

To integrate this light, we will need to make more changes in the code. Directional light accumulates in two parts: **light position** and **target**. It is made like this because we have a vector-based light. Imagine the line in 3D. This line has two points: **start** and **end**. This is how the directional light works. The target part is the part that produces the light, so each time we move the vector, we need to look at the target part. To make more visualisation for this type of light, we will introduce a special object that will help to see how the light works. This object is called a **helper**. A helper will generate visual lines on the scene, showing us where the direct light starts and what direction is configured for it. Another tool that we will introduce is normalization. We will speak in more detail about it in the next chapters, but we need to show it here as directional light is a vector-based element.

The first step is to create the required parameters, like in *Code Listing 8.5:*

```
1.  // Create light with a parameter
2.  const directLightParams = { color: 0x404040, intensity: 15 };
3.  const integratableParams = {
4.      target: { x: 0, y: 10, z: 0},
5.      position: { x: -5, y: 0, z: 0 }
6.  }
7.  const normalize = { target: false, position: false };
8.  // Add a helper variable also
9.  let light, helper = null;
```

Code Listing 8.5: Directional light parameters creation

We also need to change the initialization for the light as we have more actions to produce, like in *Code Listing 8.6:*

```
1.  const initLight = () => {
2.      light = new THREE.DirectionalLight
3.  (...Object.values(directLightParams));
4.      light.position.set(...Object.values(integratableParams.
    position));
5.      light.target.position
6.  .set(...Object.values(integratableParams.target));
7.      // This expression is required to initiate vector normalisation
8.      if (normalize.position) {
9.          light.position.normalize();
10.     }
11.     if (normalize.target) {
12.         light.target.position.normalize();
13.     }
14.     scene.add(light);
15.     scene.add(light.target);
16.     // This is a helper object that will render a wireframe for the
17.     // light. It takes the light object as a parameter
18.     // and number as size
19.     helper = new THREE.DirectionalLightHelper(light, 5);
20.     scene.add(helper);
21. };
```

Code Listing 8.6: Initialization of the directional light

In the regeneration function, we also need to add the removal of the **helper** object, as it depends on the light to have a possibility to recreate the helper too, as shown in *Code Listing 8.7*:

```
1. const regenerateLight = () => {
2.     scene.remove(light);
3.     scene.remove(helper);
4.     initLight();
5. };
6. initLight();
```

Code Listing 8.7: Changes in the regeneration function for Directional light

Finally, we need to make changes in the GUI to change the parameters. We will also group all parameters in the folders to have a more convenient visualization for the parameters, like in *Code Listing 8.8*:

```
1. const normalFolder = gui.addFolder( 'Normalizatoin' );
2. normalFolder.add( normalize, 'target')
3.         .onChange(() => regenerateLight());
4. normalFolder.add( normalize, 'position')
5.         .onChange(() => regenerateLight());
6.
7. const lightKeysAsArray = Object.keys(directLightParams);
8. const positionFolder = gui.addFolder( 'Position' );
9. const targetPositionKeysAsArray = Object.keys(integratableParams.
   position);
10. targetPositionKeysAsArray.forEach(target => {
11.     positionFolder.add( integratableParams.position, target, -50, 50)
12.         .onChange(() => regenerateLight());
13. });
14.
15. const targetFolder = gui.addFolder( 'Target' );
16. const targetTargetKeysAsArray = Object.keys(integratableParams.
    target);
17. targetTargetKeysAsArray.forEach(target => {
18.     targetFolder.add( integratableParams.target, target, -50, 50)
19.         .onChange(() => regenerateLight());
20. });
21. lightKeysAsArray.forEach(key => {
22.     if (!key.toLowerCase().includes('color')) {
23.         gui.add( directLightParams, key, 0, 50)
24.             .onChange(() => regenerateLight());
25.     }
```

```
26.    else {
27.        gui.addColor( directLightParams, key)
28.        .onChange(() => regenerateLight());
29.    }
30. });
```

Code Listing 8.8: GUI code for the debugging directional light

As a result, we will see scenes like those in *Figure 8.3*. We also see the helper vector on the screen. Using the GUI, we can play around to see how the scene reacts to changes:

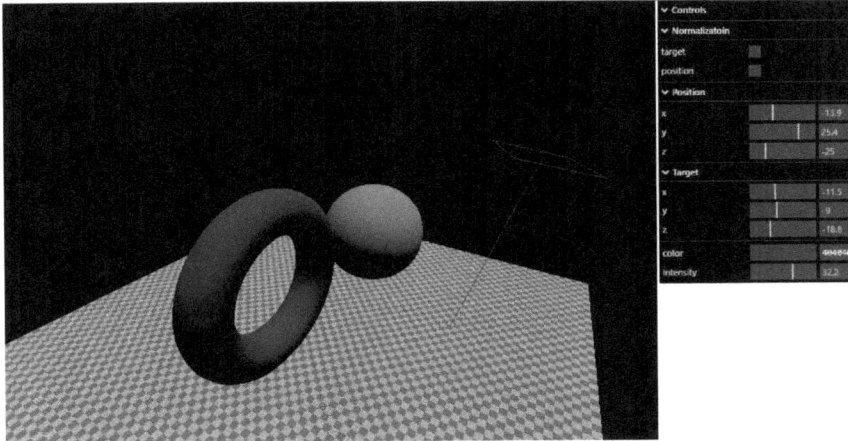

Figure 8.3: Directional light rendered scene

PointLight

In Three.js, a PointLight emits light equally in all directions from a specific point in 3D space. This type of light is often used to simulate light bulbs, lamps, or other light sources that emit light from a single, localized point. It is a common choice for indoor or local lighting within 3D scenes. The point light in Three.js has these properties:

- **Position**: We need to specify the 3D position (x, y, z) of the light source in the scene.

- **Color**: PointLights have a color attribute that defines the color of the emitted light.

- **Intensity**: This attribute controls the brightness or strength of the light. Higher intensity values create brighter lights.

- **Distance**: The distance determines how far the light reaches. The objects beyond are not illuminated by the light.

- **Decay**: It controls how much the intensity of the light diminishes with distance. For example, a decay value of 2 results in an inverse-square attenuation of light intensity.

For the point light, we do not need a target so we will not use it in the code. The only parameter that we will need as an integrative parameter is position.

Like directional light, we will also use the special helper to see the source in the scene. The code to implement is shown in *Code Listing 8.9*.

```
1.  // Create light with a parameter
2.  const lightParams = { color: 0xffffff, intensity: 300, distance: 70 };
3.  const integratableParams = {
4.      position: { x: 0, y: 25, z: 11 }
5.  };
6.
7.  let light, helper = null;
8.  // Initiation of the light type. You can follow examples from other
9.  // chapters and optimise this code using light type as a parameter
10. const initLight = () => {
11.     light = new THREE.PointLight(...Object.values(lightParams));
12.     light.position.set(...Object.values(integratableParams.position));
13.     scene.add(light);
14.     helper = new THREE.PointLightHelper(light, 5);
15.     scene.add(helper);
16. };
```

Code Listing 8.9: PointLight initiation code

The result is shown in *Figure 8.4*:

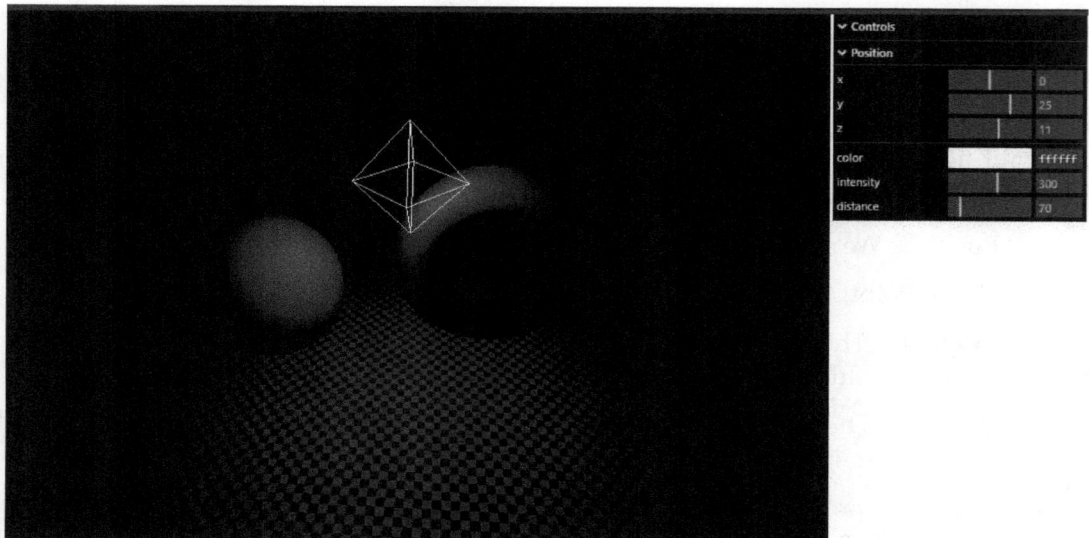

Figure 8.4: PointLight integration result

Spot light

Spotlight is a directional light source that emits light from a specific position, similar to a theater spotlight or a focused flashlight beam. They are particularly effective for creating intense, directed light in applications such as simulating car headlights, searchlights, or targeted indoor lighting.

This type of light has several key properties:

- **Position**: Defines the 3D coordinates (x, y, z) of the light source within the scene.

- **Target**: The SpotLight's `target` property determines the direction of the light beam. This is set by pointing the light at a designated object within the scene, allowing the light to consistently track this target.

- **Color**: Defines the color of the emitted light, allowing for creative control over the scene's ambiance.

- **Intensity**: Controls the brightness of the light. Higher values increase the light's strength and visibility within the scene.

- **Distance**: Determines the reach of the light. The objects located beyond this set distance will not be affected by the SpotLight.

- **Angle**: This attribute defines the spread of the light beam, measured in radians. Smaller angle values create a narrow, focused beam, while larger angles result in a broader spread of light.

- **Penumbra**: It controls the softness of the beam's edges, allowing for a gradual transition from the center of the light cone to its outer boundaries.

The unique parameter here is the **Angle**, which is measured in radians rather than degrees. Since Three.js operates in radians, any degree measurements must be converted using the formula `angle = Math.PI / <DELTA-NUMBER>`. Radians, commonly used in mathematics and physics, divide a circle into 2π (approximately 6.2832) parts rather than 360, offering a more direct method for angular calculations in programming contexts.

In Three.js, the `MathUtils` class offers a straightforward conversion method for degrees to radians. To use this, simply apply the conversion function from `MathUtils` as demonstrated in *Code Listing 8.10*. This ensures seamless integration of degree-based angles into the Three.js environment.

```
1. const radians = THREE.MathUtils.degToRad(<YOUR-DEGREE-NUMBER>)
```

Code Listing 8.10: *Converting degrees to radians*

To use the Spotlight in your scene, add code from *Code Listing 8.11* to the application:

```
1.  // Create light with a parameter
2.  const lightParams = {
3.      color: 0xffffff,
4.      intensity: 300,
5.      distance: 70,
6.      angle: THREE.MathUtils.degToRad(45),
7.      penumbra: 0.4
8.  };
9.  const ranges = {
10.     intensity: [0, 1500],
11.     distance: [1, 70],
12.     penumbra: [0, 1],
13.     angle: [0, 90]
14. };
15. const integratableParams = {
16.     target: { x: 0,  y: 10,  z: 0 },
17.     position: { x: 0,  y: 25,  z: 11 }
18. };
19.
20. let light, helper = null;
21. // Initiation of the light type. You can follow examples from other
22. // chapters and optimise this code using light type as a parameter
23. const initLight = () => {
24.     light = new THREE.SpotLight(...Object.values(lightParams));
25.     light.position.set(...Object.values(integratableParams.
    position));
26.     light.target.position.set(...Object.values(integratableParams.
    target));
27.     scene.add(light);
28.     scene.add(light.target);
29.     helper = new THREE.SpotLightHelper(light);
30.     scene.add(helper);
31. };
```

Code Listing 8.11: Code to integrate SpotLight into the scene

As we also added the target parameter and angle, having special logic, we need to make some additional changes in GUI initialization, like in *Code Listing 8.12*:

```
1.  // GUI elements to update parameters
2.  const lightKeysAsArray = Object.keys(lightParams);
3.  const positionFolder = gui.addFolder( 'Position' );
4.  const ositionKeysAsArray = Object.keys(integratableParams.position);
5.  ositionKeysAsArray.forEach(position => {
6.      positionFolder.add( integratableParams.
    position, position, -50, 50)
7.          .onChange(() => regenerateLight());
8.  });
9.
10. const targetFolder = gui.addFolder( 'Target' );
11. const targetKeysAsArray = Object.keys(integratableParams.target);
12. targetKeysAsArray.forEach(target => {
13.     targetFolder.add( integratableParams.target, target, -50, 50)
14.         .onChange(() => regenerateLight());
15. });
16.
17. lightKeysAsArray.forEach(key => {
18.     if (!key.toLowerCase().includes('color') && key !== 'angle') {
19.         gui.add( lightParams, key, ...ranges[key])
20.             .onChange(() => regenerateLight());
21.     }
22.     else if(key === 'angle') {
23.         gui.add( light, key, ...ranges[key]).name('angle')
24.             .onChange((value) => {
25.                 lightParams[key] = THREE.MathUtils.degToRad(value)
26.                 regenerateLight();
27.             });
28.     }
29.     else {
30.         gui.addColor( lightParams, key)
31.             .onChange(() => regenerateLight());
32.     }
33. });
```

Code listing 8.12: *Debug GUI for the Spotlight integration*

The result is shown in *Figure 8.5*:

Figure 8.5: *Spotlight implementation in the scene*

RectAreaLight

RectAreaLight is a light source in Three.js that simulates rectangular area lights. These lights emit light uniformly from a rectangular surface, different from point lights or spotlights that emit light from a single point or in a specific direction. This makes RectAreaLights useful for simulating lights like fluorescent lights, LED panels, or even window openings in architectural visualizations. They are commonly used to create even and soft lighting in 3D scenes. The following explains the parameters for a RectAreaLight:

- **Color**: This parameter sets the color of the light emitted by the RectAreaLight. We can define it as a hexadecimal value (e.g., 0xffffff for white) or a Three.js **Color** object.

- **Intensity**: Intensity determines the brightness of the light. Higher values denote intense light, while lower values mean dim light.

- **Width**: This parameter defines the width of the rectangular light area.

- **Height**: It specifies the height of the rectangular light area.

- **Position**: This vector is used to set the position of the RectAreaLight within the 3D scene.

- **Rotation**: This vector defines the orientation of the RectAreaLight. We can set its rotation to control the direction in which it emits light.

For the correct rendering of this type of light, we will also need a utility class called **RectAreaLightUniformsLib**. It is a part of the Three.js library that provides uniform (shaders' input variables) definitions and initializations specifically designed for the RectAreaLight. This is necessary because lighting in 3D graphics is a complex process, and it often involves shaders, which are programs run on the GPU to compute the final color of each pixel in a scene. These shaders require various parameters, including those that describe the characteristics of the light sources, like RectAreaLight.

We will also need to add a helper from the Three.js addons named **RectAreaLightHelper**. We need it as an integrated helper is not working anymore. As RectAreaLight is more powerful than other lights, it requires more attention.

To add both classes, we add the code from *Code Listing 8.13* at the top of the document:

```
1. import { RectAreaLightHelper }
2.              from 'three/addons/helpers/RectAreaLightHelper.js';
3. import { RectAreaLightUniformsLib }
4.              from 'three/addons/lights/RectAreaLightUniformsLib.js';
```

Code Listing 8.13: Importing utility classes to be used in RectArea light

To initiate light uniforms, we need to place the codes from *Code Listing 8.14* after the renderer initiation:

```
1. RectAreaLightUniformsLib.init();
```

Code Listing 8.14: Initialization of light uniform for RectArea light

If we do not initiate this utility, we could still see the scene, but it will react strangely if we add textures to the material. We will also need to change the light initiation function as in *Code Listing 8.15*:

```
1.    const initLight = () => {
2.    light = new THREE.RectAreaLight(...Object.values(lightParams));
3.    light.position.set(...Object.values(integratableParams.
   position));
4.    light.rotation.set(...Object.values(integratableParams.
   rotation));
5.    scene.add(light);
6.    helper = new RectAreaLightHelper(light);
7.    scene.add(helper);
8. };
```

Code Listing 8.15: Light initiation for the RectArea light

Next, we need to update the Debug UI to have the possibility to change values and see changes in real-time. The code for these changes is given in *Code Listing 8.16*:

```
1.  // GUI elements to update parameters
2.  const lightKeysAsArray = Object.keys(lightParams);
3.  const positionFolder = gui.addFolder( 'Position' );
4.  const ositionKeysAsArray = Object.keys(integratableParams.position);
5.  ositionKeysAsArray.forEach(position => {
6.      positionFolder.add( integratableParams.
    position, position, -50, 50)
7.          .onChange(() => regenerateLight());
8.  });
9.
10. const rotationFolder = gui.addFolder( 'rotation' );
11. const rotationKeysAsArray = Object.keys(integratableParams.
    rotation);
12. rotationKeysAsArray.forEach(rotation => {
13.     rotationFolder.add( light.rotation, rotation, -50, 50).
    name('rotation')
14.         .onChange((value) => {
15.             integratableParams.rotation[rotation] = THREE.MathUtils.
    degToRad(value);
16.             regenerateLight();
17.         });
18. });
19.
20. lightKeysAsArray.forEach(key => {
21.     if (!key.toLowerCase().includes('color') && key !== 'angle') {
22.         gui.add( lightParams, key, ...ranges[key])
23.             .onChange(() => regenerateLight());
24.     }
25.     else {
26.         gui.addColor( lightParams, key)
27.             .onChange(() => regenerateLight());
28.     }
29. });
```

Code Listing 8.16: *Changes for the Debug UI*

Finally, the result looks amazing, as shown in *Figure 8.6*:

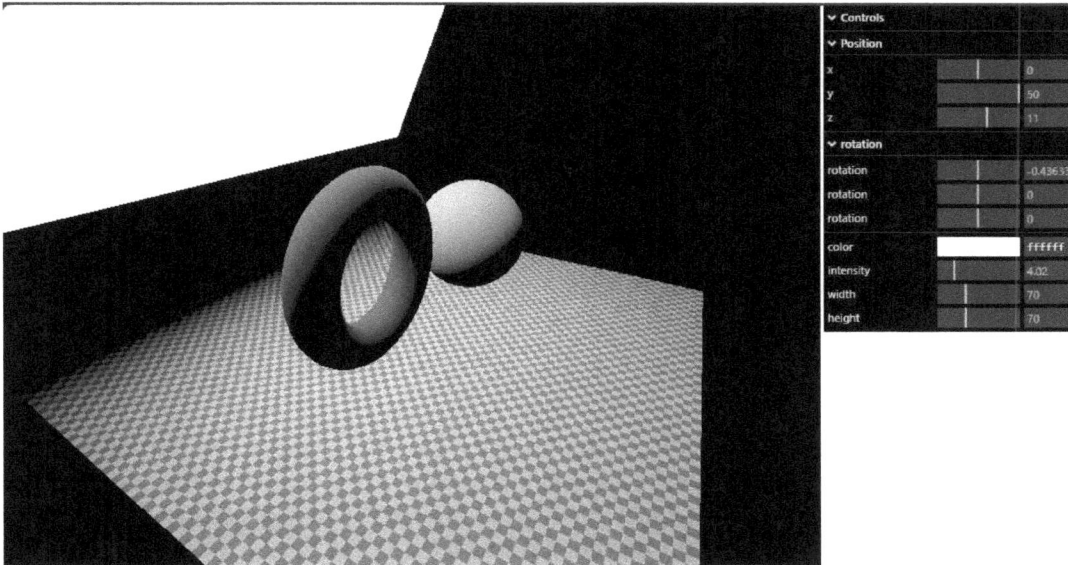

Figure 8.6: RectArea light render

Creating realistic shadows

Now that we have lights, we can proceed with shadows. Shadows are an essential aspect of 3D graphics that add realism and depth to scenes. In Three.js, we can implement shadows to create more immersive 3D environments.

Shadows are implemented using shadow casting and receiving objects, along with a light source that casts shadows. The main shadows in Three.js are:

- **Hard shadows**
- **Soft shadows**

Which we will discuss later in the *Shadow mapping* section.

In Three.js, only three types of lights support shadows: **Point light, Directional light, and Spotlight**.

In Three.js, the default method for generating shadows is through shadow maps. When we have objects set to cast shadows and lights that cast shadows, each object is rendered multiple times, once for each shadow-casting light. So, if we have 100 objects and 20 lights with shadows enabled, the entire scene will be drawn twenty-one times. All 100 objects are rendered for the first light, then for the second, and so on. Finally, the actual scene is created using data from the first several renders.

Things get more complicated when we have point lights casting shadows. In this case, the scene has to be rendered more than 20 times just because of the single light source.

Given this complexity, many developers look for alternative approaches to avoid numerous lights generating shadows. One common solution is to use multiple lights but designate only one as a directional light responsible for casting shadows.

Another option is to pre-calculate lighting effects using light maps or ambient occlusion maps. This method results in static lighting or lighting approximations, but it significantly improves performance.

A different approach involves using simulated or fake shadows. By creating a plane and applying a grayscale texture that mimics a shadow, we can place it above the ground beneath the objects.

Fake shadows

This technique creates the illusion of shadows by placing a plane beneath objects and applying a grayscale texture that resembles a shadow. By adjusting the texture and positioning, these fake shadows can effectively enhance the scene's realism without the performance cost of real-time shadow calculations.

Take a template code from *Code Example 8.2* for the scene that we will use in the implementation of the fake shadow.

```
1.  import * as THREE from 'three';
2.  import { OrbitControls } from
    'three/examples/jsm/controls/OrbitControls.js';
3.
4.  const props = {
5.      width: 800,
6.      height: 600
7.  };
8.
9.  const scene = new THREE.Scene();
10. scene.background = new THREE.Color('#ffffff');
11. const camera = new THREE.PerspectiveCamera(75, props.width /
    props.height);
12. camera.position.z = 50;
13. camera.position.y = 10;
14. camera.position.x = -30;
15. scene.add(camera);
16.
17. // This code is from the previous example to create a plane
    with texture
18. const loader = new THREE.TextureLoader();
19. loader.load(
    'https://threejs.org/manual/examples/resources/images/checker.
```

```
      png', (texture) => {
20.      texture.wrapS = THREE.RepeatWrapping;
21.      texture.wrapT = THREE.RepeatWrapping;
22.      texture.magFilter = THREE.NearestFilter;
23.      texture.colorSpace = THREE.SRGBColorSpace;
24.      const planeSize = 80;
25.      const repeats = planeSize / 2;
26.      texture.repeat.set( repeats, repeats );
27.
28.      const planeMaterial = new THREE.
      MeshStandardMaterial({ map: texture, side: THREE.DoubleSide  });
29.      const planeGeometry = new THREE.PlaneGeometry( planeSize,
       planeSize );
30.      const planeMesh = new THREE.Mesh(planeGeometry,
      planeMaterial);
31.      planeMesh.position.set(0, -5, 0);
32.      planeMesh.rotation.set(Math.PI / -2, 0, 0);
33.      planeMesh.receiveShadow = true;
34.      scene.add(planeMesh);
35. });
36.
37. // We can encapsulate blocks to unnamed closures that do not have
38. // naming intersections
39. {
40.      const skyColor = 0xB1E1FF;  // light blue
41.      const groundColor = 0xB97A20;  // brownish orange
42.      const intensity = 2;
43.      const light = new THREE.
      HemisphereLight(skyColor, groundColor, intensity);
44.      scene.add(light);
45. }
46.
47. {
48.      const color = 0xFFFFFF;
49.      const intensity = 1;
50.      const light = new THREE.DirectionalLight(color, intensity);
51.      light.position.set(0, 10, 5);
52.      light.target.position.set(-5, 0, 0);
53.      scene.add(light);
54.      scene.add(light.target);
55. }
```

```
56. const canvas = document.querySelector('#container');
57. const renderer = new THREE.WebGLRenderer({antialias: true,
    canvas});
58. renderer.setSize(props.width, props.height);
59.
60. // Here we will implement new code
61.
62. const controls = new OrbitControls( camera, renderer.domElement );
63. controls.update();
64.
65. function animate() {
66.   requestAnimationFrame( animate );
67.   controls.update();
68.   renderer.render( scene, camera );
69. }
70. animate();
```

Code example 8.2: Initial code for shadows

In Three.js, to create a group, we need a special object named **Object3D**. This object groups several objects in one. We can also add meshes and materials to this group. We will use this to create the object with a fake shadow. To initiate the scene, we will follow *Code Listing 8.17*. For the example, we will create two geometries: a plane for the shadow and a sphere as an object. We will take the sphere as the shadow texture that we will use from the Three. js example is rounded. We only need to create the shadow image with the required shape for the other geometries:

```
1.  // Objects creation
2.  const shadowTexture = loader.load('https:
    //threejs.org/manual/examples/resources/images/roundshadow.png');
3.  // In this array we will collect all grouped objects with sphere
    and plane inside
4.  const sphereShadowBases = [];
5.  const sphereParams = {
6.      radius: 1,
7.      widthDivisions: 32,
8.      heightDivisions: 16
9.  };
10. const sphereGeomerty = new THREE.SphereGeometry(...Object.
    values(sphereParams));
11. const planeSize = 1;
12. const shadowGeometry = new THREE.PlaneGeometry(planeSize,
    planeSize);
```

Code Listing 8.17: Object creation for the fake shadow

Before we see the logic of creating object groups look into how we render them. For rendering, we will put objects at different distances from the ground. To achieve this, we use trigonometrics as it is a perfect solution to operate up and down movements, jumps, or other mechanics. *Code Listing 8.18* helps create a pretty scene with several objects:

```
1.  function animate() {
2.    requestAnimationFrame( animate );
3.    controls.update();
4.      sphereShadowBases.forEach((sphereShadowBase, index) => {
5.          const { base, sphereMesh, shadowMesh, y } = sphereShadowBase;
6.
7.          const shadowIntensity = index / sphereShadowBases.length;
8.
9.          const distance = 0.2;
10.         const angle = distance + shadowIntensity * Math.PI * 2 *
    (index % 1 ? 1 : -1);
11.         const radius = Math.sin(distance - index) * 10;
12.         base.position.set(Math.cos(angle) * radius, 0,
    Math.sin(angle) * radius);
13.
14.         const yOff = Math.abs(Math.sin(5 + index));
15.         sphereMesh.position.y = y + THREE.MathUtils.lerp(-2, 2, yOff);
16.         shadowMesh.material.opacity = THREE.MathUtils.lerp(1, .25,
    yOff);
17.       });
18.   renderer.render( scene, camera );
19. }
20. animate();
```

Code Listing 8.18: Rendering of multiple objects with shadows

Finally, we create the objects shown in the scene using *Code Listing 8.19*:

```
1.  const shadowGeometry = new THREE.PlaneGeometry(planeSize, planeSize);
2.  // Put the code from below after shadow geometry creation
3.  for (let i = 0; i < 15; ++i) {
4.      // Creating the groups for objects
5.      const base = new THREE.Object3D();
6.      scene.add(base);
7.      // Creating the material for shadow using texture
8.      const shadowMaterial = new THREE.MeshBasicMaterial({
9.          map: shadowTexture,
10.         transparent: true,
11.         depthWrite: false
```

```
12.    });
13.      // Creating the shadow mesh
14.      const shadowMesh = new THREE.
    Mesh(shadowGeometry, shadowMaterial);
15.      shadowMesh.position.y = 0.001;
16.      shadowMesh.rotation.x = Math.PI * -.5;
17.
18.      const shadowSize = sphereParams.radius * 4;
19.      shadowMesh.scale.set(shadowSize, shadowSize, shadowSize);
20.      base.add(shadowMesh);
21.
22.      const sphereMaterial = new THREE.
    MeshPhongMaterial({color: '#7DAA92'});
23.      const sphereMesh = new THREE.
    Mesh(sphereGeomerty, sphereMaterial);
24.      sphereMesh.position.set(0, sphereParams.radius + 2, 0);
25.      base.add(sphereMesh);
26.      // Adding the group into the array that we will render
27.      sphereShadowBases.
    push({base, sphereMesh, shadowMesh, y: sphereMesh.position.y});
28. }
```

Code Listing 8.19: Objects creation

The result will be the same as *Figure 8.7*:

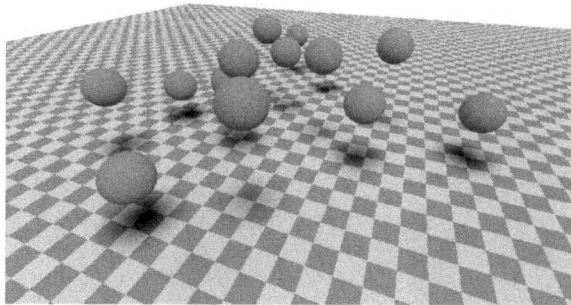

Figure 8.7: Multiple objects with fake shadows

Shadow mapping

Shadow mapping is a technique used in Three.js and other 3D rendering engines to simulate the casting and receiving of shadows in a 3D scene. This technique is vital for creating realistic and immersive 3D environments. Shadow mapping operates by rendering the scene from the perspective of the light source (point of view) into a depth map, also known as a *shadow map.* This depth map stores information about the distances between objects in the scene and the light source. Later, when rendering the scene from the camera's viewpoint, each pixel checks if it is in shadow by comparing its depth with the depth stored in the shadow map. The process is divided into two steps:

1. **Render the depth map**: The scene is rendered from the light source's perspective into a texture or frame buffer known as the shadow map. This shadow map stores the depth information.

2. **Project Shadows**: When rendering the scene from the camera's viewpoint, each fragment (*pixel*) determines its position concerning the light source. It then samples the shadow map to compare the depth of the fragment with the depth stored in the shadow map. If the pixel depth is greater (farther from the light) than the depth in the shadow map, it is in shadow; otherwise, it is lit.

The shadows in a scene are not determined by the main camera that displays the scene. Instead, each light source responsible for casting shadows has its own dedicated camera. This **shadow camera** defines the shape, range, and position of the shadows created by that specific light source.

While this setup can seem complex at first, Three.js provides **shadow camera helpers** to make it easier to understand and adjust how shadows are projected in the scene. These helpers allow you to visualize and fine-tune the shadow camera settings, giving you better control over the final shadow effects.

Let us start with a simple example and create the shadows in the scene. We will use the example with a point light so we can get back to the code (*Code Listing 8.9*) for reference (do not forget to use the general template for the lights).

As mentioned before, the shadow will need casting and receiving objects. This is done using the following steps:

1. The first step will be to initiate the shadow in the renderer. To do that, we will enable the shadow map parameter in the renderer as in *Code Listing 8.20*:

```
1. const renderer = new THREE.
   WebGLRenderer({antialias: true, canvas});
2. renderer.shadowMap.enabled = true;
```

Code Listing 8.20: Initiating the shadows in the renderer

2. The next step will be to initiate casting shadows in the light object. To do that, we need to enable the cast shadow parameter in the light as done in *Code Listing 8.21*:

```
3. const initLight = () => {
4.     light = new THREE.PointLight(...Object.
   values(lightParams));
5.     light.position.set(...Object.values(integratableParams.
   position));
```

```
6.      // Enable cast shadow in the Light objrct
7.      light.castShadow = true;
8.      scene.add(light);
9.      helper = new THREE.PointLightHelper(light, 5);
10.     scene.add(helper);
11. };
```

Code Listing 8.21: Update for the light initiation with cast shadow parameter

3. Now, we have the casting shadows light and each object on a scene should also cast and receive shadow. To make it we will need to follow the *Code Listing 8.22*:

```
1. objectsOnScene.forEach(object => {
2.      const geometry = initGeometry(object);
3.      const material = new THREE.
    MeshStandardMaterial({ color: object.color });
4.      const mesh = new THREE.Mesh(geometry, material);
5.      mesh.castShadow = true;
6.      mesh.receiveShadow = true;
7.      mesh.position.set(...object.position);
8.      scene.add(mesh);
9. });
```

Code Listing 8.22: Adding shadows to the objects

4. The result of the shadows initiation will look like in *Figure 8.8:*

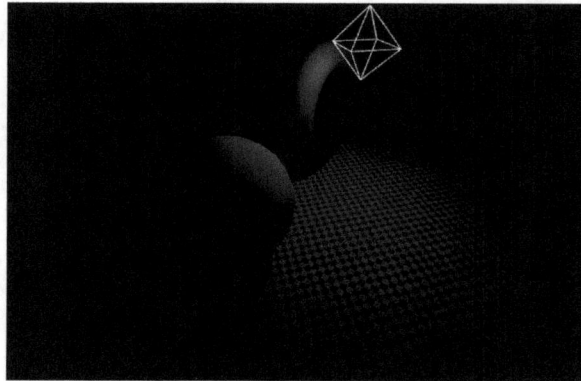

Figure 8.8: Shadows initiation render result

The shadow mapping configuration can help us decide the kind of light to use in each required case. For example, hard shadows are sharp and well-defined. They are typically used in scenarios with point light sources like the sun. To make hard shadows, we add a shadow map type parameter to make them sharper as in *Code Listing 8.23*:

```
renderer.shadowMap.type = THREE.PCFShadowMap;
```

Code Listing 8.23: Hard shadow configuration

To make shadows softer we can change this parameter to soft as in *Code Listing 8.24*. We also need to add a bias parameter to the light source:

```
1.  // Add this line into light initiation function before we add it
2.  // to the scene
3.  light.shadow.bias = -0.003;
4.
5.  // Shadow map configuration
6.  renderer.shadowMap.type = THREE.PCFSoftShadowMap;
```

Code Listing 8.24: Soft shadow configuration

The light and shadows use their camera to create the object. This means, we also can manipulate the object and see the parameters using a special helper. To create the helper for the light, we add code from *Code Listing 8.25* to the **initLight** function:

```
1.  // Update the global variables with new helper
2.  let light, helper, spotLightCameraHelper = null;
3.  // Update for the initLight function
4.  spotLightCameraHelper = new THREE.CameraHelper(light.shadow.camera);
5.  scene.add(spotLightCameraHelper);
```

Code Listing 8.25: Update for the light initiation function

Once updated, we will see a pyramid rooted in the light source, as shown in *Figure 8.9*. This is what the shadow camera looks like:

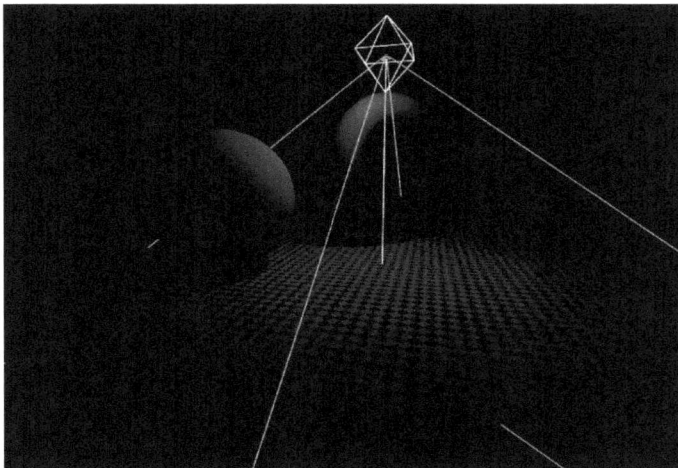

Figure 8.9: Light camera helper

In the current state, we can plan the optimization for the scene depending on what we want to see and have in the end. As we are using light shadows there is a parameter that can reduce the quality of shadow (keep in mind, we are using the web browser, and we do not need quality on the scene). The shadow quality parameter is called **mapSize**. Depending on this parameter we can change the shadow quality. To implement this parameter add the code from the *Code Listing 8.26*:

```
1. // Add this lines into initLight function after the light
   object creation
2. light.shadow.mapSize.width = 128; // default value is 512,
   you can try bigger number
3. light.shadow.mapSize.height = 128;
```

Code Listing 8.26: Map size configuration

We can also have several light sources that produce shadows in a scene. In this case, we can face the issue of overlapping shadows. As for shadows, we use cameras with a near/far parameter that overcomes such issues. To add these parameters, the code from *Code listing 8.27* has to be incorporated after the light object creation (same place as for mapSize):

```
1. // Add this lines into initLight function after the light
   object creation
2. light.shadow.camera.near = 12;
3. light.shadow.camera.far = 100;
```

Code Listing 8.27: Near far parameters initiation

Conclusion

Lighting is a crucial component of creating realistic and immersive 3D scenes. In this chapter, we have studied different types of light sources, from ambient and directional lights to point and spotlights, each with unique characteristics and use cases. By understanding how these light sources function, we learn to shape the atmosphere of our 3D environments and bring them to life.

Shadow is an essential element of realistic 3D rendering. It has been a focal point of our discussion where we have covered the concept of shadow mapping and how to implement hard and soft shadows. Whether aiming for sharp, well-defined shadows or soft, gradual transitions from light to darkness, this chapter helps create the desired shadow effects.

Moving forward in the 3D web development journey, mastering lighting and shadows will be pivotal in elevating the visual quality and realism of our projects. These skills open the door to a world of creative possibilities, allowing us to craft captivating and engaging 3D scenes that capture the imagination of the audience.

With this chapter, we have acquired a fundamental understanding of lighting and shadows and gained the tools and insights needed to apply these concepts effectively. As we proceed, these skills will serve as the building blocks for even more advanced and visually stunning 3D experiences.

In the next chapter, we will learn how to work with cameras and perspective in our scenes.

Points to remember

- Choose lights depending on your scene idea. Use only required light sources and use shadows only when necessary.

- Not all types of lights have shadow-casting.

- There is a way to fake a shadow that will be more performant than a real one.

- Configure your shadows to have optimal performance with a realistic view.

Exercises

1. Add the GUI to choose materials for the light examples. Investigate how different types of material react to light.

2. Create the scene with several objects and several spotlights. Create the GUI for the light to change the near/far points. Check how shadows overlap changing on these parameters.

Join our Discord space

Join our Discord workspace for latest updates, offers, tech happenings around the world, new releases, and sessions with the authors:

https://discord.bpbonline.com

CHAPTER 9

Camera and Perspective

Introduction

In the world of Three.js, we will now explore the environment behind the lens. The camera can be seen as a storyteller that shapes the narrative in 3D. Its artistry is similar to that of cinematography, framing scenes for an immersive experience.

Similar to a photographer employing various lenses to achieve different visual effects, **Three.js** offers a range of camera types tailored to different perspectives, from standard viewpoints to complex multi-camera setups. This chapter will discuss the configuration of camera controls, allowing for interactive experiences and creating unique viewpoints, much like a photographer capturing the essence of a scene.

As we advance through this chapter, we will explore multi-camera configurations, enabling the orchestration of intricate scenes. This approach mirrors a film director who balances visual aesthetics with performance optimization. Our goal is to achieve smooth interactions without compromising on the quality of the visual output.

Throughout this chapter, we will adopt the roles of both creator and storyteller. Utilizing cameras as our tools, we will navigate the possibilities of **Three.js**, crafting compelling visual narratives designed to engage users and draw them into the immersive worlds we create.

Structure

In this chapter, we will discuss the following topics:

- Camera types
- Configuring camera controls and interactions
- Camera optimization and performance

Objectives

By the end of this chapter, you will be equipped the reader with an adept understanding of the diverse camera types. It will help master the art of configuring camera controls, enabling seamless interactions in 3D environments. The nuances of crafting unique perspectives allow us to create compelling viewing experiences.

Further, we will discover the intricacies of multi-camera setups, honing skills in orchestrating complex scenes. The optimization and performance enhancements for cameras will be made clear, helping the reader strike a perfect balance between visual richness and computational efficiency.

Camera types

Just like in a grand theater, where the hum of anticipation echoes as the lights dim (like in *Figure 9.1*). The stage is set, and we witness a performance that weaves seamlessly between different scenes. This scenario is similar to that of Three.js cameras.

In 3D graphics, cameras are the storytellers. They frame the narrative, deciding what the audience sees and how they see it. Let us now study the different camera types, each with a distinct lens through which our story unfolds.

Figure 9.1: Grand theatre view

- **Perspective camera**: It can be visualized as the lens capturing the vastness of a landscape. The perspective camera mimics how our eyes perceive depth in the real world. It is perfect for expansive scenes, where objects in the distance appear smaller.

- **Orthographic camera**: Like a blueprint or a set design sketch, the orthographic camera is like a technical drawing, with no depth perception, just precise, parallel lines. It is ideal for scenes requiring accuracy and a more **architectural** feel.

- **Stereo camera**: Similar to slipping on 3D glasses in a cinema. The stereo camera creates a left-eye and right-eye view, adding depth to the scene. It is what makes objects pop out of the screen in 3D effects.

- **Cube camera**: It is based on reflections and refractions, where a camera encapsulated within a cube captures the panorama of a scene. The CubeCamera takes us into the world of dynamic reflections. It is a valuable asset to render environments with reflective surfaces, like mirrors or glass.

- **The array of cameras**: Sometimes, one perspective is not enough, just like having multiple cameras in a live broadcast, each focusing on a different angle. Three.js allows us to orchestrate an array of cameras, each telling its part of the story.

The provided code snippet in *Code Example 9.1* will create a scene for you, so you don't have to start from scratch. This setup allows you to focus on learning how different camera types function by simply modifying the existing scene, rather than building one yourself:

```
1.  import * as THREE from 'three';
2.  import GUI from 'lil-gui';
3.  // Init Debug UI
4.  const gui = new GUI();
5.  // Init Scene
6.  const props = { width: 800, height: 600, color: 0xff0000 };
7.  const scene = new THREE.Scene();
8.  // Setup the renderer
9.  const canvas = document.querySelector('#container');
10. const renderer = new THREE.WebGLRenderer({
11.   canvas: canvas
12. });
13. // Create some objects to play around with cameras. We will
       hardcode it here to not focus on the code at this point.
14.
15. const geometry = new THREE.SphereGeometry( 10, 32, 16 );
16. const material = new THREE.MeshStandardMaterial( { color: 0xffff00 } );
17. const sphere = new THREE.Mesh( geometry, material );
18. sphere.position.set(...[10, 10, 0]);
```

```
19. scene.add( sphere );
20.
21. // We make a ground object to see the full scene
22. const loader = new THREE.TextureLoader();
23. loader.load(
    'https://threejs.org/manual/examples/resources/images/checker.png',
    (texture) => {
24.     texture.wrapS = THREE.RepeatWrapping;
25.     texture.wrapT = THREE.RepeatWrapping;
26.     texture.magFilter = THREE.NearestFilter;
27.     texture.colorSpace = THREE.SRGBColorSpace;
28.     const planeSize = 80;
29.     const repeats = planeSize / 2;
30.     texture.repeat.set( repeats, repeats );
31.     const planeMaterial = new THREE.
    MeshStandardMaterial({ map: texture, side: THREE.DoubleSide  });
32.     const planeGeometry = new THREE.
    PlaneGeometry( planeSize, planeSize );
33.     const planeMesh = new THREE.Mesh(planeGeometry, planeMaterial);
34.     planeMesh.position.set(0, -5, 0);
35.     planeMesh.rotation.set(Math.PI / -2, 0, 0);
36.     scene.add(planeMesh);
37. });
38. const lightParams = {
39.     skyColor: 0x404040,
40.     groundColor: 0xB1E1FF,
41.     intensivity: 2
42. };
43. const light = new THREE.HemisphereLight(...Object.
    values(lightParams));
44. scene.add(light);
45.
46. // Put the camera-related code here
47.
48. renderer.setSize(props.width, props.height);
49. function animate() {
50.   requestAnimationFrame( animate );
51.   renderer.render( scene, camera );
52. }
53. animate();
54.
```

Code Example 9.1: Initial code

Perspective camera

The first type is the perspective camera. In the 3D world, this camera mimics how we perceive depth in reality.

The perspective camera replicates objects in the distance that appear smaller than those up close, just like how mountains on the horizon seem more diminutive than the ones right in front.

To add the camera to the scene, we need to add code from *Code Listing 9.1* to the block in the template code with a comment **// Put the camera-related code here.**

```
1.  // This is a default camera parameter
2.  const cameraParams = { x: 8, y: 20, z: 100 };
3.  const cameraRotation = { x: 0, y: 0, z: 0};
4.
5.  const camera = new THREE.PerspectiveCamera(
6.  45, // this is a camera frustum vertical field of view
7.  props.width / props.height, // this is a camera  frustum aspect ratio
8.  1, // this is a camera frustum near plane
9.  1000 // this is a camera frustum far plane
10. );
11. camera.position.set(...Object.values(cameraParams));
12.
13. // GUI debugger for the position and angle of the camera
14. const positionFolder = gui.addFolder( 'Position' );
15. const positionKeysAsArray = Object.keys(cameraParams);
16. positionKeysAsArray.forEach(position => {
17.     positionFolder.add( cameraParams, position, 0, 100)
18.         .onChange((value) => {
19.             camera.position[position] = value;
20.             camera.updateMatrix();
21.         });
22. });
23. const rotationFolder = gui.addFolder( 'Rotation' );
24. const rotationKeysAsArray = Object.keys(cameraRotation);
25. rotationKeysAsArray.forEach(position => {
26.     rotationFolder.add( cameraRotation, position, -100, 100)
27.         .onChange((value) => {
28.             camera.rotation[position] = THREE.MathUtils.
    degToRad(value);
29.             camera.updateMatrix();
30.         });
31. });
```

Code Listing 9.1: Perspective camera creation

Since we do not use the **OrbitControls** object for the scene, we will add a GUI interface to change parameters in real-time. After the code insertion, we will see a sphere on a plane using the created camera, like in *Figure 9.2*:

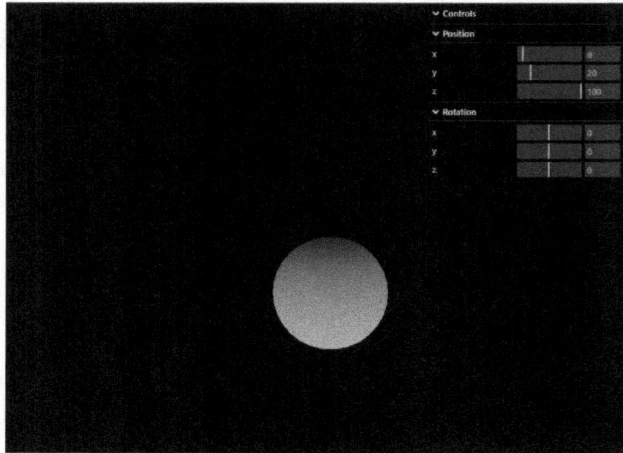

Figure 9.2: *Perspective camera render*

The camera has several parameters. Let us study in detail what they mean and how they can change the camera's view. The data types of the camera look like this:
PerspectiveCamera(fov Number, aspect: Number, near Number, far: Number)

- **Fov**: Camera frustum vertical field of view. This is the angle between the top and bottom planes of the camera frustum. It determines how much of the scene can be seen from the camera position. A larger FOV means a wider view, but also more distortion. A smaller for means a narrower view, but also less distortion. The FOV is usually between 60 and 90 degrees.

- **Aspect**: Camera frustum aspect ratio. This is the ratio between the horizontal and vertical size of the camera frustum. It affects the shape of the camera frustum and the horizontal field of view. A larger aspect means a wider horizontal view, but also more stretching. A smaller aspect means a narrower horizontal view, but also more squashing. The aspect is equal to the window width divided by the window height.

- **Near**: Camera frustum near plane. This is the minimum distance from the camera at which Three.js renders the scene. Anything closer than this distance will be clipped and not visible. A smaller near means more depth precision but more risk of z-fighting. A larger near means less depth precision but less risk of z-fighting. The near is usually a very small value, such as 0.1.

- **Far**: Camera frustum far plane. This is the maximum distance from the camera that Three.js renders the scene. Anything farther than this distance will be clipped and not visible. A smaller far means less memory usage, and more culling of distant objects. A larger far means more memory usage and less culling of distant objects. The far is usually a large value, such as 1000.

We can also learn about the **lookAt** parameter for the camera. This parameter attaches the camera view angle to the desired object position. As a parameter, it takes the coordinates when we take a sphere position as an example, the camera will follow it in whatever position we choose. Add it before the matrix update, like in *Code listing 9.2,* and on position change, the camera will rotate to the sphere:

```
1. onChange((value) => {
2.          camera.position[position] = value;
3.          camera.lookAt( sphere.
   position ); // here we will stick to sphere
4.          camera.updateMatrix();
5. });
```

Code Listing 9.2: *Code for the lookAt parameter*

Orthographic camera

Unlike its sibling, the perspective camera, which mimics human vision, the orthographic camera operates more like a top-down map view. That means that the camera will not change the view angle on position change, and the camera zoom will not distort the scene with it.

Like a surveyor mapping out a city from above, disregarding depth for a moment and concentrating solely on the layout. This is precisely what the orthographic camera achieves.

To add the camera to the scene, we need to add code from *Code Listing 9.3* to the block in the template code with a comment: **// Put the camera-related code here.**

```
1. // Put the camera-related code here
2. // This is a default camera parameter
3. const cameraParams = {
4.     delta: 20
5. };
6.
7. const cameraPosition = { x: 8, y: 20, z: 40 };
8. const cameraRotation = { x: 0, y: 0, z: 0 };
9.
10. const camera = new THREE.OrthographicCamera(
11.     props.width / - cameraParams.delta,
12.     props.width / cameraParams.delta,
13.     props.height / cameraParams.delta,
14.     props.height / - cameraParams.delta, 1, 1000 );
15. camera.position.set(...Object.values(cameraPosition));
```

```
16. camera.lookAt( sphere.position );
17.
18. // GUI debugger for the position and angle of the camera
19. const positionFolder = gui.addFolder( 'Position' );
20. const positionKeysAsArray = Object.keys(cameraPosition);
21. positionKeysAsArray.forEach(position => {
22.     positionFolder.add( cameraPosition, position, 0, 100)
23.         .onChange((value) => {
24.             camera.position[position] = value;
25.             camera.lookAt( sphere.position );
26.             camera.updateMatrix();
27.         });
28. });
```

Code Listing 9.3: *Code to insert the orthographic camera*

The data types of the camera look like this: Orthographic camera (**left : Number, right : Number, top : Number, bottom : Number, near : Number, far : Number**)

- **Left:** The coordinate of the left plane of the viewing frustum.

- **Right:** The coordinate of the right plane of the viewing frustum.

- **Top:** The coordinate of the top plane of the viewing frustum.

- **Bottom:** The coordinate of the bottom plane of the viewing frustum.

- **Near:** The distance to the near plane of the viewing frustum. Objects closer than this won't be rendered.

- **Far:** The distance to the far plane of the viewing frustum. Objects farther than this won't be rendered.

As we can see from *Code Listing 9.3,* for the plane of the viewing, we divide the number by 20. Dividing by 20 ensures that the camera frustum covers the entire width and height of the window while keeping the camera at the center of the window. It is a common practice to set up orthographic cameras in this way to create a symmetrical view centered around the camera position. That means that this 20 can be used as a delta parameter. We add code from *Code Listing 9.4* to have the possibility to change and choose the correct number:

```
1. updateMatrix const deltaFolder = gui.addFolder( 'Delta' );
2. const deltaKeysAsArray = Object.keys(cameraParams);
3. deltaKeysAsArray.forEach(delta => {
4.     deltaFolder.add( cameraParams, delta, 0, 100, 1)
5.         .onChange((value) => {
6.             camera.left = props.width / - value;
7.             camera.right = props.width / value;
```

```
8.              camera.top = props.height / value;
9.              camera.bottom = props.height / - value;
10.             camera.lookAt( sphere.position );
11.             camera.updateProjectionMatrix();
12.        });
13. });
```

Code Listing 9.4: *Code to change the delta for the camera*

We use different methods to update the camera. The reason to use it is to update different parameters for the camera:

- **updateProjectionMatrix** is specifically for cameras and updates the projection matrix based on camera properties.

- **updateMatrix** is a more general method for objects and updates the local matrix based on changes in position, rotation, or scale.

After the code insertion, we will see a sphere on a plane using the created camera, like in *Figure 9.3*:

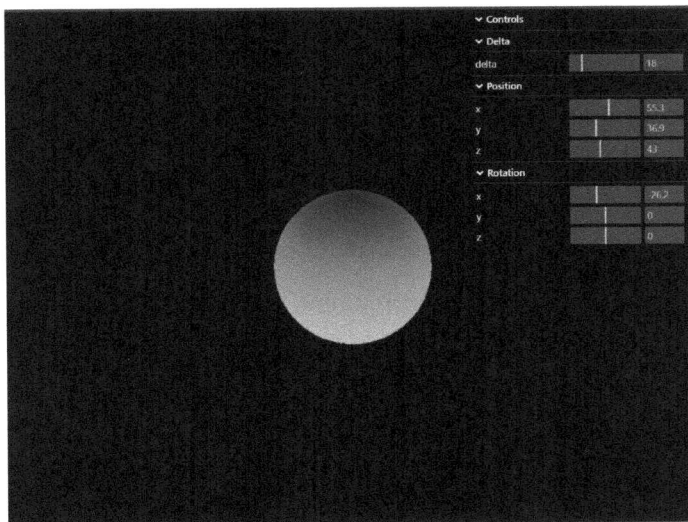

Figure 9.3: *Orthographic camera render*

Stereo camera

In Three.js, a stereo camera is a specialized camera that mimics the way human vision works, creating separate views for the left and right eyes. This is often used in **virtual reality (VR)** or immersive 3D applications to provide a realistic depth perception.

Stereo camera, Anaglyph 3D, and Parallax Barrier are interconnected elements that play pivotal roles in creating immersive 3D experiences. To render a stereo camera, we use perspective cameras with effects: *Anaglyph 3D* or *Parallax Barrier*.

Anaglyph 3D

Anaglyph 3D presents slightly offset images to each eye, usually in contrasting colors like red and cyan. When viewed through glasses with corresponding color filters, each eye perceives a different image, creating a sense of depth.

Parallax Barrier

A Parallax Barrier is a device placed in front of a display to create a stereoscopic or multiscopic 3D effect. It consists of a layer with precisely spaced slits that allow each eye to see a different set of pixels, creating the illusion of depth without the need for special glasses.

By combining the capabilities of the stereo camera with the rendering techniques of Anaglyph 3D or the technology of a Parallax Barrier display, developers can craft engaging 3D visuals that offer depth perception and enhance the overall user experience. Whether through color-filtered glasses or a dynamic barrier, these technologies bring an added dimension to virtual environments.

To see how it works in practice, we will use the example from the perspective camera. The difference will be:

- We will need to create an effect object on the scene
- Use the effect to render the scene instead of the renderer object

In *Code Listing 9.5*, we will see how to implement the Anaglyph 3D effect for the camera. To have a pure experience, we can use stereo glasses from the movie theatre, or any other ones that we may have:

```
1. // Place this line at the top of your JS file after
   the GUI object import
2. import { AnaglyphEffect } from 'three/addons/effects/AnaglyphEffect.js';
3.
4. // Place these code lines after the camera initialization part
5. const effect = new AnaglyphEffect( renderer );
6. effect.setSize( props.width, props.height );
7.
8. // In the animate() function change renderer.render
   ( scene, camera ); to this code
9. effect.render( scene, camera );
```

Code Listing 9.5: Perspective camera update to use the Anaglyph effect

After the code update, we will see the result in the browser, as in *Figure 9.4:*

Figure 9.4: Anaglyph effect in action

We may not see a big difference in the paper book. The stereo Anaglyph effect creates a color difference around the object that can not be seen in the black-and-white print. It needs to be seen in the browser.

To look at the Parallax Barrier effect, we need to change the effect from **AnaglyphEffect** to **ParallaxBarrierEffect** at the top of the **JS file,** like in *Code Listing 9.6:*

```
1.  import { AnaglyphEffect } from 'three/addons/effects/AnaglyphEffect.
    js';
2.  import { ParallaxBarrierEffect } from 'three/addons/effects/
    ParallaxBarrierEffect.js';
3.  // In a place where you add the effect, change the object name to the
    new one
4.  const effect = new ParallaxBarrierEffect( renderer );
```

Code Listing 9.6: Change effect to Parallax Barrier

The result will look as shown in *Figure 9.5:*

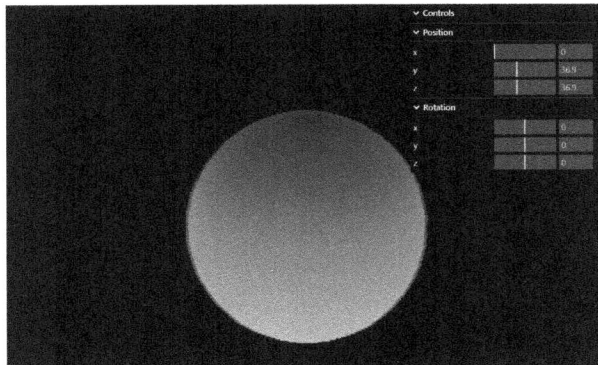

Figure 9.5: Parallax barrier effect in action

Unfortunately, to have a pure experience, we will need a TV or monitor that supports Parallax Barrier. This effect creates the stereo experience without the need to have stereo glasses. To see it in full power, we will need a special screen.

One last thing that will make our application more powerful, is stereo effects. This will create the scene separated into two parts that will allow you to look at the scene using VR devices like Oculus. To check it, we also need to change the effect, like in *Code Listing 9.7*:

```
1. // import { ParallaxBarrierEffect } from 'three/addons/
   effects/ ParallaxBarrierEffect.js';
2. import { StereoEffect } from 'three/addons/effects/ StereoEffect.js';
3. // In the place where you add the effect, change the
   object name to the new one
4. const effect = new StereoEffect( renderer );
```

Code Listing 9.7: Using the stereo effect

As a result, we will see a split into two parts screen with one scene on it, like in *Figure 9.6*:

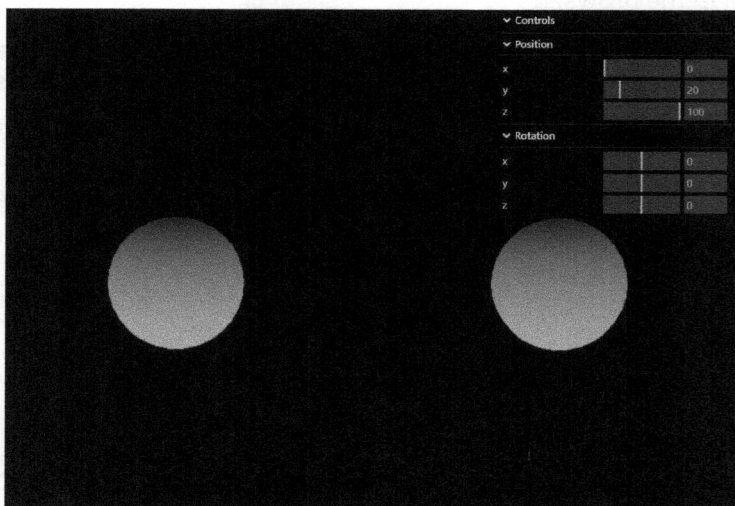

Figure 9.6: Stereo effect in action

To have a full experience with this effect, we need to have a special device. It can be a VR helmet like Oculus, or we can also use helmets that use a phone screen as a source.

Cube camera

CubeCamera is a specialized camera in Three.js designed to capture the environment in all directions. It creates a cube map. A cube map is essentially six 2D images representing the scene as viewed from the center of a cube. This cube map can then be used as an environment map for materials, creating reflections and other effects.

As a cube camera is not the camera to display but to create the effects, we will still need the camera on the scene to display. So, we will add a perspective camera on the scene as well.

To use the CubeCamera in practice, we can take the example code for the perspective camera and make some updates there, the same as in *Code Listing 9.8:*

```
1.  // Put the camera-related code here
2.  // This is a default camera parameter
3.  const camera = new THREE.PerspectiveCamera( 60, props.width / props.
    height, 1, 1000 );
4.  camera.position.z = 75;
5.
6.  const cubeRenderTarget = new THREE.WebGLCubeRenderTarget( 256 );
7.  cubeRenderTarget.texture.type = THREE.HalfFloatType;
8.  const cubeCamera = new THREE.CubeCamera(1, 1000, cubeRenderTarget);
9.  // Position the CubeCamera in the scene
10. cubeCamera.position.set(0, 5, 0);
11. scene.add(cubeCamera);
12.
13. const second_geometry = new THREE.SphereGeometry( 10, 52, 26 );
14. // Create a reflective material using the cube map
15. const reflectiveMaterial = new THREE.MeshStandardMaterial({
16.     envMap: cubeCamera.renderTarget.texture,
17.     roughness: 0.05,
18.     metalness: 1
19. });
20. // Here we will create another sphere that
    will take a Cube Camera as a
21. // material. That will create the reflections on the sphere
22. const second_sphere = new THREE.Mesh( second_geometry,
    reflectiveMaterial );
23. second_sphere.position.set(...[20, 20, 20]);
24. scene.add( second_sphere );
```

Code Listing 9.8: Code update to initiate the Cube camera

Now, we have a scene with two spheres, and one of them is reflecting the other. To have a more visual experience, we will add more improvements in the code to add more light and animate spheres like in *Code Listing 9.9:*

```
1.  // Please add intensity to light parameters to make more light
    and see more reflections
2.  const lightParams = {
```

```
3.       skyColor: 0x404040,
4.       groundColor: 0xB1E1FF,
5.       intensivity: 10
6. };
7.
8. // Update the animate function to move the
   sphere around another sphere to see reflections
9. function animate() {
10.      const time = performance.now() / 1000;
11.      requestAnimationFrame( animate );
12.      sphere.position.x = Math.cos( time + 10 ) * 30;
13.      sphere.position.y = Math.sin( time + 10 ) * 30;
14.      sphere.position.z = Math.sin( time + 10 ) * 30;
15.      cubeCamera.update(renderer, scene);
   // This will update reflections on each move
16.      renderer.render( scene, camera );
17. }
```

Code Listing 9.9: Update in code for a better experience

The result will be the same as in *Figure 9.7* (but animated):

Figure 9.7: Cube camera in action

ArrayCamera

In Three.js, ArrayCamera is a specialized camera type designed to represent an array of cameras, each capturing a different perspective of the scene. This can be useful for creating multi-view or stereoscopic effects. To create the view with multiple cameras, we will need to create an array of camera objects and render them with a loop. To create it, take the example of the perspective camera one more time and make several updates there, like in *Code Listing 9.10*:

```
1.  // Put the camera-related code here
2.  // This is a default camera parameter
3.  const AMOUNT = 4;
4.  const ASPECT_RATIO = window.innerWidth / window.innerHeight;
5.  const WIDTH = ( window.innerWidth / AMOUNT ) * window.devicePixelRatio;
6.  const HEIGHT = ( window.innerHeight / AMOUNT ) * window.devicePixelRatio;
7.  const cameras = [];
8.  for ( let y = 0; y < AMOUNT; y ++ ) {
9.      for ( let x = 0; x < AMOUNT; x ++ ) {
10.         const subcamera = new THREE.PerspectiveCamera( 120, ASPECT_RATIO, 1, 1000 );
11.         subcamera.viewport = new THREE.Vector4(
12.                 Math.floor( x * WIDTH ),
13.                 Math.floor( y * HEIGHT ),
14.                 Math.ceil( WIDTH ),
15.                 Math.ceil( HEIGHT )
16.         );
17.         subcamera.lookAt( sphere.position );
18.         subcamera.position.set(0,0,0);
19.         subcamera.updateMatrixWorld();
20.         cameras.push( subcamera );
21.     }
22. }
23. // Create an ArrayCamera using the array of cameras
24. const arrayCamera = new THREE.ArrayCamera(cameras);
25. arrayCamera.position.z = 3;
26. renderer.setPixelRatio( window.devicePixelRatio );
27. renderer.setSize( window.innerWidth, window.innerHeight );
28. renderer.shadowMap.enabled = true;
```

Code Listing 9.10: *Array of cameras code*

We will also need to update the renderer. To do that, we need to update the animate function like in *Code Listing 9.11*:

```
1. function animate() {
2.   renderer.render( scene, arrayCamera );
3.     requestAnimationFrame( animate );
4. }
```

***Code Listing 9.11:** Animate function update to render an array of cameras*

The important part of the code is using the viewport parameter. The viewport defines the portion of the screen where the camera's view will be rendered. For an ArrayCamera, this becomes particularly important because it allows us to split the screen into multiple regions, each corresponding to a different camera in the array. The result will look like *Figure 9.8*:

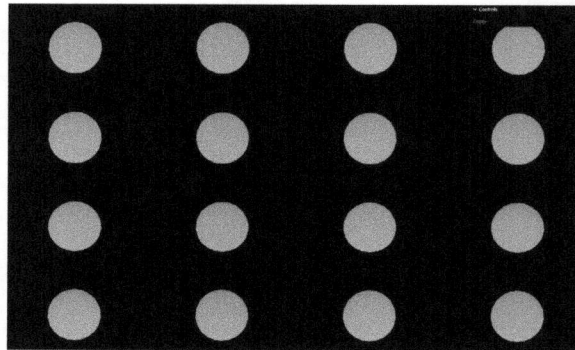

***Figure 9.8:** Array of cameras render representation*

Configuring camera controls and interactions

Configuring camera controls and interactions in Three.js involves setting up mechanisms that allow users to manipulate the camera's position, orientation, and other properties. This is crucial for creating engaging 3D scenes and applications.

Three.js provides various libraries for camera controls, such as **OrbitControls** for orbiting the camera around a target and **FlyControls** for a first-person flying experience. These libraries simplify the implementation of common camera interactions and user inputs.

Configuring controls involves defining how users can interact with the scene. This can include mouse movements, clicks, touch gestures, or keyboard inputs.

For example, **OrbitControls** allows users to rotate the camera by dragging the mouse, zoom in and out with the mouse wheel, and pan by right-clicking and dragging.

Event listeners are set up to capture user input. This involves listening for mouse movements, clicks, or touch events and updating the camera accordingly.

Event listeners can be attached to the entire document or specific HTML elements.

Depending on the application, we might need to customize controls to fit specific requirements. For instance, adjusting rotation speed, limiting zoom levels, or incorporating custom animations in response to user actions.

We already used **OrbitControls** in previous examples. Let us now figure out what interactivity we can use. We will take an example from the previous chapter, the fake shadow block. This is a good example, as several objects have already been made on screen.

We will check the limits of the zoom and smooth animation. Hence, we need to add the code from *Code Listing 9.12* to the example code at the part where we added the **OrbitControls**:

```
1.  const controls = new OrbitControls( camera, renderer.domElement );
2.  controls.enableDamping = true; // an animation loop is required
    when either damping or
3.                                 // auto-rotation are enabled
4.  controls.dampingFactor = 0.005; // This parameter manages the
    smoothness of animation
5.
6.  controls.screenSpacePanning = false;
7.
8.  controls.minDistance = 10;
9.  controls.maxDistance = 100;
10.
11. controls.maxPolarAngle = Math.PI / 2;
12. controls.update();
```

Code Listing 9.12: Code for the Orbit controls setup

After that, we will see that the camera movements and rotation became more smooth. We can play around with the **dampingFactor** parameter to achieve the required result.

The next control is **FlyControls.** This control will allow us to use the mouse and keyboard to interact with the scene. To add it to our code, we make changes in *Code Listing 9.13*:

```
1.  import { OrbitControls } from
    'three/examples/jsm/controls/OrbitControls.js';
2.  import { FlyControls } from 'three/addons/controls/FlyControls.js';
3.
4.  // const controls = new OrbitControls( camera, renderer.domElement );
5.  const controls = new FlyControls(camera, renderer.domElement);
6.  controls.movementSpeed = 10;
7.  controls.domElement = renderer.domElement;
8.  controls.rollSpeed = Math.PI / 24;
9.  controls.autoForward = false;
10. controls.dragToLook = false;
11.
```

```
12. // In animate function add the delta into controls update like this
13. controls.update(0.01);
```

Code Listing 9.13: FlyControls code update

Camera optimization and performance

Optimizing and enhancing the performance of cameras in a Three.js application is crucial for a smooth and responsive user experience. The following are some strategies and examples for optimizing camera usage:

- **Frustum culling**: Frustum culling involves excluding objects that are outside the camera's view frustum, i.e., not visible in the current scene. To use it we add this code after the camera creation: **camera.frustumCulled = true;**

- **Level of Detail (LOD):** We can add the level of detail of objects based on their distance from the camera to improve performance. We add code from *Code Listing 9.14* to manage the level of details:

```
1. const lod = new THREE.LOD();
2. // Add different levels of detail for an object
3. lod.addLevel(simpleObject, distance1);
4. lod.addLevel(detailedObject, distance2);
5. scene.add(lod);
```

Code Listing 9.14: Managing level of details code

- **Camera Clipping**: Adjust the near and far clipping planes to control the range of distances that the camera can see. This helps in discarding objects outside the specified range. We add code from *Code Listing 9.15* to manage near and far clipping planes. There are no special rules for these numbers. For each project, we will need to find the required balance:

```
1. // Adjust the near and far clipping planes
2. camera.near = 0.1;
3. camera.far = 1000;
4. camera.updateProjectionMatrix();
```

Code Listing 9.15: Managing clipping planes code

- **WebGLRenderer Performance settings**: Adjust the **pixelRatio** and antialias properties of the **WebGLRenderer** to balance performance and quality. *Code Listing 9.16* contains the required settings:

```
1. const renderer = new THREE.WebGLRenderer({ antialias: true });
2. renderer.setPixelRatio(window.devicePixelRatio);
```

Code Listing 9.16: Antialias and pixel ratio settings

- **Reuse cameras**: Instead of creating new cameras, we can use existing cameras to reduce memory consumption. As seen in the preceding code examples, we always use the camera as the variable. This variable can be reused instead of creating a new one.

- **Dispose of unused cameras:** We dispose off cameras that are no longer needed to free up resources. To achieve it, we add this code in our application logic at a time when a camera is not required anymore: `camera.dispose();`

Conclusion

Mastering the intricacies of Three.js cameras is essential for creating immersive and performant 3D experiences. From understanding different camera types, configuring controls for user interactions, and optimizing performance, we have studied key aspects that empower developers to craft engaging scenes.

We must remember that efficient camera usage contributes significantly to the overall performance of the Three.js application. The strategies, such as frustum culling, LOD, and camera clipping, provide a foundation for creating scenes that are great and also run smoothly.

In the next chapter, we will explore another critical aspect of 3D graphics, textures. We will also understand how to apply and manipulate textures, which opens infinite possibilities for adding realism and detail to 3D scenes.

Points to remember

- Do not use a perspective camera for the first point-of-view applications, as it distorts the view. We can see it in the examples that we made for the controls. We use an orthographic camera instead, as it does not have a distortion effect.

- CubeCamera is more performant for simple reflections than creating special shaders for each object.

- The VR experience is a feature of the web development. Keep it in mind for the next 10 years.

Exercise

Create the scene with multiple objects like boxes, spheres, and toruses. Add rectangle light from the previous chapter. After that, create FlyControls and add it to the scene. Add several objects with reflections using CubeCamera. Ultimately, we will have a scene we can observe using a mouse or keyboard.

Join our Discord space

Join our Discord workspace for latest updates, offers, tech happenings around the world, new releases, and sessions with the authors:

https://discord.bpbonline.com

CHAPTER 10
Textures and Mapping

Introduction

In 3D graphics, integrating textures into objects is like imparting distinct characteristics, for example, a chromatic burst and a semblance of reality. Akin to artists meticulously selecting materials for their visual opuses, 3D developers interlace textures into their creations to enrich their digital landscapes.

Imagine a digital mountain with a texture that emulates the intricate details of authentic rock formations or a 3D model of a futuristic spacecraft embellished with metallic textures that realistically reflect light. These nuances captivate users and elevate the immersive quality of 3D experiences.

In this chapter, we will study textures in 3D graphics. We will learn the intricacies of integrating textures onto 3D objects, understand the techniques of texture mapping and UV coordinates, and scrutinize effects such as specular mapping, reflection mapping, normal maps, bump mapping, and color maps. As we go through the technical aspects of texture filters and mapping modes, we aim to provide proficiency in using these tools innovatively, infusing 3D creations with depth and visual opulence.

Structure

In this chapter, we will discuss the following topics:

- Applying textures to 3D objects
- Texture mapping techniques and UV coordinates
- Texture filters for various effects

Objectives

By the end of this chapter, we will not only comprehend the complexities of texture application in 3D graphics but also possess the skills to enhance digital creations, transforming them into captivating and visually arresting experiences. Let us proceed to transform the digital canvas into a playground for technical creativity and expression.

Applying textures to 3D objects

Textures in 3D graphics are like the brush strokes on a canvas. They define the surface characteristics of objects, from the roughness of stones to the sleekness of metals. In Three. js, applying textures involves careful orchestration of images onto the surfaces of 3D models.

There are various websites with ready and free textures. We will take one from **https:// www.poliigon.com**. In this chapter, we will use different kinds of textures. For the basic example, we will use non-metal textures like *Denali Quartzite Texture* and *Gray*.

To start coding, use the template code from *Code Listing 10.1* and put your code into the section with comment **// Put your code here.**

```
1. import * as THREE from 'three';
2. import { OrbitControls } from 'three/examples/jsm/controls/
   OrbitControls.js';
3.
4. // Init Scene
5. const props = {
6.    width: 800,
7.    height: 600
8.    };
9. const scene = new THREE.Scene();
10. const camera = new THREE.PerspectiveCamera(75, props.width / props.
   height);
11. camera.position.z = 5;
12. scene.add(camera);
```

```
13.
14. // Put your code here
15.
16. // Setup the renderer
17. const canvas = document.querySelector('#container');
18. const renderer = new THREE.WebGLRenderer({ canvas: canvas });
19.
20. renderer.setSize(props.width, props.height);
21.
22. const controls = new OrbitControls( camera, renderer.domElement );
23. controls.update();
24. function animate() {
25.
26.   requestAnimationFrame( animate );
27.   controls.update();
28.   renderer.render( scene, camera );
29.
30. }
31. animate();
```

Code Listing 10.1: Initial code

We need to copy the texture file into the project to add the texture to the object. Place it into the folder with the path **/assets/<your-texture-file>**.

To add texture to the object, we can use the texture loader. The **TextureLoader** is essential for loading textures from external images or resources. It is a part of the library's core and is used to manage the asynchronous loading process of images, enabling their application as textures on 3D objects.

The stumbling block is in JavaScript as a language. If we use the texture loading directly as here: **const texture = new THREE.TextureLoader().load(<some-texture>);,** we have to ensure the following steps:

1. Use as small by weight in megabytes as possible
2. Make sure that the image will be loaded faster than the other code will be executed

To solve this situation, we must load the texture as done before, using the callback function that indicates that the texture is loaded. Once this is done, it can be installed into the mesh. *Code Listing 10.1* is a good example of how to use the loader correctly:

After the code update, we will see the sphere object with the stone texture like in *Figure 10.1*:

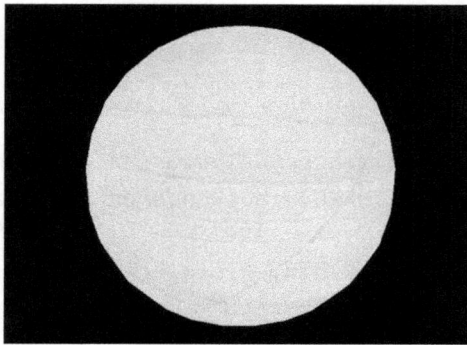

Figure 10.1: Stone texture on the Sphere object

Finally, we need to apply RGB colors to normalize texture colors. This is done by updating the texture function with the code provided in *Code Listing 10.2*.

```
1. const geometry = new THREE.SphereGeometry();
2. texture.colorSpace = THREE.
   SRGBColorSpace; // Add this line to update the code
3. const material = new THREE.MeshBasicMaterial( { map: texture } );
4. const mesh = new THREE.Mesh( geometry, material );
5. scene.add( mesh );
```

Code Listing 10.2: Adding the RGB to the texture color

Using a single image texture in **Three.js** is a straightforward approach that simplifies the process of adding surface details to 3D objects. The primary advantage of this method is its simplicity. You only need to load one image file, apply it as a texture, and your object instantly gains a more detailed appearance. This makes it an efficient choice for cases where performance and ease of implementation are prioritized. To solve this problem, we can use a special technique called **physically based rendering (PBR).**

Components of PBR textures

PBR uses multiple texture maps to simulate realistic material properties and light interactions. These textures define surface details like roughness, metallic shine, and reflections, allowing for highly lifelike 3D models under various lighting conditions. Let us examine the key components that make PBR textures:

- **Albedo (Base Color) map:**
  - Purpose: Represents the inherent color of an object.
  - It is often referred to as the **Base Color** map, defining the basic color of the material.

- **Metalness map:**
  - o Purpose: Determines which parts of the object are metal and which are **dielectric** (non-metal).
  - o A grayscale map where white indicates metal and black indicates non-metal.

- **Roughness map:**
  - o Purpose: Defines the microsurface roughness of the material.
  - o A grayscale map where white indicates a rough surface, and black indicates a smooth surface.

- **Normal map:**
  - o Purpose: Provides additional surface detail by perturbing normals.
  - o Used to simulate fine details on the surface without adding geometry.

- **Ambient Occlusion (AO) map:**
  - o Purpose: Represents areas of the object that receive less ambient light.
  - o Enhances shading realism by darkening crevices and corners.

- **Emissive map:**
  - o Purpose: Specifies areas of the material that emit light.
  - o Used to add self-illuminating elements to the material.

In resources like **https://3dtextures.me/**, we can find various packs of realistic textures. We will take one of them as an example.

Key features of LoadingManager

While a texture loader handles single images, managing multiple textures is more efficient with **LoadingManager**. This tool simplifies loading multiple images at once, optimizing performance and asset management.

- **Progress tracking**: The **LoadingManager** allows us to track the progress of multiple loading operations. As assets are loaded, the manager keeps track of the overall progress as a percentage.

- **Callback handling**: We can register callbacks to be executed when certain events occur during the loading process, such as when one or all items are loaded or when an error occurs.

- **Dependency management**: The manager supports the concept of dependencies, ensuring that certain assets are loaded before others. This is useful when one asset depends on the completion of another.

Texture mapping techniques and UV coordinates

PBR and UV mapping enable the precise application of 2D textures onto 3D models, dictating how colors, patterns, and details adorn every facet. As we move ahead, we will study the nuances of UV mapping, the coordinates that intricately define how textures seamlessly wrap around the contours of 3D objects.

Physically based render

For the texture mapping, we will need to load several files.

As you remember from the previous section, PBR texture is split into 6 parts. For each part, we will need a special file. For this section, we use *Code Listing 10.3*, which shows how to use **LoadManager** to load all required files into the application.

```
1. const loadingManager = new THREE.LoadingManager();
2. const textureLoader = new THREE.TextureLoader(loadingManager);
3. const colorTexture = textureLoader.load('assets/Glass_Window_003_
   basecolor.jpg');
4. colorTexture.colorSpace = THREE.SRGBColorSpace;
5. const alphaTexture = textureLoader.load('assets/Glass_Window_003_
   opacity.jpg');
6. const heightTexture = textureLoader.load('assets/Glass_Window_003_
   height.png');
7. const normalTexture = textureLoader.load('assets/Glass_Window_003_
   normal.jpg');
8. const ambientOcclusionTexture = textureLoader.load('assets/Glass_
   Window_003_ambientOcclusion.jpg');
9. const metalnessTexture = textureLoader.load('assets/Glass_
   Window_003_metallic.jpg');
10. const roughnessTexture = textureLoader.load('assets/Glass_
    Window_003_roughness.jpg');
```

Code Listing 10.3: Loading of PBR-compliant files into the application

Now, we need to add all maps to the material following *Code Listing 10.4:*

```
1. const geometry = new THREE.SphereGeometry();
2. const material = new THREE.MeshBasicMaterial( {
3.     map: colorTexture,
4.     metalnessMap: metalnessTexture,
5.     roughnessMap: roughnessTexture,
6.     normalMap: normalTexture,
```

```
7.        aoMap: ambientOcclusionTexture,
8.        alphaMap: alphaTexture,
9.        heightTexture
10. } );
11.
12. const mesh = new THREE.Mesh( geometry, material );
13. scene.add( mesh );
```

Code Listing 10.4: Adding maps to the material

In the code, an important line is the **heightTexture**. This texture manages the height of small details, and we see it in action later. If we update the code, we will see the result as shown in *Figure 10.2:*

Figure 10.2: Representation of adding the mapped texture

As we are using **MeshBasicMaterial**, we cannot see all the magic of the mapping. If we zoom in closer to the sphere, we can see some shadows, which make the sphere more detailed. However, it does not show all the features of the mapping. To see more details, we need to add light and change the material to one that reacts to the light. Follow *Code Listing 10.5* to add light and material:

```
1. const lightParams = {
2.        color: 0xffffff,
3.        intensity: 500,
4.        distance: 70
5. };
6. const integratableParams = {
7.        position: {
8.                x: 0,
9.                y: 25,
10.               z: 11
11.       }
12. };
```

```
13. const light = new THREE.PointLight(...Object.values(lightParams));
14. light.position.set(...Object.values(integratableParams.position));
15. scene.add(light);
16.
17. // Your map loader is here. Copy it from  Code Listing 10.4
18.
19. const geometry = new THREE.SphereGeometry();
20. const material = new THREE.MeshStandardMaterial( {
21.    map: colorTexture,
22.    metalnessMap: metalnessTexture,
23.    roughnessMap: roughnessTexture,
24.    normalMap: normalTexture,
25.    aoMap: ambientOcclusionTexture,
26.    alphaMap: alphaTexture,
27.    heightTexture
28. } );
29.
30. const mesh = new THREE.Mesh( geometry, material );
31. scene.add( mesh );
```

Code Listing 10.5: Update code with light and standard material

The result will be the same as in *Figure 10.3:*

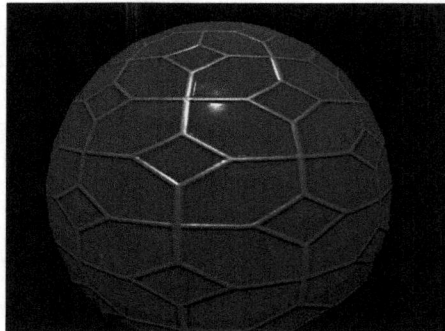

Figure 10.3: Result of adding the light into the scene

As we see, the sphere becomes more realistic. The small details are magnified, and the sphere looks like it contains small details.

UV coordinates

UV mapping is a technique used in 3D computer graphics to map 2D textures onto 3D objects. UV coordinates (u, v) represent the 2D coordinate system applied to the surface of a 3D model. To apply the current part of texture to the object we need to use specific coordinates taken from the texture image. Technically we split texture into blocks like in *Figure 10.4* and then use them with UV coordinates.

UV coordinates are a pair of values (u, v) assigned to each vertex of a 3D model. These coordinates determine how the 2D texture is applied to the model's surface. The (0, 0) point corresponds to the bottom-left corner of the texture, and (1, 1) corresponds to the top-right corner.

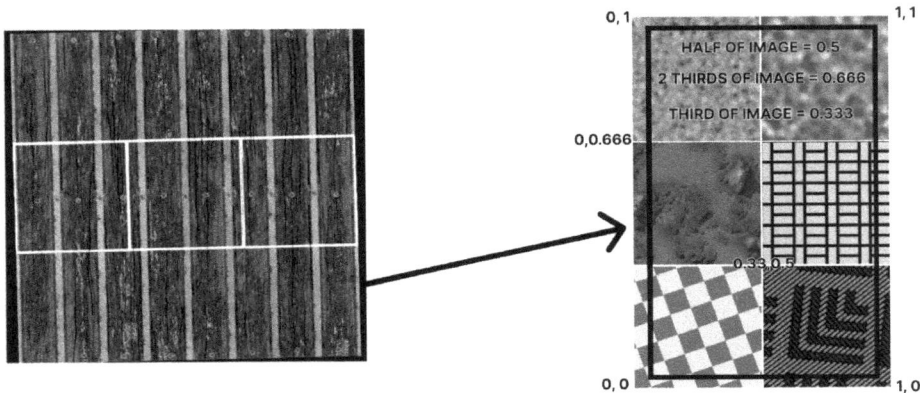

Figure 10.4: Representation of UV blocks on the texture

As per the classical explanation, we should visually split the texture into rectangular blocks, like in *Figure 10.4* on the left side. However, it would be more informative if we showed several rectangles with different textures on the right side of the picture. This makes it clear why we would need to use UV coordinates in practice.

For example, we have a box geometry that must be wrapped with each rectangle on each side. If we just put the texture on it we will see the result in *Figure 10.5* which is incorrect.

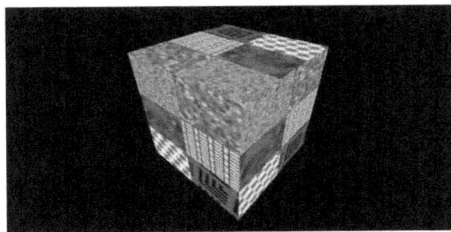

Figure 10.5: Incorrect texture wrapping

For a correct wrap, we need to extend the UV coordinates of the box using the logic from *Figure 10.4:*

- Divide the texture into blocks
- Each block contains half of the picture by width and a third by height

Follow the code from *Code Listing 10.6* to unleash the UV coordinates:

```
1.  const geometry = new THREE.BoxGeometry(2, 2, 2);
2.  const texture = new THREE.TextureLoader().
    load('assets/uv-collection.png');
3.  texture.colorSpace = THREE.SRGBColorSpace;
4.
5.  const uvAttribute = geometry.getAttribute("uv");
    // Unwrap the UV coordinates
6.  const uvArray = uvAttribute.array;
7.  let isLeft = true;
8.  let cornerStep = 0;
9.  let delta = 0;
10. for (let i = 0; i < uvArray.length; i += 2) {
11.     if (i > 0 && i % 8 === 0) { isLeft = !isLeft; }
12.     // Checking if there is any left box
13.     if (i > 0 && i % 16 === 0) { delta += 1/3 }
14.     // If we step into the next level, we increase the delta
15.     if (isLeft) {
16.       uvArray[i + 0] = cornerStep === 1 || cornerStep === 2 ? 0.5 : 0;
17.     } else {
18.       uvArray[i + 0] = cornerStep === 1 || cornerStep === 2 ? 1 : 0.5;
19.     }
20.     uvArray[i + 1] = cornerStep === 0 || cornerStep === 1 ?
    1 - delta - 1/3 : 1 - delta;
21. // delta  indicates on what third of the texture we are right now
22.     cornerStep ++;
23.     if (cornerStep > 3) { cornerStep = 0; }
24. }
25.
26. uvAttribute.needsUpdate = true;
27. const material = new THREE.MeshBasicMaterial({ map: texture });
28. const mesh = new THREE.Mesh( geometry, material );
29. mesh.position.set(0.0, 0.0);
30. scene.add( mesh );
```

Code Listing 10.6: The unwrapping of the texture into blocks

In this code, we iterate UV coordinates by the logic that we take each rectangle from the top left, then the top right, switching to the lower level, and so on. Each box iterates like this:

- Bottom left corner
- Bottom right corner

- Top right corner
- Top left corner

As a result, we will see a box like in *Figure 10.6:*

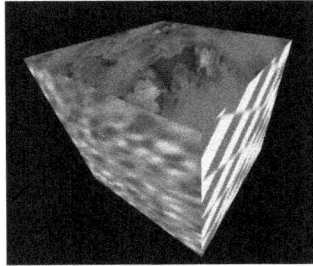

Figure 10.6: Unwrapped texture using UV coordinates

UV coordinates are important to apply the textures to the object. For example, we can try to use the non-rectangular object for the presented texture, and we will see that the result is incorrect, as seen in *Figure 10.7*:

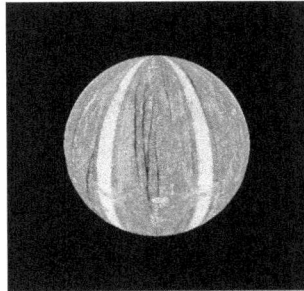

Figure 10.7: Using wooden texture on the sphere object

Taking a more complex example, we take the image of an eye, as shown in *Figure 10.8,* and take a look at the result in *Figure 10.9*. This is not the desired output, and we can fix the situation with UV mapping:

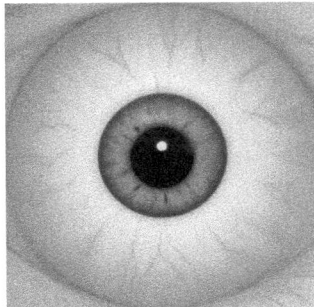

Figure 10.8: An eye texture for the sphere

Figure 10.9: *Result of applying texture to a sphere*

If we change the mapping of the image, like in *Code Listing 10.7*, it will make a better result than that seen in *Figure 10.10*:

```
1. const eyeTexture = new THREE.TextureLoader().load('assets/eye.jpg');
2. eyeTexture.colorSpace = THREE.SRGBColorSpace;
3. eyeTexture.repeat.x = 2;
4. eyeTexture.repeat.y = 1;
```

Code Listing 10.7: *Update for the better texture alignment*

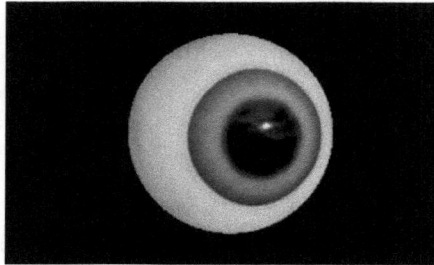

Figure 10.10: *The better texture placement*

To get perfect results, we have to use a technique that is out of the scope of this book, as it requires knowledge of shaders and its special language.

To achieve it, we need to follow the code from *Code Listing 10.8*:

```
1. const geometry = new THREE.SphereGeometry(1, 32, 32);
2. const eyeTexture = new THREE.TextureLoader().load('assets/eye.jpg');
3. eyeTexture.colorSpace = THREE.SRGBColorSpace;
4. const uniforms = {
5.   "tex": { value: eyeTexture }
6. };
7.
8. const vertex_shader = `
```

```
9.  varying vec3 vNormal;
10. void main() {
11.   vNormal = normal;
12.   gl_Position = projectionMatrix * modelViewMatrix
      * vec4( position, 1.0 );
13. }
14. `;
15. const fragment_shader = `
16. uniform sampler2D tex;
17. varying vec3 vNormal;
18. void main() {
19.   vec2 uv = normalize( vNormal ).xy * 0.5 + 0.5;
20.   vec3 color = texture2D( tex, uv ).rgb;
21.   if ( vNormal.z < - 0.85 ) color = vec3( 0.777, 0.74, 0.74 );
22.   gl_FragColor = vec4( color, 1.0 );
23. }
24. `;
25.
26. const material = new THREE.ShaderMaterial({
27.   uniforms        : uniforms,
28.   vertexShader    : vertex_shader,
29.   fragmentShader  : fragment_shader
30. });
31.
32. const sphere = new THREE.Mesh(geometry, material);
33. scene.add(sphere);
```

Code Listing 10.8: *UV mapping code using shaders*

The result will be way better than before, as can be seen in *Figure 10.11*:

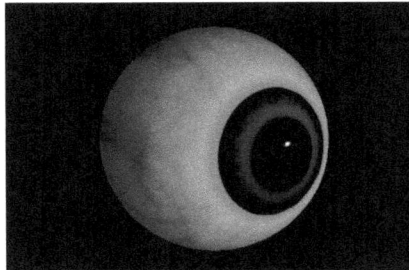

Figure 10.11: *Eye texture mapped on the sphere using the shaders method*

Texture filters for various effects

Texture filters in Three.js are essential tools for manipulating how textures appear on 3D objects. The filters affect the details of the texture. We do not commonly see them on the scene, so to make a better example, we will need to use simple images for the details. In this case, we will take one from the Three.js examples containing colored rectangles.

The filters control how the texture is sampled, displayed, and interpolated. The following are some commonly used texture filters and their effects:

Nearest filter

This filter uses the color value of the nearest pixel. It results in a blocky, pixelated appearance, suitable for a retro or low-resolution aesthetic.

To check the result of this filter, add code from *Code Listing 10.9* into the section with comment **// Put your code here.** We will create two objects with and without filters to see the difference:

```
1.  // Put your code here
2.  const texture = new THREE.TextureLoader().load('assets/low-poly-
    texture.png');
3.  texture.magFilter = THREE.NearestFilter; // Initiation of the filter
4.  texture.minFilter = THREE.NearestFilter; // Initiation of the filter
5.
6.  const geometry = new THREE.BoxGeometry(1, 1, 1);
7.  const material = new THREE.MeshBasicMaterial( { map: texture } );
8.  const cube = new THREE.Mesh( geometry, material );
9.  scene.add( cube );
10.
11. const textureNonFiltered = new THREE.TextureLoader().load('assets/
    low-poly-texture.png');
12. const nonFilteredGeometry = new THREE.BoxGeometry(1, 1, 1);
13. const materialNonFiltered = new THREE.
    MeshBasicMaterial( { map: textureNonFiltered } );
14. const cubeNoneFiltered = new THREE.
    Mesh( nonFilteredGeometry, materialNonFiltered );
15. cubeNoneFiltered.position.set(...[2, 0, 0]);
16.
17. scene.add( cubeNoneFiltered );
```

***Code Listing 10.9**: The initiation of the Nearest filter*

In *Figure 10.12*, we will see the result of the code. As mentioned, it will not be easily visible. We will need to zoom in on the box to see the result. The main idea is that texture will look sharper in detail than without filters.

For the next several filters, we will need to change only lines that are marked with comment **//Initiation of the filter** in *Code Listing 10.9*:

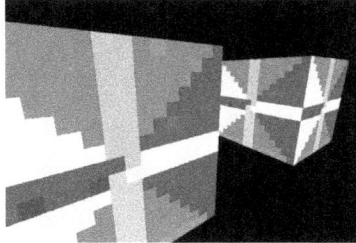

Figure 10.12: *Nearest filter result*

Linear filter

This filter takes the weighted average of surrounding pixels and produces smoother transitions between pixels. It offers a more visually appealing and realistic look.

To add this filter, change the filter initiation code to the one provided in *Code Listing 10.10*, and the result will be like in *Figure 10.13*:

```
1. texture.magFilter = THREE.LinearFilter;
2. texture.minFilter = THREE.LinearFilter;
```

Code Listing 10.10: *Code for Linear filter initiation*

Figure 10.13: *Smooth edges with Linear filter*

MipMap filter

MipMapping involves creating a series of pre-scaled versions of a texture. It is used to prevent aliasing artifacts and improve rendering quality at various distances, and is suitable for improving texture quality in different viewing scenarios.

To add this filter, change the filter initiation code to the one provided in *Code Listing 10.11*, and the result will be like in *Figure 10.14*:

```
1.  texture.magFilter = THREE.LinearFilter;
2.  texture.minFilter = THREE.LinearMipMapLinearFilter;
```

Code Listing 10.11: *MipMap filter code initiation*

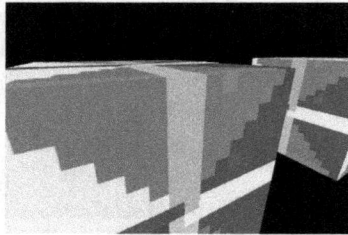

Figure 10.14: *MipMap filter using a result*

Anisotropic filter

Anisotropic filtering enhances texture clarity in oblique views. It improves the appearance of textures on surfaces at acute angles and is useful for maintaining texture quality across various viewing angles.

To add the filter, we use the code from *Code Listing 10.12*. The texture we use will not have any visible improvements, so we will take the texture from the previous example to see that the texture is more detailed after the filter. The result is shown in *Figure 10.15*:

```
1.  texture.anisotropy = renderer.capabilities.getMaxAnisotropy();
```

Code Listing 10.12: *Code for the anisotropy filter*

Figure 10.15: *More details in the box after using the anisotropy filter*

Wrapping

Wrapping determines how the texture repeats or clamps outside its original UV coordinates:

- **RepeatWrapping** creates a tiled pattern.

- **MirroredRepeatWrapping** tiles the texture with mirroring.

- **ClampToEdgeWrapping** clamps the texture at the edges.

We use the code from *Code Listing 10.13* to add the wrapping filter. We will use repeat wrapping to show how to change the pattern inside the box. The result is shown in *Figure 10.16*:

```
1. texture.wrapS = THREE.RepeatWrapping;
2. texture.wrapT = THREE.RepeatWrapping;
3. const timesToRepeatHorizontally = 4;
4. const timesToRepeatVertically = 2;
5. texture. Repeat.
   set(timesToRepeatHorizontally, timesToRepeatVertically);
```

Code Listing 10.13: *The code for wrapping filter initiation*

Figure 10.16: *Change the repeat pattern with filter representation*

Custom filters

Custom filters can be implemented using shaders. They allow for more advanced and tailored visual effects. Shaders enable developers to create unique and complex texture manipulations.

As we can see from *Figure 10.17,* the shader visibly affects the box and makes it look more solid:

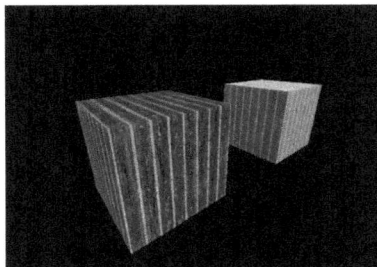

Figure 10.17: Shaders *on texture result*

To use this shader in practice, we take the code from *Code Listing 10.14*. We must keep in mind that this is the basic usage of the shaders. We can learn more about shaders at **https://thebookofshaders.com/.**

```
1. const geometry = new THREE.BoxGeometry(1, 1, 1, 10, 10, 10);
2. const texture =  new THREE.TextureLoader().load
   ('assets/uv_mapping.jpg');
3. const uniforms = {
4.   "tex": { value: texture }
5. };
6. const vertexShader = `
7. varying vec2 vUv; // This is an important declaration to make
   vUv work in the fragment
8. void main() {
9.   vUv = uv;
10.  gl_Position = projectionMatrix * modelViewMatrix *
   vec4(position, 1.0);
11. }
12. `;
13.
14. const customFilterShader = `
15. varying vec2 vUv;
16. uniform sampler2D tex; // name in uniforms should be the same as here
17.
18. void main()
19. {
20.     vec4 color = texture2D(tex, vUv); // Apply the shader in texture
21.     gl_FragColor = color;
22. }
23. `;
24.
25. const material = new THREE.ShaderMaterial({
26.   uniforms,
27.   fragmentShader: customFilterShader,
28.   vertexShader: vertexShader
29. });
30.
31. const cube = new THREE.Mesh( geometry, material );
32. scene.add( cube );
```

*Code Listing 10.14: **Custom** shader filter code*

Conclusion

Throughout this chapter, we studied various topics from the foundational concepts of texture incorporation onto 3D objects to the intricacies of texture mapping techniques and UV coordinates. We discussed the effects of specular mapping, reflection mapping, normal maps, bump mapping, and color maps.

Navigating the technical intricacies of texture filters and mapping modes, we have equipped ourselves with the tools to creatively manipulate and enhance our 3D creations. Textures, in their myriad forms, have proven to be indispensable in adding a touch of realism and individuality to our digital masterpieces.

With this newfound knowledge, we are ready to proceed to the next chapter, where we unravel the intricacies of user input manipulation and controls.

Points to remember

- Use the function inside the load() function for textures. This avoids black textures.
- Carefully prepare textures for each geometry. Remember that each geometry reacts differently to images.

Exercises

1. Use textures from this chapter to create a simple model of a building from stone and add several doors using the wooden texture.

Join our Discord space

Join our Discord workspace for latest updates, offers, tech happenings around the world, new releases, and sessions with the authors:

https://discord.bpbonline.com

CHAPTER 11

Interaction and User Input

.

Introduction

In the digital world, user interaction breathes life into the static world of 3D graphics. When we navigate a virtual landscape, the mouse or touch gestures seamlessly translate into movements within a Three.js scene. The thrill of exploration is quite literally at our fingertips.

This chapter will explain the art of interaction and user input in Three.js, where the boundaries between the real and virtual worlds blur. Imagine sculpting a 3D masterpiece not just with code but with gestures. We will look into the intricacies of handling user interactions in this chapter.

Structure

The chapter includes the following topics:

- Handling user interactions through mouse events
- Implementing controls for camera movements

Objectives

By the end of this chapter, you will be able to understand how to harness mouse events for responsive user interactions. You will also learn to implement keyboard controls to add another layer of user interaction.

Handling user interactions through mouse and touch events

User interactions are the threads that weave digital experiences. Mouse and touch events are identical to brushstrokes, allowing users to navigate and engage with 3D scenes. These interactions breathe life into the virtual landscapes, providing a better user experience.

In this chapter, we will need a starter scene with the box to add some interactions. Use the code from *Code Example 11.1* to have a smooth start:

```
1.  import * as THREE from 'three';
2.  let scene, camera, cube;
3.  let raycaster, mouse, renderer;
4.  const props = { width: 800, height: 600 };
5.
6.  function init() {
7.      // Init Scene
8.      scene = new THREE.Scene();
9.      camera = new THREE.PerspectiveCamera(75, props.width / props.
    height);
10.     camera.position.z = 3;
11.     camera.position.y = 3;
12.     camera.position.x = 3;
13.     camera.lookAt( 0, 0, 0 );
14.     scene.add(camera);
15.
16.     // This helper will create the grid on the scene
17.     // We will need it to see how elements are located in the scene
18.     const gridHelper = new THREE.GridHelper( props.width, props.
    width );
19.     scene.add( gridHelper );
20.
21.     const geometry = new THREE.BoxGeometry(1, 1, 1);
22.     const material = new THREE.MeshBasicMaterial
    ({ color: 0x00ff00, opacity: 0.5, transparent: true });
23.     cube = new THREE.Mesh(geometry, material);
```

```
24.      cube.position.set(1,1,1);
25.      // Your code will be here. The event listener will be
   aligned to a cube
26.
27.      scene.add(cube);
28.      // Raycaster to handle mouse events
29.      raycaster = new THREE.Raycaster();
30.      mouse = new THREE.Vector2();
31.
32.      // Setup the renderer
33.      const canvas = document.querySelector('#container');
34.      renderer = new THREE.WebGLRenderer({ canvas: canvas });
35.      renderer.setSize(props.width, props.height);
36.      // Add click event listener to the document
37.      document.addEventListener('click', onMouseClick, false);
38.      document.addEventListener('pointermove', onMouserMove, false);
39. }
40.
41. // Handle mouse click
42. // Your code will be here
43. function onMouseClick(event) {}
44. function onMouseMove( event ) {}
45.
46. // This function will create a random color.
47. // We will use it to show the interactions
48. function getRandomColor() {
49.      const letters = '0123456789ABCDEF';
50.      let color = '#';
51.      for (let i = 0; i < 6; i++) {
52.          color += letters[Math.floor(Math.random() * 16)];
53.      }
54.      return color;
55. }
56.
57. function render() { renderer.render( scene, camera ); }
58. init();
59. render();
```

Code Example 11.1: Initial code

As we will use 3D objects in Canvas, we cannot just align events on the object. To open the possibility of doing that in Three.js we have the **raycaster.**

In Three.js, the **raycaster** is a powerful tool that enables precise interactions in 3D scenes. Think of it as a virtual beam extending from the camera into the scene. It allows us to cast rays and detect intersections with objects, making it a fundamental component for handling user interactions like picking or clicking on objects.

The following is how it works:

- **Origin**: The raycaster starts from a specified origin, usually the camera's position.

- **Direction**: It has a defined direction in which it extends, determined by the camera's orientation.

- **Casting rays**: When we use the **raycaster.intersectObjects**(objects) method, casts rays into the scene and checks for intersections with specified objects.

- **Intersections**: If an intersection is detected, we get information about what object was intersected, the point of intersection, and more.

This mechanism is crucial for scenarios like object picking, where we determine which 3D object the user is interacting with.

Another object that we will use is called **userData**. The **userData** property in Three.js allows us to attach custom data to a Three.js object. It also allows us to make direct changes to the objects. The following are the advantages of **userData**:

- **Custom information storage**: We can store any custom information related to an object that is not part of its inherent properties. This could be user-specific data, application-specific metadata, or any other details.

- **Maintaining state**: We can use **userData** to maintain the state of an object. For example, if we are handling user interactions and want to remember certain properties or states for an object, **userData** provides a convenient way to store and retrieve this information.

- **Ease of use**: It is a simple and direct way to associate data with an object. The data can be of any type, making it flexible for various use cases.

As in the starter code, we had a function that generated a random color. We will use that function to introduce the on-click function. Each time the user clicks on the box object, we will change its color.

To add this user event to your code, we will add the code from *Code Listing 11.1* to the section that expects the event listener code:

```
1. cube.userData.onClick = function (object) {
2.        // Your click event logic here
3.        object.material.color.set(getRandomColor());
4.        console.log('Box clicked!');
5. };
```

Code Listing 11.1: Event for clicking the box object

When we use an object as a function parameter, we send the cube there as an object. That logic is required, as in the **userData** section, we have no access to the object itself. We can only align the additional parameters.

In the function for the click event, we will use the code from *Code Listing 11.2*:

```
1.  // Handle mouse click
2.  function onMouseClick(event) {
3.      event.preventDefault();
4.      // Calculate mouse position in normalized device coordinates
5.      mouse.set(
6.  (event.clientX / props.width) * 2 - 1,
7.  - ( event.clientY / props.height) * 2 + 1
8.  );
9.      // Check for intersections
10.     // We need an array of objects that will intersect
11.     const intersects = raycaster.intersectObjects([cube], false);
12.     if (intersects.length > 0) {
13.         // Trigger the click event
14.         intersects[0].object.userData.onClick(intersects[0].object);
15.         render();
16.     }
17. }
```

Code Listing 11.2: Function to manage click event

This function might seem confusing at first glance. It normalizes the coordinates because, instead of working directly with the screen or **DOM** elements, we operate within the Canvas created by the **WebGL engine**. The multiplication by 2 and the addition or subtraction of 1 are necessary to transform the mouse's screen coordinates into **normalized device coordinates** (**NDC**) that range from -1 to 1, which is required by **WebGL** for accurate interaction. The following is why we need it:

- Multiplying by 2:
  - In the NDC system used in WebGL and Three.js, the visible range for coordinates along the x and y axes is from -1 to 1.
  - The multiplication by 2 expands the range from its original window or canvas coordinates to a range that extends from -2 to 2.

- Adding or subtracting 1:
  - After the multiplication, the range is now from -2 to 2. By subtracting 1, the range is shifted from -1 to 1.
  - For the y-coordinate, there is an additional subtraction of 1 after the multiplication and a negation of the result (-). This is because the y-coordinate

in typical screen coordinates has its origin (0,0) at the top-left corner, whereas in NDC, the origin is often at the center of the screen. So, the subtraction and negation adjust for this difference in coordinate systems.

Last but not least, we need to check if the mouse intersects any objects when we click. The tricky part is that we can not just align the click event on the object like in classical DOM; we have to check if the mouse intersects the required object.

As you can see we align the objects for the intersection in this part of the code: **const intersects = raycaster.intersectObjects([cube], false);** Because we have only one object here, we can use simple logic to take the first possible object in the intersection and call any function. And after that, we will re-render the scene.

In this example, we will not use the animation function. This is why we need to re-render the scene.

If we start your project and try to click on the box, nothing will happen, and the intersection array will be empty, like in *Figure 11.1*:

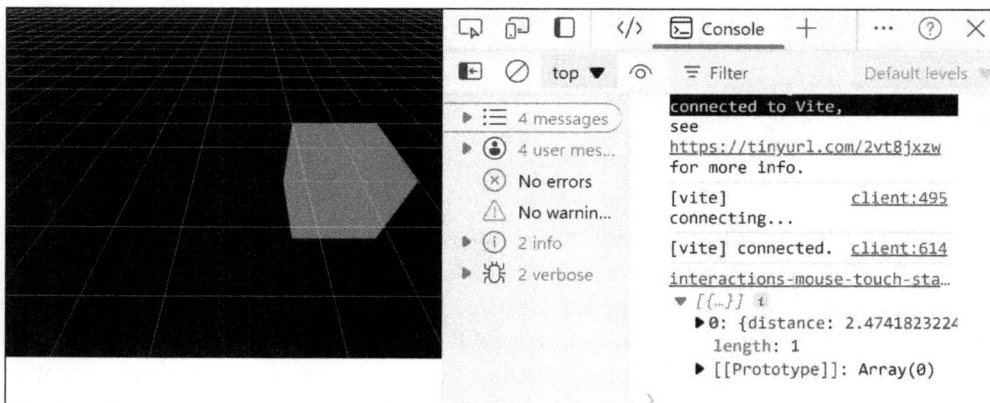

Figure 11.1: Empty intersection array

This is because, on each mouse move, we do not have normalized coordinates of the mouse. As we can see in the starter code, we also have the **onMouserMove** function. In that function, we will put the code from *Code Listing 11.3*:

```
1. function onMouserMove( event ) {
2.   mouse.set(
3.       ( event.clientX / props.width ) * 2 - 1,
4.       - ( event.clientY / props.height ) * 2 + 1 );
5.     // The raycaster is required here to align the mouse to the
  camera
6.     raycaster.setFromCamera( mouse, camera );
7. }
```

Code Listing 11.3: Function to align each mouse move into raycaster coordinates

Post this, we can try to click the box. Each click will change the box color on the scene, thus we can align click events to any object on the scene.

Implementing controls for camera movements

Implementing controls for camera movements in Three.js is crucial for creating interactive and engaging 3D scenes. We can use various control libraries that simplify the handling of user inputs, such as mouse movements and touch gestures, to manipulate the camera. Several internal libraries provide camera control possibilities. We will start with a simple one, **OrbitControls**. We can manage its position using mouse events. We will take the previous code and add some logic to move the camera by clicking on the **Box** object.

OrbitControl

The first step is to create the animate function. To have any animated movements, we need to align them to have the possibility of creating the animation logic.

Instead of calling the **render()** function at the end of the code, we will create the animation function like in *Code Listing 11.4*:

```
1.  init();
2.  // render(); this function we not need here anymore
3.
4.  function animate() {
5.    requestAnimationFrame( animate );
6.        // Put animation logic here
7.    render();
8.  }
9.  animate();
```

Code Listing 11.4: Animation function to render the scene dynamically

The next step will be to import **OrbitControls** and introduce some variables to store the data. We follow *Code Listing 11.5* to get the updates:

```
1.  // At the top of the file, add importing
2.  import { OrbitControls } from 'three/examples/jsm/controls/
    OrbitControls.js';
3.
4.  let scene, camera, cube; // this is old code
5.  let raycaster, mouse, renderer; // this is old code
6.  let controls, startAnimation, x, delta, mod; // this is new code
```

Code Listing 11.5: Introducing OrbitControls and new variables

The variables we will need are:

- **controls**: Will contain **OrbitControls** object. We will implement it into the **init()** function. In the *Code Listing 11.6* you can see the code for it.

  o **startAnimation:** Boolean value that indicates that the animation has started

  o **x**: The coordinates for the controls that we will change

  o **delta:** Value that will be used to change the x position

  o **mod:** In our example, the camera will move left and right on each click, so this value will contain the Boolean value that will be true to move it right and false for the left

```
1. // This is the old code
2. renderer = new THREE.WebGLRenderer({ canvas: canvas });
3. renderer.setSize(props.width, props.height);
4.
5. // This is the new code to implement controls
6. controls = new OrbitControls( camera, renderer.domElement );
7. controls.update();
```

Code Listing 11.6: Implementing OrbitControls at the scene in the init() function

To change the click event, we need to change the **startAnimation** status to true and change the **mod** value. Follow *Code Listing 11.7* to align the **onMouseClick** function:

```
1. // Handle mouse click
2. function onMouseClick(event) {
3.     event.preventDefault();
4.
5.     // Calculate mouse position in normalized device coordinates
6.     mouse.set(
7.         ( event.clientX / props.width) * 2 - 1,
8.         - ( event.clientY / props.height) * 2 + 1 );
9.
10.    // Check for intersections
11.    const intersects = raycaster.intersectObjects([cube], false);
12.    if (intersects.length > 0) {
13.        x = 0; // Do not forget to initiate x value
14.        mod = !mod;
15.        delta = 0.01 * (mod? 1: -1);
16.        startAnimation = true;
17.    }
18. }
```

Code Listing 11.7: Updated mouse click function

Finally, the animation logic will work like this: we will update the **OrbitControl** coordinates using delta and stop the animation. We will use *Code Listing 11.8* for the animation code and put it in the required place of *Code Listing 11.4*:

```
1.  if(startAnimation) {
2.        controls.target = new THREE.Vector3 (x, 0, 0);
3.        controls.update(); // Update controls to apply the changes
4.        x +=delta;
5.        if (x >= 1 || x <= -1) {
6.            x = 0;
7.            startAnimation = false;
8.        }
9.    }
10. controls.update();
```

Code Listing 11.8: Animation logic

As a result, we can click on the box, and the camera will change the position. If we click the box one more time, the camera position will move in the opposite direction.

There is a similar control with a small difference in behavior, called **TrackballControls**.

TrackballControls allows users to rotate, zoom, and pan a 3D scene with freeform motion. It enables unrestricted camera movement, offering a natural, fluid exploration experience. Ideal for applications requiring full freedom of interaction, like scientific visualizations or games.

Comparison with OrbitControls:

- **Rotation:** **TrackballControls** allows free, unconstrained rotation; **OrbitControls** limits rotation to a defined polar angle.

- **Ease of use: OrbitControls** is simpler and more user-friendly; **TrackballControls** can feel more complex due to its freedom.

- **Best use: TrackballControls** is suited for unrestricted exploration, while **OrbitControls** works best for targeted viewing around a specific object.

Follow the exercise requirements to play around with it.

FlyControls

FlyControls in Three.js is a control scheme that allows the camera to move as if it is flying, providing a first-person perspective with the ability to move in all directions. We follow the *Code Listing 11.9* to add it to the scene:

```
1.  // import { OrbitControls } from 'three/examples/jsm/controls/
    OrbitControls.js';
2.  import { FlyControls } from 'three/examples/jsm/controls/FlyControls.js';
```

```
3.
4.  // old code is here
5.  function init() {
6.  // old code here
7.  controls = new FlyControls( camera, renderer.domElement );
8.  controls.movementSpeed = 0.02;
9.  controls.rollSpeed = 0.002;
10. // old code here
11. }
12. // old code is here
13. function animate() {
14.  requestAnimationFrame( animate );
15.  controls.update(1); // 1 is a delta parameter to align control changes
16.  render();
17. }
```

Code Listing 11.9: Updates in the code to initiate FlyControls

When the scene has restarted, we can use our mouse to fly in the scene using the mouse and keyboard. We can use **WSAD** keys(like in video games) to move the camera, and **Q** and **E** keys to rotate the camera. The mouse movement will be aligned to the camera view, and clicking will make it move forward or back.

PointerLockControls

PointerLockControls allow for an immersive first-person navigation experience by locking the mouse cursor to the canvas. This is particularly useful for applications where we want to provide FPS-style navigation.

In the next example, we will make a scene that will do the animation move for the camera. On click, we will lock the camera and have the possibility to look around. Identical to video games with a security camera (Metal Gear Solid or Cyberpunk 2077), there is a function to connect to the security camera. We will make something similar. The updated code from *Code Listing 11.10* creates such functionality:

```
1.  // import { FlyControls } from 'three/examples/jsm/controls/
    FlyControls.js';
2.  import { PointerLockControls } from 'three/addons/controls/
    PointerLockControls.js';
3.
4.  // old code is here
5.  function init() {
6.    // old code is here
```

```
7.    controls = new PointerLockControls( camera, renderer.domElement );
8.    // controls.movementSpeed = 0.02;
9.    // controls.rollSpeed = 0.002;
10. }
11. // old code is here
12.
13. // Handle mouse click
14. function onMouseClick(event) {
15.     event.preventDefault();
16.     // Calculate mouse position in normalized device coordinates
17.     mouse.set(
18.         ( event.clientX / props.width) * 2 - 1,
19.         - ( event.clientY / props.height) * 2 + 1 );
20.     controls.lock();
21. }
22. x = 0;
23. function animate() {
24.     requestAnimationFrame( animate );
25.     if (controls.getObject().position.x < 1) {
26.         x += 0.00001;
27.     }
28.     else if(controls.getObject().position.x > 1) {
29.         x -= 0.00001;
30.     }
31.     controls.getObject().position.x += ( x ); // new behavior
32.     render();
33. }
```

Code Listing 11.10: *Code update for the pointer lock control*

This update will allow us to click on the scene and use a mouse to turn around the camera. The update has several important parts:

- On click event we need to use the lock function: **controls.lock();**. This will activate the locking functionality. To exit the lock we need to press the *Esc* button.

- For the animation, we will move the camera by the X-axis. The interesting fact is that locking does not affect the animation and it will proceed with changing position, while we can look around.

- To set a new position for the camera, we need to manually set the coordinates for it with this function: **controls.getObject().position.x += (x);**

Conclusion

By delving into mouse events, we empower our scenes with responsiveness, creating a seamless bridge between the digital world and the user's gestures. Controls, ranging from orbit to fly, offer avenues for users to explore and interact with the 3D space.

The chapter showcased the versatility and customization options available in Three.js through different control libraries, from **OrbitControls** to **FlyControls**. These controls provide avenues for users to explore and interact with the 3D space.

In the next chapter, we will study movement and dynamism, exploring the techniques that breathe life into our 3D scenes.

Points to remember

- There is a list of controls that work similarly to those presented in this chapter. Follow the exercise section to try them. The full list is:
    - o ArcballControl
    - o TrackballControl
    - o OrbitControl
    - o DragControl
    - o FlyControl
    - o MapControl
    - o PointerLockControl
- Three.js does not have proper native support for mobile events (touch and device orientation. It was fully removed from the last update. This happened during a lot of problems using it across devices. Unfortunately, for each case, we must create our solution depending on the device's requirements.

Exercises

1. Add more objects and create the click event on them using the first part of the chapter.

2. Try all the controls from the list on your scene. The logic of using is to change the control object in the init() function and follow the update logic from this chapter.

CHAPTER 12

Animation and Particle Systems

Introduction

This chapter is like the fulfillment of a childhood dream. It is the digital atelier where the storyteller breathes life into the still canvases of 3D scenes. Imagine transforming static objects into lively characters, orchestrating movements that echo the graceful play of yesteryears.

We will study the tools and techniques that once seemed magical, now tangible in Three. js. This chapter bridges the playfulness of our early years and the boundless possibilities of the digital canvas.

Structure

In this chapter, we will discuss the following topics:

- Tween animations
- Particle systems
- Advanced animation techmiques

Objectives

By the end of this chapter, we will possess the technical know-how to animate objects in Three.js and the creative prowess to craft narratives that unfold seamlessly in the digital space. During the chapter, we will unveil the power of **TWEEN,** a versatile library for creating smooth transitions and animations. Explore particle effects and emitters, mastering the art of controlled chaos and elevating animations with advanced techniques tailored for dynamic scenes.

Tween animations

In the vast landscape of animation, where the digital canvas is painted with pixels and polygons, the concept of tweening stands as a cornerstone for crafting fluid and captivating motion. Short for **in-betweening**, tweening is an animation technique that generates intermediate frames between two keyframes, allowing for a graceful and seamless transition from one state to another.

At its core, tweening transforms static scenes into dynamic narratives. It bridges the gap between keyframes, ensuring that the journey from point A to point B (*Figure 12.1*) is a smooth, elegant, and visually pleasing experience. A ball rolling down a hill or a character gracefully transitioning from a walk to a run are the fruits of the tweening process.

In the context of animation, Tweens are the specific instances or sequences that define the transition between keyframes. These sequences dictate how a property or set of properties evolves. Whether it is the position of an object, the intensity of light, or the color of a surface, tweens orchestrate the dance of transformation.

In the Three.js development, we do not have internal tools to make tween animations. We can, however, introduce third-party tools that smoothly support the canvas and, in our case, Three.js.

Tween.js (you can collect it from this link **https://tweenjs.github.io/tween.js/** or use the given CLI command) emerges as a powerful and versatile library for implementing tween animations. Compatible with various rendering engines. It simplifies the process of defining and executing tweens. Lightweight nature with a straightforward syntax, it is a favorite among developers for creating engaging animations with minimal effort.

To add this library to the project, use npm install (or yarn, whatever you prefer):

```
1. npm install -D @tweenjs/tween.js
```

Functions to create animations

Let us start with basic examples. We will take a simple **div** layout and change its coordinates. Before we begin, we need to introduce some functions that will help us create the animations.

Initialization

To begin, we initialize Tween.js and set the initial state of the property we want to animate. For example, we want to move the object by coordinates. The code for this case will look like:

```
1. const tween = new TWEEN.Tween(object.position)
2.   .to({ x: 200, y: 100, z: 50 }, 2000)
3.   .start();
```

The following explains the code breakup:

- new TWEEN.Tween(object.position): This initializes a new Tween object, specifying that the animation will target the *position* property of the provided object. In Three. js, the **position** property typically represents the 3D coordinates *(x, y, z)* of an object in the scene.

- .to({ x: 200, y: 100, z: 50 }, 2000): This method sets the destination values for the **position** property. The object will move from its current position to the specified destination (x: 200, y: 100, z: 50) in 2000 milliseconds (or 2 seconds).

- **.start**(): This initiates the tween animation. Once initiated, the Tween.js library will handle the transition of the object's position from its initial state to the defined destination.

Chaining Tweens

Tween.js allows the chaining of multiple tweens, enabling the creation of intricate animations by linking sequences. The code for this will look like the following:

```
1. const firstTween = new TWEEN.Tween(object.position)
2.                              .to({ x: 200 }, 1000);
3. const secondTween = new TWEEN.Tween(object.position)
4.                              .to({ y: 100 }, 1000);
5.
6. firstTween.chain(secondTween);
7. firstTween.start();
```

To chain the animations, we need to connect one to another with the **.chain()** function. If we connect the second tween to the first, we can create the loop:

secondTween.chain(firstTween).

Easing functions

These functions control the acceleration or deceleration of the tween. In the library, there are various options for easing. We will use one in our examples. We must take a different one for exercise. To connect easing, we will use the function:

.easing(TWEEN.Easing.Elastic.InOut).

Update loop

Integration into the animation loop is essential for Tween.js to work its magic consistently. The code for the update will look like :

```
1. function animate() {
2.     requestAnimationFrame(animate);
3.     TWEEN.update();
4. }
```

When we have all the basics for Tween.js, we can begin. Our first example will be to create the basic layout and move it smoothly on the screen (like in *Figure 12.1*)

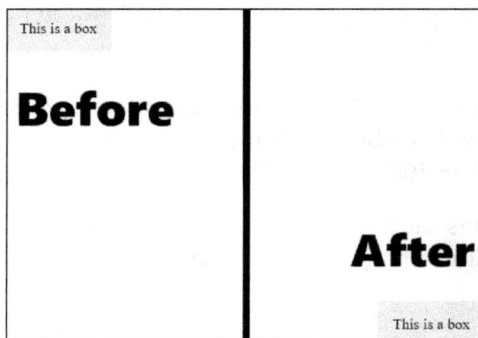

Figure 12.1: Example animation structure

```
1.  import * as TWEEN from '@tweenjs/tween.js';
2.
3.  const box = document.getElementById('box');
4.  const coords = { x: 0, y: 0 };
5.  let tween, tweenChain;
6.
7.  function init() {
8.      tween = new TWEEN.Tween(coords)
9.          .to({x: 500, y: 500}, 2000)
10.         .easing(TWEEN.Easing.Quadratic.InOut)
11.         .delay(1000)
12.         .onUpdate(update);
13.
14.     tweenChain = new TWEEN.Tween(coords)
15.         .to({x: 0, y: 0}, 3000)
16.         .easing(TWEEN.Easing.Quadratic.InOut)
17.         .onUpdate(update);
18.     tween.chain(tweenChain);
19.     tweenChain.chain(tween);
```

```
20.    tween.start();
21.}
22.
23.function animate(time) {
24.    requestAnimationFrame(animate);
25.    const result = tween.update(time);
26.    if (!result) cancelAnimationFrame(box)
27.}
28.
29.function update() {
30.    box.style.transform = `translate(${coords.x}px, ${coords.y}px)`;
31.}
32.
33.init();
34.animate();
```

Code Listing 12.1: Basic animation

To create such an animation, take the code from *Code Listing 12.1*. In this example, we will use all the basics to create such an animation. To make it work, we create the *HTML code* in the **index.html** file. We will take the code from *Code Listing 12.2* to update the **index. html** file:

```
1.  <!DOCTYPE html>
2.  <html lang="en">
3.  <body>
4.  <script type="module"
5.  src="basic-animations.js"></script> // this is your JS file
6.    <div id="box" style="transform: translate(0, 0);
7.            position: absolute; padding: 1rem;
8.            background-color:yellow;
9.            color: black;
10.           width: fit-content;"> This is a box </div>
11.</body>
12.</html>
```

Code Listing 12.2: HTML code for the animation

Now we have the basic tween animation. Let us add some animations to the ThreeJS project.

To add animations to the Three.js project, we will create this scene:

1. We will create the plane, the box, and the basic light

2. On each click box will move to the mouse position with ease

We will need the following list of **requirements**:

- Import Three.js and Tween.js into the project
- Create the plane in the scene
- Create the sphere in the scene
- Create the light
- Align click event (we will use double click for safety, as we will also use OrbitControls)

Similar to the previous chapter, we need a raycaster object to align actions.

First, we will need a simple scene as described in the **requirements**. To create one, we will use *Code Listing 12.3*:

```
1.  import * as THREE from 'three';
2.  import * as TWEEN from '@tweenjs/tween.js';
3.  import { OrbitControls } from 'three/examples/jsm/controls/
    OrbitControls.js';
4.
5.  const props = { width: 800, height: 600 };
6.  const canvas = document.querySelector('#container');
7.  const renderer = new THREE.WebGLRenderer({ canvas: canvas });
8.  const scene = new THREE.Scene();
9.  const camera = new THREE.PerspectiveCamera(75, props.width / props.
    height);
10. let tween;
11. camera.position.z = 6;
12. scene.add(camera);
13.
14. const planeMaterial = new THREE.
    MeshBasicMaterial({ color: '#ebebeb', side: THREE.DoubleSide});
15. const planeGeometry = new THREE.PlaneGeometry( props.width, props.
    width );
16. const planeMesh = new THREE.Mesh(planeGeometry, planeMaterial);
17. planeMesh.position.set(0, -5, 0);
18. planeMesh.rotation.set(Math.PI / -2, 0, 0);
19. scene.add(planeMesh);
20.
21. const geometry = new THREE.SphereGeometry( 10, 32, 16 );
22. const material = new THREE.MeshBasicMaterial( { color: 0xffff00 } );
23. const sphere = new THREE.Mesh( geometry, material );
24. sphere.position.set(...[10, 10, 0]);
```

```
25. scene.add( sphere );
26.
27. renderer.setSize(props.width, props.height);
28. const controls = new OrbitControls( camera, renderer.domElement );
29. // your code goes here
30. function animate() {
31.   requestAnimationFrame( animate );
32.   controls.update();
33.   renderer.render( scene, camera );
34. }
35. animate();
```

Code Listing 12.3: Scene with plane and sphere

To simplify this example, we will use basic materials.

We can add some tweening animation to make this scene more interactive. Follow the code from *Code Listing 12.4* to add interactivity:

```
1.  const raycaster = new THREE.Raycaster();
2.  const mouse = new THREE.Vector2();
3.
4.  function onDoubleClick(event) {
5.      console.log('click');
6.      mouse.set(
7.          (event.clientX / renderer.domElement.clientWidth) * 2 - 1,
8.          - (event.clientY / renderer.domElement.clientHeight) * 2 + 1
9.      );
10.     raycaster.setFromCamera(mouse, camera);
11.     const intersects = raycaster.intersectObjects(scene.
    children, false);
12.
13.     if (intersects.length > 0) {
14.         const point = intersects[0].point;
15.         tween = new TWEEN.Tween(sphere.position)
16.             .to({ x: point.x, z: point.z }, 500).start()
17.     }
18. }
19.
20. renderer.domElement.
    addEventListener('dblclick', onDoubleClick, false);
```

Code Listing 12.4: Adding Tween animations into the scene

If we reload the scene, we will see that nothing has happened. We aligned the animation and got coordinates from the raycaster.

We also need to assign a **TWEEN** object to the animation function. If we add it there like :

```
1.  function animate() {
2.      requestAnimationFrame(animate);
3.      controls.update();
4.      tween?.update();
5.      renderer.render(scene, camera);
6.  }
```

Everything will start working correctly. We can double-click the plane, and we see that the sphere bounces to the required place.

As seen from *Code Listing 12.4,* tweening is pretty simple and works with ThreeJS like a charm.

Particle systems

Particle systems in Three.js provide a powerful way to simulate and render large numbers of small objects, known as particles, in a scene. These particles often represent effects like fire, smoke, rain, or any other scenario where individual elements create a collective visual impact.

Particle effects and emitters

A particle system is a collection of tiny particles that move independently within a specified space. These particles collectively create visual effects through their combined behavior. In Three.js, creating a particle system involves defining the properties and appearance of individual particles, their movement, and their interaction with the scene.

Particle systems in Three.js offer a versatile way to create dynamic and visually engaging effects in 3D scenes. Whether simulating a natural phenomenon or adding decorative elements, particle systems provide a flexible and efficient solution for a range of applications.

To create an example, we will take an already familiar part of the code from *Code Listing 12.5*:

```
1.  import * as THREE from 'three';
2.  import { OrbitControls } from 'three/examples/jsm/controls/
    OrbitControls.js';
3.  const props = {
4.      width: 800,
5.      height: 600
```

```
6.  };
7.  const scene = new THREE.Scene();
8.  const camera = new THREE.PerspectiveCamera(75, props.width / props.
    height);
9.  camera.position.z = 1; camera.position.y = 1; camera.position.x = 1;
10. const canvas = document.querySelector('#container');
11. const renderer = new THREE.WebGLRenderer({canvas: canvas });
12. renderer.setSize( props.width,  props.height);
13. document.body.appendChild(renderer.domElement);
14.
15. //Your code goes here
16.
17. const controls = new OrbitControls( camera, renderer.domElement );
18.
19. function animate() {
20.  requestAnimationFrame( animate );
21.  controls.update();
22.  renderer.render( scene, camera );
23. }
24. animate();
```

Code Listing 12.5: Particles starter

Now, we can create some particles here. In this example, we will create a lot of dots, using the box geometry to organize them.

We use the code from *Code Listing 12.7* and insert it into the code slot from *Code Listing 12.6*:

```
1.  const particlesGeometry = new THREE.BoxGeometry(1, 1, 1, 7, 7, 7);
2.  const particlesMaterial = new THREE.PointsMaterial();
3.  particlesMaterial.size = 0.02;
4.  particlesMaterial.sizeAttenuation = true;
5.
6.  const particles = new THREE.
    Points(particlesGeometry, particlesMaterial);
7.  scene.add(particles);
```

Code Listing 12.6: Adding particles to the scene

We need to have material and geometry, but in the case of particles, we will not render the geometry; we will render a lot of dots using this geometry, like in *Figure 12.2*:

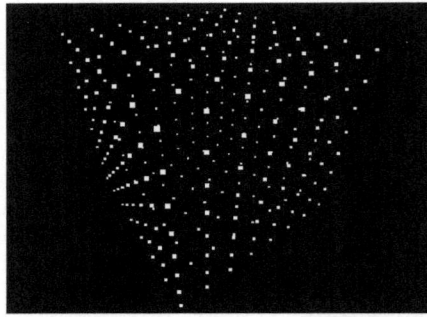

Figure 12.2: Particle system in box geometry

The following are two important points:

- **particlesMaterial**: The size parameter will introduce the size of each particle here
- **new THREE.BoxGeometry(1, 1, 1, 7, 7,7)**: The last three numbers will introduce the number of points as we are using the geometry itself

Another way to create the system is by using custom geometry. In this case, we can create randomly located points. We update the code using *Code Listing 12.7* to get the result shown in *Figure 12.3*:

```
1.  const particlesGeometry = new THREE.BufferGeometry();
2.  particlesGeometry.computeBoundingSphere();
3.  const count = 1500;
4.  const positions = new Float32Array(count);
5.  for(let i = 0; i < count; i++) {
6.      positions[i] = (Math.random() - 0.5) * 10;
7.  }
8.  particlesGeometry.setAttribute('position', new THREE.
    BufferAttribute(positions, 2));
```

Code Listing 12.7: Custom geometry for particles

Figure 12.3: Custom geometry render

The following is an important point:

- **new THREE.BufferAttribute(positions, 2)**: Number two will be responsible for the number of dimensions. To create more dimensions, just increase this number; 4 will be the maximum.

Particle animations

Animations in particles are the same as anything else. Having a particle animation on a scene can add a lot of atmosphere. For example, let us try to make a rotation animation for the particle that we already made in the last example. We will post number 3 into the Buffer attribute to create more volume.

We can update the animation function using code from *Code Listing 12.8*:

```
1. function animate() {
2.     requestAnimationFrame( animate );
3.     controls.update();
4.     particles.rotation.x += 0.005;
5.     particles.rotation.y += 0.005;
6.     renderer.render( scene, camera );
7. }
```

Code Listing 12.8: Simple particle animation

Now, when we restart the project we can see the deep space with a lot of stars and the camera will turn around like we are flying in this internal space.

Advanced animation techniques

In Three.js, an **AnimationClip** is a container that holds animation data. It defines how an object should change over time by specifying a set of keyframes for various properties such as position, rotation, and scale. Essentially, it is a way to describe a series of transformations or changes that an object should undergo during an animation.

Here are the key components of an `AnimationClip`:

- **Name**: An identifier for the animation clip.

- **Duration**: The total time taken for the animation.

- **Tracks**: It defines how specific properties of an object change over time. For example, you might have a position track, a rotation track, and a scale track. Each track is responsible for a particular property's animation.

- **Interpolation**: Interpolation determines how values between keyframes are calculated. Common types include linear interpolation, step interpolation, and smooth interpolation.

The objects in Three.js can be complex or taken from 3D modeling software. In another example, we also have complex objects like bones in Three.js. For the bone, we mostly use 3D model objects, exported from files (like Blender or 3DsMax), but it is also can be a possibility. In both cases, using third-party software for the animation could become impossible. For these cases, it is more convenient to use the **AnimationClip** approach.

To make the first animation clip, use the code from *Code Listing 12.9*:

```
1.  import * as THREE from 'three';
2.  const scene = new THREE.Scene();
3.  const camera = new THREE.PerspectiveCamera(75, window.
    innerWidth / window.innerHeight, 0.1, 1000);
4.  const renderer = new THREE.WebGLRenderer();
5.  renderer.setSize(window.innerWidth, window.innerHeight);
6.  document.body.appendChild(renderer.domElement);
7.  const cubeGeometry = new THREE.BoxGeometry();
8.  const cubeMaterial = new THREE.
    MeshBasicMaterial({ color: 0x00ff00 });
9.  const cube = new THREE.Mesh(cubeGeometry, cubeMaterial);
10. scene.add(cube);
11. camera.position.z = 5;
12. // your code goes here
13. function animate() {
14.   requestAnimationFrame(animate);
15.   // your code goes here
16.   renderer.render(scene, camera);
17. }
18. animate();
```

Code Listing 12.9: Starter code to create an animation clip

Now we can put the code to create the animation clip. First, we will need keyframes. It is an array of data that contains the current state and time that will be used for the animation. In our example, it will be positioned so your code will look like in *Code Listing 12.11*:

```
1.  const keyframes = [
2.    { pos: new THREE.Vector3(0, 0, 0), time: 0 },
3.    { pos: new THREE.Vector3(0, 2, 0), time: 2 },
4.    { pos: new THREE.Vector3(0, 0, 0), time: 4 },
5.  ];
6.
```

Code Listing 12.10: Adding keyframes

Now, we can create the clip like in *Code Listing 12.11*:

```
1. const positionTrack = new THREE.VectorKeyframeTrack(
2.     '.position',
3.         keyframes.map(kf => kf.time),
4.         keyframes.flatMap(kf => kf.pos.toArray()));
5.
6. const clip = new THREE.
   AnimationClip('cubeAnimation', -1, [positionTrack]);
7.
```

Code Listing 12.11: Creating the clip

The important part here is the type of animation that here indicated, like **cubeAnimation.** This -1 number indicates that the animation will loop indefinitely.

Finally, we need to create the object to manage the animation. It is called a mixer in Three.js, and to add it, we do it like in *Code Listing 12.12*:

```
1. const mixer = new THREE.AnimationMixer(cube);
2. const action = mixer.clipAction(clip);
3. action.play();
```

Code Listing 12.12: Mixer code example

The last thing is to update the animation function to update the mixer on each tick, like in *Code Listing 12.13*:

```
1. function animate() {
2.   requestAnimationFrame(animate);
3.   mixer.update(0.01); // Update the animation mixer
4.   renderer.render(scene, camera);
5. }
```

Code Listing 12.13: Animation function update

As a result, we will see a smooth animated box that moves up and down using the configuration from the preceding code.

Conclusion

In this chapter, we have unraveled the magic behind infusing life into digital realms. From keyframes and tweens to particle systems and advanced animation techniques, this chapter has elaborated on the tools to breathe motion into 3D scenes.

In the next chapter, we will study the integration of Three.js with React and Next.js. The seamless blend of the powerful Three.js library with the versatility of React and the dynamic capabilities of Next.js opens new horizons for immersive web experiences.

Points to remember

- Use TWEEN animation for the simple scenes; it is simpler to configure.
- We can animate the bones' bodies in Three.js with AnimationClip.
- Particle systems have limitations if we want to have millions of points. In this case, we need to use shaders.

Exercises

1. Create the particle system with spherical geometry.
2. Create the click animation with other geometry(we had a sphere).
3. Add light and shadows to the scene using the previous chapters.

Join our Discord space

Join our Discord workspace for latest updates, offers, tech happenings around the world, new releases, and sessions with the authors:

https://discord.bpbonline.com

CHAPTER 13

Introduction to Next.js and Three.js Integration

Introduction

In web development, my experience with React was akin to discovering a new language—expressive, modular, and, most importantly, scalable. Thanks to React's declarative nature and component-based architecture, crafting interactive and dynamic user interfaces became thrilling.

As the pages of my projects grew, so did the realization that the orchestration of React's Fiber architecture was a game-changer. Just like a seamless performance, where intricate user interfaces danced effortlessly across screens. React Fiber optimized rendering and enabled the creation of complex, yet nimble, applications.

This chapter explores the fusion of React, Three.js, and Next.js, introducing React Fiber's unique role in the marriage of server-side rendering and 3D visualizations. With R3F, a React binding for Three.js, we delve into an immersive experience where React's composability meets Three.js' visual prowess.

In this chapter, we will study the harmonious integration of React's familiar syntax, Next.js' streamlined workflows, and the artistic canvas of Three.js. The union of React and Three.js opens doors to a new dimension of web development.

Structure

The chapter includes the following topics:

- Setting the stage
- Setting up the development environment
- R3F basics and Three.js in a React environment
- Integrating Three.js scenes into Next.js pages
- Manipulating 3D objects with R3F
- Uploading and manipulating 3D models

Objectives

In this chapter, we will study the fusion of Next.js and Three.js, setting the stage with a brief overview. By the end, we will configure a development environment for their seamless integration, translate Three.js concepts into React components, and weave 3D magic into Next.js pages. We will craft dynamic 3D scenes, connect them to Next.js pages, and manipulate 3D objects using R3F. By the end of the chapter, we will be able to apply animations, handle user interactions, and even test the robustness of React Fiber-driven 3D scenes.

Setting the stage

This section is like the stage where React, Next.js, and Three.js harmonize to create a performance of digital brilliance. We set the scene by providing a brief overview of Next.js and introducing R3F, the React binding for Three.js. We will explore why this is a powerful combination, understanding how Next.js orchestrates server-side rendering, while R3F serves as a guide in merging React and Three.js. Together, they form a dynamic duo, promising a seamless integration that elevates 3D production.

Brief overview of Next.js and R3F library

Next.js is a popular React framework for building fast, scalable web applications with features like server-side rendering and static site generation. **React Three Fiber (R3F)**, on the other hand, is a React-based library for integrating Three.js, enabling the creation of stunning 3D visuals directly in React components. Together, they simplify the development of immersive, high-performance 3D web experiences.

Next.js features

Next.js features the power of client-side rendering. It is like a dynamic gallery where each page transition feels like turning the pages of a book. With dynamic routes, we sculpt scenes that load seamlessly, offering an uninterrupted narrative. This experience is similar to a virtual art exhibition where the audience navigates effortlessly between pieces, experiencing the story at their own pace.

Since we will use Three.js as a library that generates the canvas, we will need a lot of features from Next.js, except the server-side rendering (basically, we cannot make an animation or 3D dynamic and render it once). The following is the list of features we will take from Next.js:

- **Client-side routing:**
    - o **Description:** Next.js provides a straightforward approach to client-side routing. Pages are dynamically loaded and rendered on the client side, allowing smooth and optimized navigation.
    - o **Example usage:** Using the `Link` component to navigate between pages without a full page reload.

- **Static Site Generation (SSG):**
    - o **Description:** Next.js supports SSG, allowing us to pre-render pages at build time. This results in faster page loads as static HTML files are served.
    - o **Example usage:** Generating static pages for a blog or documentation site at build time.

- **Dynamic routes:**
    - o **Description:** Next.js enables dynamic route parameters, allowing us to create pages with variable paths.
    - o **Example usage:** Building a product page with a dynamic route parameter for each product.

- **API routes:**
    - o **Description:** We can create API routes within the Next.js project, providing a serverless function that can be invoked from the client side.
    - o **Example usage:** Implementing a contact form with an API route to handle form submissions.

- **Client-side data fetching:**
    - o **Description:** Next.js allows for client-side data fetching, enabling components to fetch and display data after the initial page load.
    - o **Example usage:** Fetching data from an external API using `useEffect` or similar hooks.

- **File-based routing:**
  - o **Description:** Next.js simplifies routing by following a file-based approach. Each file in the **pages/app** directory corresponds to a route.
  - o **Example usage:** Creating a new page by adding a new file to the **pages/app directory**.

- **Automatic code splitting:**
  - o **Description:** Next.js automatically performs a code splitting function, ensuring that only the necessary JavaScript is sent to the client, optimizing performance.
  - o **Example usage:** Breaking down large components into smaller ones and letting Next.js handle the code splitting.

React Fiber library capabilities

R3F (React Fiber) is the technical artist. With components like **<Canvas>** and **<OrbitControls>**, R3F transforms our digital canvas into an interactive masterpiece. The **<Canvas>** component, akin to an empty stage, is where we craft our 3D scenes. With **<OrbitControls>**, the audience (users) play a part, navigating and interacting with the scenes as though exploring an art installation.

Combining Next.js with Three.js for interactive 3D web applications

The synergy between Next.js and Three.js is a storytelling revolution. Imagine a digital museum where each exhibit, powered by Three.js, comes to life with client-side rendering. The user, armed with the dynamic routes of Next.js, walks through this museum, exploring narratives seamlessly woven into each 3D masterpiece.

By the end of the chapter, we will not just understand these tools but efficiently use them to create an immersive gallery of digital experiences. Dynamic routes, client-side rendering, and interactive 3D scenes will harmonize to craft a virtual performance that blurs the lines between user and spectator.

The following is a list of features we will take from React Fiber:

- **Declarative Three.js in React:** R3F introduces a declarative way to work with Three.js within a React environment. It aligns with React's component-based architecture, making it easier to manage and reuse components.

- **React suspense and concurrent mode support:** R3F is designed to work seamlessly with React's suspense and concurrent mode features. This ensures efficient rendering and loading of 3D scenes without blocking the user interface.

- **Hooks-based API:** R3F provides a set of hooks that allow us to interact with the Three.js scene in a React-friendly manner. For example, we can use the `useEffect` hook to perform side effects like fetching data.

- **Responsive design:** R3F makes it easier to create responsive 3D scenes. It adapts well to different screen sizes and can be integrated into responsive web designs.

- **Dynamic imports and code splitting:** R3F leverages dynamic imports and code splitting, ensuring that only the necessary parts of the 3D scene are loaded when needed. This is beneficial for performance, especially in large applications.

- **Component-based architecture:** R3F encourages a component-based approach to building 3D scenes. Each Three.js object or group of objects can be encapsulated within a React component, promoting reusability.

- **Custom hooks for animation:** R3F provides custom hooks for handling animations. For instance, the `useSpring` hook simplifies creating animated effects in response to user interactions or changes in data.

- **Built-in components**: R3F includes built-in components like `<Canvas>` and `<OrbitControls>`, which abstract away some of the complexity of setting up a Three.js scene. These components can be easily integrated into React applications.

- **TypeScript support:** R3F supports TypeScript, providing type safety for React components and ensuring a smoother development experience.

Combining Next.js with Three.js offers a compelling synergy, unlocking many advantages that enhance the development experience and end-user satisfaction. Here are reasons why this amalgamation is a strategic move:

1. **Seamless integration of 3D graphics and web development**: Next.js, a popular React framework, seamlessly integrates with Three.js, a powerful 3D graphics library. This combination allows developers to effortlessly incorporate immersive 3D elements into web applications, offering users a rich and engaging experience.

2. **React's component-based architecture for 3D scenes**: React's component-based architecture aligns well with Three.js through the R3F library. This approach allows developers to create reusable and modular components for 3D scenes, enhancing code organization and maintainability.

3. **Leveraging the React ecosystem:** By incorporating Three.js into the React ecosystem, developers can leverage the vast array of tools, libraries, and best practices established within the React community. This results in a more efficient and collaborative development process.

4. **Responsive and dynamic web design:** Next.js provides features like dynamic routing and server-side rendering, which can be beneficial when creating responsive and dynamic web designs. Combined with Three.js, it allows for creating adaptive

and visually stunning 3D scenes that respond to user interactions and different screen sizes.

5. **Optimized performance with code splitting:** Next.js supports code splitting, allowing developers to load only the necessary parts of the application when needed. This is particularly advantageous when working with Three.js scenes, as it optimizes performance by reducing initial loading times.

6. **React hooks and state management**: Next.js and React offer powerful features like React hooks and state management, which can be seamlessly integrated into developing 3D scenes. This enables developers to manage complex state logic and user interactions effectively.

7. **Community support and resources:** Combining Next.js and Three.js benefits from the robust support and resources available within both communities. Developers can find documentation, tutorials, and solutions for common challenges, fostering a collaborative and informed development environment.

In summary, the marriage of Next.js and Three.js creates a powerful synergy, merging the strengths of a versatile web framework with a cutting-edge 3D graphics library. This combination creates new possibilities for visually stunning and highly interactive web applications. By leveraging the strengths of each technology, developers can deliver immersive experiences that seamlessly integrate 3D graphics into the world of web development.

Setting up the development environment

To initiate the Next.js project, follow *Chapter 4, Setting up all tools for the QuickStart of the development.* The next step will be to add the React Fiber library to the project. To add the React Fiber library to the project, we need to enter this command in the project root:

```
npm install three @types/three @react-three/fiber
or
yarn add three @types/three @react-three/fiber
```

As we are using Next.js and version at the current version is 14 (or higher), we need to add one line to the configuration file. It will work without it, but it is highly recommended to have it for optimization reasons. In the **next.config.js** file, please add this line into the configuration section like so:

```
const nextConfig = {
    transpilePackages: ['three']
};

module.exports = nextConfig;
```

After this, we can add a short code in our page file to see the magic. Before we start, we will create the list of objects that we want to see on the scene:

- We need to create a canvas
- We need to create the mesh object that will contain the box geometry and the material
- We need to create some light in the scene

We will check the React Fiber code in *Code Listing 13.1*:

```
1.  'use client';
2.  // As we use canvas, it will render only on the client side
3.  import React from "react";
4.  import { Canvas } from "@react-three/fiber";
5.
6.  export default function Home() {
7.    return (
8.    <main className="flex min-h-screen flex-col items-center p-24">
9.      <Canvas>
10.       <ambientLight intensity={Math.PI / 2} />
11.       <spotLight
12.         position={[10, 10, 10]}
13.         angle={0.15}
14.         penumbra={1}
15.         decay={0}
16.         intensity {Math.PI} />
17.       <pointLight
18.          position={[-10, -10, -10]}
19.         decay={0}
20.         intensity={Math.PI} />
21.       <mesh position={[-1.2, 0, 0]}>
22.         <boxGeometry args={[4, 4, 4]} />
23.         <meshStandardMaterial color="orange" />
24.       </mesh>
25.     </Canvas>
26.   </main>
27.   )
28. };
29.
```

Code Listing 13.1: Our first React Fiber component

Let us study this code in detail for a parallel understanding of what we did before with pure Three.js.

```
<Canvas>{/* ... */}</Canvas>
```

This part of the code will create the scene, which will require rendering 3D objects. In this object, React Fiber will initiate the renderer. In simple words, this is an object closure that will contain all our scenes.

```
<ambientLight … />
<spotLight …/>
<pointLight …/>
```

These components represent the light types. We can read about light types in Three.js in *Chapter 8, Lights and Shadows.* As you can see, all light parameters are used as React props that make creating lights on the scene convenient and fast.

The last and most interesting part is creating the mesh:

```
<mesh>
        <YOUR-GEOMETRY />
        <YOUR-MATERIAL />
</mesh>
```

As we can see, we have a declarative way of creating the 3D object. We create the mesh components that take geometry and the material as children. As a result, after the project starts, we will see an orange box like in *Figure 13.1*:

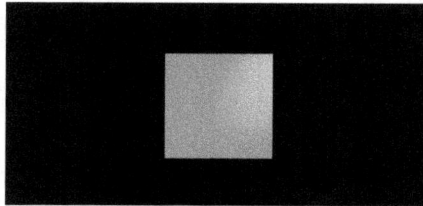

Figure 13.1: Render result

The next tool required for us is **Drei.** It is a collection of helpers that will be most important in the field of industrial applications. It contains a lot of useful tools like already familiar controls (like orbit controls) or cameras, and special elements like portals that allow us to render one scene with multiple cameras using one renderer.

To add this tool to the project, use this command:

```
npm install @react-three/drei
or
yarn add @react-three/drei
```

Note: **Be aware that at the current moment Next.js works stable only with version 9.6.0. Place this version in your package.json file to avoid conflicts.**

Now, if we add the **<OrbitControls />** as a child in the **<Canvas />** component there will be a possibility to use it as we have seen in the previous chapter so we could rotate and zoom our box as shown in *Figure 13.2*:

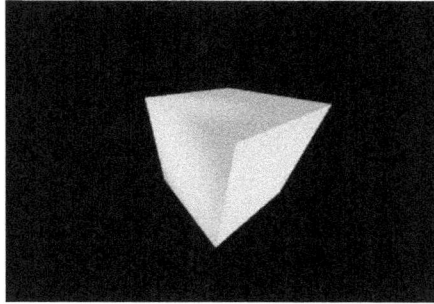

Figure 13.2: *Adding orbit controls to the canvas*

R3F basics and Three.js in a React environment

In this section, we will study the fundamental concepts of working with Three.js in a React environment using the R3F library. The following are the key components and practices:

Translating Three.js concepts to React components

We will start from the basics and take a look at the canvas object. As you can remember from the first chapters, we had to align the size of the scene for canvas and the renderer. Using the R3F library will save time as it uses the parent element size and fills it in 100%.

Let us take the code from *Code Listing 13.1* and make several changes to make a canvas and main object full screen, and also add the border color for better visualization:

```
<main className="h-screen border-8 border-neutral-50">
    <Canvas
        className="border-rose-700 border-8"
    >
    {/* old code here */}
    </Canvas>
</main>
```

We use Tailwind as a styling engine; thus, we will take a look at the class names to understand the changes:

- The main layout now covers the full height of the screen

- We added borders to the main layout and canvas

- The main border is white, and the canvas border is red

- Both borders are 8px

After this update, if we start the project, we will see the page as shown in *Figure 13.3*:

Figure 13.3: Border around the canvas with 100% height

Let us also take a look at other properties that will be useful in daily practice:

Property	Description	Example
`children`	Three.js JSX elements or regular components	`{}`
`camera`	Props for the default camera or your own `THREE.Camera`	`{ fov: 75, near: 0.1, far: 1000, position: [0, 0, 5] }`
`scene`	Props for the default scene or your own `THREE.Scene`	`{}`
`shadows`	Props for `gl.shadowMap`, set true for `PCFsoft`, or use 'basic', 'percentage', 'soft', 'variance'	`false`
`raycaster`	Props for the default raycaster	`{}`
`resize`	Resize configuration, see react-use-measure's options	`{ scroll: true, debounce: { scroll: 50, resize: 0 } }`
`orthographic`	Creates an orthographic camera	`false`
`dpr`	Pixel-ratio, use `window.devicePixelRatio`, or `automatic: [min, max]`	`[1, 2]`
`linear`	Switch off automatic sRGB color space and gamma correction	`false`
`events`	Configuration for the event manager, as a function of state	`import { events } from "@react-three/fiber"`
`eventSource`	The source where events are being subscribed to, `HTMLElement`	`React.MutableRefObject<HTMLElement>, gl.domElement.parentNode`

Property	Description	Example
eventPrefix	The event prefix is cast into canvas pointer x/y events	**offset**
flat	Use **THREE.NoToneMapping** instead of **THREE.ACESFilmicToneMapping**	**false**
onCreated	Callback after the canvas has been rendered (but not yet committed)	**(state) => {}**
onPointerMissed	Response for pointer clicks that have missed any target	**(event) => {}**

Table 13.1: Useful properties from Three.js

As we see, the canvas object contains everything that we need to use to render the scene. The most critical properties are:

- **linear property:** As we can use not only the colors but also real textures this switch comes in handy.

- **flat** is used to optimize rendering by disabling certain Three.js features like tone mapping and gamma correction. When set to true, it simplifies the rendering process, making it more lightweight and performant.

- **onCreated:** Provides access to the underlying Three.js state object, including the **gl** renderer, **scene**, and **camera**. Having the event on the scene load could make a smooth page loading effect.

- **orthographic:** This flag creates the orthographic type of camera for the view.

Each component in React Fiber has a lot of properties. But we looked at the canvas because of React hooks that are used in the library. **Important note: React Fiber hooks can be used inside the Canvas, as we need the canvas context.** So, to use the hook, we would need to create some component with it like this:

```
function HookActor() {
  const { size } = useThree();
  ...
}
...
<main className="h-screen border-8 border-neutral-50">
    <Canvas
        className="border-rose-700 border-8"
    >
    <HookActor />
```

```
    {/* old code here */}
    </Canvas>
</main>
```

After that, we can operate with Canvas as we want using the **HookActor** component. This limitation creates a good architecture in the end.

Integrating Three.js scenes into Next.js pages

This section breaks down the steps of blending Next.js with R3F to craft dynamic and interactive pages. We will learn how to effortlessly weave 3D scenes into Next.js applications, from setting up the development environment to playing with 3D objects and adding animations.

Creating dynamic 3D scenes as React components

The main idea of this section is to create a Next.js page with several 3D objects on it. We will take a look at the integration process and also at the possibilities of using one renderer for several 3D objects on the page in different situations.

To have a good structure for educational purposes, we will create the **components** folder in our **src** folder, where we collect all our React components. The folder structure should look like that in *Figure 13.4*:

Figure 13.4: Project structure with the new folder

The following are the requirements that we will follow to create the page in Next.js:

- The page will contain several blocks with a structure:

    o Top navigation

    o Introduction block with H1, the paragraph at one side and 3D objects on another side

    o We will create several blocks with text and 3D objects (let us take 3 for now, and leave it for the exercise part for now)

- We will use each block as a component, which will be used on a separate page

The mock-up for the page that we will create will look like *Figure 13.5*:

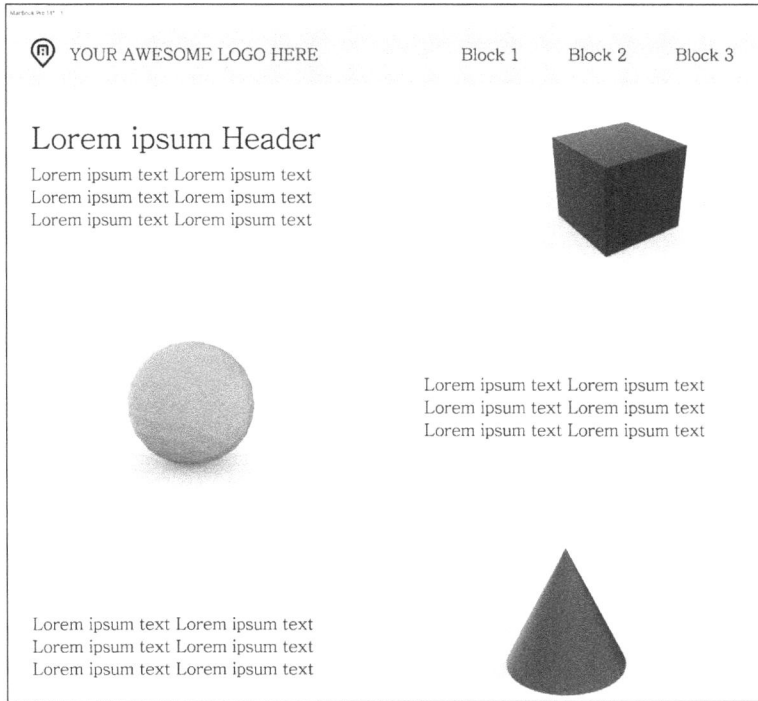

Figure 13.5: Mock-up for the page

Following the requirements, we will create the component for each required block. So, in the end, the file structure should follow *Figure 13.6*:

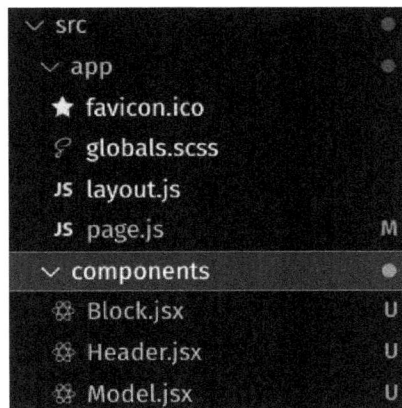

Figure 13.6: Components file structure

For our basic example, we will ignore the **Model** file. In that file, we will create the upload of the 3D object later. To create the header, follow the *Code Listing 13.2*:

```
1.  import Link from 'next/link';
2.  export default function Header() {
3.    return (
4.   <header>
5.      <div className="flex items-center justify-between gap-2">
6.          <div className="flex items-center justify-start gap-2">
7.              <div>
8.    <PUT-YOUR-SVG-LOGO-HERE>
9.              </div>
10.             <div>
11.                 Your super logo here
12.             </div>
13.          </div>
14.          <nav>
15.              <ul className="max-w-screen-xl flex flex-wrap gap-
    4 items-center justify-between mx-auto p-4">
16.                  <li>
17.                      <Link href="#">Block 1</Link>
18.                  </li>
19.                  <li>
20.                      <Link href="#">Block 2</Link>
21.                  </li>
22.                  <li>
23.                      <Link href="#">Block 3</Link>
24.                  </li>
25.              </ul>
26.          </nav>
27.      </div>
28.   </header>
29.   )
30. };
```

Code Listing 13.2: Header component code

For the **Block** component, follow *Code Listing 13.3*:

```
1.  'use client';
2.  import { Canvas } from "@react-three/fiber";
3.  import { OrbitControls } from "@react-three/drei";
4.
5.  export default function Block({ reverse }) {
6.    return (
7.   <div className={`my-6 flex items-center ${reverse ? 'flex-row-
    reverse' : ''}`}>
```

```
8.          <div><h1>Lorem ipsum Header</h1>
9.              <p> Lorem ipsum text Lorem ipsum text Lorem ipsum text
    Lorem ipsum text Lorem ipsum text Lorem ipsum text
10.             </p></div>
11.         <div>
12.         <Canvas>
13.             <ambientLight intensity={Math.PI / 2} />
14.             <spotLight
15.                 position={[10, 10, 10]}
16.                  angle={0.15}
17.                  penumbra={1}
18.                 decay={0}
19.                  intensity={Math.PI} />
20.             <pointLight
21.                 position={[-10, -10, -10]}
22.                 decay={0}
23.                  intensity={Math.PI} />
24.             <mesh position={[-1.2, 0, 0]}>
25.                 <boxGeometry args={[4, 4, 4]} />
26.                 <meshStandardMaterial color="orange" />
27.             </mesh>
28.             <OrbitControls />
29.         </Canvas>
30.         </div>
31. </div>
32.  )};
```

Code Listing 13.3: *Code for the block component*

The next step will be to put all components on the page, like in *Code Listing 13.4*:

```
1.  'use client';
2.
3.  import Header from "@/components/Header";
4.  import Block from "@/components/Block";
5.
6.  export default function Home() {
7.    return (
8.    <main className="max-w-[1000px] m-auto">
9.        <Header />
10.       <Block  />
11.       <Block reverse />
12.       <Block />
```

```
13. </main>
14.  )
15. };
```

Code Listing 13.4: Page component

The result will be the same as shown in *Figure 13.7*:

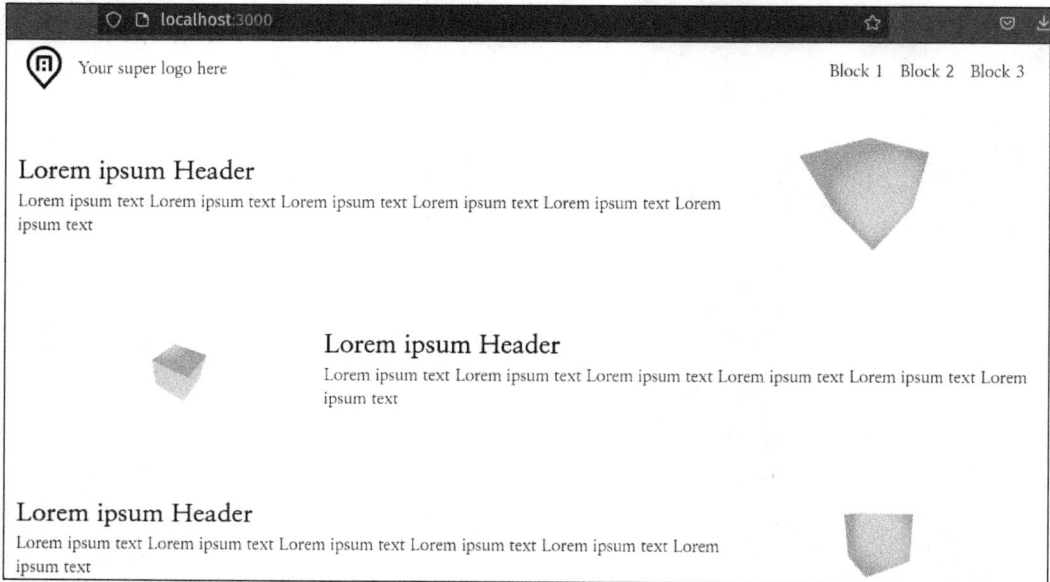

Figure 13.7: Page after updates

Connecting scenes to Next.js pages

We already have a great result and can render several canvas elements on the page. From the optimization perspective, we are overloading the browser. There is a way to translate one renderer for several objects, this possibility is called **Portals** from the **Drei** library. Several objects can be used as Portals. For our example, we will take the **Views** component.

Views employ **gl.scissor(native WEB GL function)** to partition the viewport into segments. We associate a view with a tracking **div**, which subsequently manages the position and boundaries of the viewport. This approach enables the creation of multiple views utilizing a single, efficient canvas. These views seamlessly track their corresponding elements, accommodating scrolling, resizing, and more.

It is recommended to re-establish the event system connection to a parent element, encompassing both the canvas and HTML content. This guarantees accessibility and selection for both. It additionally permits the mounting of controls or deeper integrations into the view.

Using **Views** will connect several independent scenes to the page. On the page, we will see that the canvas will contain all the pages, but we will load small portions of the scene in different places.

That will allow us to create a page with multiple 3D elements, or use multiple camera angles for one.

As we mentioned before, Views will use **gl.scissors**. The **Drei** library contains the package that will allow us to use it. It is called a **tunnel-rat**. Tunnel-rat package logic is pretty same as in any tunnel, it has **IN** and **OUT**. In the case of a library, it can have multiple **IN** and one **OUT**. That means we will open a tunnel for each model and render it in the end.

In refactoring, the first place where we will need to make changes is the **layout.js**. We need to wrap **children** with a component like this:

```
<body>
    <CanvasLayout>
        {children}
    </CanvasLayout>
</body>
```

Check *Code Listing 13.5* to collect the code for this component:

```
1.
    'use client';
2.
3. import { Canvas } from '@react-three/fiber';
4. import { Preload } from '@react-three/drei';
5. import { Tunnel } from "@/components/Model";
6. import { useRef } from 'react';
7.
8. export default function CanvasLayout({ children }) {
9.   const ref = useRef();
10.
11.   return (
12. <div
13.          ref={ref}
14.  >
15.      { children }
16.      <Canvas
17.       style={{
18.          position: 'fixed',
19.          top: 0,
20.          left: 0,
```

```
21.          width: ‹100vw',
22.          height: ‹100vh',
23.          pointerEvents: ‹none',
24.     }}
25.     eventSource={ref}>
26.          <Tunnel.Out />
27.          <Preload all />
28.     </Canvas>
29. </div>
30. )
31. };
```

Code Listing 13.5: CanvasLayout component

As we can see, there is another dependency here called a **tunnel.** This component is exactly the open tunnel inside that we mentioned before. *Code Listing 13.6* helps to follow the new codebase. The next update will be in the file **Model.jsx**:

```
1.  'use client';
2.  import { OrbitControls, PerspectiveCamera, View } from
    '@react-three/drei';
3.  import tunnel from 'tunnel-rat';
4.  import { useRef } from 'react'
5.
6.  export const Tunnel = tunnel();
7.  const TunnelWrapper = ({ children }) => {
8.    {/* Here we open the portal tunnel for each
9.  3D element that will be rendered  */}
10.   return <Tunnel.In>{children}</Tunnel.In>
11.   }
12.
13. export function General () {
14. {/* This component is made for simplicity,
15.     you can create an individual scene for each 3D model*/}
16.   return (
17.     <>
18.       <ambientLight />
19.       <pointLight position={[20, 30, 10]} intensity={3} decay={0.2} />
20.       <pointLight position={[-10, -10, -10]} color='blue'
    decay={0.2} />
21.       <PerspectiveCamera makeDefault  position={[12.5, 5, 5]}
    fov={35} />
22.     </>
```

```
23.  );
24. }
25.
26. export function Model ({ children, orbit, ...props }) {
27.   const ref = useRef();
28.
29.   return (
30.     <>
31.       <div ref={ref} {...props} />
32. {/* We need a ref object to align the target to some HTML element */}
33.       <TunnelWrapper>
34.           <View track={ref}>
35.               {orbit && <OrbitControls />}
36.               { children }
37.           </View>
38.       </TunnelWrapper>
39.     </>
40.   )
41. };
```

Code Listing 13.6: Model file updates

We check *Code Listing 13.7* to update the **Block.jsx** component. We will remove **Canvas** and replace it with the **Model** component:

```
1.
    'use client';
2. import { Model, General } from "@/components/Model";
3.
4. export default function Block({ reverse }) {
5.   return (
6.   <div className={`my-6 flex items-center ${reverse ? 'flex-row-
    reverse' : ''}`}>
7.       <div>
8.           <h1>Lorem ipsum Header</h1>
9.           <p>
10.              Lorem ipsum text Lorem ipsum text
11.              Lorem ipsum text Lorem ipsum text
12.              Lorem ipsum text Lorem ipsum text
13.          </p>
14.      </div>
15.      <div className='w-full text-center md:w--3/5'>
16.          <Model orbit className='flex h-96 w-full flex-col items-
```

```
      center justify-center'>
17.              <General />
18.              <mesh position={[-1.2, 0, 0]}>
19.                  <boxGeometry args={[4, 4, 4]} />
20.                  <meshStandardMaterial color="orange" />
21.              </mesh>
22.          </Model>
23.      </div>
24. </div>
25.  )
26. };
```

Code Listing 13.7: Adding the 3D objects to the scene using the Model component

Now, after the page update, we will see the same result as shown in *Figure 13.8*:

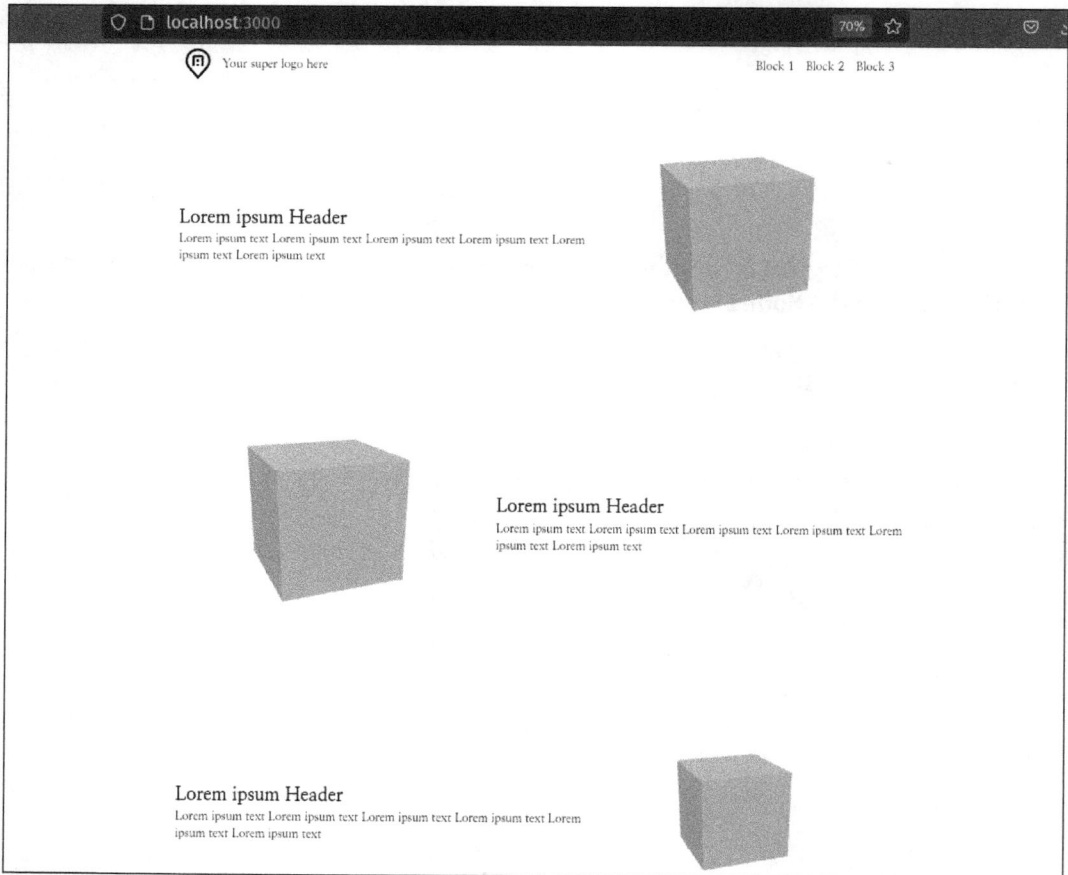

Figure 13.8: Result after code update

Visually, there is no difference from the boxes before. If we now open the developer tools we will see that the Canvas covers the whole page and each box uses it. That means we saved a lot of memory in our browser to better invest in model details and lights.

Manipulating 3D objects with R3F

Manipulating the 3D objects happens because of the object called Raycaster (as studied in the preceding chapters). As we are now in a React environment, these actions will be easier to implement.

Basic object interactions in a React environment

On each hover on the box on our page, we change the material's color. We align the color of the material with the variable that will be changed on the mouse event, as we do in any React component. Follow the *Code Listing 13.8* to add actions to the 3D objects:

```
1.  'use client';
2.  import { Model, General } from "@/components/Model";
3.  import { useState } from 'react';
4.
5.  export default function Block({ reverse, index }) {
6.    const [hover, setHover] = useState(false);
7.    const [clicked, click] = useState(false);
8.
9.
10.   const interaction = (e, state) => {
11.   e.stopPropagation();
12.   setHover(state);
13.   }
14.
15.   return (
16.   <div className={`my-6 flex items-center ${reverse ? 'flex-row-
      reverse' : ''}`}>
17.       <div>
18.           <h1>Lorem ipsum Header</h1>
19.           <p>
20.               Lorem ipsum text Lorem ipsum text
21.               Lorem ipsum text Lorem ipsum text
22.               Lorem ipsum text Lorem ipsum text
23.           </p>
24.       </div>
25.       <div className='w-full text-center md:w--3/5'>
26.           <Model orbit className='flex h-96 w-full flex-col
      items-center justify-center'>
```

```
27.                    <General />
28.                  <mesh
29.                    scale={clicked ? 1.5 : 1}
30.                    position={[-1.2, 0, 0]}
31.                    rotation={[Math.PI / 2, 0, 0]}
32.                    onClick={() => click(!clicked)}
33.                    onPointerOver={(e) => pointerAction(e, true)}
34.                    onPointerOut={(e) =>  pointerAction(e, false)}
35.                  >
36.                    <boxGeometry args={[4, 4, 4]} />
37.                    <meshStandardMaterial color={hover ? ‹blue' :
       ‹orange'} />
38.                  </mesh>
39.                </Model>
40.          </div>
41.  </div>
42.    )
43. };
```

Code Listing 13.8: Adding actions to the objects

Now, if we hover over any box it will change the color to blue, and on clicking, it will change the size. This is way easier than done before with Raycasting.

Applying animation and Tweens with R3F

Using the animations in the tunnels is not recommended, as it can generate a lot of issues with performance. It has a strict purpose to render elements inside the page but complex interactions will overload the page as we need to postpone the animation data through the tunnels in the end.

To add the animation packages, we use the following command:

```
npm install three @react-spring/three
or
yarn add three @react-spring/three
```

To try animations, we will create a new page in Next.js. We will call it **basic-animations**. To create the new page, we added the basic-animations folder and put the page.js file inside. Check *Code Listing 13.9* for the basic animation example:

```
1.
    'use client';
2.  import { useState, useRef } from 'react';
3.  import { Canvas, useFrame } from "@react-three/fiber";
4.  import { useSpring, animated, config } from "@react-spring/three";
```

```
5.
6.  function RotatingBox() {
7.    const mesh = useRef();
8.    const [active, setActive] = useState(false);
9.
10.   const { scale } = useSpring({
11.     scale: active ? 1.5 : 1,
12.     config: config.wobbly,
13.   });
14.
15.   useFrame(({ clock }) => {
16.     const a = clock.getElapsedTime();
17.     mesh.current.rotation.x = a;
18.   });
19.
20.   return (
21.     <animated.mesh
22.       scale={scale}
23.       onClick={() => { setActive(!active); console.log(active)}}
24.       ref={mesh}
25.     >
26.         <boxGeometry args={[2, 2, 2]} />
27.         <meshPhongMaterial color="orange" />
28.     </animated.mesh>
29.   );
30.   }
31.
32. export default function BasicAnimations() {
33.   return (
34.   <main className="max-w-[1000px] m-auto">
35.    <div className="App">
36.     <Canvas>
37.       <RotatingBox />
38.        <ambientLight intensity={0.1} />
39.       <directionalLight />
40.     </Canvas>
41.   </div>
42.   </main>
43.   )
44. }
```

Code Listing 13.9: Basic animation

The following is an important part of the code. This is the rotation hook for the box on the screen:

```
useFrame(({ clock }) => {
      const a = clock.getElapsedTime();
      mesh.current.rotation.x = a;
});
```

We can use this hook only in the separated component that is used as a child in **Canvas**. In another case, it will lead to an issue. This is the reason why we cannot use this animation in the tunnels because the components are rendered outside of the canvas and then moved inside using the tunnel.

As we can see, another animation on clicks using the **React Spring** library. It is free to use everywhere, even in tunnels (follow the exercise requirements to try it on the previous page).

The trick you can use for the animation is managing the time. You can take the time or connect to the ticks (depending on your needs). Check *Code Listing 13.10* for the trick:

```
1.  function RotatingBox() {
2.    const mesh = useRef();
3.    const [active, setActive] = useState(false);
4.    const [y, setY] = useState(0);
5.
6.    const { scale } = useSpring({
7.      scale: active ? 1.5 : 1,
8.      config: config.wobbly,
9.    });
10.
11.  // useFrame(({ clock }) => {
12.  //   const a = clock.getElapsedTime();
13.  //   mesh.current.rotation.x = a;
14.  // });
15.
16.  setInterval(() => {
17.      setY(Date.now() / 1000);
18.  }, 1);
19.
20.  return (
21.    <animated.mesh
22.      scale={scale}
23.      onClick={() => { setActive(!active); console.log(active)}}
24.      ref={mesh}
25.      rotation={[1, y, 4]}
```

```
26.  >
27.    <boxGeometry args={[2, 2, 2]} />
28.    <meshPhongMaterial color="orange" />
29.  </animated.mesh>
30. );
31. }
```

Code Listing 13.10: Animation trick

We will see that the box is rotating. This animation trick can also be used in the tunnels because it is not linked to the **Canvas** object.

Uploading and manipulating 3D models

In the creative process of developing web applications using Three.js, we did not always use shape primitives. There is a task to upload the 3D model into the scene and manage it.

Importing external 3D models into a scene

There are two ways of importing the 3D model into the scene. The first one supports several file types: GLTF, FBX, and OBJ. Let`s take the ***.gltf** file and try to import it. To make an example, we will create a new page. For the new page, we will create a folder with the name **upload-model** that must contain a file page.js (this is a Next.js rule). Download and put the file in the public folder. We will name ours just **scene.gltf**. Follow the *Code Listing 13.11* to render the uploaded file on the screen:

```
1.
   'use client';
2. import { Canvas, useLoader } from "@react-three/fiber";
3. import { Environment } from "@react-three/drei";
4. import { GLTFLoader } from "three/examples/jsm/loaders/GLTFLoader";
5. import { Suspense } from "react";
6.
7. const Model = () => {
8.   const ref = useRef();
9.
10. const gltf = useLoader(GLTFLoader, "./scene.gltf");
11. return (
12.   <>
13.     <mesh
14.         scale={1}
15.         ref={ref}
16.     >
17.         <primitive
```

```
18.               receiveShadow
19.               castShadow
20.               object={gltf.scene}
21.               />
22.       </mesh>
23.    </>
24.  );
25. };
26.
27. export default function UploadModel() {
28.   return (
29.  <main className="w-full h-svh m-auto»>
30.    <Canvas>
31.       <Suspense fallback={null}>
32.              <Model />
33.              <ambientLight intensity={0.1} />
34.              <directionalLight />
35.              <Environment preset="city" background />
36.       </Suspense>
37.    </Canvas>
38.  </main>
39.   )
40. };
```

Code Listing 13.11: Code to render the 3D file in the browser

There are several important moments in this code:

- In the official documentation examples, we will find direct use of **the <primitive />** object. Using it without **<mesh />** will not allow us to use mouse events.

- **<Environment />** object is a very useful tool. It will allow us to create the background for the scene. In this case, we use an out-of-the-box solution with an image, but we can upload any image there, and even the scene. The following is an example of its usage:

```
1.  <Environment
2.     background={false} // can be true, false, or "only"
       (which only sets the background) (default: false)
3.     blur={0} // blur factor between 0 and 1
       (default: 0, only works with three 0.146 and up)
4.     files={['px.png', 'nx.png', 'py.png', 'ny.png', 'pz.png',
       'nz.png']}
5.     path="/"
6.     preset={null}
```

7. scene={undefined} *// adds the ability to pass a custom THREE.Scene can also be a ref*
8. encoding={undefined} *// adds the ability to pass a custom THREE.TextureEncoding (default: THREE.sRGBEncoding for an array of files and THREE.LinearEncoding for a single texture)*
9. />

Once we reload the project, the page will look as shown in *Figure 13.9*:

Figure 13.9: *Uploaded 3D model in the scene from the Drei documentation*

The next method is to use a hook from the Drei library. It will allow us to use **FBX** files. Make

The following updates are required to load this type of object:

```
1. // const gltf = useLoader(GLTFLoader, "./scene.gltf");
2. //    return (
3. //      <>
4. //      <mesh
5. //  .    scale={scale}
6. //        ref={ref}
7. //      >
8. //      <primitive
9. //          receiveShadow
10. //          castShadow
11. //          object={gltf.scene}
12. //        />
13. //      </mesh>
14. //      </>
15. //    );
```

```
16. const fbx = useFBX('/room.fbx');
17. return <mesh
18.          scale={0.005}
19.          ref={ref}
20. >
21.    <primitive object={fbx} />
22. </mesh>;
23.
```

This update will look the same as in *Figure 13.10*:

Figure 13.10: *Upload fbx model into the scene*

Manipulating and animating imported models

Having the scene with the 3D model will lead us to have some manipulations with it. Using the knowledge that we used for primitive objects, we can also use it for the uploaded file. The first one is to use **OrbitControls**. To make an update, just put it in Canvas after the light object, like the following:

```
<Model />
<ambientLight intensity={0.1} />
<directionalLight />
<OrbitControls />
<Environment preset="city" background />
```

Now, we will be able to use the mouse to rotate the scene. The next step is to integrate the **React Spring** animation. For this, we need to update the **Model** object with code from *Code Listing 13.12*:

```
1.  import { Canvas, useLoader } from "@react-three/fiber";
2.  import { Environment, OrbitControls, useFBX } from "@react-three/
    drei";
3.  import { GLTFLoader } from "three/examples/jsm/loaders/GLTFLoader";
4.  import { Suspense } from "react";
5.  import { useSpring, animated, config } from "@react-spring/three";
6.  import { useState, useRef } from 'react';
7.
8.  const Model = () => {
9.    const ref = useRef();
10.   const [clicked, click] = useState(false);
11.   const { scale } = useSpring({
12.       scale: clicked ? 0.003 : 0.0005,
13.       config: config.wobbly
14.   });
15.
16.   const gltf = useLoader(GLTFLoader, "./scene.gltf");
17.   return (
18.     <>
19.       <animated.mesh
20.           scale={scale}
21.           onClick={() => click(!clicked)}
22.           ref={ref}
23.       >
24.           <primitive
25.               receiveShadow
26.               castShadow
27.               object={gltf.scene}
28.               />
29.       </animated.mesh>
30.     </>
31.   );
32.   };
```

Code Listing 13.12: Update to add Spring animation for scaling

After the project restarts, we will be able to click on the object as we did for the boxes to smoothly increase the scale of the mesh.

Conclusion

In this chapter, we have closely studied the fusion of Next.js and Three.js. These technologies offer endless possibilities. Whether we create virtual environments or interactive product showcases, the combination of Next.js and Three.js provides the tools and flexibility to bring ideas to life.

In the next chapter, we will cover the fundamentals of Next.js, including file conventions, the file-based routing system, middleware for handling requests, and API routes for creating serverless endpoints.

Points to remember

- Helper library contains almost everything we need to create a clean and creative 3D scene in the browser. It must not be ignored.

- There are various ways to animate the scene, and each option has its pros and cons. In React we will mostly use the Spring animations, but if we need to use the tick animation, the codebase needs to be organized to avoid tunnels. For the tick animations, it is better to avoid tunnels.

Exercises

1. **Create the page with several blocks:**
   a. Use different geometries
   b. Use the uploaded 3D file

2. **Create different pages with 3D objects**Add hover and click animations to the objects

Join our Discord space

Join our Discord workspace for latest updates, offers, tech happenings around the world, new releases, and sessions with the authors:

https://discord.bpbonline.com

CHAPTER 14

Next.js Fundamentals

Introduction

As a developer constantly striving to stay ahead of the curve and deliver cutting-edge solutions, the ever-growing complexity of web development and keeping up with the latest trends and technologies can take time and effort. This is where Next.js can help, offering a robust and intuitive platform to build modern, performant web applications easily.

What sets Next.js apart from other frameworks is not just the features. Though Next.js boasts an impressive array of capabilities, what truly sets Next.js apart is its ability to simplify the development process, providing developers with a seamless and intuitive experience that enhances productivity and unleashes creativity.

With Next.js, we can bid the complexities of configuration and setup goodbye, and say hello to a world where building sophisticated web applications is as easy as writing a few lines of code. Whether a seasoned developer or just starting the coding journey, Next.js has something for everyone, from its intuitive file conventions to its powerful routing system and flexible data fetching capabilities.

Structure

In this chapter, we will discuss the following topic:

- Fundamentals of Next.js

Objectives

In our exploration, we will study the fundamental concepts of Next.js, tracing the pathways of its file conventions, navigating through routing, and unraveling the threads of data fetching techniques. From file organization to server-side rendering and client-side data fetching, we will try to grasp the essence of Next.js development. As we proceed, we will come across the middleware concept, which steers requests, processes data, and enlivens custom server-side logic. We will also discover the power of API routes, bridging the gap between client and server, and enabling seamless communication with external services and databases.

This chapter will give us the required knowledge and skills to master the fundamentals of Next.js development.

Fundamentals of Next.js

We will begin this chapter by exploring the basics of Next.js, a robust framework driving dynamic web development. We will navigate through organizing files, routing, and seamless data fetching. We will study the essentials and unleash the potential of Next.js for our web projects!

File conventions

Next.js uses a filebase core, so we need to understand the file convention. This is an important part of using the framework. The file conventions are split into top-level folders, files, and routes. The first two parts are used to configure and structure the base project.

In the top-level folders, we will find the following:

`app`	App router
`pages`	Pages router
`public`	Static assets to be served
`src`	Optional application source folder

Table 14.1: Main folders of Next.js

In Next.js, there are several ways of the base structure:

- Using the app folder as the root

- Using the pages folder as the root

- Using the **src** folder as root, one will still be required to choose the **app** or **pares** as the initial

We should remember that only one kind of routing (app or pages) will work in the application, thus, it should be chosen in the beginning.

Choosing the **src** folder does not affect fundamental changes and can be used or ignored. We will use the **app** folder for the routes in our examples and exercises.

Important files at the root level are:

`next.config.js`	Configuration file for Next.js. This file is used to connect various plugins, change WebPack configuration, or add special headers to the application.
`instrumentation.ts`	OpenTelemetry and Instrumentation file. That file can be used to connect monitoring tools like LogRocket, DataDog, or Dynatrace to monitor the application usage and performance in real-time.
`middleware.ts`	Next.js request middleware. This file can contain functions that will be triggered before any request in the application. As a most efficient example of usage, we can mention the authorization check before each request for data. This function can contain logic that will be triggered if the user is not authorized or the session is over.
`next-env.d.ts`	TypeScript declaration file for Next.js (if you plan to use TypeScript)
`.env`	Environment variables. Can be separated into several files for different environments e.g. env.local, .env.production, etc.

Table 14.2: Important files in the root folder of the Next.js application

The next part of the file convention is related to the routing.

Routing

Routing in Next.js is based on files. We need to align with the rules to use it correctly. Generally, each page endpoint should have a folder in the project structure. In each folder, we need to have these files to render the page correctly:

| layout | **Layout**. This file contains the shared code that wraps the pages that come inside as props. All pages, by default, have named **children** in the code. We can use other names to provide them in parallel routes (please follow this section to understand this functionality). As a basic example for the layout, we can use this code:<br><br>```js
export default function RootLayout({
  children,
}: {
  children: React.ReactNode
}) {
  return <section>{children}</section>
}
```<br><br>The name for the layout component (we use **RootLayout** here) can be any that you like.<br><br>By the file convention, the layout file can exist in each page folder. That means we can align specific sub-layouts for each page in the project. |
page	**Page**. This is the main file that is required to create the page. The rendered data from the page instance will be used as children in the layout.
loading	**Loading UI**. This component is used in case we use **Suspense** from the latest React version.
not-found	**Not found UI**. This component will be used if we try to call a page that does not exist.
error	**Error UI**. This is a wrapper that uses the same logic as the loading mechanism. In the routing section, we will take a look at the example.
global-error	**Global error UI**. Same as the previous one, but used for the root
route	**API endpoint**. As Next.js can create the API gateway, this file is used to create the API endpoint in the desired folder.
template	**Re-rendered layout**. This file is used in case we need to have a different behavior for the layout. It will re-render the content at each route change.
default	Parallel route fallback page. In this section, we will introduce a powerful possibility named Parallel Routes. This possibility, in general, allows preloading the application as a route. But in case we can't load the component, we need to show something. This "something" will be taken from the **default.js/jsx** file.

Table 14.3: Table of the file naming convention for the Next.js application

The file type for this list can be any of these:

js/jsx or ts/tsx.

In this chapter, we will use TSX files to demonstrate the possibility of using different file resolutions. We will not introduce or use TypeScript constructions.
```

For example, we need to create several pages, including the main page. As we plan to work with 3D models, let us name them like this:

- Main page
- Car model
- Trains the model
- Edit models

The project structure should be the same as in *Figure 14.1*:

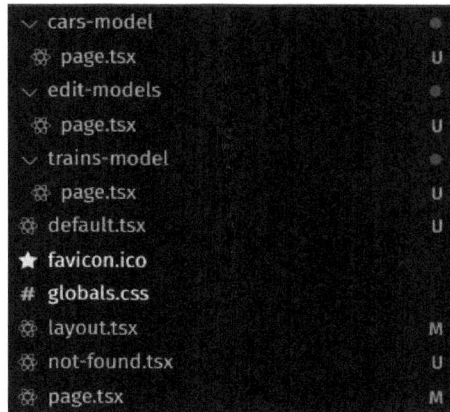

Figure 14.1: Project structure

The next important thing we need to know about routing is dynamic routing. For example, we need to create sub-pages for each kind of model. To solve it, we need to create the folder in **cars-model** that follows the pattern **[<any-name-you-want>]** to make it look like in *Figure 14.2*:

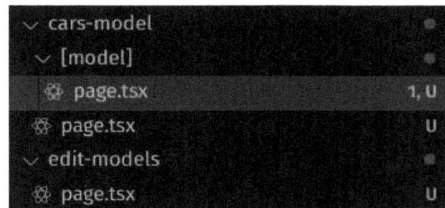

Figure 14.2: Subpage example

The next powerful tool for routing is **parallel routes**. Using parallel routes, we can dynamically load several mini-applications on the page. This can be a good tool to create micro frontend architecture using Next.js. One important thing to remember is that micro-frontend is just an architecture, which means using this architecture in the project does not automatically mean the possibility to use different frameworks. It means we can split our applications into several smaller applications and implement them dynamically.

The following are the steps to create the parallel route:

1. The route name is a named slot that will be implemented in the layout.

2. The name must contain **@** this symbol as the first character.

3. The Route folder should contain the **default.js/jsx** file, as it is required in case we reload the page manually.

For practice, we will create the file structure the same as shown in *Figure 14.3*:

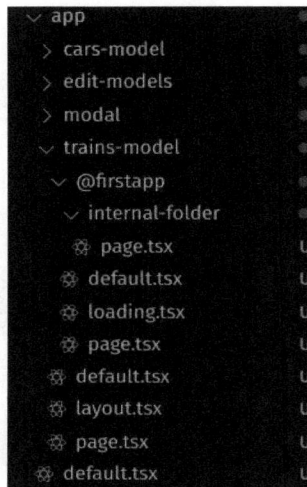

Figure 14.3: Adding a parallel route to the application

As seen in the preceding image, we will require these folders:

- **@firstapp** folder as a root for the parallel route

- **default.tsx** file (**or js or jsx**. This is just an example that will contain default logic in case we can`t reach the route file for some reason

- **loading.tsx** file that will contain the loader component that will be rendered before the page for the **@firstapp** is loaded

- **page.tsx** file that will contain the page itself

- **internal-folder** folder with a sub-route with a page file inside

We are now ready to code. *Code Listings 14.1-14.4* have all the required codes for the files:

```
1. import Link from "next/link";
2.
3. export default async function Page() {
4.   // This code will emulate loading
5.   await new Promise(resolve => setTimeout(resolve, 8000));
6.
```

```
7.  return (
8.     <div className="p-24 bg-slate-400">
9.       Gray app<br />
10.        <Link href="/trains-model/internal-folder">open internal</Link>
11.    </div>
12.  );
13. }
```

Code Listing 14.1: *Code for the page located in @firstapp/page.tsx*

For the loading component, we will use the following code:

```
1.  export default function Loading() {
2.   return <p className="p-24">LOADING Gray App...</p>
3.  }
```

Code Listing 14.2: *Code for the page located in @firstapp/loading.tsx*

For the default view, we can use any visual data we want. If we do not need to show anything in case the page is not reachable, we then use the code from *Code Listing 14.3*:

```
1.  export default function Default() {
2.   return null;
3.  }
```

Code Listing 14.3: Code for the page located in @firstapp/default.tsx

In this case, we will not render anything.

For the internal page, we will use *Code Listing 14.4*. This page will be loaded in the same slot where we render the **@firstapp** page. Thus, it will show the powerful possibilities of parallel routing and how it can be used.

```
1.  export default async function Page() {
2.   return (
3.     <div className="p-24 bg-slate-400">
4.       Gray internal folder
5.     </div>
6.   );
7.  }
```

Code Listing 14.4: *Code for the page located in @firstapp/internal-folder/page.tsx*

The final changes should be done in the layout file. As we make the changes in the **trains-model** folder, it should be a file from **/trains-mode/layout.tsx**. The code for the layout file is in *Code Listing 14.5*:

```
1.  import type { Metadata } from "next";
2.  import { Inter } from "next/font/google";
3.  import { Suspense } from "react";
4.  import Loading from "./@firstapp/loading";
5.
6.  const inter = Inter({ subsets: ["latin"] });
7.
8.  export const metadata: Metadata = {
9.    title: "Create Next App",
10.   description: "Generated by creating the next app",
11. };
12.
13. export default function TrainsLayout({
14.   children,
15.   firstapp
16. }: Readonly<{
17.   children: React.ReactNode,
18.   firstapp: React.ReactNode
19. }>) {
20.   return (
21. <div className="flex">
22.     <div>
23.         <Suspense fallback={<Loading />}>{firstapp}</Suspense>
24.     </div>
25.     <div>
26.         {children}
27.     </div>
28. </div>
29.   );
30. }
```

Code Listing 14.5: Code for the layout file

We add the parameter into layout variables and pass them into the **Suspense** component with **Loading** fallback, which means that we load **@firstapp** as a micro application into any page that will be loaded using this layout. In addition, if we do not use **Suspense** here, the component will be loaded as a server-side rendered component. This will depend on the application requirements. In this case, we do not need such a requirement as we are working with **Canvas**.

As a result, we will see the application view as shown in *Figure 14.4* for the root page and *Figure 14.5* for the internal page:

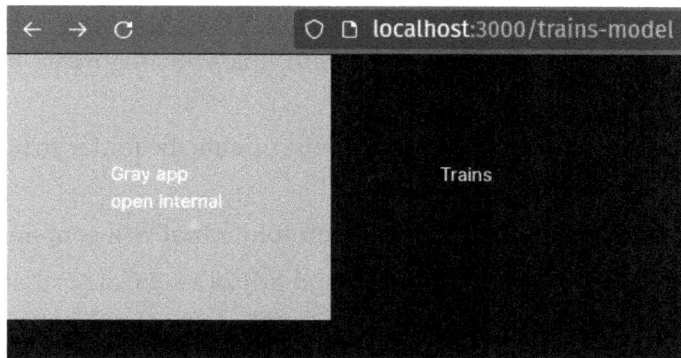

Figure 14.4: Root page of the Trains page with parallel route

As you can see, the right part stays the same. The only change happens in the gray block:

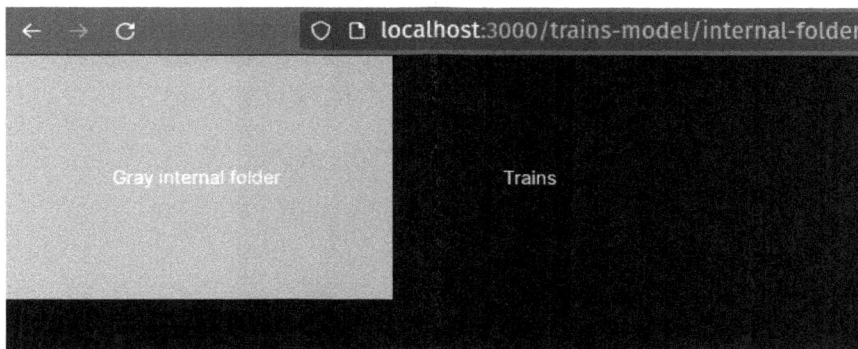

Figure 14.5: Internal page of the Trains page with parallel route

Parallel routing happens only on the client side of the application. That means that when we open the internal page of **@firstapp** and then reload the page, we will see content only related to the **@firstapp**. This behavior exists because the server routers do not know the current children to load into the layout. The children part is not loaded and does not break the page because we have **default.tsx** file, that renders nothing.

The next route feature that can be useful in parallel routes is **intercepting routes**. This feature is not related directly to parallel routes and can be used independently. We take the context from another page and provide it in the current route. It means, we can have one general route and several interceptors that can provide different content. The most popular example is using a modal window with the possibility to share the content by link.

The convention for folder naming looks like this:

- Use **(.)** before the folder name to link with segments at the same level.
- Utilize **(..)** before the folder name to link with segments one level above.

- Apply **(..)(..)** before the folder name to link with segments two levels above.
- Utilize **(...)** before the folder name to link with segments from the root app directory.

To make the realization of intercepting route, let us update the folder structure with several elements:

- **modal** folder in the root and [id] as a sub-folder that will contain the page file.
- **(..)modal** folder in **@firstapp** folder and [id] as a sub-folder that will also contain the page file.

The structure should follow *Figure 14.6*:

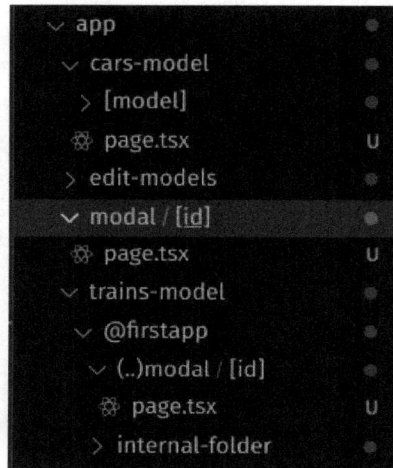

Figure 14.6: Updated folder structure

We will create the basic content inside to make a difference between routes in the root and the **@firstapp**. To make it interactive, we will add the link to open the modal to **trains-model/page.tsx** like:

```
<div className="p-24 bg-slate-400">
    Gray app<br />
        <Link href="/modal/123">open modal</Link><br />
        <Link href="/trains-model/internal-folder">open internal</Link>
</div>
```

After the project reloads, we can navigate to the **/modal/123**. The folder structure should lead us to the modal folder in the root. We use an interceptor here, and the content for this route will be used from the **(..modal)** folder. The result is the same, as shown in *Figure 14.7*:

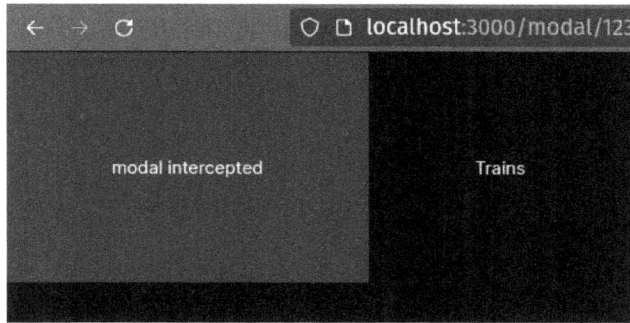

Figure 14.7: Intercepted modal result

Intercepting also happens on the client side only, which means that if we reload the page, or share the link, we will see the content of the modal page from the root that we created in the structure. The application architecture should have connections between intercepting routes and real ones to have a better user experience.

Middleware

Middleware enables the execution of code before a request is finalized. Subsequently, leveraging the incoming request, we can alter the response through actions such as rewriting, redirecting, adjusting request or response headers, or directly providing a response.

To create the middleware for our project, we will need to create the **middleware.js** (or **ts**) file in the root (that means, the file should be at the same level as **package.json**). The *Code Listing 14.6* helps create our first middleware:

```
1. import { NextResponse } from 'next/server'
2. import type { NextRequest } from 'next/server'
3.
4. export function middleware(request: NextRequest) {
5.   return NextResponse.redirect(new URL('/', request.url));
6. }
7.
8. export const config = {
9.   matcher: '/special-url',
10. }
```

Code Listing 14.6: Middleware file content

When we try to open **/special-url** in our browser, we will be redirected to the main page. The matcher in the config object can follow these rules:

- It can be a string or an array of strings.

- The string can be a direct link or regular expression like this **/your-page/(.*)** or like this **/about/:path***

The **middleware** function triggers on each router call. That means we can put any expression inside and check the request directly. The most important example we would need to use is to check the auth on each route. The basic example can look like in *Code Listing 14.7*:

```
1. export function middleware(request: NextRequest) {
2.    // Call our authentication function to check the request
3.    if (!isAuthenticated(request)) {
4.    // Respond with JSON indicating an error message
5.    return Response. json (
6.       { success: false, message: 'authentication failed' },
7.       { status: 401 }
8.    )
9.    }
10. }
```

Code Listing 14.7: Middleware function to manage each call

API routes

Route Handlers enable the creation of customized request handlers for a specific route, utilizing the web request and response APIs. In Next.js, there are two ways of project creation: with app folder and with the pages folder.

For the app folder, we need to define a **route.js**(or **ts**) file. The rule for this file is that it can follow any route we want, but it should not have a **page.js(ts)** file. It can be an API folder or any other name. As an example, we can have the **GET** request in the routes file like *Code Listing 14.8*:

```
1. export async function GET() {
2.    const data = 'some data';
3.    return Response.json({ data })
4. }
```

Code Listing 14.8: Simple code for the GET request using the app router

The function names are related to the HTTP method and include **GET, POST, PUT, PATCH, DELETE, HEAD, and OPTIONS**. In case an unsupported method is called, Next.js will respond with a 405 Method Not Allowed status.

For the pages folder option, we need to have **api** folder with files that define the route. For example,**/api/hello-world**. As a code example, we can see in *Code Listing 14.9*:

```
1.  import type { NextApiRequest, NextApiResponse } from 'next'
2.
3.  export default function handler(req, res) {
4.    res.status(200).json({ message: 'Hello World!' });
5.  }
```

Code Listing 14.9: *Simple code for the GET request using the pages router*

This will automatically create the GET request. To have other types of requests here, we need to update the call like in *Code Listing 14.10*:

```
1.  import type { NextApiRequest, NextApiResponse } from 'next'
2.
3.  export default function handler(req, res) {
4.    if (req.method === 'POST') {
5.        // Make a POST request
6.    }
7.
8.    res.status(200).json({ message: 'Hello World!' });
9.  }
```

Code Listing 14.10: *Simple code for the POST request using the pages router*

Conclusion

In this chapter, we have studied the fundamental aspects of Next.js, exploring its file conventions, routing system, and middleware functionalities. We have learned how to organize files effectively, navigate routes seamlessly, and utilize middleware to customize request handling. By understanding these core concepts, you are now equipped with the essential knowledge to build robust and dynamic web applications with Next.js. These principles and techniques will enable us to create powerful and efficient web solutions.

In the next chapter, we will focus on managing data and state in a Next.js application. We will begin by exploring how to fetch data in Next.js, followed by techniques for data manipulation and handling mutations. We will also cover using a data context to manage state across components. Additionally, we will look at how to communicate and share data between Next.js and Three.js components to create interactive 3D experiences.

Points to remember

- Take your time to create the correct file structure that follows your system requirements.

- Keep in mind that router magic, like parallel routes and intersections, works only if you have the information about the previous route.

- It is possible to create the correct system with magic routes using middleware.

- API routes is a powerful feature that can help you to create a backend-less system in a short time.

Exercises

Using the knowledge from this chapter and the previous ones, please create the following application:

1. Create an application that has three parts.

   a. The main part that will render the next two components: 3D model component from previous chapters as the children's route.

      i. Menu part as the parallel route that will contain a list of models.

2. Make a basic API gateway that will return a list of 3D models for the menu.

Join our Discord space

Join our Discord workspace for latest updates, offers, tech happenings around the world, new releases, and sessions with the authors:

https://discord.bpbonline.com

Data Management and State in Next.js

Introduction

In Next.js development, data and state management are the cornerstone of robust and dynamic applications. They are the foundation of a bustling digital world with a seamless flow of information. This chapter will introduce managing data and state in a Next.js application. From fetching data to manipulating and sharing it across components, we will explore the intricacies of data management and harness the power of Next.js to create engaging and responsive user experiences.

Structure

In this chapter, we will discuss the following topics:

- Managing data and state in a Next.js application
- Communicating and sharing data between components

Objectives

By the end of this chapter, we will learn how to fetch data in a Next.js application, understand the concept of data context in Next.js and its role in providing global state management across components, and explore strategies to communicate and share data between Next.js and Three.js components. This will enable us to create interactive and data-driven 3D experiences seamlessly.

Managing data and state in a Next.js application

Next.js for seamless data handling and state management. In this section, we will explore Next.js and its versatile data fetching mechanisms, catering to client and server-side needs. Additionally, we will study the data context, discovering how Next.js facilitates state sharing across components without third-party libraries.

Fetching data in Next.js

Fetching data is an essential aspect of application development. This section explores the process of fetching, caching, and revalidating data in React and Next.js.

The following are the four primary methods for fetching data:

- Server-side fetching using the built-in fetch function.
- Server-side fetching with third-party libraries.
- Client-side fetching.
- Client-side fetching with third-party libraries.

Let us start with server-side fetching. Next.js extends the native fetch web API to enable customization of caching and revalidation behaviors for each fetch request on the server. Additionally, React extends fetch to automatically cache fetch requests during the rendering process of a React component tree.

When we build an application that shows each item of the factory tool as a 3D object. This 3D object contains some information, like the model and its status. We have a lot of such elements in our factory that we need to monitor and manage. The requirements for the development of such an application will be to create a page that contains a list of such elements that shows the data for each one, with the possibility to get into one item and edit it. We do not need to show any interactive elements on this page, so we can use the Next. js server-rendered page opportunity here.

The logical structure for such an example will be like the following:

```
async function getData() {
  const res = await fetch("some-api-url")
  return res.json()
}

export default async function Page() {
```

```
  const data = await getData()
  return <main></main>
}
```

Let us use this template to create an example for our case. We follow *Code Listing 15.1* to create the page. We first need to create two files and two folders to follow the example:

- First is the folder with the API endpoint of **/api** route. In this folder, we will place the file with the name **route.js**. In Next.js the file convention file with the name route.js will create the API endpoint. The main rule is not to place this file with the **page.js** file.

- The second folder is with the page itself. We will name it **data-fetch** and place the **page.js(**or **jsx** or **ts/tsx)** file inside.

As a result, the folder structure should look like *Figure 15.1*:

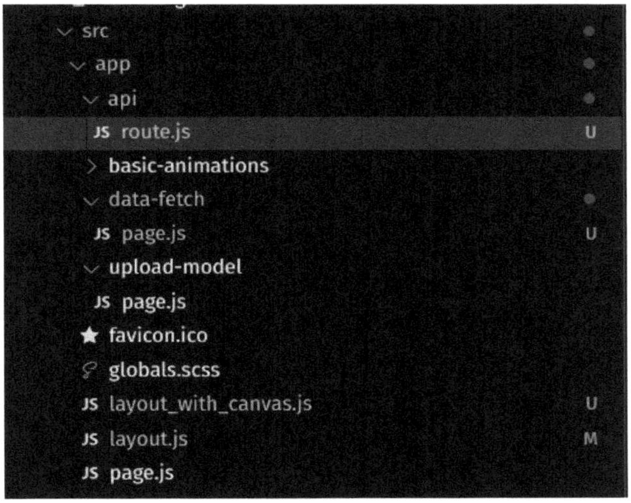

Figure 15.1: Updated folder structure

The code in *Code Listing 15.1* demonstrates how to fetch data from an API in a Next.js application and display it in a responsive and styled table. It includes error handling for failed API calls, showcases asynchronous functions for data retrieval, and implements a dynamic rendering approach to traverse the data and populate table rows, providing an editable interface for user interactions.

```
// We will create the function outside of the component to avoid hydration:
1. import Link from "next/link";
2.
3. async function getData() {
4.    // We will also put the API mock is also in the application
5.      // Check the Code Listing 10.2 to collect the code for it
```

```
6.    const res = await fetch('http://localhost:3001/api');
7.    if (!res.ok) {
8.            throw new Error('Failed to fetch data');
9.    }
10.
11.   return res.json()
12.  }
13.
14.  export default async function DataFetch() {
15.   // Now we call this function to get the data
16.  // Aware that your page function should be async
17.   const { data } = await getData();
18.
19.   return (
20.   <main className="w-full h-svh m-auto p-4»>
21.   <div className="relative overflow-x-auto shadow-md sm:rounded-lg">
22.       <table className="w-full text-sm text-left rtl:text-right text-gray-500
23.                              dark:text-gray-400»>
24.         <thead className="text-xs text-gray-700 uppercase bg-gray-50
25.                              dark:bg-gray-700 dark:text-gray-400»>
26.           <tr>
27.             <th scope="col" className="px-6 py-3">
28.                Model ID
29.             </th>
30.             <th scope="col" className="px-6 py-3">
31.                Name
32.             </th>
33.             <th scope="col" className="px-6 py-3">
34.                Type
35.             </th>
36.             <th scope="col" className="px-6 py-3">
37.                Status
38.             </th>
39.             <th scope="col" className="px-6 py-3">
40.                Action
41.             </th>
42.           </tr>
43.         </thead>
44.         <tbody>
45.           {
```

```
46.             data &&
47.             data.map(item => (
48.               <tr key={item.id}
49. className="odd:bg-white odd:dark:bg-gray-900
50.     even:bg-gray-50
51.                                 even:dark:bg-gray-800 border-b
52. dark:border-gray-700
53. hover:bg-gray-50
54. dark:hover:bg-gray-600">
55.               <th scope="row" className="px-6 py-4
56. font-medium
57.       text-gray-900
58.                                 whitespace-nowrap
59.                                  dark:text-white»>
60.               {item.id}
61.             </th>
62.             <td className="px-6 py-4">
63.               {item.name}
64.             </td>
65.             <td className="px-6 py-4">
66.               {item.type}
67.             </td>
68.             <td className="px-6 py-4">
69.               {item.status}
70.             </td>
71.             <td className="px-6 py-4">
72.               <Link href="#" className="font-medium
73.                   text-blue-600 dark:text-blue-500
74.                   hover:underline">Edit</Link>
75.             </td>
76.           </tr>
77.         ))
78.       }
79.       </tbody>
80.     </table>
81. </div>
82.
83. </main>
84. )
85. }
```

Code Listing 15.1: Page with fetched data

The code in *Code Listing 15.2* demonstrates how to define a mock API endpoint in a Next. js application using the **NextResponse** object. It returns a JSON response containing mock data with appropriate status headers, making it useful for testing and simulating API interactions during development.

```
1.  import { NextResponse } from 'next/server';
2.  export async function GET(request, context) {
3.  const mockData = [
4.    {
5.      "id": "g1oxhn4nv",
6.      "name": "Object 1",
7.      "type": "motion",
8.      "status": "active"
9.    },
10.   // Add more data here, just follow the pattern of the first element
11.  ];
12.  // This operator will return the object as a server response
13.  // We use NextResponse because it also creates a status header
14.  return NextResponse.json({ data: mockData }, { status: 200 });
```

Code Listing 15.2: Route.js file

If we start the project and open the page, we will see the data table from the API call. The whole page is rendered on the server, which will give more performance on the caching stage. The result is visible in *Figure 15.2*:

MODEL ID	NAME	TYPE	STATUS	ACTION
g1oxhn4nv	Object 1	motion	active	Edit
p5t6lkqj3	Object 2	handler	not active	Edit
8izw3qrj0	Object 3	motion	not active	Edit
m4a8kq5hr	Object 4	device	active	Edit
n2j7cr4l9	Object 5	handler	active	Edit
h9o1ky3dt	Object 6	device	not active	Edit
l7wj3zfgx	Object 7	device	active	Edit
q6akyr9wl	Object 8	motion	active	Edit

Figure 15.2: Result of page render for the data fetching

The important feature is that each request is cached using the Next.js mechanism. We will not see it if we run the application in **DEV** mode. If we build a project and start the production option using the **yarn start** command (or **npm run start**), we will see that data is cached, and even if we update the data and reload the page, it will still not be updated. To see this as an example (as in our case, we connect to an internal mock API), let us add a function that will get data outside, like in *Code Listing 15.3*:

```
1.  async function getTime() {
2.    const res = await
3.        fetch('https://timeapi.io/api/time/current/
    zone?timeZone=Asia%2FKolkata');
4.    if (!res.ok) {
5.          throw new Error('Failed to fetch data');
6.    }
7.    return res.json();
8.  }
```

Code Listing 15.3: Function to get data from an API endpoint

After this, we will add this function call where we get the data before:

```
const { data } = await getData();
const { datetime } = await getTime();
```

If we put this data into a template and run the application in production mode, we will see that the data is not changing anymore. If we need updated data in each call, we will need to add a special parameter in the fetch function to let Next.js know that we do not need to store the data in the cache. For example, let us take the following code:

```
1.  const res = await fetch(
2.    'https://timeapi.io/api/time/current/zone?timeZone=Asia%2FKolkat,
3.    { cache:  'no-store'}
4.  );
```

Code Listing 15.4: Cache flag to revalidate every reload

If we still need the cache for only some time, like five minutes to an hour, we will need to update the parameter with a **revalidate** flag like the following:

```
1.  const res = await fetch(
2.    'https://timeapi.io/api/time/current/zone?timeZone=Asia%2FKolkata',
3.    { next:  {revalidate: 3}}
4.  );
```

Code Listing 15.5: Cache flag to indicate revalidation period

In this code, we have a number value. This number is **seconds**. It means we can update the cache now for the required time. In our case, the time will be updated every 3 seconds.

This works only in case we have a **fetch** function in the code. If we use a third-party library that does not have fetch, it uses Axios instead, and then each request will be cached. For this case, we can use the special variable that must be placed in the **layout.js** file (use the root layout or create one on a specific page). For example, our page looks like that in *Code Listing 15.6:*

```
1.  async function getTime() {
2.   const res = axios.get('https://timeapi.io/api/time/current/
    zone?timeZone=Asia%2FKolkata');
3.   return await res;
4.  }
5.
6.  export default async function DataFetch() {
7.   const { data } = await getTime();
8.   return (
9.    <main>
10.      { data.datetime }
11.           <main/>
12.      )
13. }
```

Code Listing 15.6: Example page for Axios

Now, the root layout will look like the following:

```
1.  import './globals.scss';
2.  export const revalidate = 3;
3.
4.  export default function RootLayout({ children }) {
5.    return (
6.   <html lang="en">
7.     <body>{children}</body>
8.   </html>
9.    )
10. }
```

Code Listing 15.7: Layout file to show the place for the revalidation parameter

This will help to make the same trick for the third-party way. Now, the page will be revalidated every 3 seconds.

It is not necessary to use an async component page. We can use a hook for it. The hook is called **use()**. You can change **await** for data like this, and it will still work:

```
import { use } from 'react';
// code from the previous example here
export default function DataFetch() {
    const { data } = use(getData());
        // code from the previous example here
}
```

The next step is to check how we can use the same trick on the client side, as working with React Fiber will lead us to mostly client-side rendered components. For this case, we can use regular React fetching like the following:

```
1. 'use client';
2. import { useEffect, useState } from 'react';
3. export default function DataFetch() {
4.   let [data, setData] = useState([]);
5.   useEffect(() => {
6.       const getData = async () => {
7.           const res = (await fetch('http://localhost:3000/api')).
   json();
8.           const { data } = await res;
9.           setData(data);
10.       };
11.       getData();
12. },[]);
13. // Code from the previous example
14. }
```

Code Listing 15.8: Get data on the client with fetch

As shown, we added the **use client** parameter at the top, which made the page client-rendered. Now, the result will be the same as in *Figure 15.2*.

In case we want to use third-party libraries like SWR, fetching code will not need many changes and will look like in *Code Listing 15.9*:

```
1. 'use client';
2. import useSWR from 'swr';
3.
4. const fetcher = (url) => fetch(url).then((res) => res.json());
5. export default function DataFetch() {
6.   const { data, error, isLoading } = useSWR('http://localhost:3000/
   api', fetcher);
7.   if (error) return <div>failed to load</div>;
8.   if (isLoading) return <div>loading...</div>;
9.
10.  return (
11.  <main className="w-full h-svh m-auto p-4">
12.  // Code from the previous example
13.          {
14.              data.data &&
15.              data.data.map(item => (
16.              // Code from the previous example
```

```
17. </main>
18. )
19. }
```

Code Listing 15.9: Using the SWR library to fetch data on the client

In this example, we use the SWR library to fetch, which allows us to improve the fetching logic and add a loading and error state check. It can be a good alternative to regular fetch for the client component.

Data manipulation and mutations

Apart from knowing how to get the data, we also need to know how to send data back. There are two ways to achieve that. We can use the same way as we did on the client, using fetch (or third-party libraries like Axios) or using one more modern feature from Next.js that calls **server actions**. We will create a new page with the name **data-manipulation** (follow the guide from the previous block to make it: create the folder and page file).

The following is what we need to do:

- Take a previous example with data fetch to get the list.
  - o Keep getting data functions outside of the component just to show that it is possible to have it outside (in another file or structure)
- Add input for the new data.
- Add a button that will call to API and add some data to the list.
- Update the list.

To update the API endpoints, follow these steps:

1. The first step is to update API endpoints. For this, we will open the **api/routes. js** file and make a copy function from *Code Listing 15.10* into it:

```
1. export async function POST(request, _) {
2.   const data = await request.json();
3.   mockData.push({
4.   "id": "newID-123",
5.   "name": data.name,
6.   "type": "motion",
7.   "status": "not active"
8.   })
9.   return NextResponse.json({ status: "OK" }, { status: 200 });
10. }
```

Code Listing 15.10: Put this code into api/route.js

2. The next step will be to send data and revalidate the page. We need to remember that the API endpoint can be located anywhere, not only in our internal system. This is where **server actions** come into play. Let us look at the code in *Code Listing 15.11*, where we will update the page code and inject the server action inside:

```
1.  import { revalidatePath } from "next/cache";
2.
3.  async function getData() {
4.    const res = await fetch('http://localhost:3000/api');
5.    if (!res.ok) {
6.        throw new Error('Failed to fetch data');
7.    }
8.    return res.json();
9.  }
10.
11. export default async function DataManipulation() {
12.   const { data } = await getData();
13.
14.   async function callToAction(formData) {
15.     // This flag is required to set the function to be a
          server action
16.       'use server';
17.       await fetch('http://localhost:3000/api', {
18.           method: "POST",
19.           body: JSON.stringify({name: formData.get('name')})
20.       });
21.       // This function is required to set the revalidate page
      after the server call
22.       revalidatePath('/data-manipulation');
23.   }
24.
25.   return (
26.       <main className="max-w-[1000px] m-auto">
27.           Server actions!
28.           <div>
29.               <form action={callToAction}>
30.                   <div><input name="name"
      placeholder="enter the name" /></div>
31.                   <button type="submit">click me!</button>
32.               </form>
33.           </div>
34.
```

```
35.        <div className="relative overflow-x-auto shadow-md
   sm:rounded-lg">
36.          <table className="w-full text-sm
   text-left rtl:text-right text-gray-500 dark:text-gray-400">
37.            <thead className="text-xs text-gray-700
   uppercase bg-gray-50 dark:bg-gray-700 dark:text-gray-400">
38.              <tr>
39.                <th scope="col" className="px-6 py-3">
40.                  Model ID
41.                </th>
42.                <th scope="col" className="px-6 py-3">
43.                  Name
44.                </th>
45.                <th scope="col" className="px-6 py-3">
46.                  Type
47.                </th>
48.                <th scope="col" className="px-6 py-3">
49.                  Status
50.                </th>
51.                <th scope="col" className="px-6 py-3">
52.                  Action
53.                </th>
54.              </tr>
55.            </thead>
56.            <tbody>
57.            {
58.              data &&
59.              data.map(item => (
60.                <tr key={item.id} className="odd:bg-
   white odd:dark:bg-gray-900 even:bg-gray-50
61.                                    even:dark:bg-
   gray-800 border-b dark:border-gray-700
62.                                    hover:bg-
   gray-50 dark:hover:bg-gray-600">
63.                  <th scope="row" className="px-6
   py-4 font-medium text-gray-900 whitespace-nowrap dark:text-white">
64.                    {item.id}
65.                  </th>
66.                  <td className="px-6 py-4">
67.                    {item.name}
68.                  </td>
69.                  <td className="px-6 py-4">
70.                    {item.type}
```

```
71.                                    </td>
72.                                    <td className="px-6 py-4">
73.                                        {item.status}
74.                                    </td>
75.                                    <td className="px-6 py-4">
76.                                        <a href="#"
    className="font-medium text-blue-600 dark:text-
    blue-500 hover:underline">Edit</a>
77.                                    </td>
78.                                </tr>
79.                            ))
80.                        }
81.                    </tbody>
82.                </table>
83.            </div>
84.
85.        </main>
86.    )
87. }
```

Code Listing 15.11: Page component with server action inside

We have marked important parts as **bold**. The following is what we see:

```
async function callToAction(formData) {
        'use server';
        await fetch('http://localhost:3000/api', {
                method: "POST",
                body: JSON.stringify({name: formData.get('name')})
        });
        revalidatePath('/data-manipulation');
}
```

First, we tell the framework to look at this function as a server action, which means it will trigger on the server side. We then revalidate the current path, which will lead to re-rendering the component and getting all the data from the API again against all cache mechanisms.

The most important part here is that at the current time (probably at the moment when this book will be published, it will be updated), this feature is set as experimental, so we need to turn it on.

To make this, open the file **next.config.js** and set it like in *Code Listing 15.12*:

```
1. const nextConfig = {
2.   transpilePackages: ['three'],
```

```
3.   experimental: {
4.        serverActions: true,
5.   },
6.   }
7.   module.exports = nextConfig
```

Code Listing 15.12: Updates for the configuration to enable server actions

As we see, the flag is set as **experimental**. It is ok to use experimental features.

Data context

In Next.js, data context is a feature that allows us to manage the global state and share data across components without having to pass props manually through every level of the component tree. It is particularly useful for managing application-level state that needs to be accessed by multiple components.

Here is how data context works in Next.js:

1. **Create a context**: We start by creating a context using the **createContext** function from React. This creates a new context object that we can use to share data.

2. **Provide context value**: We then provide a value for the context using a **Context. Provider** component. This component wraps the part of the component tree where we want the context to be available.

3. **Consume context value**: Components that need access to the context can consume their value using the **useContext** hook. This hook allows us to access the current context value within a functional component.

To add the context to our application, let us add the code to the file with the name **data-context.js**. We will follow *Code Listing 15.13* to add the context functionality to our application:

```
1.   // The data context will work only on the client side.
     This flag is mandatory
2.   'use client';
3.
4.
5.   import React, { createContext, useState } from 'react';
6.   const DataContext = createContext();
7.
8.   export default function DataContextAPI({ children }) {
9.     const [data, setData] = useState('Initial Data');
10.
11.    return (
```

```
12.    <DataContext.Provider value={{ data, setData }}>
13.        {children}
14.    </DataContext.Provider>
15.  )
16. }
```

Code Listing 15.13: Wrapping application with data context

Now, we can pass the data to the context and get data from this context back. This mechanism looks like any third-party state library, like Redux, but is simpler to use. In case we do not need any complex solutions in data sharing, context will be the best choice.

To see it in action, let us proceed to the next section.

Communicating and sharing data between components

As a simple example of usage data sharing, let us align with these requirements:

- We will create a page that will contain two components

    o 3D model (let us take the box component, which we used in all chapters before)

    o The button that will change the material color on clicked

- The button and the box will be in different files and will not know each other's state

Creating communication between components will require following these steps:

1. To start, we will follow the *Code Listing 15.14* to create the page (check previous examples to check how to do that. Create the folder and page file):

```
1. export default function DataShare() {
2.   return (
3.       <main className="max-w-[1000px] m-auto">
4.           <div className="flex">
5.               <div><BoxModel /></div>
6.               <div><Actions /></div>
7.           </div>
8.       </main>
9.   )
10. }
```

Code Listing 15.14: Initial page component for the data share example

2. Now, we need to connect the context to this page. To do that, we will create the file data **context.js** in the page folder (it can be a global state for the whole application. In that case, we need to wrap our layout with data context). The *Code Listing 15.15* contains information about the context provider that we will need:

```
1.  'use client';
2.  import { createContext, useEffect, useState } from 'react';
3.  // Init the context with empty data. We need state and
    actions, same as in Redux
4.  const AppDataContext = createContext({state: {}, actions: {}});
5.
6.  const AppDataProvider = ({ children }) => {
7.    const [appData, setAppData] = useState({});
8.
9.    // Init the context information. We can create as many as
    we want for each component
10.   // So it will look like a state: { appData, some-component, …},
11.   const value = {
12.   state: { appData },
13.   actions: { setAppData },
14.   };
15.
16.   useEffect(() => {
17.   // Setting the color of the box as a global state
18.   setAppData({color: 'orange'});
19.   },[]);
20.
21.   return (
22.   <AppDataContext.Provider value={value}>
23.     {children}
24.   </AppDataContext.Provider>
25.   )
26. }
27. export { AppDataProvider, AppDataContext};
```

Code Listing 15.15: Context file to share state

3. Now, we can wrap the code with context and along with the possibility to share the data. The code for the update is in *Code Listing 15.16*:

```
1.  import BoxModel from './components/BoxModel';
2.  import Actions from './components/Actions';
3.  import { AppDataProvider } from './data-context';
4.
5.  export default function DataShare() {
```

```
6.  return (
7.      <main className="max-w-[1000px] m-auto">
8.          <AppDataProvider>
9.              <div className="flex">
10.                  <div><BoxModel /></div>
11.                  <div><Actions /></div>
12.              </div>
13.          </AppDataProvider>
14.      </main>
15. )
16. }
17.
```

Code Listing 15.16: Update the page code to connect the data provider

4. The next step is to collect and change the state of the components. Let us create the box component. We collect the code from *Code Listing 15.17* to create the simple box component with data context:

```
1.  'use client';
2.
3.  import { Canvas } from '@react-three/fiber';
4.  import { OrbitControls } from '@react-three/drei';
5.  import { AppDataContext } from '@/app/data-share/data-context';
6.  import { useContext } from 'react';
7.
8.  export default function BoxModel() {
9.  const { state } = useContext(AppDataContext);
10. return (
11.     <section>
12.         <Canvas>
13.             <ambientLight intensity={0.1} />
14.             <directionalLight position={[0, 0, 5]} />
15.             <mesh>
16.                 <boxGeometry args={[2, 2, 2]} />
17.                 <meshStandardMaterial color={state.appData.
    color}/>
18.             </mesh>
19.             <OrbitControls />
20.         </Canvas>
21.     </section>
22. )
23. }
```

Code Listing 15.17: Box component with data context inside

5. For the actions, we need to have a button and a click to send this data into context. The example code can be taken from *Code Listing 15.18*:

```
1.  'use client';
2.
3.  import { AppDataContext } from '@/app/data-share/data-context';
4.  import { useContext } from 'react';
5.
6.  export default function Actions() {
7.    const { state, actions } = useContext(AppDataContext);
8.    const changeColor = () => {
9.        if (state.appData.color === 'orange') {
10.           actions.setAppData({color: 'blue'});
11.       } else  {
12.           actions.setAppData({color: 'orange'});
13.       }
14. };
15.
16.  return (
17.      <section>
18.          <button class="bg-blue-500 hover:bg-blue-700 text-
    white font-bold py-2 px-4 rounded"
19.          onClick={changeColor}>change color</button>
20.      </section>
21.  )
22. }
```

Code Listing 15.18: Actions component

6. Finally, when we try to use it, we will see that we have two independent components: the first contains a 3D model, and the second is an action button. Clicking on the button leads to a change in the material color, as shown in *Figure 15.3*:

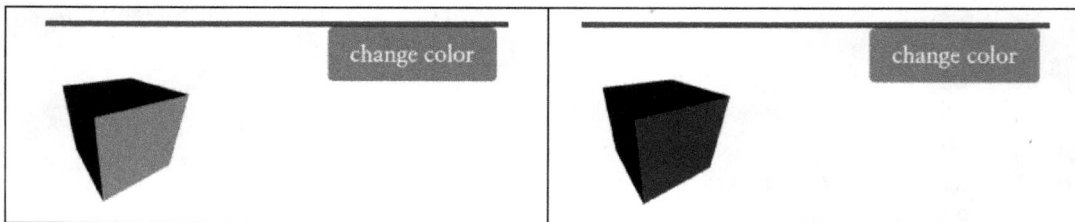

Figure 15.3: Context data sharing from the action component to the 3D model

Conclusion

In this chapter, we studied the intricacies of managing data and state within a Next.js application, exploring various techniques and strategies to handle data effectively. We started with understanding the fundamentals of fetching data in Next.js, exploring server-side rendering, static site generation, and client-side data fetching methods.

Moving forward, we explored data manipulation and mutations, learning how to update and modify data within our Next.js application to meet our specific requirements. We discussed the importance of data context in managing the global state across components, leveraging the power of context providers and consumers to share data seamlessly.

Furthermore, we explored techniques for communicating and sharing data between Next.js and Three.js components, enabling collaboration and data exchange between different parts of our application. By harnessing the capabilities of Next.js and Three.js together, we can create dynamic and interactive web experiences that engage users and provide rich, immersive content.

We have now equipped ourselves with the knowledge and tools necessary to effectively manage data and state in our Next.js applications. By applying these techniques and principles, we can build robust and scalable applications that deliver exceptional user experiences and drive business success.

In the next chapter, we will focus on implementing interactive controls for camera movements and object interactions. We will start by exploring camera controls and navigation, followed by techniques for manipulating and transforming objects. We will also cover creating interactive UI elements to enhance user engagement. Additionally, we will discuss accessibility and inclusive user interactions to ensure your application is usable for everyone.

Points to remember

- **Next.js supports both server-side and client-side data fetching**, each with specific use cases—server-side for performance/SEO, client-side for interactivity.

- **Caching and revalidation are built into Next.js fetch**, allowing you to control how fresh your data is by using cache: 'no-store' or revalidate options.

- **Server actions in Next.js (experimental) allow secure**, server-side data mutations directly from form actions, combined with path revalidation for fresh UI updates.

- **React Context is a simple built-in solution for global state management**, useful for sharing state across components without extra libraries like Redux.

- **Next.js can seamlessly integrate with Three.js**, using context to share data between UI components and 3D models for dynamic visual interactions.

Exercises

As an exercise, improve the last example with more manipulation data for the 3D model by these requirements:

1. Create an API endpoint with default information that contains:

   a. Material color

   b. Light position

   c. Light intensity

   d. Model position

2. Collect this data in the context of initiation.

3. Create a layout with buttons and inputs to change the 3D model information.

Join our Discord space

Join our Discord workspace for latest updates, offers, tech happenings around the world, new releases, and sessions with the authors:

https://discord.bpbonline.com

User Interactions and Controls

Introduction

In this chapter, we will get into practice and learn about user interactions. To make it more practice-oriented, we will make a small project covering interesting topics. It will help to create and support our first 3D web application. In this chapter, we will study moving cameras, manipulating object properties, using animation with React Spring, and important topics in the web, Web Accessibility, and how to use it in 3D development.

Structure

- Implementing interactive camera and object control
- Accessibility and inclusive user interactions and control
- Adding transitions using React Spring

Objectives

By the end of this chapter, we will learn how to create interactive scenes with camera controls. These controls will appear as UI elements as well as 3D objects. We will also learn how to manipulate objects and add basic animations to the scene. At the end of the chapter, we will implement accessible elements to the scene and will be able to understand and use Web Accessibility principles in 3D development.

Implementing interactive camera and object control

This chapter is more practice-oriented, thus, we will proceed to the requirements of what application we will create in this chapter, and what the application should look like, as well as the functionality it should provide.

First, we will make a scene with the box introducing the building with three floors. Each floor will contain some object (to keep the example as simple as possible, we will put a box inside each floor). The building itself will look like *Figure 16.1*. To create the example, we made this object in Blender, to have the possibility to get a 3D object that Three.js supports:

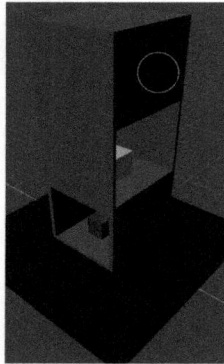

Figure 16.1: *The Object that will introduce our building*

The scene should follow these requirements:

- The screen should contain UI elements to manage the camera control of the scene.
    - o HTML inputs should be on the screen.
    - o 3D elements should act like buttons and move the camera.
- The camera, on each click, should change the floor of the building position and show the selected floor.
    - o The scene should also contain an independent 3D model attached to the floor.
    - o On click, we should be able to change the material.
    - o On input change, we should be able to change the size of the object.
- The scene should contain 3D objects that act like buttons.
    - o On click, we should change the camera position to the selected floor.
    - o Each object should follow Web Accessibility rules and have a voice announce and the possibility to use the *Tab* button to switch between objects.

As a result, we should have a scene that looks like *Figure 16.2*:

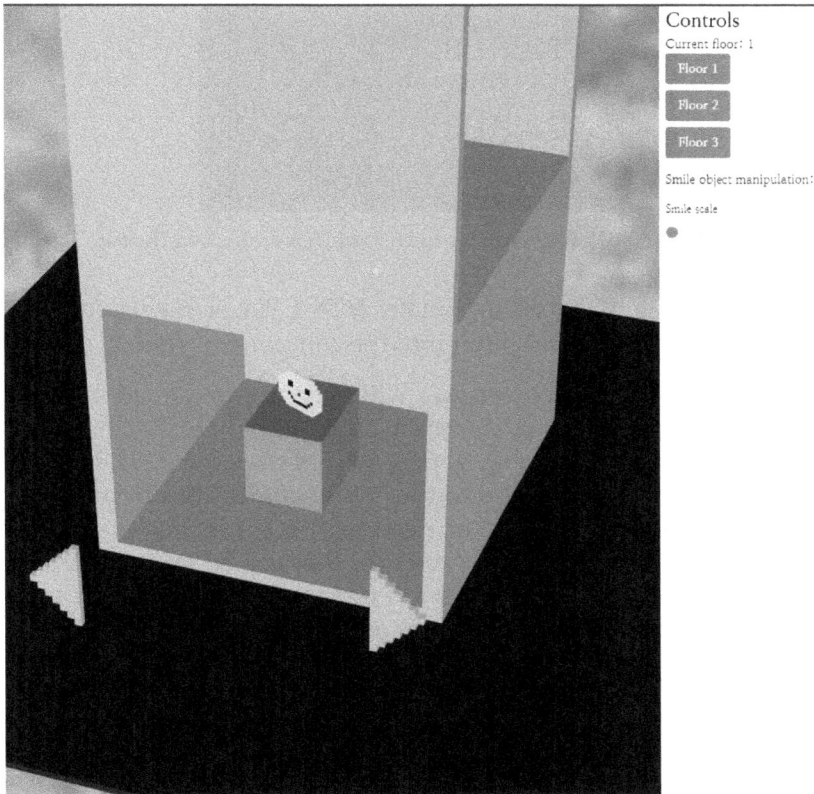

Figure 16.2: Expected result by the end of this chapter

Camera controls and camera navigation

Let us start with camera controls and positioning. In this block, we will create the scene page and add UI controls to move the camera. As done earlier, we will create the page folder, we can use any name. In this case, we will name it **boxes**. This folder should contain several files:

- **page.jsx**: The page file that will contain the canvas (*Code Listing 16.1*)
- **layout.jsx**: We will need it to create the context wrapper to pass the data between components (*Code Listing 16.2*)
- **data-provider.jsx**: This file will contain the context provider (*Code Listing 16.3*)
- **defaults.js**: Here, we will store all the coordinates of the objects (*Code Listing 16.4*)

We will not use any functional logic for changing coordinates, but it must be done in the exercises at the end of the chapter.

As a result, the file structure should look as shown in *Figure 16.3*:

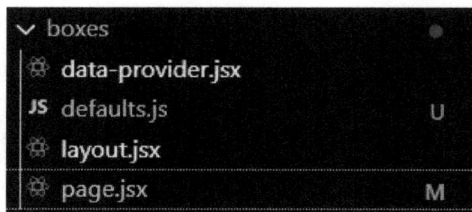

Figure 16.3: Updated file structure that is valid for the current chapter

We will require a component that will contain HTML UI elements. We will name it **Controls.jsx** (*Code Listing 16.5*) and put it into the components folder.

As we will work with external 3D objects, we will need to implement them. We can use the guide from the previous chapter to insert the object into the scene. Here we will see a convenient way of implementation using a special NPM package. This package is named **gltfjsx** and can be collected from this repository **https://github.com/pmndrs/gltfjsx**. To use it, we will need the **npx** command, so no need to install it manually; the script will do that by itself. The script supports various file types that can be taken from 3D modeling software like Blender (. **glb or. gltf**). This is not mandatory, and we can still use the previous chapters as a guide to insert 3D objects manually.

To use the script, run this command:

```
npx gltfjsx <PATH-TO-YOUR-FILE/FILE-NAME> --transform
```

The script will automatically generate the component. The script will generate a new model object at the same place, containing a normalized coordinates object. We can rename it or keep it as is. We will name the primary object component as **BoxModel.jsx** (*Code Listing 16.6*) and place it into the components folder. In the end, the components folder should look like *Figure 16.4*:

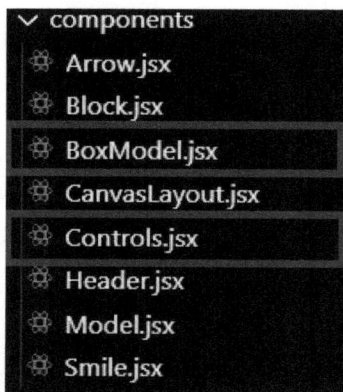

Figure 16.4: Components folder update

We are ready to code our application, and start with the **page.jsx** file:

```
1.  'use client';
2.  import React, { useContext, useState, useEffect, Suspense } from
    'react';
3.  import { Canvas } from '@react-three/fiber';
4.  import { Environment } from '@react-three/drei';
5.  import { BoxModel } from '@/components/BoxModel';
6.  import { PresentationControls, PerspectiveCamera } from
    '@react-three/drei';
7.  import { AppDataContext } from './data-provider';
8.  import Controls from '@/components/Controls';
9.  import { cameraPositions, cameraAngles} from "./defaults";
10.
11. export default function Boxes() {
12.     const { state, actions } = useContext(AppDataContext);
13.
14.     const [cameraAngle, setCameraAngle] = useState(cameraAngles[0]);
15.     const [cameraPosition, setCameraPosition] =
    useState(cameraPositions[0]);
16.
17.     useEffect(() => {
18.       /*5*/setCameraAngle(cameraAngles[state.appData.floor - 1]);
19.       /*5*/setCameraPosition(cameraPositions[state.appData.floor - 1]);
20.     }, [state.appData.floor]);
21.
22.     return (
23.       <main className="h-screen">
24.         <div className="flex h-screen w-full gap-2 ">
25.           <div className="w-[50%]">
26.             <Canvas shadows flat dpr={[2, 2]}
27.     camera={{ fov: 25, position: [20, 20, 20] }}>
28.               <Suspense fallback={null}>
29.         /*1*/<PresentationControls snap global
    rotation={cameraAngle} >
30.                 /*2*/<PerspectiveCamera position={cameraPosition}>
31.                   <BoxModel />
32.                   /*3*/<Environment preset="dawn" background />
33.                 </PerspectiveCamera>
34.               </PresentationControls>
35.             </Suspense>
36.           </Canvas>
```

```
37.                    </div>
38.                <div>
39.                    <h1>Controls</h1>
40.                    /*4*/<Controls />
41.                </div>
42.            </div>
43.        </main>
44.    )
45. }
```

Code Listing 16.1: *Code for the page.jsx file*

We made numbered anchors in *Code Listing 16.1* to make explanations more straightforward:

- /*1*/ At this point, we use the **PresentationControls** wrapper. As mentioned in *Chapter 9, Camera and Perspective,* in Three.js, we have different camera controls like **OrbitControls**. This one we take from the **@react-three/drei library.** It allows us to create a possibility to turn the camera smoothly, and after that, it will return to the first position. Using this, we will be able to create a smooth camera movement animation. By default, we set the rotation angle to show the exact floor. Considering that these controls allow us only to turn the camera around, to change the camera position along the Y axis, we will need to have a camera.

- /*2*/ At this point, we added the camera that will allow us to change the position of the view along the Y axis, which means we could see floors higher than the first one.

- /*3*/ Here, we add an environment around. This object is used to simplify the scene. In the exercise, we will be required to manually add lights and background to the scene. The environment object automatically adds background and lights.

- /*4*/ We add HTML controls to the scene, allowing us to manage parameters used to render the scene.

- /*5*/ Here, we listen for the context data changes and set the values to the scene. As we will use an array to store the default values, we will use each floor number as an index, reduced by 1.

The next step will be to add code to the **layout.jsx** file. Its code can be collected in *Code Listing 16.2:*

```
1. 'use client';
2. import { AppDataProvider } from './data-provider';
3. export default function BoxesLayout({ children }) {
4.     return (
5.         <AppDataProvider>
6.             {children}
```

```
7.            </AppDataProvider>
8.      )
9. };
```

Code Listing 16.2: Code for the layout component

This part just needs to be copied and pasted into the file.

The next step is to create the data context we will use on the page. Consider creating one global context and not breaking it into parts for each page. We will keep this as an example that it is possible to have no global context. Code for the file **data-provider.jsx** can be collected from *Code Listing 16.3*:

```
1.  'use client';
2.  import { createContext, useEffect, useState } from 'react';
3.
4.  const AppDataContext = createContext({state: {}, actions: {}});
5.  export default function AppDataProvider({ children }) {
6.      const [appData, setAppData] = useState({});
7.
8.      /*1*/const value = {
9.        state: { appData },
10.       actions: { setAppData },
11.     };
12.
13.     useEffect(() => {
14.       /*2*/setAppData({floor: 1})
15.     },[]);
16.     return (
17.         <AppDataContext.Provider value={value}>
18.             {children}
19.         </AppDataContext.Provider>
20.   )
21. };
22.
23. export { AppDataProvider, AppDataContext };
```

Code Listing 16.3: Code for the data context wrapper

We made numbered anchors in *Code Listing 16.3* to make the explanation clearer:

- /*1*/ We created an object that will contain the state and actions for the context. This will be required to use the context at each component that will call to state or state mutation.

- /*2*/ At this point, we assign a default value that will be set at each page reload as a starting point.

We need to add the default values in the file **defaults.js**. The code can be collected from *Code Listing 16.4*. As mentioned before, the default values will contain coordinates and values for each floor without calculations. We will need to just copy and paste them:

```
1.  const cameraAngles = [
2.      [0, 2, 0],
3.      [0, 1, 0],
4.      [0, -0.5, 0],
5.  ];
6.
7.  const cameraPositions = [
8.      [0, 0, 0],
9.      [0, -3, 0],
10.     [0, -6, 0]
11. ];
12.
13. export { cameraPositions, cameraAngles };
```

Code Listing 16.4: Default values

Now, we can proceed with the components. The first component will be the HTML UI controls layout that we named **Controls.jsx.** The code from it can be collected from *Code Listing 16.5*:

```
1.  import { useContext, useState, useEffect } from 'react';
2.  import { AppDataContext } from '../app/boxes/data-provider';
3.
4.  export default function Controls() {
5.  /*1*/ const { state, actions } = useContext(AppDataContext);
6.
7.  const setFloor = (floor) => {
8.      /*2*/ actions.setAppData({...state.appData, ...{floor}});
9.  }
10.
11. return (
12.     <div>
13.       Current floor: {state.appData.floor}
14.     <ul>
15.         <li className="mb-2">
16.             <button onClick={/*3*/() => setFloor(1)} className=»bg-
    blue-500 hover:bg-blue-700 text-white font-bold py-2 px-4 rounded»>
```

```
17.              Floor 1
18.            </button>
19.          </li>
20.          <li className="mb-2">
21.            <button onClick={() => setFloor(2)} className=»bg-
    blue-500 hover:bg-blue-700 text-white font-bold py-2 px-4 rounded»>
22.              Floor 2
23.            </button>
24.          </li>
25.          <li className="mb-2">
26.            <button onClick={() => setFloor(3)} className=»bg-
    blue-500 hover:bg-blue-700 text-white font-bold py-2 px-4 rounded»>
27.              Floor 3
28.            </button>
29.          </li>
30.      </ul>
31.        </div>
32.    )
33. }
```

Code Listing 16.5: *Code for the Controls.jsx component*

We made numbered anchors in *Code Listing 16.5* to make the explanations more straightforward:

- /*1*/ At this point, we create the connection to the context to share data between components. In the current one, there are three buttons, each button will set the current floor. This floor data will be used to set the camera position.

- /*2*/ Here, we set the floor value in the context.

- /*3*/ We call the function to set the floor value on click. We also hardcoded the list of buttons here. Changing this logic to a loop will also be a part of the exercise.

The only step left to have our first run and play around with the 3D model is to create the box with the floors themselves. The code for the **BoxModel.jsx** file is located in *Code Listing 16.6*:

```
1. import React, { useRef, useContext, useState, useEffect }
   from 'react';
2. import { useGLTF } from '@react-three/drei';
3.
4. export function BoxModel(props) {
5.   const groupRef = useRef();
6.   /*1*/const { nodes, materials } = useGLTF('/box-transformed.glb');
```

```
7.
8.   return (
9.       <group ref={groupRef} {...props} dispose={null}>
10.         <mesh receiveShadow
11.             geometry={nodes.Untitled.geometry}
12.             material={materials.palette}
13.             position={[0, 0, 0]}
14.             rotation={[Math.PI / 2, 0, 0]}
15.         />
16.     </group>
17.   )
18. }
19.
20. /*2*/useGLTF.preload('/box-transformed.glb');
```

Code Listing 16.6: Code for the BoxModel.jsx component

We made numbered anchors in *Code Listing 16.6* to make the explanation more straightforward:

- /*1*/ We align to the hook that loads the 3D object and ger nodes, and material data for our mesh.

- /*2*/ At this point, we also use the hook to preload the 3D object into the scene.

After we run the application, we see that clicking on the UI buttons leads to an animated camera position change. We cannot show animation on the screenshot, but we can see floors like in *Figures 16.5(a)-16.5(c)*:

Figure 16.5 (a): Camera position on the first floor of the building

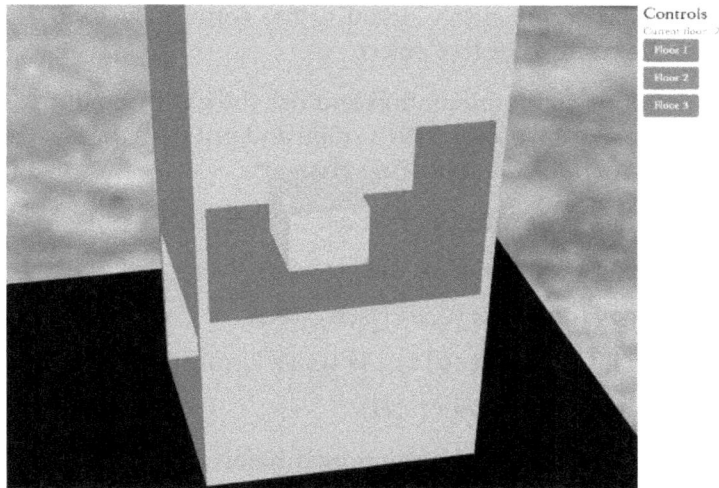

Figure 16.5 (b): Camera position on the second floor of the building

Figure 16.5 (c): Camera position on the third floor of the building

Object manipulation and transformations

In the next block, we will add another 3D object to the scene. It will be a simple object with a smile on it. For each floor, we will change the position of the object and move it with the camera. As we need to learn manipulation and transformation in this block, we will also add the following functionalities to this object:

- On object click, we will change the material to green color, which will indicate the action.

- We will add a range slider to the HTML UI to resize the object.

- As the **Controls** component is linked to the context, we will also need to add some data to the context for this object.

We will follow the previous recommendation and use the **gltfjsx** library to generate the component. We will take a small object with a smile and put it on the selected floor. To add the object, we will need to make the following changes:

- Add default values in **defaults.js** (*Code Listing 16.7*)

- Add component **Smile.jsx** (*Code Listing 16.8*)

- Update **data provider.jsx** (*Code Listing 16.9*)

- Implement HTML UI in **Controls.jsx** (*Code Listing 16.10*)

- Add object to **page** (*Code Listing 16.11*)

Let us start with default values. As we mentioned before, all values will be hard-coded into variables, and we will create the math functionality to calculate them:

```
1.  const cameraAngles = [
2.      [0, 2, 0],
3.      [0, 1, 0],
4.      [0, -0.5, 0],
5.  ];
6.
7.  const cameraPositions = [
8.      [0, 0, 0],
9.      [0, -3, 0],
10.     [0, -6, 0]
11. ];
12.
13. const smileProps = [
14.     {
15.         position: [-0.3, 2, -0.2],
16.         rotation: [Math.PI, 2, 0],
17.     },
18.     {
19.         position: [0.5, 6.5, 0],
20.         rotation: [Math.PI, 3, 0],
21.     },
22.     {
23.         position: [1, 11.5, -0.1],
24.         rotation: [Math.PI, 2, 0],
25.     }
26. ];
27. export {smileProps, cameraPositions, cameraAngles};
```

Code Listing 16.7: Update for the default values

The next step will be to create the 3D object file. We cannot provide the source code of the object. Here, we can use any that we would like to see on the scene or take one that is provided with this book in the code repository:

```
1.  import React, { useState, useContext } from 'react';
2.  import { MeshStandardMaterial } from "three";
3.  import { useGLTF } from '@react-three/drei';
4.  import { AppDataContext } from '../app/boxes/data-provider';
5.
6.  export function Smile(props) {
7.    const { nodes, materials } = useGLTF('/smile.glb');
8.    const [isGreen, setIsGreen] = useState(false);
9.    const { state } = useContext(AppDataContext);
10.
11.   const smileClicked = () => {
12.     /*4*/ setIsGreen(!isGreen);
13.   }
14.
15.   return (
16.     <group dispose={null} onClick={/*4*/smileClicked}>
17.       <mesh geometry={nodes.Untitled.geometry}
18.             /*1*/material={!isGreen ? materials.
      palette : new MeshStandardMaterial({ color: 0x0ff000 })}
19.             /*2*/ position={props.position}
20.             /*2*/ rotation={props.rotation}
21.             /*3*/ scale={state.appData.smileScale}
22.             />
23.     </group>
24.   )
25. }
26.
27. useGLTF.preload('/smile.glb');
```

Code Listing 16.8: Smile object implementation

We made numbered anchors in *Code Listing 16.8* to make the explanations more straightforward:

- /*1*/ We will check if the user clicked on the object or not. If the user makes a click, we will change the object material to green.

- /*2*/ We will get position and rotation data from props. There is no advantage or disadvantage to the question, where we will set the object data: inside or outside. This was made to show an example of different data store approaches.

- /*3*/ Here, we will get the scale data from the context. The context will be updated by the range slider in the HTML UI component.

- /*4*/ At this point, we will update the local state and change the material of the object.

Now, we need to update the **data provider.jsx** file to add the object parameter:

```
1.  'use client';
2.  import { createContext, useEffect, useState } from 'react';
3.
4.  const AppDataContext = createContext({state: {}, actions: {}});
5.  export default function AppDataProvider({ children }) {
6.      const [appData, setAppData] = useState({});
7.
8.      const value = {
9.        state: { appData },
10.       actions: { setAppData },
11.     };
12.
13.     useEffect(() => {
14.       setAppData({floor: 1, /*1*/ smileScale: 0.5})
15.     },[]);
16.     return (
17.         <AppDataContext.Provider value={value}>
18.             {children}
19.         </AppDataContext.Provider>
20.   )
21. };
22.
23. export { AppDataProvider, AppDataContext };
```

Code Listing 16.9: Data provider update

At point /*1*/ we add the scale parameter that will be updated by the HTML UI.

The next step is to add some controls in **Controls.jsx**:

```
1.  import { useContext, useState, useEffect } from 'react';
2.  import { AppDataContext } from '../app/boxes/data-provider';
3.  export default function Controls() {
4.    const { state, actions } = useContext(AppDataContext);
5.    const [rangeValue, setRangeValue] = useState(0.5);
6.
7.    const setFloor = (floor) => {
8.      actions.setAppData({...state.appData, ...{floor}});
```

```
9.    }
10.   /*1*/const setRange = (value) => {
11.     setRangeValue(value);
12.   }
13.
14.   /*2*/useEffect(() => {
15.     actions.setAppData({...state.appData, ...
  {smileScale: rangeValue}});
16.   }, [rangeValue]);
17.
18.   return (
19.     <div>
20.     Current floor: {state.appData.floor}
21.     <ul>
22.         <li className="mb-2">
23.           <button onClick={() => setFloor(1)} className=»bg-
  blue-500 hover:bg-blue-700 text-white font-bold py-2 px-4 rounded»>
24.             Floor 1
25.           </button>
26.         </li>
27.         <li className="mb-2">
28.           <button onClick={() => setFloor(2)} className=»bg-
  blue-500 hover:bg-blue-700 text-white font-bold py-2 px-4 rounded»>
29.             Floor 2
30.           </button>
31.         </li>
32.         <li className="mb-2">
33.           <button onClick={() => setFloor(3)} className=»bg-
  blue-500 hover:bg-blue-700 text-white font-bold py-2 px-4 rounded»>
34.             Floor 3
35.           </button>
36.         </li>
37.     </ul>
38.     <div className="mt-4">
39.       Smile object manipulation:
40.       <ul className="mt-4">
41.         <li>
42.           <label htmlFor="scale" className="block mb-2 text-sm font-
  medium text-gray-900">Smile scale</label>
43.           <input id="scale"
44.                 value={/*3*/rangeValue}
45.                 onChange={/*4*/(event) => setRange(event.target.
  value)}
```

```
46.                  step=»0.1»
47.                  min=»0.5»
48.                  max=»2»
49.                  type=»range»
50.                  className=»w-full h-2 bg-gray-200 rounded-
    lg appearance-none cursor-pointer «
51.              />
52.            </li>
53.          </ul>
54.        </div>
55.      </div>
56.    )
57. }
```

Code Listing 16.10: Update for the HTML UI controls

We made numbered anchors in *Code Listing 16.10* to make the explanations clearer:

- /*1*/ At this point, we create the function to set the range value locally in the current component. We just do not update the context and use the context value. If we do so, we will create an uncontrollable state change for the range slider, and React will break in issue at this point. Thus, the correct usage will be to change the value in the local state and then, on change, push this data into context.

- /*2*/ We will follow the local state changes to push them into context. Yes, we could do that in one function with local changes, but we do not know the component scale at this point, and safer to separate them.

- /*3*/ Here, we initialize the range slider value with local state data.

- /*4*/ And on value change, we call the function from point /*1*/.

Finally, we need to put the object on the page to see changes:

```
1.  'use client';
2.  import React, { useContext, useState, useEffect, Suspense } from
    'react';
3.  import { Canvas } from '@react-three/fiber';
4.  import { Environment } from '@react-three/drei';
5.  import { BoxModel } from '@/components/BoxModel';
6.  import { PresentationControls, PerspectiveCamera } from
    '@react-three/drei';
7.  import { AppDataContext } from './data-provider';
8.  import Controls from '@/components/Controls';
9.  import { Smile } from '@/components/Smile';
10. import { cameraPositions, cameraAngles} from "./defaults";
11.
```

```
12. export default function Boxes() {
13.     const { state, actions } = useContext(AppDataContext);
14.
15.     const [cameraAngle, setCameraAngle] = useState(cameraAngles[0]);
16.     const [cameraPosition, setCameraPosition] =
    useState(cameraPositions[0]);
17.     const [smileProperties, setSmileProperties] =
    useState(smileProps[0]);
18.
19.     useEffect(() => {
20.       setCameraAngle(cameraAngles[state.appData.floor - 1]);
21.       setCameraPosition(cameraPositions[state.appData.floor - 1]);
22.       /*1*/setSmileProperties(smileProps[state.appData.floor - 1]);
23.     }, [state.appData.floor]);
24.
25.     return (
26.       <main className="h-screen">
27.           <div className="flex h-screen w-full gap-2 ">
28.             <div className="w-[50%]">
29.               <Canvas shadows flat dpr={[2, 2]}
30.     camera={{ fov: 25, position: [20, 20, 20] }}>
31.                 <Suspense fallback={null}>
32.                   <PresentationControls snap global
    rotation={cameraAngle} >
33.                     <PerspectiveCamera position={cameraPosition}>
34.                       <BoxModel />
35./*2*/<Smile {...smileProperties} />
36.                       <Environment preset="dawn" background />
37.                     </PerspectiveCamera>
38.                   </PresentationControls>
39.                 </Suspense>
40.               </Canvas>
41.             </div>
42.             <div>
43.               <h1>Controls</h1>
44.               <Controls />
45.             </div>
46.           </div>
47.       </main>
48.     )
49. }
```

Code Listing 16.11: Update for the page component

We made numbered anchors in *Code Listing 16.11* to make the explanations clearer:

- /*1*/ At this point, we set new values for the smile position on each floor change.
- /*2*/ Here, we implement the smile object.

In the end, we will have a picture like in *Figure 16.6 (a)*, *(b)*, and *(c)* where on each floor change the smile object will appear on the selected floor. Also, the range slider will give us the possibility to change the scale of it:

Figure 16.6 (a): Smile object position on the first floor of the building

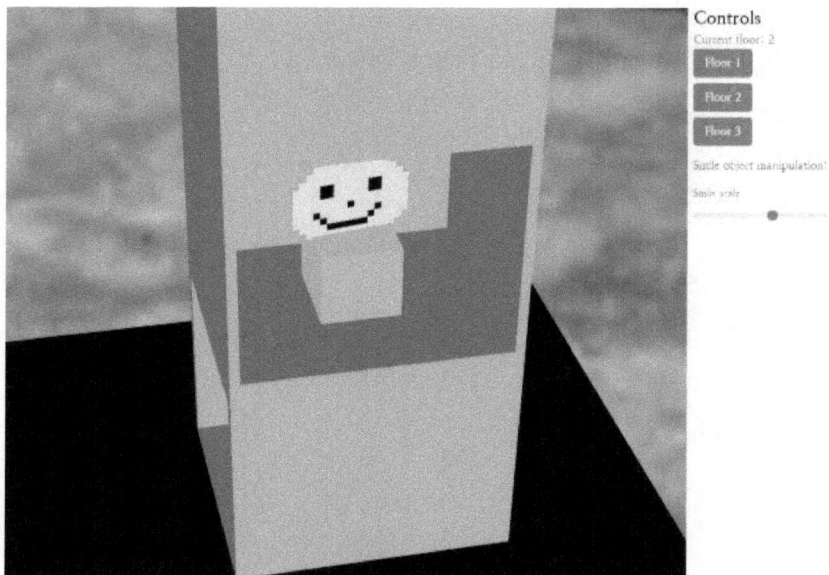

Figure 16.6 (b): Smile object position on the second floor of the building

Figure 16.6 (c): *Smile object position on the third floor of the building*

Interactive UI elements

It is great to have an HTML UI element in our application, but if we need to create 3D UI objects that will be able to make the same actions, we will add 3D arrows that will change the floor number and camera position, the same as the UI buttons we made before.

We will follow the previous recommendation and use the **gltfjsx** library one more time to generate the component. We will take a small object with an arrow to the left and right and put it on the selected floor. To add the objects, we will need to make the following changes:

- Add default values in **defaults.js** (*Code Listing 16.12*)
- Add component **Arrow.jsx** (*Code Listing 16.13*)
- Add objects to the **page** (*Code Listing 16.14*)

Let us start with default values and update the **defaults.js** file:

```
1.  const cameraAngles = [
2.      [0, 2, 0],
3.      [0, 1, 0],
4.      [0, -0.5, 0],
5.  ];
6.
7.  const cameraPositions = [
8.      [0, 0, 0],
9.      [0, -3, 0],
```

```
10.      [0, -6, 0]
11. ];
12.
13. const smileProps = [
14.      {
15.          position: [-0.3, 2, -0.2],
16.          rotation: [Math.PI, 2, 0],
17.      },
18.      {
19.          position: [0.5, 6.5, 0],
20.          rotation: [Math.PI, 3, 0],
21.      },
22.      {
23.          position: [1, 11.5, -0.1],
24.          rotation: [Math.PI, 2, 0],
25.      }
26. ];
27.
28. const arrowProps = {
29.      left: [
30.          {
31.              position: [-5, 2, 3],
32.              rotation: [Math.PI / 2, Math.PI / 2, Math.PI / 2]
33.          },
34.          {
35.              position: [3, 6.5, 3],
36.              rotation: [0, 0 , 0]
37.          },
38.          {
39.              position: [5, 12, -2],
40.              rotation: [-Math.PI / 2, Math.PI / 2, Math.PI / 2]
41.          }
42.      ],
43.      right: [
44.          {
45.              position: [-5, 2, -2],
46.              rotation: [-Math.PI / 2, Math.PI / 2, Math.PI / 2]
47.          },
48.          {
49.              position: [-1.5, 6.5, 3],
50.              rotation: [0, -Math.PI , 0]
51.          },
52.          {
53.              position: [5, 11, 2.5],
```

```
54.             rotation: [Math.PI / 2, Math.PI / 2, Math.PI / 2]
55.         }
56.     ]
57. };
58.
59. export {arrowProps, smileProps, cameraPositions, cameraAngles};
```

Code Listing 16.12: Default values update with arrow positions

The next step is to add the arrow object. We will use the same object for the left and right arrows, with one difference: the rotation value.

```
1.  import React, { useRef } from 'react';
2.  import { useGLTF } from '@react-three/drei';
3.
4.  export function Arrow(props) {
5.    const { nodes, materials } = useGLTF('/arrow.glb');
6.
7.    return (
8.      <group dispose={null}>
9.        <animated.mesh castShadow geometry={nodes.Untitled.geometry}
10.                rotation={props.rotation}
11.                position={props.position}
12.                scale={1}
13.            >
14.                <meshStandardMaterial
15.                  metalness={1}
16.                  roughness={0.8}
17.                  color={"#0088ee"}
18.                />
19.        </animated.mesh>
20.      </group>
21.    )
22. }
23.
24. useGLTF.preload('/arrow.glb');
```

Code Listing 16.13: Arrow object

Finally, we need to add these objects to the scene and update the page component:

```
1.  'use client';
2.  import React, { useContext, useState, useEffect, Suspense } from
    'react';
3.  import { Canvas } from '@react-three/fiber';
4.  import { Environment } from '@react-three/drei';
```

```
 5. import { BoxModel } from '@/components/BoxModel';
 6. import { PresentationControls, PerspectiveCamera } from
    '@react-three/drei';
 7. import { AppDataContext } from './data-provider';
 8. import Controls from '@/components/Controls';
 9. import { Smile } from '@/components/Smile';
10. import { Arrow } from '@/components/Arrow';
11. import { A11yAnnouncer, A11y } from '@react-three/a11y';
12. import {arrowProps, smileProps, cameraPositions, cameraAngles} from
    "./defaults";
13.
14. export default function Boxes() {
15.     const { state, actions } = useContext(AppDataContext);
16.
17.     const [cameraAngle, setCameraAngle] = useState(cameraAngles[0]);
18.     const [cameraPosition, setCameraPosition] =
    useState(cameraPositions[0]);
19.     const [smileProperties, setSmileProperties] =
    useState(smileProps[0]);
20.     const [leftArrowProperties, setLeftArrowProperties] =
    useState(arrowProps.left[0]);
21.     const [rightArrowProperties, setRightArrowProperties] =
    useState(arrowProps.right[0]);
22.
23.   useEffect(() => {
24.       setCameraAngle(cameraAngles[state.appData.floor - 1]);
25.       setCameraPosition(cameraPositions[state.appData.floor - 1]);
26.       setSmileProperties(smileProps[state.appData.floor - 1]);
27.       setLeftArrowProperties(arrowProps.left[state.appData.floor - 1]);
28.       setRightArrowProperties(arrowProps.right[state.appData.floor - 1]);
29.   }, [state.appData.floor]);
30.
31.   return (
32.     <main className="h-screen">
33.       <div className="flex h-screen w-full gap-2 ">
34.         <div className="w-[50%]">
35.           <Canvas shadows  flat dpr={[2, 2]}
    camera={{ fov: 25, position: [20, 20, 20] }}>
36.             <Suspense fallback={null}>
37.               <PresentationControls snap global
    rotation={cameraAngle} >
38.                 <PerspectiveCamera position={cameraPosition}>
39.                   <BoxModel />
```

```
40.                          <Smile {...smileProperties} />
41.                      <Arrow position={leftArrowProperties?.position}
     rotation={leftArrowProperties?.rotation}/>
42.                      <Arrow position={rightArrowProperties?.position}
     rotation={rightArrowProperties?.rotation} />
43.                  <Environment preset="dawn" background />
44.                  </PerspectiveCamera>
45.                  </PresentationControls>
46.              </Suspense>
47.            </Canvas>
48.            <A11yAnnouncer />
49.          </div>
50.          <div>
51.            <h1>Controls</h1>
52.            <Controls />
53.          </div>
54.        </div>
55.      </main>
56.    )
57. }
```

Code Listing 16.14: *Implement arrow elements in the scene*

As a result, we will see arrow elements, as shown in *Figure 16.7*:

Figure 16.7: *Arrow elements on the scene*

For interactivity, we can use the same functionality on the smile object when clicking. There is one more possibility of creating clickable elements in the scene. It will also be covered in Web Accessibility.

Accessibility and inclusive user interactions and control

Web Content Accessibility Guidelines (WCAG) is a set of guidelines and standards developed by the **World Wide Web Consortium (W3C)** to ensure that web content is accessible to people with disabilities. The main goal of WCAG is to make web content more perceivable, operable, understandable, and robust for all users, including those with disabilities.

WCAG provides a framework for web developers, designers, content creators, and other stakeholders to follow when creating or updating web content. It covers a wide range of accessibility issues and provides techniques and best practices for addressing them.

In our example, we will need several elements of the WCAG standards:

- Voice announcer to announce the focused element.
- Button elements that will exist in the 3D scene.

We will use another helper library for it called **React Three A11y,** which can be collected from this repository **https://github.com/pmndrs/react-three-a11y.** This must be added to the project with **npm** or **yarn.** This library will give us the possibility to add these functionalities to our scene:

- Focus and focus indication
- Tab index and keyboard navigation
- Screen reader support and alt-text
- Roles and cursor shapes
- Descriptive links

In the previous block, we made a scene with 3D buttons. Our next step will be to turn objects into buttons and add some functionality to them. The updated code for the page can be collected in *Code Listing 16.15* and *Code Listing 16.16* for the arrow object:

```
1. 'use client';
2. import React, { useContext, useState, useEffect, Suspense } from
   'react';
3. import { Canvas } from '@react-three/fiber';
4. import { Environment } from '@react-three/drei';
5. import { BoxModel } from '@/components/BoxModel';
```

```
6.  import { PresentationControls, PerspectiveCamera } from
    '@react-three/drei';
7.  import { AppDataContext } from './data-provider';
8.  import Controls from '@/components/Controls';
9.  import { Smile } from '@/components/Smile';
10. import { Arrow } from '@/components/Arrow';
11. import { A11yAnnouncer, A11y } from '@react-three/a11y';
12. import {arrowProps, smileProps, cameraPositions, cameraAngles} from
    "./defaults";
13.
14. export default function Boxes() {
15.     const { state, actions } = useContext(AppDataContext);
16.
17.     const [cameraAngle, setCameraAngle] = useState(cameraAngles[0]);
18.     const [cameraPosition, setCameraPosition] =
    useState(cameraPositions[0]);
19.     const [smileProperties, setSmileProperties] =
    useState(smileProps[0]);
20.     const [leftArrowProperties, setLeftArrowProperties] =
useState(arrowProps.left[0]);
21.     const [rightArrowProperties, setRightArrowProperties] =
    useState(arrowProps.right[0]);
22.
23.
24.     /*1*/const setFloor = (toRight) => {
25.       let floor = state.appData.floor;
26.       if(toRight && floor < 3) {
27.         floor +=1;
28.       }
29.       else if(toRight && floor === 3) {
30.         floor = 1;
31.       }
32.       else if(!toRight && floor >= 2) {
33.         floor -=1;
34.       }
35.       else if(!toRight && floor === 1) {
36.         floor = 3;
37.       }
38.       actions.setAppData({...state.appData, ...{floor}});
39.     }
40.
```

```
41.    useEffect(() => {
42.       setCameraAngle(cameraAngles[state.appData.floor - 1]);
43.       setCameraPosition(cameraPositions[state.appData.floor - 1]);
44.       setSmileProperties(smileProps[state.appData.floor - 1]);
45.       setLeftArrowProperties(arrowProps.left[state.appData.floor - 1]);
46.       setRightArrowProperties(arrowProps.right[state.appData.floor - 1]);
47.    }, [state.appData.floor]);
48.
49.    return (
50.       <main className="h-screen">
51.          <div className="flex h-screen w-full gap-2 ">
52.             <div className="w-[50%]">
53.                <Canvas shadows  flat dpr={[2, 2]} camera={{ fov: 25,
       position: [20, 20, 20] }}>
54.                   <Suspense fallback={null}>
55.                      <PresentationControls snap global
       rotation={cameraAngle} >
56.                         <PerspectiveCamera position={cameraPosition}>
57.                            <BoxModel />
58.                            <Smile {...smileProperties} />
59.                            /*2*/<A11y role="button" tabIndex={0}
       actionCall={() => {setFloor(true)}}>
60.                               <Arrow position={leftArrowProperties?.position}
61.          rotation={leftArrowProperties?.rotation}/>
62.                            </A11y>
63.                            <A11y role="button" tabIndex={1} actionCall={()
       => {setFloor(false)}}>
64.                               <Arrow position={rightArrowProperties?.position}
65.                                  rotation={rightArrowProperties?.rotation} />
66.                            </A11y>
67.                            <Environment preset="dawn" background />
68.                         </PerspectiveCamera>
69.                      </PresentationControls>
70.                   </Suspense>
71.                </Canvas>
72.                /*3*/<A11yAnnouncer />
73.             </div>
74.             <div>
75.                <h1>Controls</h1>
76.                <Controls />
77.             </div>
```

```
78.              </div>
79.          </main>
80.      )
81. }
```

Code Listing 16.15: Updated code for the page

We made numbered anchors in *Code Listing 16.15* to make the explanations clearer:

- /*1*/ This is a basic logic for the floor changing. We could use the same logic for the buttons, but in the case of arrows, we do not have the information for what floor the current button is working by default. This logic is too complex. In the exercise part, we will reduce the complexity of this function. There are several ways to solve it, using an array.

- /*2*/ This is a special wrapper that turns a 3D object into any WCAG-valid element. It has several important parameters:

  o **role**: Stands for the current role of the element. It can be content, button (or toggle), or the link.

  o **tabindex**: Is taking the queue number. It means we could set what element would be focused next on each *Tab* button press.

  o **actionCall**: This is what we needed in the previous block. It is a function that will be called on clicking or pressing the Enter button on the keyboard. (Note that we do not need to make a specific action for the keyboard here. The library makes this automatically.

- /*3*/ This is the special announcement component that will trigger a voice announcement for each component.

We will also require some minor changes in the arrow object, as we now have a focus on the element and need to indicate which object is in focus:

```
1.  import React, { useRef } from 'react';
2.  import { useGLTF } from '@react-three/drei';
3.  import { useA11y } from "@react-three/a11y";
4.
5.
6.  export function Arrow(props) {
7.    const { nodes, materials } = useGLTF('/arrow.glb');
8.    const a11y = useA11y();
9.    return (
10.     <group dispose={null}>
11.       <animated.mesh castShadow geometry={nodes.Untitled.geometry}
12.             rotation={props.rotation}
```

```
13.           position={props.position}
14.           scale={1}
15.        >
16.          <meshStandardMaterial
17.            metalness={1}
18.            roughness={0.8}
19.            color={"#0088ee"}
20.            /*1*/emissive={a11y.focus ? «#cc4444" : a11y.
     hover ? «#44bb44" : «#0088ee"}
21.          />
22.      </animated.mesh>
23.      </group>
24.    )
25. }
```

Code Listing 16.16: Updated code for the arrow object

We made numbered anchors in *Code Listing 16.16* to make the explanation clearer:

- /*1*/ This parameter sets a material color for the focus and hover actions. When we start the project, we will see that hover material will take colors from this parameter, and on tab focus also.

Adding transitions using React Spring

The last thing we will do in this chapter is add a small animation to our arrows. As we have already made all the required functionality, we will make the arrow bounce on the hover action. We will use the React Spring library. To add it to our project, we will use this command (as we need three.js support):

```
npm install three @react-spring/three
or yarn add three @react-spring/three
```

React Spring is a JavaScript library used to create animations in React applications. It is built on top of the Spring physics-based animation library, providing a simple and flexible API for animating components and elements in React. It can be used for:

- **Physics-based animations**: React Spring utilizes a physics-based animation system, which allows for more natural and fluid animations compared to traditional linear or easing-based animations. This system simulates real-world physics principles such as mass, spring force, and friction, resulting in animations that feel more lifelike.

- **Interpolations**: The library supports interpolating animated values, allowing developers to smoothly transition between different states or values over time.

This can be particularly useful for creating complex animations with multiple components or properties that need to be synchronized.

- **Hooks and components**: React Spring provides hooks and components that integrate seamlessly with React functional components and class components. These include hooks like **useSpring**, **useTransition**, and **useTrail**, as well as components like **<Spring>**, **<Transition>**, and **<Trail>**, which make it easy to add animations to React applications with minimal boilerplate code.

To add it, follow the updated code in *Code Listing 16.17:*

```
1.  import React, { useRef } from 'react';
2.  import { useGLTF } from '@react-three/drei';
3.  import { useA11y } from "@react-three/a11y";
4.  import { useSpring, animated } from '@react-spring/three';
5.
6.  export function Arrow(props) {
7.    const { nodes, materials } = useGLTF('/arrow.glb');
8.    const a11y = useA11y();
9.
10.   /*1*/ const [springs, api] = useSpring(
11.     () => ({
12.       scale: 1,
13.       config: key => {
14.         switch (key) {
15.           case 'scale':
16.             return {
17.               mass: 1,
18.               friction: 3,
19.             }
20.           default:
21.             return {}
22.         }
23.       },
24.     }),
25.     []
26.   )
27.
28.   /*1*/ const handlePointerEnter = () => {
29.     api.start({
30.       scale: 1.1,
31.     })
32.   }
33.
```

```
34.  /*2*/ const handlePointerLeave = () => {
35.     api.start({
36.        scale: 1,
37.     })
38.  }
39.
40.  return (
41.     <group dispose={null}>
42.        <animated.mesh castShadow geometry={nodes.Untitled.geometry}
43.             rotation={props.rotation}
44.             position={props.position}
45.             /*3*/ scale={springs.scale}
46.             /*4*/ onPointerEnter={handlePointerEnter}
47.             /*4*/ onPointerLeave={handlePointerLeave}
48.          >
49.             <meshStandardMaterial
50.                metalness={1}
51.                roughness={0.8}
52.                color={"#0088ee"}
53.                emissive={a11y.focus ? «#cc4444" : a11y.
     hover ? «#44bb44" : «#0088ee"}
54.             />
55.        </animated.mesh>
56.     </group>
57.  )
58. }
59.
60. useGLTF.preload('/arrow.glb');
```

Code Listing 16.17: Updated code for the arrow object with animation

We made numbered anchors in *Code Listing 16.17* to make the explanations clearer:

- /*1*/ This is the most important part, here we create the hook with parameters that will be used and animated in the object. We do not change the object physically, but change the values. We set the scale value. Scale value is just a variable name, so it is not linked to a real scale and can be named any name we like. After that, we set the animation for the key to be used. It is needed in case we have several objects and need to have different animations for them. Mass and friction parameters are part of the animation. Mass means how physically heavy the object is and how friction is related to the bouncing process.

- /*2*/ We set the functions that align the new state with the action. If we hover the object, we increase the scale to a 1.1 value. It will smoothly change the value depending on the mass value from the configuration. The backward process is working the same way.

- /*3*/ We align the property of the Spring object as a scale value. It will be changed on each mouse hover and out.

- /*4*/ We align what function will be triggered on the mouse enter and leave the event. After that, we will trigger the animation process from point /*2*/.

As a result, we will see a bouncing animation on each mouse enter and leave event for the arrow objects.

Conclusion

This chapter has provided a comprehensive exploration of implementing interactive controls, object manipulation, UI elements, accessibility considerations, and transitions in Three.js applications.

We began by delving into camera controls and navigation techniques, enabling users to navigate smoothly through 3D scenes. We then explored object manipulation and transformations, allowing users to interact with and dynamically modify objects within the scene.

The chapter also covered the integration of interactive UI elements, enhancing user engagement, and providing intuitive controls for various functionalities. Additionally, we discussed the importance of accessibility and inclusive user interactions, ensuring that our applications are accessible to all users. Furthermore, we explored how to add smooth transitions and animations using React Spring, enhancing the visual appeal and user experience of our Three.js applications.

In the next chapter, we will discuss the critical aspects of performance profiling and debugging in a Three.js application. We will explore performance monitoring tools that help identify bottlenecks, examine strategies for optimizing application performance across various devices, and address mobile performance considerations. Additionally, we will discuss ensuring browser compatibility, testing applications effectively, and wrapping up with best practices to maintain a high-performing and robust web 3D project.

Points to remember

- Creating the scene is a hard process. In our example, we made it very precise just to learn the basics. In a real example, we can take a longer time just to align the camera angle correctly.

- As we can use HTML UI objects, it means that we could use any third-party libraries to create any kind of required UI to manage the 3D object.

- WCAG is an important topic, you should read and learn the basics; it will be useful in real-life projects.

Exercises

For the current application, make the following improvements to your skills:

1. Create the math functionality for the objects to calculate position and rotation angle to get rid of hardcoded values.

2. Remove the environment object and create the lights and shadows for your scene using knowledge from previous chapters.

3. Create an array of buttons instead of a hardcoded list.

4. Reduce the complexity of the changing floor algorithm. Use any logic from your experience (changing an image in a gallery with an array, for example).

5. Add more animation to your scene by adding bouncing to the smile object.

Join our Discord space

Join our Discord workspace for latest updates, offers, tech happenings around the world, new releases, and sessions with the authors:

https://discord.bpbonline.com

CHAPTER 17
Optimization and Performance Consideration

Introduction

Optimization is crucial in ensuring React applications' smooth and efficient functioning. Optimizing their performance as applications grow in complexity and scale becomes increasingly important to deliver a seamless user experience. In this chapter, we will explore the fundamentals of optimization techniques in React Fiber and study the significance of optimizing React applications for better performance.

Structure

In this chapter, we will discuss the following topics:

- Performance profiling and debugging
- Application performance
- Mobile performance
- Browser compatibility
- Testing the application

Objectives

By the end of this chapter, we will gain a solid understanding and hands-on experience in key topics such as component reusability, component memorization, performance profiling, and debugging. Additionally, we will explore important considerations for optimizing application performance, particularly on mobile devices, ensuring a smoother and more efficient user experience across platforms.

Performance profiling and debugging

Performance profiling involves analyzing the execution time and resource usage of different parts of our application to identify performance bottlenecks. Profiling React applications can pinpoint areas that consume excessive CPU, memory, or network resources and optimize them for better performance.

Debugging involves identifying and fixing issues or bugs in our application that may impact performance. This includes identifying unnecessary re-renders, inefficient data fetching, or poorly optimized components. Debugging tools such as **React DevTools** and **Chrome DevTools** provide insights into component lifecycles, state changes, and performance metrics, allowing us to diagnose and fix performance issues efficiently.

To get deep into both topics we will require some tools to help us get information from the scene. We will start with performance.

Performance monitoring tools

As we work with Canvas, we will need some tools that will show how many resources we use at the moment. We need to know these resource usages:

- **CPU**: Central processing unit
- **GPU**: Graphics processing unit
- System memory

Stats

First, we can use a helper already in the **Drei** plugin that we used to have helpers for the React Fiber. This helper is named **Stats**. The Stats helper is a component that will create the screen's special layout with performance information. To see it in action, we will create a new page.

On this page, we must create the object to measure performance. If we just put the object on the page, it will not produce much performance information.

To check this functionality, we will add code from *Code Listing 17.1* to the newly created page. Please ensure that you have made all the installations from *Chapter 13, Introduction to Next.js and Three.js Integration.* In *Chapter 13,* you will find out how to install Drei and Fiber packages:

```
1.  'use client';
2.  import { OrbitControls } from "@react-three/drei";
3.  import { Canvas, useFrame } from "@react-three/fiber";
4.  import { useRef } from "react";
5.
6.
7.  const Box = () => {
8.      const ref = useRef();
9.      useFrame((_, delta) => {
10.         ref.current.rotation.x += 1 * delta;
11.         ref.current.rotation.y += 0.5 * delta;
12.     });
13.
14.     return (
15.         <mesh ref={ref}>
16.             <boxGeometry args={[2, 2, 2]}/>
17.             <meshStandardMaterial/>
18.         </mesh>
19.     );
20. };
21.
22. export default function Optimisation() {
23.     return (
24.         <main className="m-auto h-screen">
25.             <Canvas>
26.                 <ambientLight intensity={0.1} />
27.                 <directionalLight color="red" position={[0, 0, 5]} />
28.                 <Box />
29.                 <OrbitControls />
30.             </Canvas>
31.         </main>
32.     );
33. }
```

Code Listing 17.1: Starter code for adding optimization

As mentioned earlier, just adding the object to the page will not produce much performance. To check the performance, we need to add some actions. For example, we will add a simple animation by following these steps:

1. To add animation, we will need the **useRef** hook. This hook will wrap the **requestAnimationFrame** function that we used in the previous part of the book.

2. Next, we can add the **Stats** from **Drei,** and it will be very simple. We use *Code Listing 17.2* to add the **Stats** to the page:

```
1.  'use client';
2.  {/*code from Code Listing 17.1*/}
3.  import { Stats } from '@react-three/drei';
4.
5.
6.  const Box = () => {
7.  {/*code from Code Listing 17.1*/}
8.  export default function Optimisation() {
9.      return (
10.         <main className="m-auto h-screen">
11.             <Canvas>
12.                 {/*code from Code Listing 17.1*/}
13.                 <Stats />
14.             </Canvas>
15.         </main>
16.     );
17. }
```

Code Listing 17.2: Update code to add Stats (lines 3 and 13)

3. The result will be the same as shown in *Figure 17.1*. We will see the tool in the top left corner:

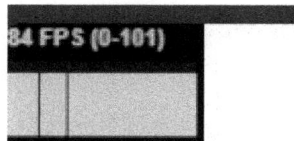

Figure 17.1: Result after adding the component to the page

R3-Perf

Another useful tool that we can use is a library called **R3-Perf**. This library can be collected by the link **https://github.com/utsuboco/r3f-perf.** To add it to the project, use this command:

```
npm install r3f-perf --save-dev or yarn add install r3f-perf --save-dev
```

Next, we can put it into the scene as a component. An example of the code can be seen in *Code Listing 17.3:*

```
1.  'use client';
2.  {/*old code*/}
3.  import { Perf } from 'r3f-perf';
4.
5.  const Box = () => {
6.  {/*old code*/}
7.
8.  export default function Optimisation() {
9.      return (
10.         <main className="m-auto h-screen">
11.             <Canvas>
12.                 {/*old code*/}
13.                 <Perf position="top-right" />
14.             </Canvas>
15.         </main>
16.     );
17. }
```

Code Listing 17.3: Update code to add R3-Perf (lines 3 and 13)

This library will provide us with more information than Stats. It has the following points:

- GPU information
- CPU information
- FPS information
- Number of calls that are helpful in debugging
- Number of triangles on the page (as any object is made with triangles)
- Number of geometries on page
- Number of textures on the page
- Number of shaders on page
- Number of lines
- Number of points

The result can be seen in *Figure 17.2*:

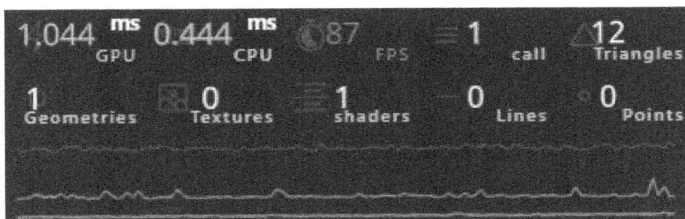

Figure 17.2: Result after adding the component to the page

As we can see, it has maximum information to help us measure and debug the performance of the scene.

Spector.js

Another useful tool to debug WebGL applications is a Chrome (or Firefox) extension, **Spector.js** **(https://chromewebstore.google.com/detail/ denbgaamihkadbghdceggmchnflmhpmk).**

This extension makes a recording of the canvas and provides all the required information with all possible screenshots. The performance tools that we used before also create the canvas, so to avoid confusion, they need to be removed from the scene if this extension is used.

One more thing to consider is that this tool is not **React Three Fiber** (**R3F**) or Three.js related; it is a WebGL debugging tool used when we see a possibility of finding an issue at this level. An example of the result screen can be seen in *Figure 17.3*:

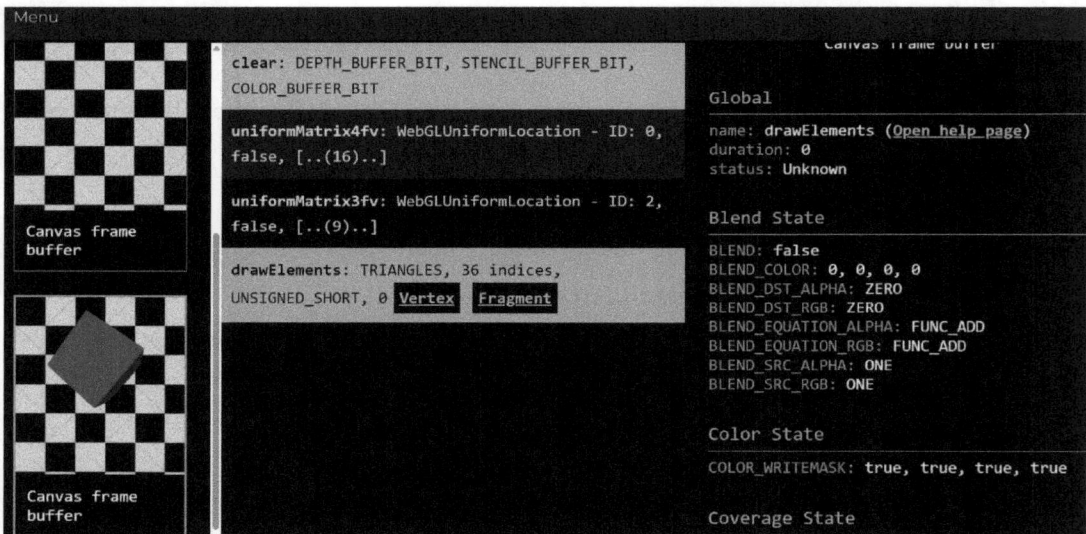

Figure 17.3: Debug page for Spector.js extension

The extension itself is very powerful but not simple. Let us try to understand its possibilities.

- The first useful information we can get is a stack trace to understand which function made a call to render and from which file. With R3F, we will see links to the library, but in the case of using pure Three.js or other tools, the result will be different. An example can be seen in *Figure 17.4*:

```
Stack Trace

0: WebGLIndexedBufferRenderer.render (webpack-internal:///(app-pages-browser)/../../node_modules/t
hree/build/three.module.js:11742:12)
1: WebGLRenderer.renderBufferDirect (webpack-internal:///(app-pages-browser)/../../node_modules/th
ree/build/three.module.js:18832:26)
2: renderObject (webpack-internal:///(app-pages-browser)/../../node_modules/three/build/three.modu
le.js:19201:23)
3: renderObjects (webpack-internal:///(app-pages-browser)/../../node_modules/three/build/three.mod
ule.js:19183:21)
4: renderScene (webpack-internal:///(app-pages-browser)/../../node_modules/three/build/three.modul
e.js:19099:43)
5: WebGLRenderer.render (webpack-internal:///(app-pages-browser)/../../node_modules/three/build/th
ree.module.js:19005:17)
6: render$1 (webpack-internal:///(app-pages-browser)/../../node_modules/@react-three/fiber/dist/in
dex-8afac004.esm.js:1586:61)
7: loop (webpack-internal:///(app-pages-browser)/../../node_modules/@react-three/fiber/dist/index-
8afac004.esm.js:1610:19)
```

Figure 17.4: *Stack trace information from the extension*

- Another useful information will be if we use shaders. In this case, we will see the special block with information about it and a link to the source code of the shader itself. The example can be seen in *Figure 17.5* and *Figure 17.6*:

```
Shaders(1)

shader: WebGLShader - ID: 15
COMPILE_STATUS: true
DELETE_STATUS: true
SHADER_TYPE: FRAGMENT_SHADER
source: Click to Open.
```

Figure 17.5: *Shader's information in the extension*

Clicking on the **Click to Open** link will lead to the shader code that is presented in *Figure 17.6*:

```
#version 300 es
#define NUM_BONE_INFLUENCERS 0

precision highp float;
precision highp int;
in vec3 vNormalV;
in vec4 vViewPos;
#ifdef ALPHATEST
    in vec2 vUV;
    uniform sampler2D diffuseSampler;
#endif
layout(location = 0) out vec4 color0;
layout(location = 1) out vec4 color1;
void main() {
    #ifdef ALPHATEST
        if (texture(diffuseSampler, vUV).a<0.4)
        discard;
    #endif
    color0 = vec4(vViewPos.z/vViewPos.w, 0.0, 0.0, 0.0);
    color1 = vec4(normalize(vNormalV), 1.0);
}
```

Figure 17.6: *Shaders source code*

Application performance

Since we now have all the tools to monitor and debug our scenes, we can proceed with using React to increase the performance of our animated scenes. As done previously, we can use React Spring or any other animation tools. This way of using animation is optimized by default in case our animation is controllable by the user. If our scene is an animation by default and should act on interactions while the animation is changing the state, we should use the **useFrame**. In this case, the animation is working by default. Using multiple objects on the scene can lead to uncontrollable results and a lack of performance. In this section, we will find out how to cover such cases and fix possible issues with performance.

The techniques that we will use in this block are not the ultimate solution, and we should first use debugging tools to find out the real problem.

Let us take an example from *Code Listing 17.3*, where we had a box object on the scene and also a performance monitor to check the changes.

useMemo

The first technique to increase application performance is using the **useMemo** hook to initialize the geometry. This method allows us to not only save some memory but also help to change the geometry itself without hard usage of the memory in our components. Changes for the code are introduced in *Code Listing 17.4*:

```
1.  import * as THREE from 'three';
2.
3.  const Box = memo( ({ position }) => {
4.      {/* old code here */}
5.      const geometry = useMemo(() => new THREE.BoxGeometry(), []);
6.      {/* old code here */}
7.
8.      return (
9.          <mesh ref={ref} position={position} geometry={geometry}>
10.             <meshStandardMaterial/>
11.         </mesh>
12.     );
13. });
```

Code Listing 17.4: Usage of the useMemo hook

As we can see, on *lines 1* and *5*, we use a direct call of the geometry from the Three.js library and cache it in the page cache. It means that we will not re-render any geometry, even if we re-render the whole component or even the page.

The next react-related update will be wrapping the component itself in **React.memo** function. That will also save us from re-rendering actions if we do not change anything in props or components themselves.

While the **useMemo** hook in React can improve performance by avoiding unnecessary recalculations, it's not a one-size-fits-all solution, especially in the context of Three.js applications using **@react-three/fiber**.

In Three.js, scenes often depend on continuous updates and dynamic values. Animations, user interactions, and physics-based changes typically occur on every frame. In these cases, applying useMemo too aggressively can lead to confusing code without any meaningful performance improvement.

Imagine you're building a particle system where the position of each particle changes every frame based on velocity, gravity, or user interaction. If you wrap the particle data in **useMemo** thinking it'll optimize the system, you'll lock the data and prevent it from updating correctly. The values inside **useMemo** are only recalculated when their dependencies change, which might not happen every frame. This leads to stale values and broken behavior.

Moreover, even in less dynamic cases, if the calculation is cheap (like setting a simple color or vector), memoizing it adds unnecessary complexity without noticeable gain. React's rendering is already fast; unless profiling shows a bottleneck, it's better to keep the logic straightforward.

useMemo is best reserved for static or semi-static values—like geometry definitions, configuration objects, or textures that don't change frequently. For example, if you're creating a custom geometry once and reusing it across re-renders, memoizing it can prevent re-instantiation and save memory.

Note: **Use useMemo for expensive calculations or large static objects.**

Avoid it for values that change every frame or rely on animation.

useCallback

Another update for the component will be using the **useCallback** hook for the animation changes. This will save some bytes of code in memory as well. The **useCallback** hook is used to memorize a callback function, ensuring that the function does not get recreated unnecessarily during re-renders. This helps prevent unintended behavior and improves performance by isolating the function from changes unless its dependencies explicitly change. It is very helpful while doing actions in parallel with animation, like clicking on an object. This is what we will add to our scene. Clicking on the box will lead to changing the geometry to a **torus**. The source code for these changes is shown in *Code Listing 17.5*:

```
1.  'use client';
2.  import { OrbitControls } from "@react-three/drei";
3.  import { Canvas, useFrame } from "@react-three/fiber";
4.  import { Perf } from 'r3f-perf';
5.  import { memo, useCallback, useMemo, useRef, useState } from "react";
6.  import * as THREE from 'three';
7.
8.  const Box = memo( ({ position }) => {
```

```
9.      const ref = useRef();
10.     const [currentGeometry, setCurrentGeometry] = useState(0);
11.     const geometry = useMemo(
12.       () =>  [
13.           new THREE.BoxGeometry(),
14.           new THREE.TorusGeometry(1)],
15.     []);
16.
17.     const updateRotation = useCallback((delta) => {
18.         ref.current.rotation.x += 1 * delta;
19.         ref.current.rotation.y += 0.5 * delta;
20.     }, []);
21.
22.     useFrame((_, delta) => {
23.         updateRotation(delta);
24.     });
25.
26.     return (
27.         <mesh ref={ref}
28.               position={position}
29.               geometry={geometry[currentGeometry]}
30.               onClick={() => currentGeometry === 0 ?
    setCurrentGeometry(1) : setCurrentGeometry(0)}
31.         >
32.             <meshStandardMaterial/>
33.         </mesh>
34.     );
35. });
36. Box.displayName = 'Box';
37.
38. export default function Optimisation() {
39.     return (
40.         <main className="m-auto h-screen">
41.             <Canvas>
42.                 <ambientLight intensity={0.1} />
43.                 <directionalLight color="red" position={[0, 0, 5]} />
44.                 <Box position={[1, 2, 3]} />
45.                 <Box position={[4, 5, 6]}/>
46.                 <Box position={[7, 8, 9]}/>
47.                 <OrbitControls />
48.                 <Perf position="top-right" />
49.             </Canvas>
50.         </main>
51.     );
```

Code Listing 17.5: Updates to follow the memoization updates

Let us see the explanations for this code:

- The **Box** component is a memorized functional component that renders a box or a torus geometry based on the **currentGeometry** state.

- It uses a ref to reference the mesh object and updates its rotation using the **updateRotation** callback function.

- The **useFrame** hook calls the **updateRotation** function on each frame, providing the delta time as an argument.

- The component renders a **<mesh>** with the specified position and geometry and toggles between box and torus geometries on click.

- As we use the **memo** as a wrapper, your linter will probably complain that we use an unnamed component. For this situation, we added the **displayName** property to the component.

- Delta can be any number you like; we added it here to allow you to play around in practice.

Note: **Creating the geometries before using them is a very useful method. It will allow us to share the pre-created geometries across the application and save resources that will make our application smoother on various devices.**

This method can increase the chances of our components not being optimized and having an optimization issue. In other cases, the performance increase will be very low. Minor performance improvements are also important and lead us to the next block.

The **useCallback** hook is often introduced as a way to prevent unnecessary re-renders by memoizing function definitions. While this can be useful in certain scenarios, overusing **useCallback**—especially in a real-time rendering environment like Three.js—can lead to code that's harder to read without any actual performance gain.

Let's say you're handling mouse movement to rotate a camera or trigger animations. You might be tempted to wrap your handler in **useCallback** to "optimize" it. However, this function likely needs to change when any of the values inside it change, like camera state, animation timing, or pointer position. In practice, this often leads to listing several dependencies and still re-creating the function on every render, defeating the purpose of memoization.

In animation-heavy contexts or within **useFrame**, these functions are frequently short-lived and lightweight. The cost of re-declaring them is negligible compared to the complexity of managing their dependencies properly.

When **useCallback** is worth using? If you pass a function deep into a component tree—especially into memoized or pure components—**useCallback** can help prevent unnecessary re-renders. For example, if you pass an event handler to a Canvas overlay or UI component that doesn't need to re-render unless the callback changes, memoizing that function can be beneficial.

But in most cases where the function is declared and used locally (within the same component or nearby logic), there's no performance benefit.

> Note: **Use useCallback when passing stable functions into memoized child components. Avoid it for short, local functions that change frequently or aren't triggering re-renders.**

React Fiber offscreen

Another technique that will help us optimize the application is using **React Fiber Offscreen**. This will allow us to move extensive CPU operations into the Web worker.

Web Workers are a browser feature that enables concurrent execution of JavaScript code in the background, separate from the main execution thread of a web page. They provide a way to perform computationally intensive tasks, such as data processing, without blocking the user interface or causing slowdowns in the main thread.

To add this possibility to our project, we use the following command:

npm install @react-three/offscreen

or

yarn add @react-three/offscreen

We will use the code from the last example located in *Code Listing 17.5*. In this code, we will move all scene-related objects, except the canvas, to a separate file. We will name this file **scene.js,** and it will contain code from *Code Listing 17.6*:

```
1.  'use client';
2.
3.  import { OrbitControls } from "@react-three/drei";
4.  import { useFrame } from "@react-three/fiber";
5.  import { Perf } from "r3f-perf";
6.  import { memo, useCallback, useMemo, useRef, useState } from "react";
7.  import * as THREE from "three";
8.
9.  const Box = memo( ({ position }) => {
10.     const ref = useRef();
11.     const [currentGeometry, setCurrentGeometry] = useState(0);
12.     const geometry = useMemo(() =>  [new THREE.BoxGeometry(),
    new THREE.TorusGeometry(1)], []);
13.
14.     const updateRotation = useCallback((delta) => {
15.         ref.current.rotation.x += 1 * delta;
16.         ref.current.rotation.y += 0.5 * delta;
17.     }, []);
18.
```

```
19.     useFrame((_, delta) => {
20.         updateRotation(delta);
21.     });
22.
23.     return (
24.         <mesh ref={ref}
25.                 position={position}
26.                 geometry={geometry[currentGeometry]}
27.                 onClick={() => currentGeometry === 0 ?
   setCurrentGeometry(1) : setCurrentGeometry(0)}
28.         >
29.             <meshStandardMaterial/>
30.         </mesh>
31.     );
32. });
33. Box.displayName = 'Box';
34.
35. export default function Scene () {
36.     return (
37.         <>
38.             <ambientLight intensity={0.1}/>
39.             <directionalLight color="red" position={[0, 0, 5]}/>
40.             <Box position={[1, 2, 3]}/>
41.             <Box position={[4, 5, 6]}/>
42.             <Box position={[7, 8, 9]}/>
43.             <OrbitControls/>
44.             <Perf position="top-right"/>
45.         </>
46.     );
47. };
```

Code Listing 17.6 *Code for the Scene component*

The next step will be to add workers to your project. For this, we will create a file **worker. js** with code from *Code Listing 17.7*:

```
1. "use client";
2.
3. import { render } from "@react-three/offscreen";
4.
5. import Scene from "@/app/optimisation/components/scene";
6.
7. render(<Scene />);
```

Code Listing 17.7: *Code for the Scene component*

We take render from the offscreen helper to render the React component. Next, we need to create the model renderer for our page. We will create a new file with the name **renderer. js**. For the code, follow *Code Listing 17.8*:

```
1.  'use client';
2.
3.  import { Canvas } from "@react-three/offscreen";
4.  import React, { lazy, Suspense } from "react";
5.
6.  const Scene = lazy(() => import("./scene"));
7.
8.  const worker = new Worker(new URL("./worker.js", import.meta.url), {
9.      type: "module",
10. });
11. export default function Renderer() {
12.     return (
13.         <Suspense
14.             fallback={
15.                 <div className="w-full flex items-center justify-
    center h-[calc(100vh-300px)] font-bold text-[30px] font-mono text-
    white">
16.                     loading...
17.                 </div>
18.             }
19.         >
20.             <Canvas
21.                 worker={worker}
22.                 fallback={<Scene />}
23.             >
24.             </Canvas>
25.         </Suspense>
26.     );
27. }
```

Code Listing 17.8: Renderer for the model using workers

Here are some explanations for the updated code:

- We use the **Canvas** object from the Offscreen helper. It will allow us to bring all render computations into the worker.

- We use lazy loading to improve performance in *line 5*.

- We created the new web worker (it is JavaScript native, so there are no imports for it).

- Canvas object takes the newly created worker as a **worker** property.

- Canvas uses the lazy loaded scene as a fallback property, which means that we automatically use a suspense component. (Check how we loaded 3D models in previous chapters. The process is the same)

Finally, we need to update the **page.js** file to render everything from the worker. We *take Code Listing 17.9* for the updated code for the page:

```
1.  'use client';
2.
3.  import dynamic from "next/dynamic";
4.
5.  const Renderer = dynamic(() => import("../../components/
    renderer"), {
6.      ssr: false
7.  });
8.
9.  export default function Optimisation() {
10.     return (
11.         <main className="m-auto h-screen">
12.             <Renderer />
13.         </main>
14.     );
15. }
```

Code Listing 17.9: Updated page code

As we can see from *Code Listing 17.9,* we also dynamically load the **renderer** component to improve loading performance.

This method will lead to GPU and CPU performance increase as well and it will generally improve our page load.

After we build our project using workers, we see an error that says window is not defined. There is no method to get rid of this error. It happens because, in the Next.js build stage, we put an additional option in the configuration file. Open **next.config.js** and see the line **transpilePackages: ['three']**. We removed it, as it conflicts with a Web Worker option. Some additional packages may require this option, so we use this optimization method only in case of bad performance or other requirements.

Mobile performance

Most users use web applications with their phones or tablets. Even though they have huge resources to render and use 3D graphics on the web, these devices have a limited battery life. That is directly linked to the resources. Thus, for mobile devices, we need to think about reducing all possible usage, to save device battery.

There are several methods that we could follow to reduce resources and battery usage in addition to what we already learned in the previous section.

- **Use low-poly models**: Mobile devices have limited resources compared to desktop computers, so it is essential to use low-poly models with fewer vertices and simpler geometries. Avoid using highly detailed models that can strain the device's GPU and CPU.

- **Minimize texture sizes**: Reduce the resolution and size of textures used in 3D models to conserve memory and improve loading times. Use texture compression formats like JPEG or WebP to further reduce file sizes without sacrificing quality. For example, *Code Listing 17.10*:

```
1. const texture = useLoader(THREE.TextureLoader, 'texture.jpg');
2. texture.encoding = THREE.sRGBEncoding;
3. texture.anisotropy = 4;
```

Code Listing 17.10: Configure your texture to be less detailed

- **Optimize rendering pipeline**: Implement techniques such as **frustum culling, occlusion culling**, and **level-of-detail (LOD)** to optimize the rendering pipeline. These techniques help reduce the number of objects and polygons rendered on screen, improving performance on mobile devices. For this, we can use special components from the **Drei** helpers and reduce the detail level. This is a wrapper around the Three.js level of details module. An example of usage can be collected in *Code Listing 17.11*. In the example, we use distance as a property to switch the level of detail. We can use any property that can be created in the React component.

- **Avoid heavy shaders**: Complex shaders can tax mobile GPUs, leading to performance issues. Use simpler shaders with fewer calculations and avoid using features like reflections, refractions, and real-time shadows unless necessary.

```
1. <Detailed distances={[0, 10, 20]} {...props}>
2.   <mesh geometry={highDetail} />
3.   <mesh geometry={mediumDetail} />
4.   <mesh geometry={lowDetail} />
5. </Detailed>
```

Code Listing 17.11: Level of detail usage from the Drei helpers

Browser compatibility

Ensuring browser compatibility is crucial when developing applications with R3F, especially for web-based 3D experiences. There can be several issues related to browser compatibility using R3F, Three.js, or WebGL directly.

First, we must ensure that the target browser supports WebGL. We can do this with different tools, for example, **webglreport.com**. Opening this link in the target browser will lead us to the page with reports about what was added or updated in WebGL at the current time. The most important information for us will be supportability. We will see the top layout shown in *Figure 17.7*:

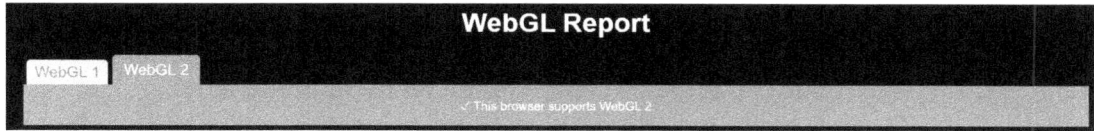

Figure 17.7: Browser computability check

In case we get an error that the browser does not support this feature, we can try to use special polyfills. Here is a short list of polyfills examples that we can use:

- **Core-js**: A modular standard library for JavaScript that includes polyfills for ECMAScript features.

- **Babel polyfill:** A collection of polyfills that replicate browser APIs for modern ECMAScript features.

- **Web components polyfills**: Polyfills for Web Components APIs, which may be required for certain R3F components or features.

Another important thing is that React Three Finer uses web workers, which R3F uses for offloading expensive computations. You can use a polyfill like **comlink** to add web workers' support for browsers that do not support it natively.

Testing application

Similar to any other application, testing plays a crucial role in the release process of an application, ensuring its reliability and quality before it goes live. With R3F, we can utilize the React Three Test Renderer to accomplish this task.

Using R3F, we will have a regular React application so we can use the same techniques we use for testing it.

When it comes to testing in a React + Three.js environment, **Jest** is widely adopted and recommended as a foundational testing library. It offers a robust and flexible framework that integrates well with modern JavaScript applications, particularly those built with React.

The following are the reasons for choosing Jest:

- Jest is a standard choice in the React ecosystem. It is maintained by the team behind React, which ensures compatibility and long-term support.

- It supports snapshot and DOM testing, working well with tools like **@testing-library/react** to validate component output and user interactions.

- Tests run quickly and in isolation, which is especially beneficial for continuous integration workflows and local development.

- Jest has a strong plugin ecosystem, making it easy to extend with mocking tools, code coverage reports, or visual testing utilities.

For testing **React Three Fiber** components, we also need a way to render 3D components in a test environment. Since these components rely on a WebGL context, traditional React test setups won't be sufficient. This is where the **@react-three/test-renderer** package comes in—it allows you to pre-render 3D components in a virtual scene without requiring an actual canvas. To add it, we use this command:

```
npm install @react-three/test-renderer --save-dev
```

or

```
yarn add @react-three/test-renderer --save-dev
```

Next, we can create a file with the name **your-first-test.test.js** with code from *Code Listing 17.12*:

```
1. import ReactThreeTestRenderer from '@react-three/test-renderer';
2. import { Box } from '@components/Box';
3.
4. test('Your first test', async () => {
5.   const renderer = await ReactThreeTestRenderer.create(<Box />);
6. });
```

Code Listing 17.12: *Starter code for our first test*

As a basic example, we can check if the component is rendered in the component. To add such a test, we will use a regular technique that we use in every Jest test. We need to create the component and create the expectation logic for it. *Code Listing 17.13* has the updated code:

```
1. import ReactThreeTestRenderer from '@react-three/test-renderer';
2. import { Box } from '@components/Box';
3.
4. test('Your first test', async () => {
5.   const renderer = await ReactThreeTestRenderer.create(<Box />);
6.   const box = container.querySelector('mesh');
7.   expect(box).toBeInTheDocument();
8. });
```

Code Listing 17.13: *Code that checks that the box is rendered correctly*

The next example will be to check if we created the correct properties on the render sage. As seen in *Code Listing 17.13,* we create the box object as a JS object. This means we can get properties from it and create assertions to check it. *Code Listing 17.14* has the updated example:

```
1. import ReactThreeTestRenderer from '@react-three/test-renderer';
2. import { Box } from '@components/Box';
```

```
 3.
 4. test('Your first test', async () => {
 5.   const renderer = await ReactThreeTestRenderer.create(<Box />);
 6.   const box = container.querySelector('mesh');
 7.   expect(box).toBeInTheDocument();
 8.   expect(box.props.scale).toBe(1);
 9. });
```

Code Listing 17.14: Assert test to check the box properties

In Three.js (and by extension, R3F), every 3D object has a scale property that determines its size along the X, Y, and Z axes. By default, a scale of 1 means the object retains its original dimensions—no scaling is applied. If the scale were set to 2, the object would appear twice as large in that axis direction.

In the context of this test, we're rendering a **Box** component and checking two things:

1. A mesh exists in the scene, confirming the component renders a valid 3D object.

2. The mesh has a scale of 1, which ensures the object is rendered at its intended size without unintended transformations.

Testing the **scale** property helps validate that the Box component is being initialized correctly and hasn't been affected by unexpected props or logic that might alter its visual size in the scene.

This kind of assertion is especially useful when components are meant to maintain strict dimensions—such as UI elements in 3D, physics bodies, or objects that interact with others in predictable ways.

What we also want to check is that our properties are set to new values on the event. Let us check that adding the click event to the test is like in *Code Listing 17.15*:

```
 1. import ReactThreeTestRenderer from '@react-three/test-renderer';
 2. import { Box } from '@components/Box';
 3.
 4. test('Your first test', async () => {
 5.   const renderer = await ReactThreeTestRenderer.create(<Box />);
 6.   const box = container.querySelector('mesh');
 7.   expect(box).toBeInTheDocument();
 8.   expect(box.props.scale).toBe(1);
 9.   await renderer.fireEvent(box, 'click');
10.   expect(box.props.scale).toBe(2);
11. });
```

Code Listing 17.15: Assert test to check the box properties changed on click

Conclusion

In this chapter, we get into an important topic, performance profiling and debugging in R3F applications. We explored various performance monitoring tools to gain insights into the performance of our applications and identify areas for optimization. By focusing on application and mobile performance, and ensuring browser compatibility, we equipped ourselves with the knowledge and tools needed to create high-performing and accessible 3D web applications.

Additionally, we emphasized the importance of testing our applications to ensure reliability and robustness, leveraging tools like React Three Test Renderer to streamline the testing process.

It is essential to recognize that performance optimization and testing are ongoing endeavors. By integrating these practices into our development workflow, we can create immersive and engaging 3D experiences across different devices and browsers.

In the next chapter, we will explore AWS Amplify and its role in simplifying cloud-powered application development. We will begin with an introduction to AWS Amplify, followed by a step-by-step guide to setting it up for your projects. Additionally, we will cover essential topics such as security and access control to safeguard your applications, and delve into Amplify's powerful extensions and integrations to enhance functionality and scalability.

Points to remember

- Use all listed optimization techniques according to the project requirements. Some of them will work better, some of them not. Align to the project requirements and what Three.js elements you plan to use in your application.

- Stick to the testing or create tests before coding, as it is a good practice for coding.

- Use performance monitoring in the development stage, and it will help you to find heavy loading before you deploy the project to production.

Exercises

As an exercise for the current chapter, take the application from *Chapter 16, User Interactions and Controls,* and complete these tasks:

1. Make all models load dynamically and use special hooks (memo, useMemo, useCallback) for the optimization.

2. Use workers to optimize application load.

3. Cover application with small tests: check that the model is rendered and check the state change on action.

CHAPTER 18

Introduction to AWS Amplify

Introduction

In today's fast-paced tech landscape, the demand for scalable and reliable applications has never been higher. As developers, delivering applications is not just about local development. It is about ensuring robustness and scalability throughout the entire development lifecycle.

AWS Amplify emerges as a powerful ally in this endeavor, offering a comprehensive suite of tools and services designed to simplify the development and deployment of full-stack applications. By leveraging Amplify, developers can streamline their workflows, access managed backend services, and seamlessly integrate with other AWS offerings.

In this chapter, we will study AWS Amplify, exploring its features, benefits, and practical applications in the context of Three.js and Next.js development. We will uncover how Amplify empowers developers to focus on crafting immersive experiences while AWS handles the heavy lifting of infrastructure management.

Structure

In this chapter, we will discuss the following topics:

- Introduction to AWS Amplify
- Setting up AWS Amplify

- Security and access control
- Amplify extensions and integrations

Objectives

By the end of this chapter, we will have a theoretical knowledge of using AWS Amplify as a Cloud hosting and delivery system. We will understand the important topics in the user management field and will be able to set up our working environment.

Introduction to AWS Amplify

AWS Amplify is a platform that offers many tools and services to streamline the development, deployment, and management of web applications. Combined with Next. js, a popular React framework for building server-side rendered and statically generated applications, AWS Amplify empowers developers to create robust, feature-rich applications with ease. In this section, we will explore the advantages and disadvantages of using AWS Amplify with Next.js, along with important cost considerations.

Advantages of AWS Amplify

The following list highlights the key benefits of using AWS Amplify, showcasing its seamless integration, scalability, security features, serverless architecture, and extensive ecosystem of services and integrations:

- **Seamless integration**: AWS Amplify seamlessly integrates with Next.js, providing developers with a unified development experience. With Amplify CLI, developers can easily configure backend resources such as authentication, storage, and databases, and integrate them into their Next.js applications.

- **Scalability**: One of the key advantages of AWS Amplify is its scalability. By leveraging AWS's global infrastructure, Amplify applications can effortlessly handle fluctuations in traffic and scale dynamically to accommodate growing user bases.

- **Security**: It offers robust security features, including built-in authentication and authorization mechanisms. With features like Amazon Cognito for user authentication and AWS **Identity and Access Management (IAM)** for access control, developers can ensure that their Next.js applications are secure.

- **Serverless architecture**: It embraces a serverless architecture, eliminating the need for developers to manage servers or infrastructure. This allows developers to focus on writing code and building features, rather than worrying about provisioning and scaling servers.

- **Rich ecosystem**: AWS Amplify has a rich ecosystem of services and integrations, including **AWS Lambda, Amazon DynamoDB, Amazon S3,** and more. This enables developers to leverage many tools and resources to build powerful, feature-rich applications.

Disadvantages of AWS Amplify

The following list outlines some potential challenges associated with using AWS Amplify, including the learning curve for new users, the risk of vendor lock-in within the AWS ecosystem, and the complexity of managing resources as applications scale:

- **Learning curve**: While AWS Amplify simplifies many aspects of application development, it also comes with a learning curve. Developers may need to learn the ins and outs of Amplify's features and best practices, especially if they are new to AWS.

- **Vendor lock-in**: Using AWS Amplify ties developers to the AWS ecosystem, which can be a disadvantage for some. While AWS offers a comprehensive set of services, developers should realize the potential for vendor lock-in and consider the long-term implications.

- **Complexity**: As applications grow in complexity, managing and configuring Amplify resources can become challenging. Developers may need to carefully architect their applications and adopt best practices to ensure scalability, reliability, and maintainability.

Cost considerations of AWS Amplify

The following list highlights the cost-related aspects of using AWS Amplify, including the availability of a generous free tier for experimentation, a pay-as-you-go pricing model for scalability, and strategies for cost optimization. It also emphasizes the importance of monitoring and analyzing usage with AWS tools to maintain cost efficiency and avoid unexpected expenses:

- **Free tier**: AWS offers a generous free tier for many services, including AWS Amplify. Developers can take advantage of this free tier to experiment with Amplify and build small-scale applications at no cost.

- **Pay-as-you-go pricing**: For applications that exceed the limits of the free tier, AWS operates on a pay-as-you-go pricing model. Developers are charged based on their usage of AWS services, including computing, storage, and data transfer.

- **Cost optimization**: To minimize costs, developers should optimize their applications for performance and efficiency. This may involve leveraging caching mechanisms, optimizing database queries, and implementing cost-effective solutions.

- **Monitoring and analysis**: AWS provides tools for monitoring and analyzing usage and costs, such as **AWS Cost Explorer** and **AWS Budgets**. Developers should regularly monitor their usage and adjust their resources to avoid unexpected costs.

Setting up AWS Amplify

As studied in *Chapter 4, Setting up all tools for the QuickStart of the development,* we already made an initial setup of the service to have the possibility to use it immediately. In this section, we will look into the most important services that we will use to create a professional web application.

As we already have a project, let us proceed with code delivery. Our main goal here will be to connect the code repository to the initiated project. To achieve it, we will need to follow these steps:

1. In the project link, choose the **Hosting environments** tab, as shown in *Figure 18.1*:

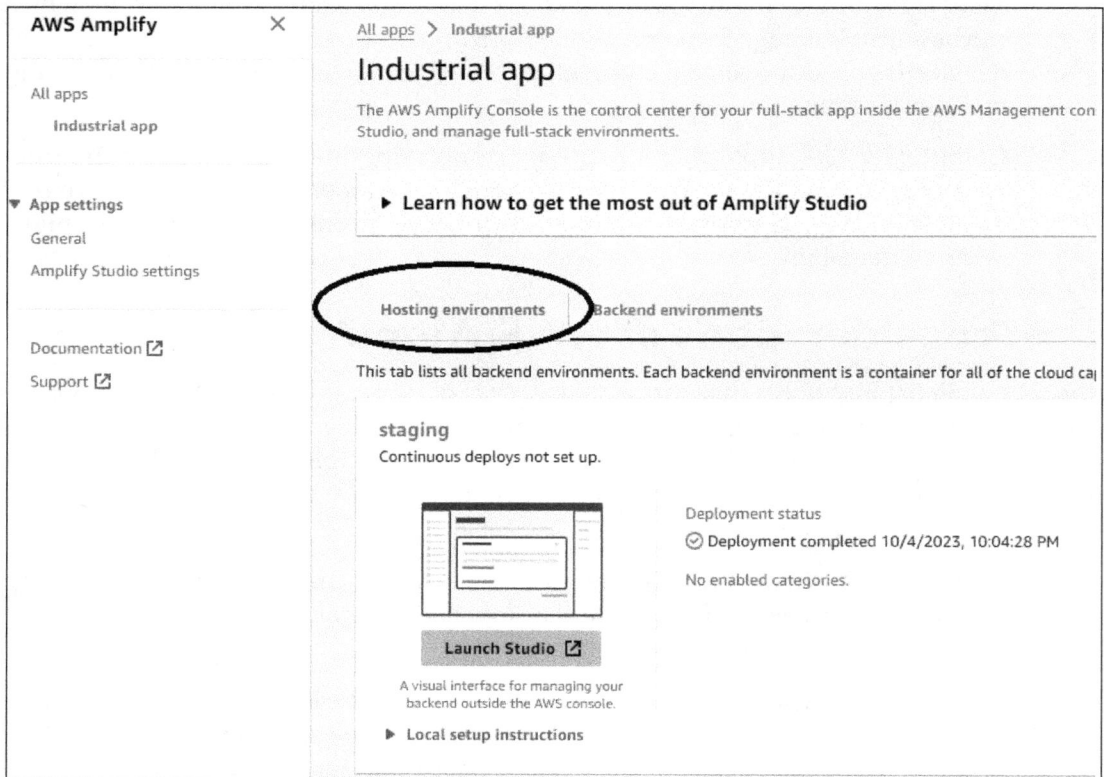

Figure 18.1: Hosting environment tab in AWS Amplify project

2. In the newly opened tab, we need to choose the git repository provider that we plan to use as a source, like in *Figure 18.2:*

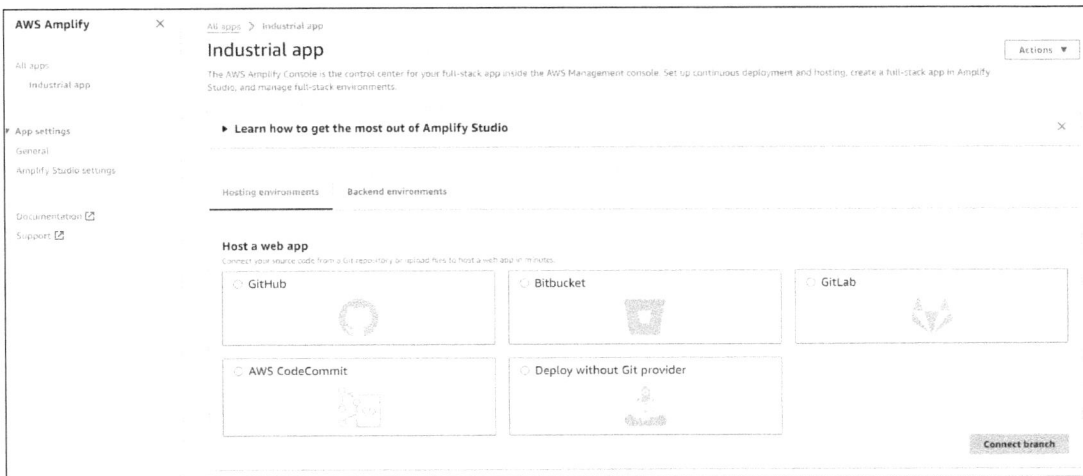

Figure 18.2: *Choosing the git repository provider*

Each git repository source has its own permission-providing mechanism. Follow the instructions to access each one. In our example, we will use a GitHub account. To connect it, we just need to allow access on the chosen step.

3. After that, we can choose your repository from the dropdown list and click the **Next** button, like in *Figure 18.3*:

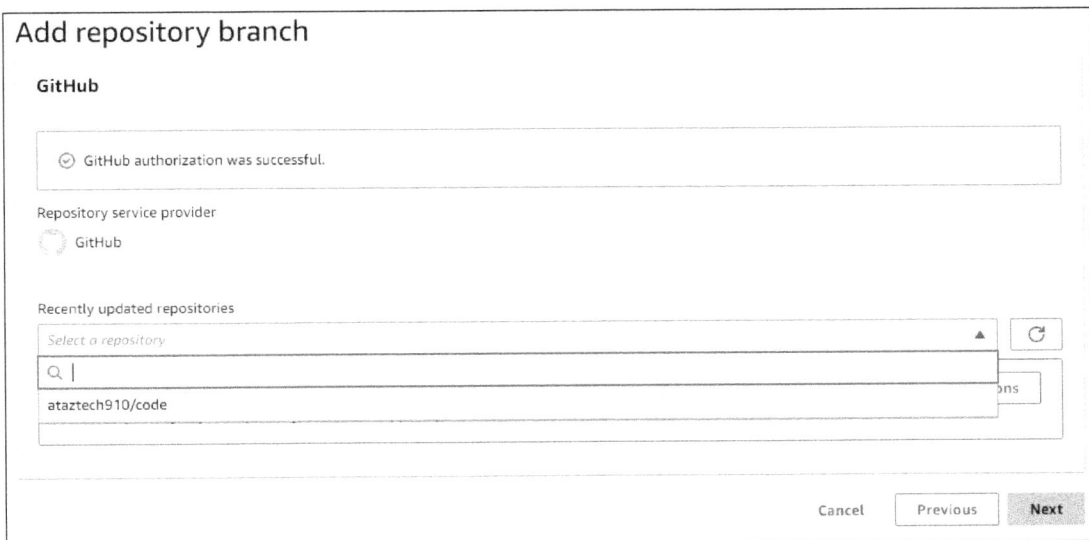

Figure 18.3: *Choosing the git repository*

4. The next step will be to choose the branch to be used for the deployment. We also need to choose our application folder in case we use a Monorepo. As an example,

we made a mono repo application (Turborepo from Vercel is used) to show the configuration in this case. It is shown in Figure *18.4*:

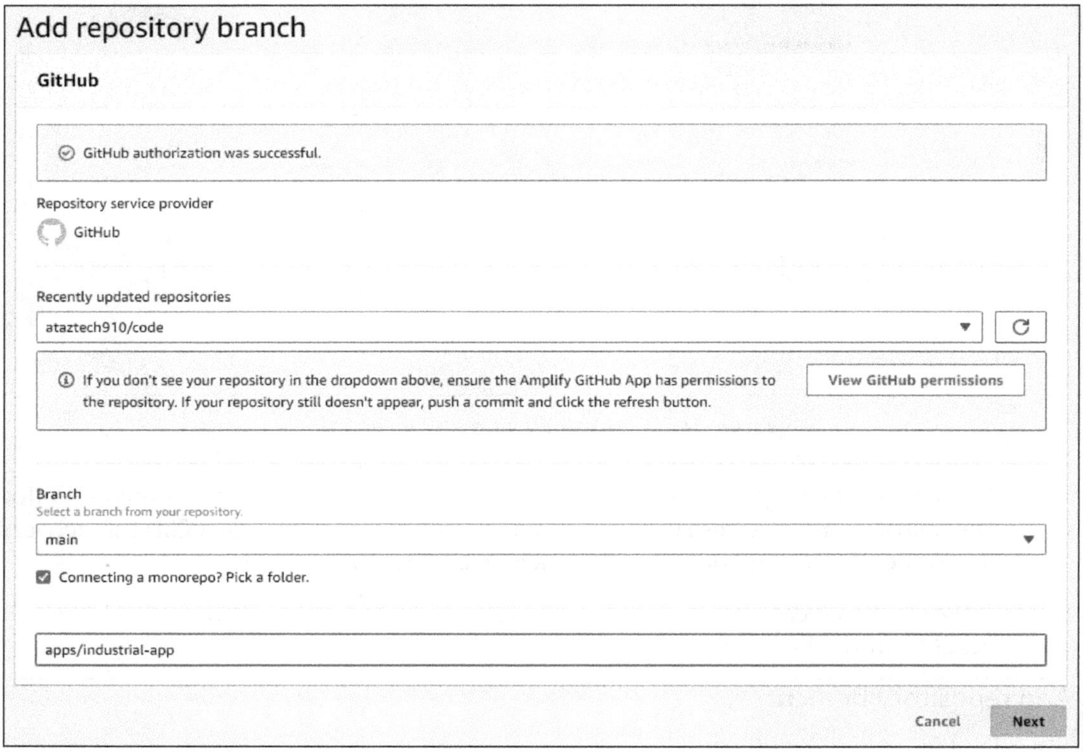

Figure 18.4: *Choosing the branch and folder for the monorepo*

Amplify can create the project with only backend environment, without setting up a fronted part. This feature can be used in case we have several front-end projects that use one back-end infrastructure, e.g. multitenant system with different purposes.

To align the backend, at the next stage, we need to choose what project will be used for it. At this stage, we also need to choose the environment. The environments can be variable, just **Development** and **Production**, or have **Stage,** or even more complicated.

5.   Another configuration to choose from is a service role. In the next section, we will speak about user management. Currently, we will just choose one that is created automatically by Amplify. An example of this configuration is shown in *Figure 18.5*:

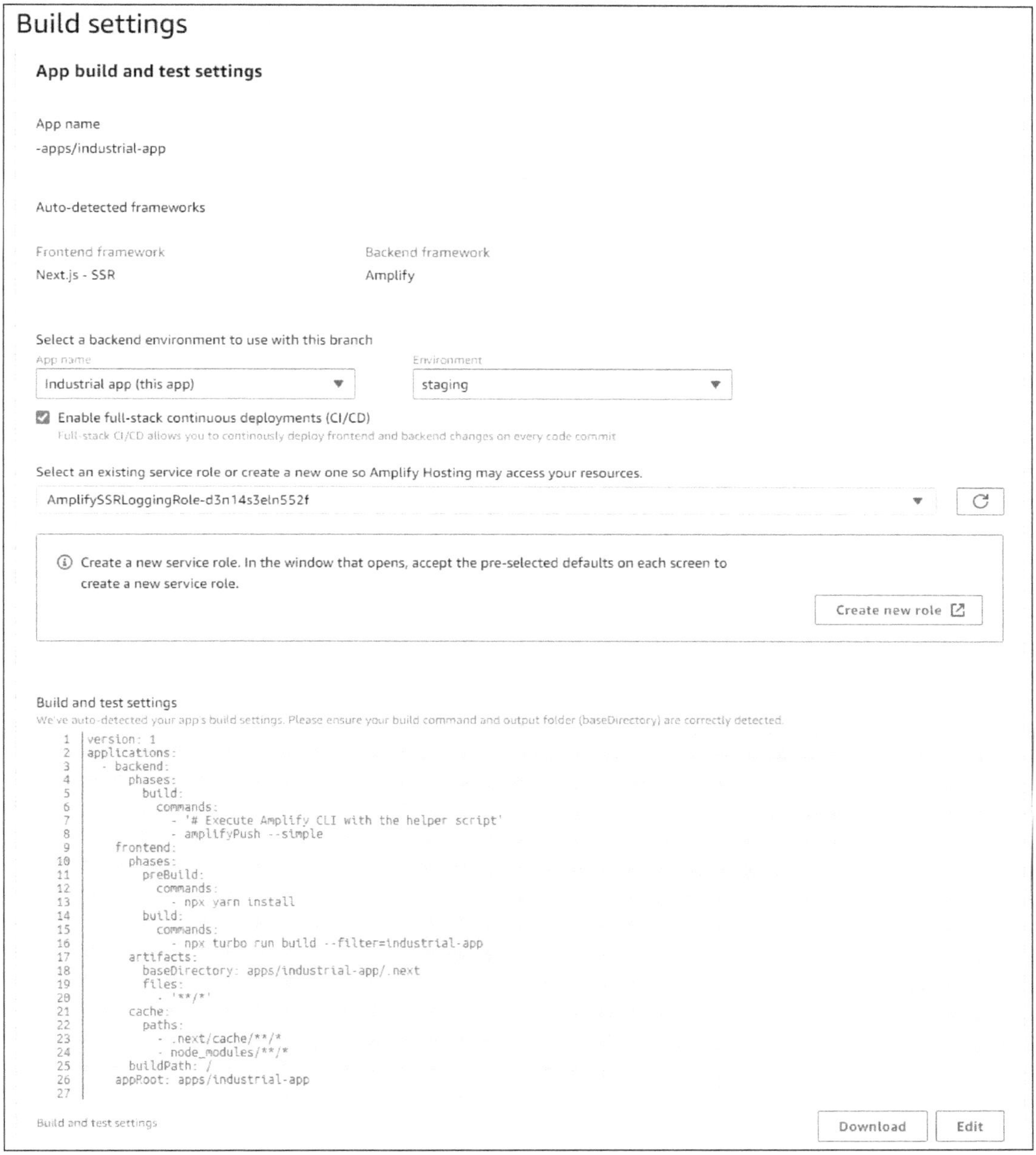

Build settings

App build and test settings

App name
-apps/industrial-app

Auto-detected frameworks

Frontend framework
Next.js - SSR

Backend framework
Amplify

Select a backend environment to use with this branch

App name

| Industrial app (this app) ▼ |

Environment

| staging ▼ |

☑ Enable full-stack continuous deployments (CI/CD)
Full-stack CI/CD allows you to continuously deploy frontend and backend changes on every code commit

Select an existing service role or create a new one so Amplify Hosting may access your resources.

| AmplifySSRLoggingRole-d3n14s3eln552f ▼ | C |

> ⓘ Create a new service role. In the window that opens, accept the pre-selected defaults on each screen to
> create a new service role.
>
> Create new role ↗

Build and test settings
We've auto-detected your app's build settings. Please ensure your build command and output folder (baseDirectory) are correctly detected.

```
 1  version: 1
 2  applications:
 3    - backend:
 4        phases:
 5          build:
 6            commands:
 7              - '# Execute Amplify CLI with the helper script'
 8              - amplifyPush --simple
 9      frontend:
10        phases:
11          preBuild:
12            commands:
13              - npx yarn install
14          build:
15            commands:
16              - npx turbo run build --filter=industrial-app
17        artifacts:
18          baseDirectory: apps/industrial-app/.next
19          files:
20            - '**/*'
21        cache:
22          paths:
23            - .next/cache/**/*
24            - node_modules/**/*
25      buildPath: /
26      appRoot: apps/industrial-app
27
```

Build and test settings | Download | Edit |

Figure 18.5: Choosing the back-end and environment for the project

6. The last configuration step on this screen is to align the **Environment Variables**. These variables are a set of secrets that we will use in your project (For example, Headless CMS API keys, like Contentful or Storyblock), as shown in *Figure 18.6*. If there are no secrets, skip this step.

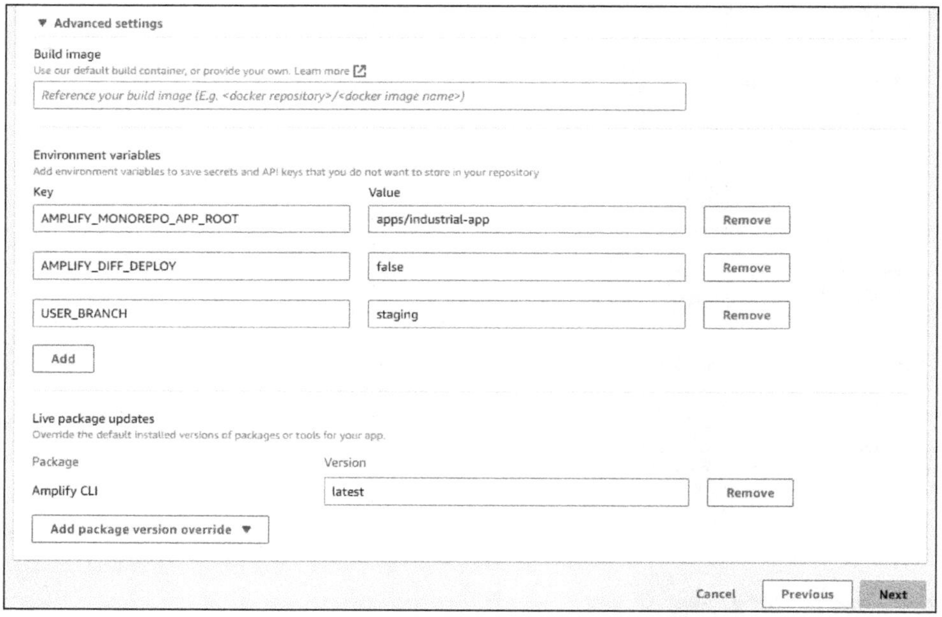

Figure 18.6: Choosing the environment variables

7. Now, we need to review our setup and check if all configurations are set correctly. After everything is in order (shown in *Figure 18.7*), we click the **Save and Deploy** button to start the deployment process:

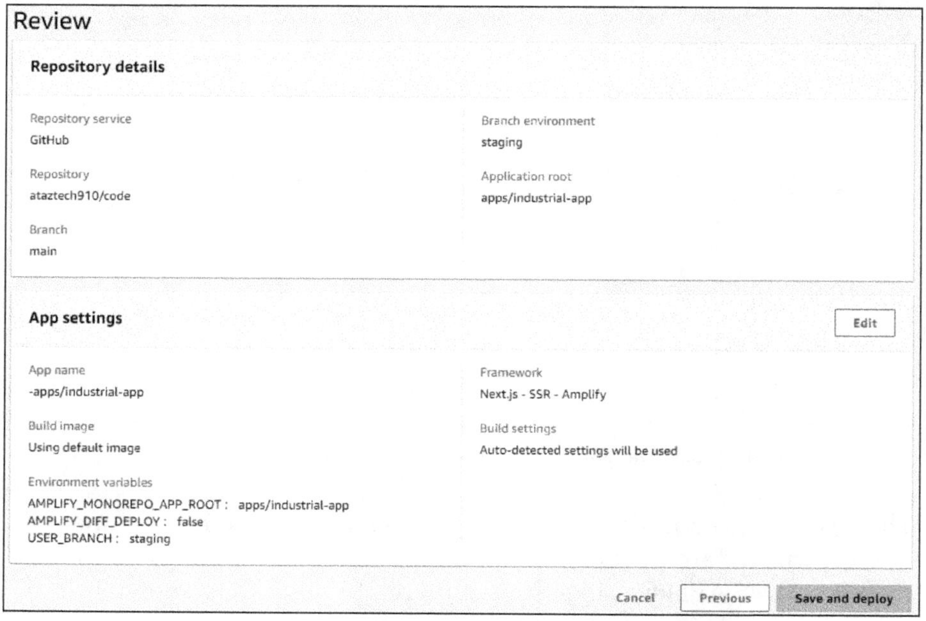

Figure 18.7: Configuration review and deployment

8. As a result, we will see the process monitoring screen like in *Figure 18.8,* which will be green if the build was successful and red in the opposite case.

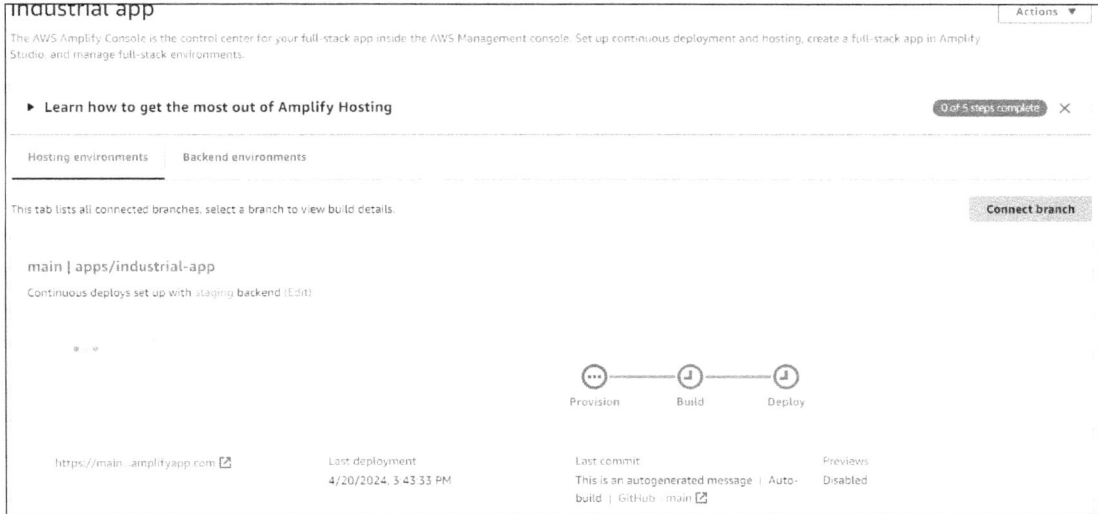

Figure 18.8: Build and deploy process

Several issues can be triggered in the build stage:

- If we use the Monorepo approach, ensure that we place the Amplify configuration in the project root

- The role of the build in the Amplify project can be misconfigured. To fix that, we create a new role and use the new one

- Ensure that the build framework is selected **Next.js - SSR - Amplify**

As a result, we will see all green circles that indicate successful build and deployment, and will have the link to the project that we can connect to our domain or use as is (*Figure 18.9*):

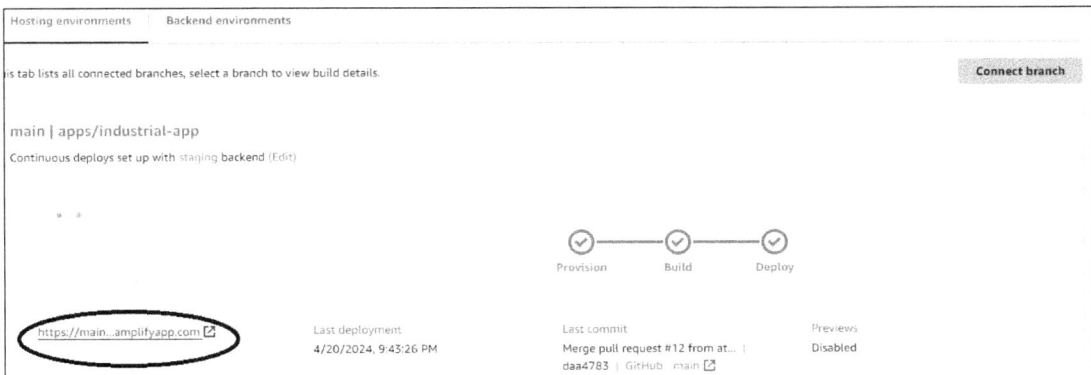

Figure 18.9: Result and link to the web app

Security and access control

Access management is essential in AWS Amplify for safeguarding applications and data, ensuring compliance with regulatory requirements, preventing data breaches, adhering to the principle of least privilege, optimizing resource usage, and maintaining centralized control and visibility over the AWS environment.

In this section, we will check two access management configurations in Amplify:

- The first one will allow us to configure access to the web application globally.

- The second one will allow us to configure the authorization at the application level.

Amplify allows the creation of steps for building different branches and environments. This situation could globally close the application using login and password for all branches or selected ones. To initiate this possibility, follow these steps:

1. Open the **Access control** tab and click on the **Manage access** button, as shown in *Figure 18.10*:

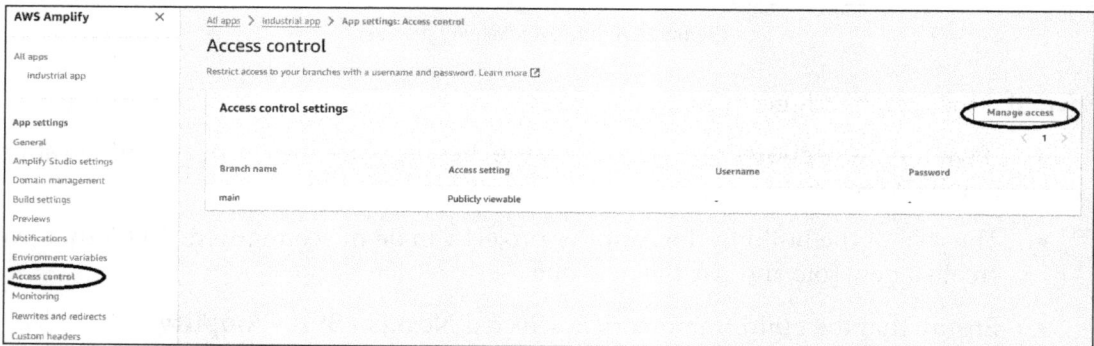

Figure 18.10: Access control tab and Manage access button

2. Now we have the selection to enable password access for all branches globally for all branches or for any selected branch, as shown in *Figure 18.11*:

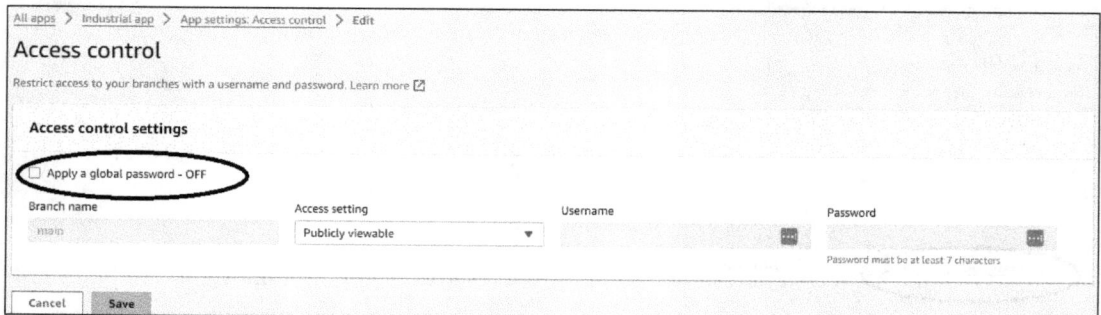

Figure 18.11: Access control settings interface

3. As a result, if we set access to be restricted by the password, we will see a confirmation form related to the selected branch, same as in *Figure 18.12*:

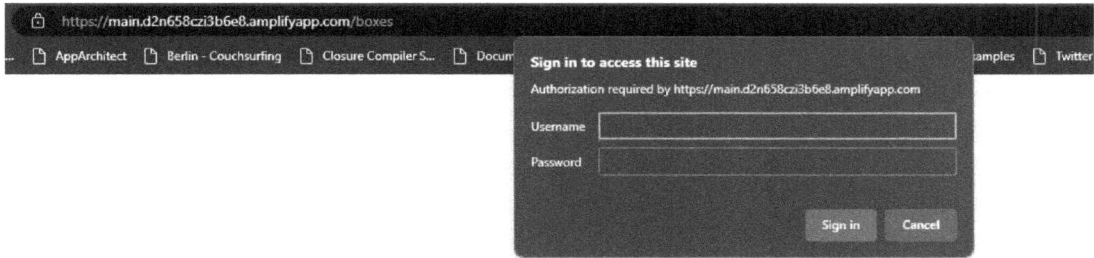

Figure 18.12: Authorization access form for the restricted link

4. For the authorization at the application level, we need to enter the backend studio (*Figure 18.13*). A detailed description is given in *Chapter 20, User Authentication with AWS Amplify,* as this chapter is related to the auth process and configuration. For now, we will check where it is located to fulfill the theoretical knowledge here:

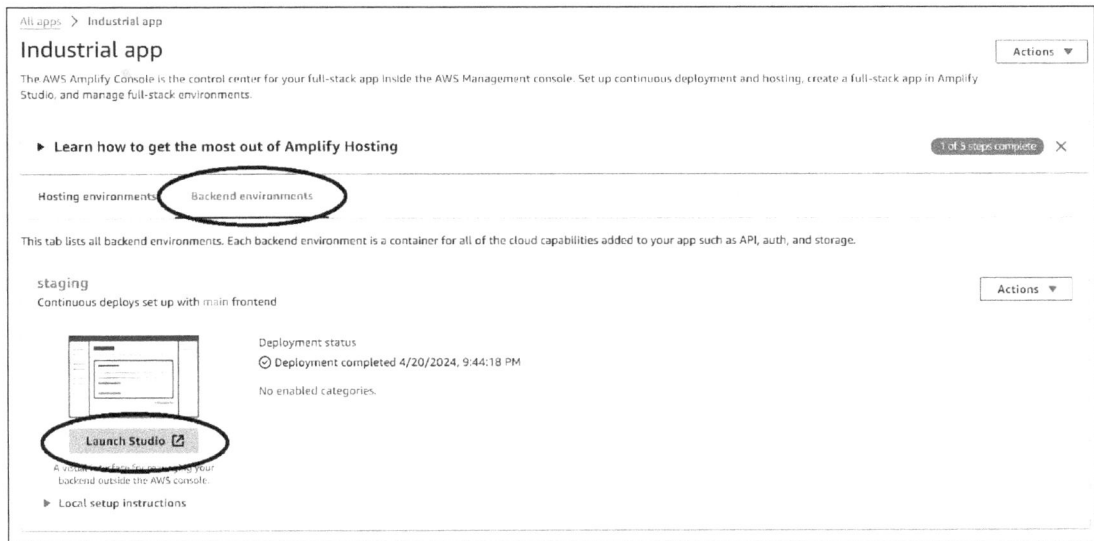

Figure 18.13: Access to the backend studio

5. After entering the studio, we will have only one step to complete the current task. Click on the **User management** tab, and then we will have the possibility to configure it (detailed instructions given in *Chapter 20, User Authentication with AWS Amplify*). The screen for it is shown in *Figure 18.14*:

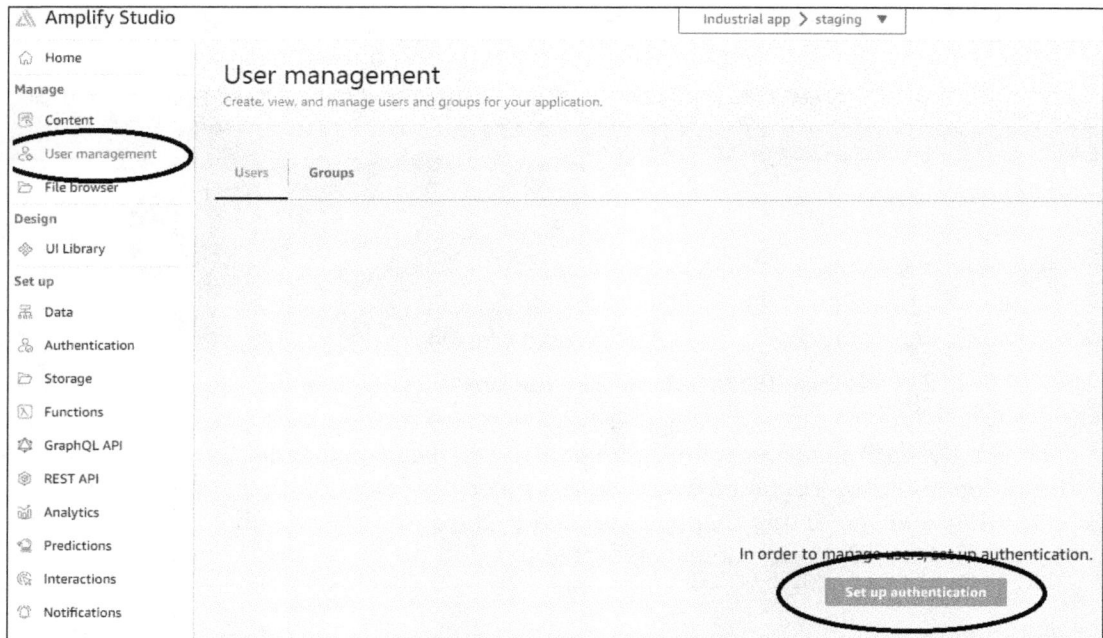

Figure 18.14: User management tab with configuration button

Amplify extensions and integrations

AWS Amplify extensions are pre-built, customizable solutions that extend the functionality of AWS Amplify, enabling developers to easily integrate additional features into their applications. These extensions cover a wide range of use cases, including authentication, storage, analytics, and more, and can be seamlessly integrated with Amplify projects.

The following are some examples of AWS Amplify extensions and integrations:

- **Amplify authentication**: Amplify provides built-in authentication capabilities, including authentication with Amazon Cognito, social sign-in with providers like Google and Facebook, and **multi-factor authentication (MFA).** Developers can further enhance authentication workflows by integrating extensions such as:

  o **Auth0 integration**: Allows developers to leverage Auth0's identity platform for user authentication and authorization. This extension provides seamless integration with Amplify's authentication features, enabling developers to use Auth0 alongside other authentication providers supported by Amplify.

  o **Okta integration**: Enables developers to integrate Okta's identity management platform with Amplify for user authentication and authorization. With this extension, developers can leverage Okta's advanced features, such as **single sign-on (SSO)** and adaptive MFA, within their Amplify applications.

- **Amplify DataStore**: Amplify DataStore provides a simplified interface for working with data in offline and online scenarios, with automatic sync capabilities powered by GraphQL. Developers can extend DataStore functionality with integrations such as:

  o **Amazon DynamoDB Accelerator (DAX)**: Integrates DAX with Amplify DataStore to improve read performance and reduce latency for data queries. By caching frequently accessed data in memory, DAX accelerates database access and enhances the responsiveness of DataStore-powered applications.

  o **Amazon Elasticsearch Service (Amazon ES)**: Enables full-text search capabilities in Amplify DataStore applications by integrating with Amazon ES. Developers can leverage Amazon ES to perform complex search queries on structured and unstructured data stored in DataStore, providing users with powerful search functionality.

- **Amplify analytics:** Amplify analytics allows developers to collect, analyze, and visualize user engagement metrics and application usage patterns. Extensions and integrations in this category include:

  o **Amazon Pinpoint Integration**: Integrates Amazon Pinpoint with Amplify Analytics to capture user engagement data, such as user sessions, events, and campaign metrics. This extension provides insights into user behavior and helps developers optimize their applications for better user experiences.

  o **Amazon Kinesis Integration**: Enables real-time streaming of application telemetry data to Amazon Kinesis for advanced analytics and processing. With this integration, developers can analyze large volumes of streaming data in real-time and gain actionable insights into application performance and user behavior.

Conclusion

AWS Amplify is a comprehensive platform that simplifies the development, deployment, and management of modern web and mobile applications. With features like authentication, data storage, and analytics, it empowers developers to create scalable, secure applications with less effort. This chapter examined how AWS Amplify integrates with Next.js to streamline workflows. While Amplify offers pre-configured solutions and seamless integrations, it's important to consider challenges such as cost, access management, and the complexity of scaling resources. Amplify's built-in tools for authentication and authorization ensure secure access control, protecting sensitive data and safeguarding applications from unauthorized use. Amplify's extensions and integrations allow developers to tailor their applications to specific needs. Whether it's integrating with third-party identity providers, enhancing storage capabilities, or tracking user engagement, these tools offer flexibility for building feature-rich solutions. By combining AWS Amplify with

Next.js, developers can leverage a powerful set of tools to accelerate development, scale effortlessly, and deliver polished, user-friendly applications. Amplify not only simplifies cloud resource management but also enhances the developer experience, enabling teams to focus on building innovative features and delivering value to their users.

In the next chapter, we will dive into the critical aspects of data storage and management for 3D applications. We will begin by exploring the core principles of data storage and how to design effective model schemas specifically for managing 3D objects. From there, we will walk through implementing **Create, Read, Update, Delete (CRUD)** operations to manage 3D data seamlessly. Finally, we'll tackle the challenges of file storage for 3D objects, discussing best practices for efficient and scalable solutions. This chapter will equip you with the tools and strategies to handle complex data workflows in 3D application development.

Points to remember

- AWS services are powerful enough to create end-to-end applications, avoiding any third-party solutions, only in special cases or specific requirements
- Using AWS can be expensive without proper monitoring and configuration
- Align with free tier pricing on the requirement stage

Exercises

1. Follow the guide from this chapter and initiate the environment that will be needed in further chapters.

Join our Discord space

Join our Discord workspace for latest updates, offers, tech happenings around the world, new releases, and sessions with the authors:

https://discord.bpbonline.com

CHAPTER 19
Host Web Application with AWS Amplify

Introduction

With the development of web applications, the need for reliable and scalable hosting solutions becomes increasingly crucial. In the era of cloud computing, services like AWS Amplify offer comprehensive solutions for deploying and managing web applications with ease. In this chapter, we will study the process of hosting web applications with AWS Amplify, exploring its capabilities for environment management, custom domain setup, CI/CD automation, and performance monitoring.

Structure

In this chapter, we will discuss the following topics:

- Environments and deployment
- Custom domain, SSL, and CDN settings
- CI/CD automation
- Performance monitoring

Objectives

By the end of this chapter, you will gain a comprehensive understanding of setting up and managing environments for deploying web applications using AWS Amplify, enabling seamless development workflows and efficient deployment processes. You will learn how to configure custom domains, SSL certificates, and CDN settings to enhance the security and performance of hosted applications. By the end of this chapter, you will also understand how to automate the CI/CD pipeline with AWS Amplify, streamlining deployments while embracing modern continuous integration and delivery practices. Finally, you will learn the strategies for monitoring and optimizing the performance of web applications, leveraging AWS Amplify's built-in tools and analytics to ensure a reliable and high-quality user experience.

Environments and deployment

Before deploying a web application, it is crucial to have separate environments for development, staging, and production. This ensures that changes can be thoroughly tested before being released to users. In this chapter, we will explore how AWS Amplify simplifies the process of managing environments and deploying web applications.

In the previous chapter, we made a basic deployment into AWS hosting. We will now proceed with deeper configuration. First, we will create different environments. Environments are connected to various branches in the git repository. The default branch selected for the environment that we already have is main (or master, depending on the default configuration in GIT). To create the deployment flow, follow these steps:

1. To create the new environment, we have two options (**Branch settings** and **Add branch**), as shown in *Figure 19.1*:

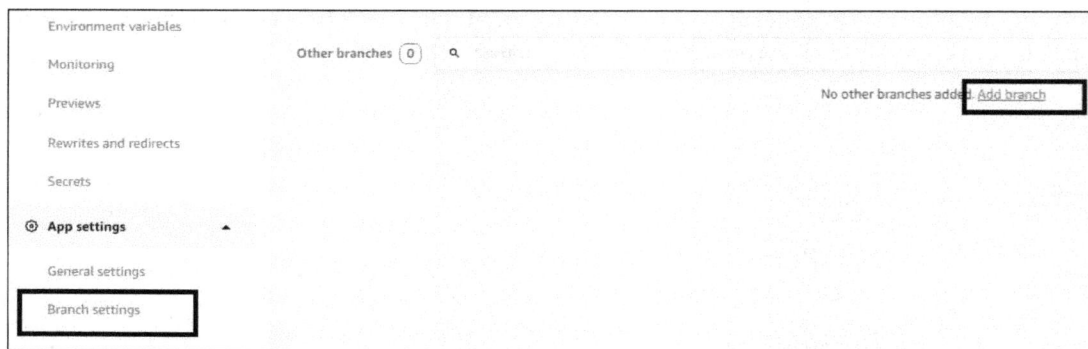

Figure 19.1: Options to choose from for creating environments

2. Now, we can choose the branch to create a new environment. This selection is shown in *Figure 19.2*:

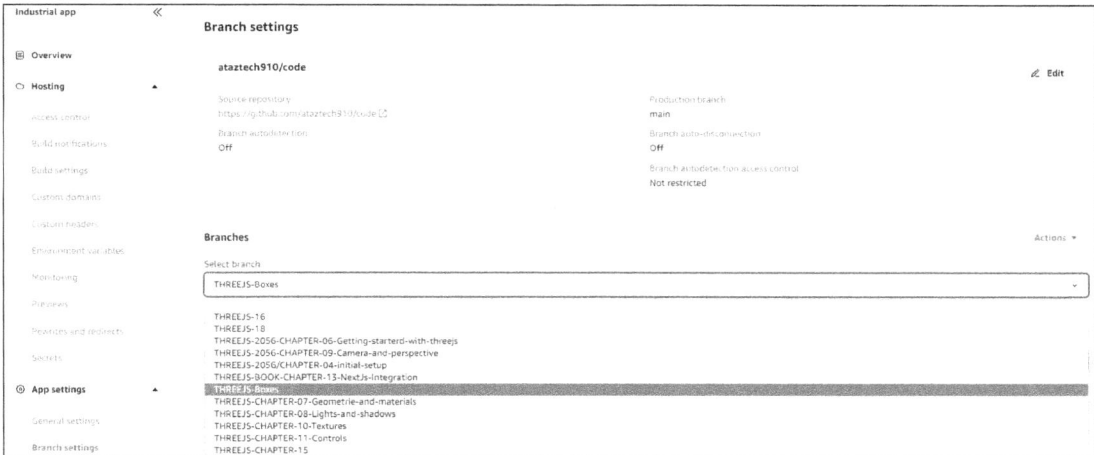

Figure 19.2: Creating the new environment

3. Next, we will see our branch in a list, as shown in *Figure 19.3*. We can choose to connect the backend environment:

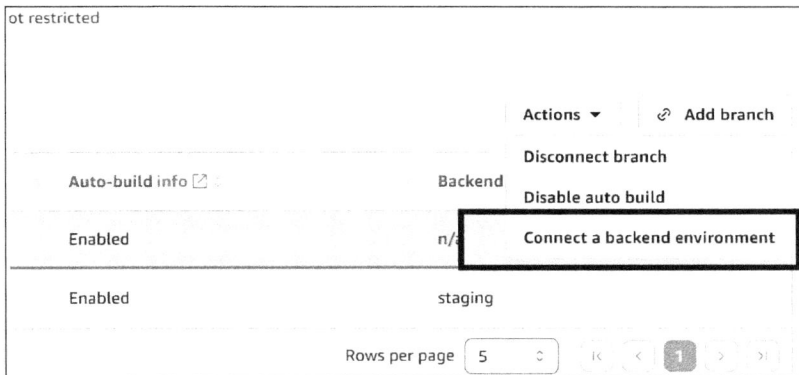

Figure 19.3: Connecting the environment

4. Now we have the frontend branch separately hosted and can connect backend environment. By default, we will see **staging**. After deployment, Amplify will automatically create a new environment that we can choose by name, like in *Figure 19.4* :

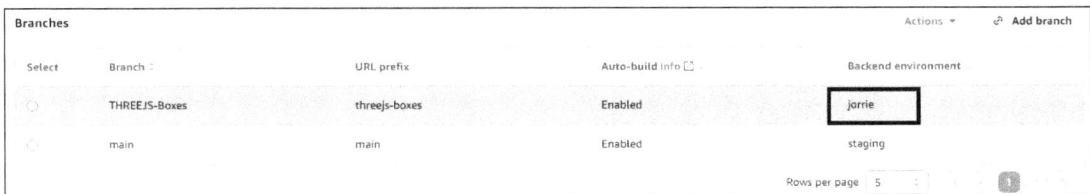

Figure 19.4: New environment

5. As a result, we will see another environment in the list that will have the link we can use to manage the application and move it into the regular Agile process. An example is shown in *Figure 19.5:*

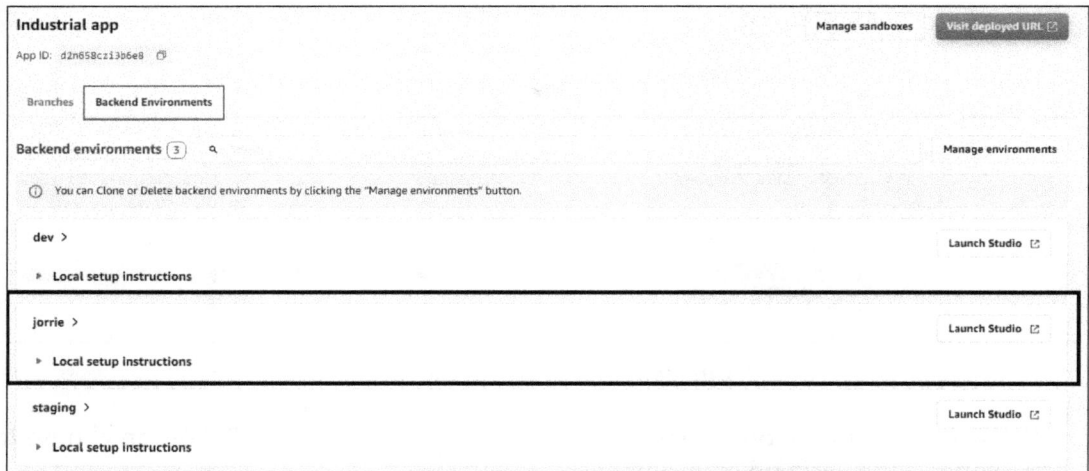

Figure 19.5: New environment in the list

In specific cases, we may face issues in the build stage if AWS does not see the configuration files in the branch. To solve it, pull the environment into the branch with the command: `amplify pull --appId YOUR_APP_ID --envName YOUR_ENVIRONMENT_NAME`. This will pull the environment data. After that push these changes into the branch. Note that we should be in the project root when we run the command in the CLI.

Custom domain, SSL, and CDN settings

The custom domain is essential for establishing a strong online presence, building brand credibility, improving search engine visibility, and providing a memorable and trustworthy user experience. It is a foundational element of web development that contributes to the success and longevity of a website. Adding a custom domain will require following these steps:

1. To align a custom domain to the project in the AWS Amplify Console, choose the **Hosting** panel and select the **Custom domain** tab, like in *Figure 19.6:*

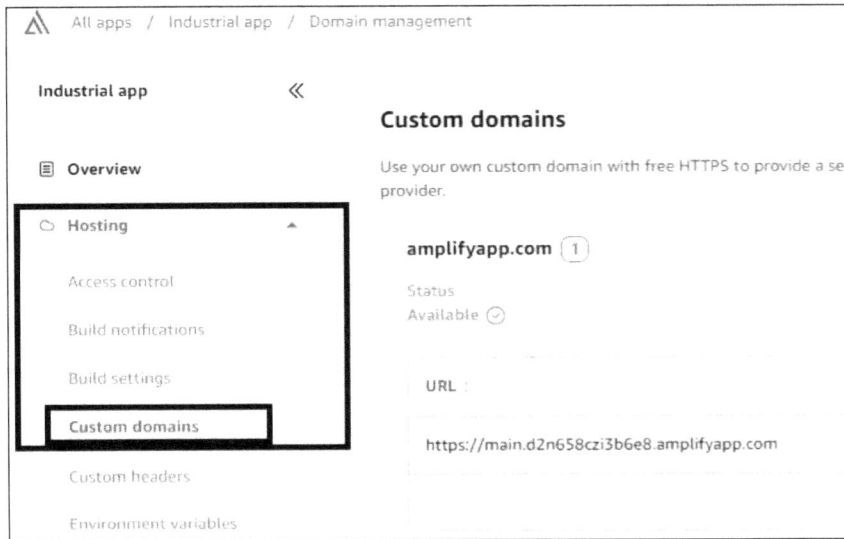

Figure 19.6: Enter the custom domains screen in AWS Amplify

2. Next, we can press the **Add domain** button and enter the required domain in the input field or use the Amazon Route53 service as described in *Figure 19.7*:

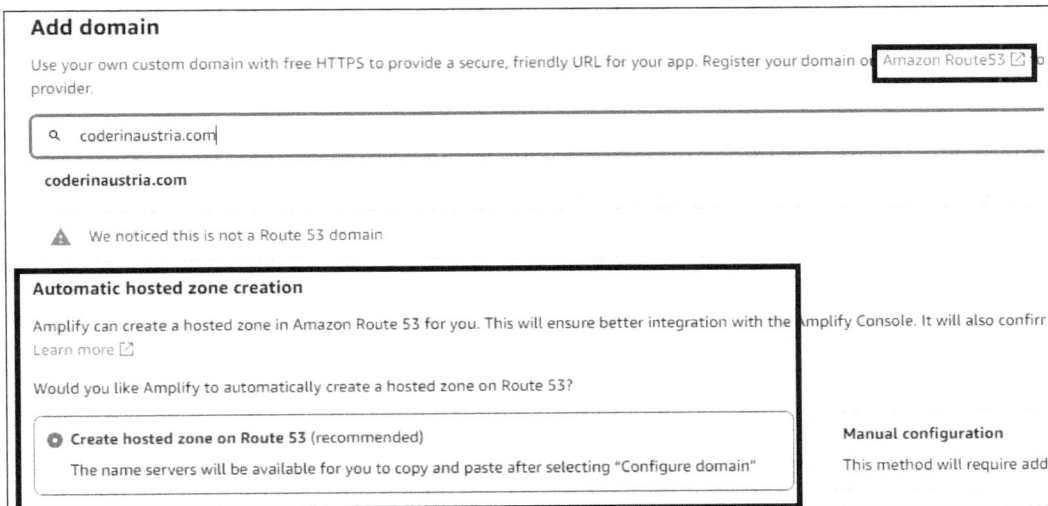

Figure 19.7: Adding the custom domain in AWS Amplify

3. The last step is configuring the zone name servers in the domain panel. Unfortunately, each domain service has its own configuration. The following example is with the **Namecheap** service. The one you will choose will have a different view screen, so please read the documentation from your domain holder first.

4. After clicking on the **Configure domain** button from *Figure 19.7,* we will see the screen where we can collect the list of Name servers (*Figure 19.8*) that we will use in domain configuration (*Figure 19.9*):

The domain configuration screen is shown in *Figure 19.8*. On this screen need to check the checkbox with the label **I have added the above name servers to my domain registry**:

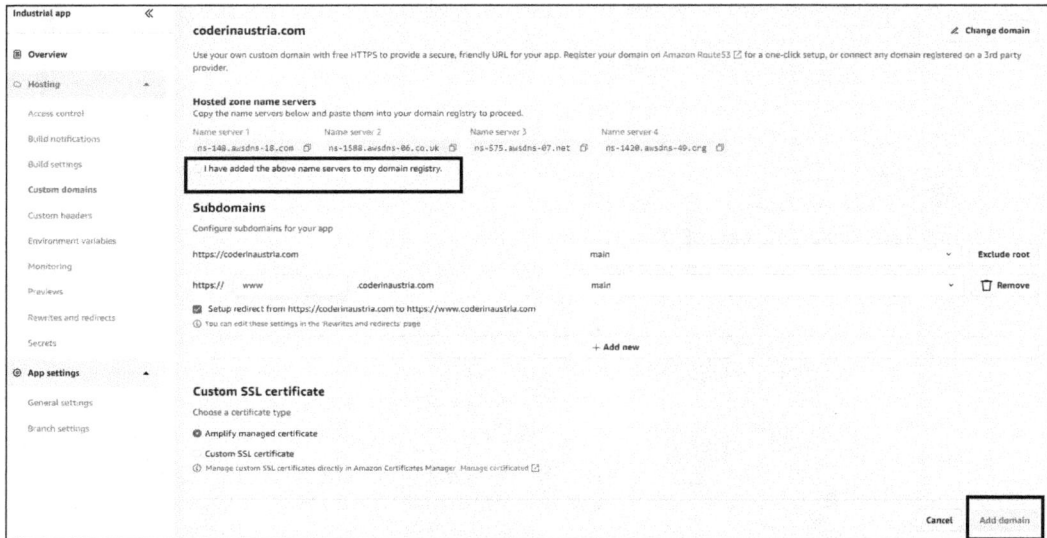

Figure 19.8: Domain configuration in AWS Amplify

5. When we fill in all the **Name servers** in the domain system from *Figure 19.8,* we can press the checkbox shown in *Figure 19.9* and click the **Add Domain** button.

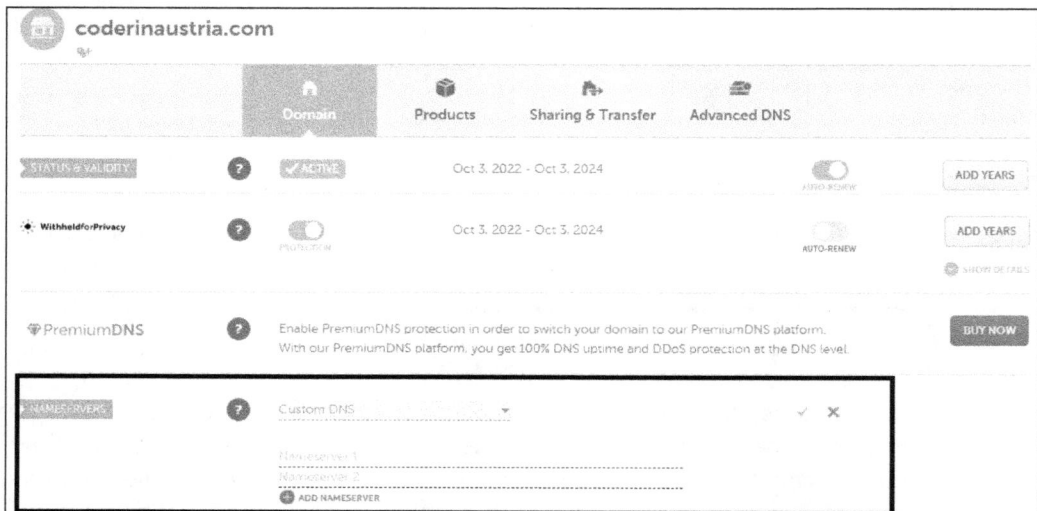

Figure 19.9: Domain configuration in Namecheap domain system

6. Using AWS Amplify in production is very convenient in the case of custom domains. As we can see in *Figure 19.8,* there is a section for choosing a **Secure Sockets Layer** (**SSL**) certificate. We can find the specific section in *Figure 19.10*:

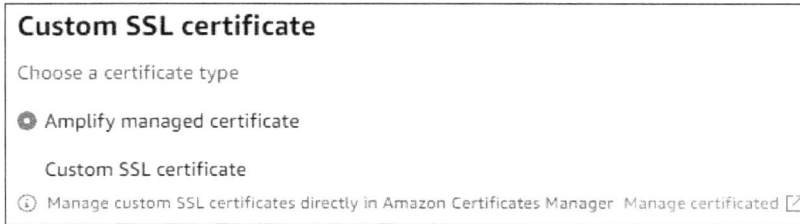

Custom SSL certificate

Choose a certificate type

● Amplify managed certificate

Custom SSL certificate

ⓘ Manage custom SSL certificates directly in Amazon Certificates Manager Manage certificated ↗

Figure 19.10: SSL configuration in AWS Amplify

7. For most cases, we should choose an automatic SSL certificate connection. We must choose the manual way if we have specific certificates from the DevOps team or the client.

8. The last screen is an automatic configuration of the domain in Amplify, shown in *Figure 19.11:*

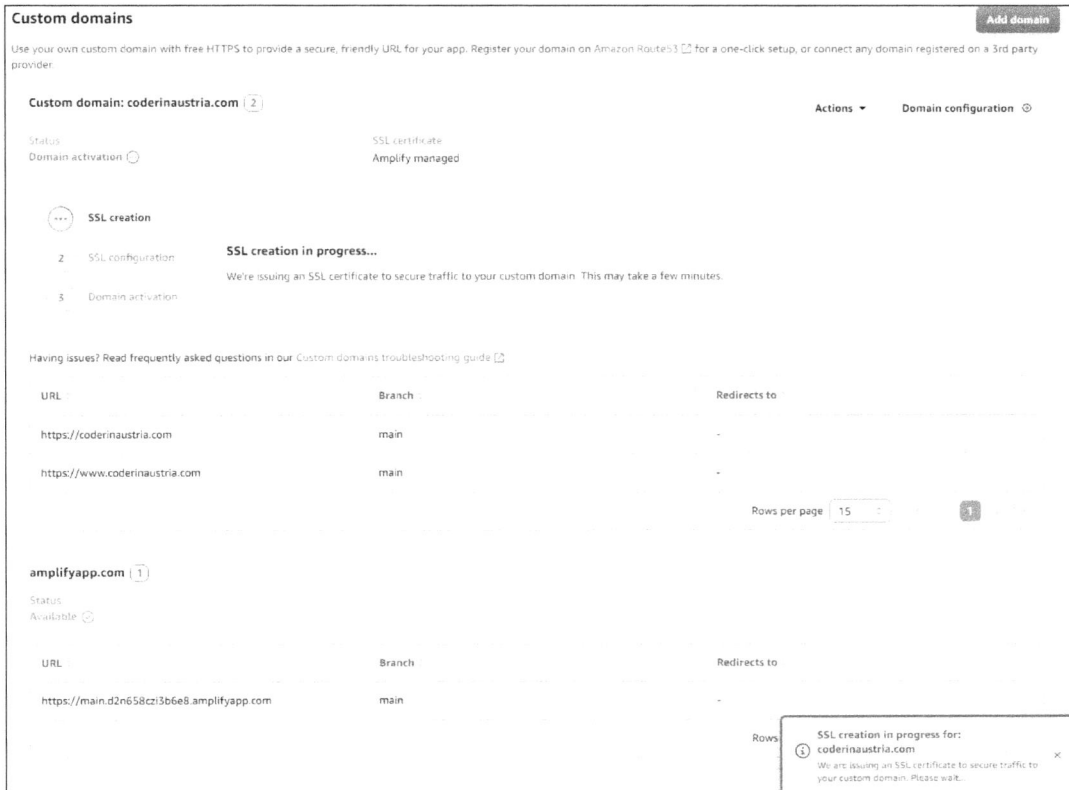

Figure 19.11: Domain initiation in AWS Amplify

Note: SSL certificates facilitate secure communication between the web browser and the website's server by delivering encryption and authentication.

Since AWS Amplify is fully automated to set the **Content Delivery Network** (**CDN**), we can make some configurations using **Custom headers**. To get into the section, choose the menu tab with the **Custom headers** label, as shown in *Figure 19.12*:

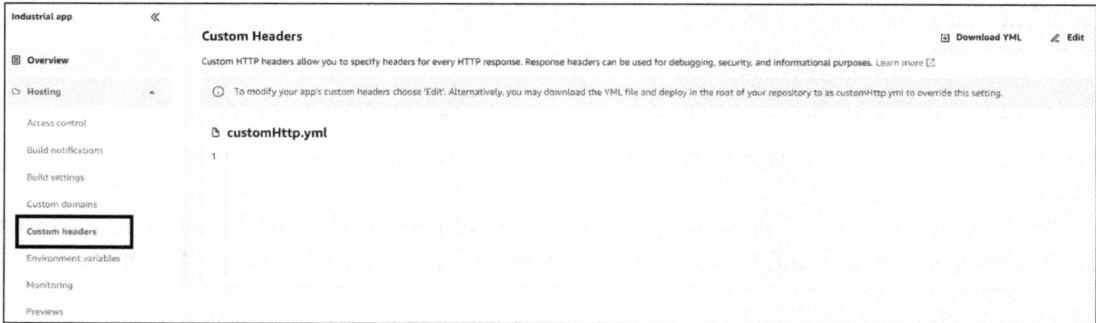

Figure 19.12: Custom headers in AWS Amplify

For example, if we need to update cache control for the images, we can add some custom headers in specific fields. Put the code from *Code Listing 19.1* into the specific field on the **Custom headers** page:

```
1.  customHeaders:
2.    - pattern: '/img/*'
3.      headers:
4.        - key: 'Cache-Control'
5.          value: 's-maxage=3600'
```

Code Listing 19.1: Custom headers code example

This example keeps the associated content cached at the edge for 3600 seconds (one hour).

CI/CD automation

Continuous Integration/Continuous Deployment (CI/CD) is a crucial aspect of modern software development, streamlining the process from code creation to deployment. Here, we will study what CI/CD entails, its significance in software development, and how it is implemented with AWS Amplify for automated deployment workflows.

CI/CD is a software development practice that enables developers to automate integration, testing, and deployment of code changes. Here is a breakdown of its core components:

- **Continuous Integration (CI):** Developers frequently merge their code changes into a shared repository, triggering automated builds and tests. This ensures that new code integrates smoothly with the existing codebase and catches errors early in the development cycle.

- **Continuous Deployment (CD):** After code changes pass the CI process, they are automatically deployed to production or staging environments. CD ensures that tested and validated code is swiftly delivered to users, reducing manual intervention and deployment errors.

AWS Amplify provides a comprehensive suite of tools for implementing CI/CD pipelines seamlessly. This is how it works:

1. **Code repository integration**: Amplify integrates with popular code repositories like GitHub, Bitbucket, and GitLab, enabling automatic triggers for build and deployment pipelines.

2. **Build and test automation**: Once triggered, Amplify builds and tests the application using predefined scripts and configurations. Developers can define custom-built settings and testing environments to suit their requirements.

3. **Deployment options**: Amplify supports various deployment options, including automatic deployment to AWS services like Amazon S3, AWS Lambda, and Amazon CloudFront. Developers can also configure custom deployment settings and environment variables.

4. **Monitoring and rollback**: Amplify provides monitoring and logging capabilities, allowing developers to track deployment progress and performance metrics. In case of deployment failures or errors, Amplify supports automatic rollback to the previous working version.

Performance monitoring

AWS Amplify Monitoring is a comprehensive monitoring solution that provides visibility into the performance and health of applications deployed using AWS Amplify. It offers real-time metrics, logs, and alerts to help developers and operators monitor, troubleshoot, and optimize their applications effectively.

Features of AWS Amplify Monitoring

Some features of AWS Amplify Monitoring are as follows:

- **Real-time metrics**: Amplify Monitoring collects and aggregates real-time metrics related to application performance, including latency, error rates, and request throughput. These metrics provide valuable insights into the overall health and performance of the application.

- **Logs and traces**: Amplify Monitoring offers logging and tracing capabilities, allowing developers to track application activity, diagnose errors, and identify performance bottlenecks. Developers can view logs generated by various AWS services, as well as custom application logs.

- **Alerting and notifications**: Amplify Monitoring supports alerting and notification mechanisms, enabling developers to set up alarms based on predefined thresholds or conditions. Alerts can be configured to notify developers via email, SMS, or other channels when specific metrics or events occur.

- **Dashboard and visualization**: Amplify Monitoring provides customizable dashboards and visualization tools to help developers visualize and analyze application metrics and logs. Developers can create custom dashboards tailored to their specific monitoring needs, making it easier to track key performance indicators and troubleshoot issues.

Benefits of effective monitoring

Some benefits of effective monitoring are as follows:

- **Performance optimization**: Monitoring allows developers to identify performance bottlenecks and optimize application performance. By tracking key metrics like latency and error rates, developers can pinpoint areas for improvement and optimize resource utilization.

- **Proactive issue detection**: Monitoring enables proactive detection of issues and errors before they impact end users. Setting up alerts and notifications helps developers respond quickly to critical events and minimize downtime.

- **Capacity planning**: Monitoring provides insights into resource usage and capacity requirements, helping developers plan and scale their infrastructure effectively. Tracking resource utilization metrics helps developers anticipate future capacity needs and scale resources accordingly.

- **Troubleshooting and debugging**: Monitoring facilitates troubleshooting and debugging by providing access to logs, traces, and other diagnostic information. Developers can use monitoring data to identify the root cause of issues and implement timely fixes.

The view of monitoring can be found in the menu tab, as shown in *Figure 19.13:*

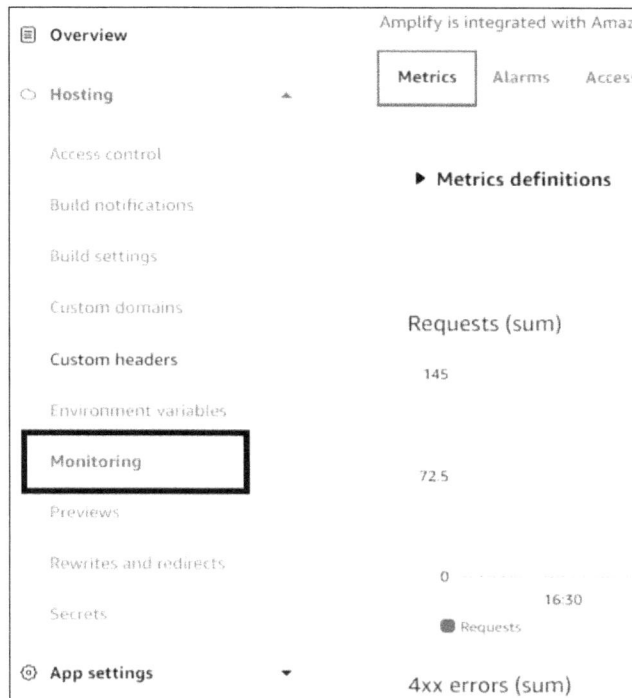

Figure 19.13: Monitoring in AWS Amplify

Conclusion

This chapter provides a comprehensive overview of hosting web applications with AWS Amplify. From managing environments and deployments to configuring custom domains, SSL certificates, and CDN settings, we have studied the key steps involved in deploying and managing web applications on the Amplify platform. We have also seen the importance of CI/CD automation and performance monitoring in ensuring the reliability, security, and performance of deployed applications.

By leveraging AWS Amplify's powerful features and integrations, developers can streamline the deployment process, automate repetitive tasks, and gain valuable insights into their application's performance. With CI/CD automation, developers can accelerate the release cycle, reduce manual errors, and maintain consistency across environments. Meanwhile, performance monitoring enables developers to proactively identify and address performance issues, optimize resource utilization, and deliver an exceptional user experience.

As organizations increasingly adopt cloud-native development practices, AWS Amplify emerges as a valuable tool for modern web development workflows. Its seamless integration with AWS services, intuitive interface, and robust feature set make it an ideal choice for developers looking to build, deploy, and scale web applications with ease. By mastering the concepts covered in this chapter, developers can harness the full potential of AWS Amplify to accelerate their development lifecycle, enhance application reliability, and deliver exceptional user experiences.

In the next chapter, we will discuss the critical aspects of user management within modern web applications. We will begin by developing a solid understanding of user management principles, including how to handle authentication and authorization effectively. From there, we will explore the implementation of user sign-in and sign-up workflows, ensuring a secure and seamless user experience. Next, we will focus on customizing the authorization form's UI to align with your application's branding and design needs. Finally, we will tackle multi-factor authentication, a vital security feature that adds an extra layer of protection for user accounts. This chapter will provide the foundation and practical skills to create secure, user-friendly authentication systems.

Points to remember

- AWS Amplify provides a streamlined approach to managing deployment environments, allowing for efficient workflows and consistent application states across development, staging, and production.

- Custom domains, SSL certificates, and CDN configurations enhance security and performance, ensuring fast and reliable access to your application.

- Automating the CI/CD pipeline in AWS Amplify simplifies the deployment process, reducing manual effort and minimizing errors.

- Performance monitoring tools in AWS Amplify help track application health, optimize load times, and detect issues before they impact users.

- Implementing best practices for scalability and security ensures that your Next.js application remains performant and secure as it grows.

Exercises

These exercises will reinforce key concepts and give you hands-on experience with AWS Amplify's deployment and management features. Let me know if you'd like any adjustments! Create a new environment in AWS Amplify and deploy your Next.js application.

1. Connect a custom domain to your Amplify-hosted application.
2. Set up a repository on GitHub, GitLab, or Bitbucket and link it to AWS Amplify.
3. Enable monitoring tools in AWS Amplify and analyze performance metrics.

CHAPTER 20
User Authentication with AWS Amplify

Introduction

Managing users effectively is a cornerstone of any successful web application. AWS Amplify offers a robust suite of tools and services designed to simplify and enhance user management, making it easier for developers to implement secure authentication and authorization mechanisms. This chapter dives into the essentials of user management with AWS Amplify, covering everything from user sign-in and sign-up to advanced security features like multi-factor authentication. By leveraging these capabilities, developers can create a seamless and secure user experience, ensuring that their applications meet functional and security requirements.

Structure

In this chapter, we will discuss the following topics:

- Understanding user management
- Implementation of user sign-in and sign-up
- Authorization form UI customization
- Multi-factor authentication

Objectives

By the end of this chapter, you will have a thorough understanding of user management in AWS Amplify, including its core functionalities and why it is essential for modern applications. You will learn how to implement secure user sign-in and sign-up features, providing a strong foundation for managing access to your application. Additionally, we will cover techniques for customizing the authorization form UI, enabling you to align it seamlessly with your application's design and branding. Finally, you will learn how to set up **multi-factor authentication** (**MFA**), enhancing your application's security by adding an extra layer of protection to the user authentication process. This chapter will equip you with the knowledge and tools to build secure and user-friendly authentication systems.

Understanding user management

User management and authorization are fundamental aspects of web and application development, ensuring that users can securely access resources and perform actions based on their permissions.

User management refers to the processes and tools used to handle user accounts and their associated data within an application. It encompasses several key functions:

- **User registration**:
    - o Allows new users to create accounts.
    - o Typically involves collecting user information such as username, email, and password.
    - o May include email verification to confirm the user's identity.

- **Authentication**:
    - o The process of verifying a user's identity.
    - o Common methods include username/password pairs, MFA, and OAuth.
    - o Once authenticated, users are usually issued a token (e.g., JWT) for subsequent requests.

- **User profiles**:
    - o Managing user-specific information such as personal details, preferences, and settings.
    - o Users should be able to view and update their profiles.

- **Password management**:
    - o Functions for changing passwords, resetting forgotten passwords, and enforcing password policies (e.g., complexity requirements).

      o   Store passwords securely using hashing algorithms.

- **Account management**:
  - o   Functions for updating user information, deactivating accounts, and deleting accounts.
  - o   Admin might have additional capabilities to manage other users' accounts.

- **Roles and Permissions**:
  - o   Defining different roles (e.g., user, admin) and the permissions associated with each role.
  - o   Users can be assigned roles that determine their access level within the application.

All these functionalities exist in AWS Amplify out of the box. Let us study user management in detail. To start working with user management, we need to enter the Amplify studio. For this, follow these steps:

1. Select the **Backend Environments** tab and enter the Studio in the environment that we want to use, as shown in *Figure 20.1*:

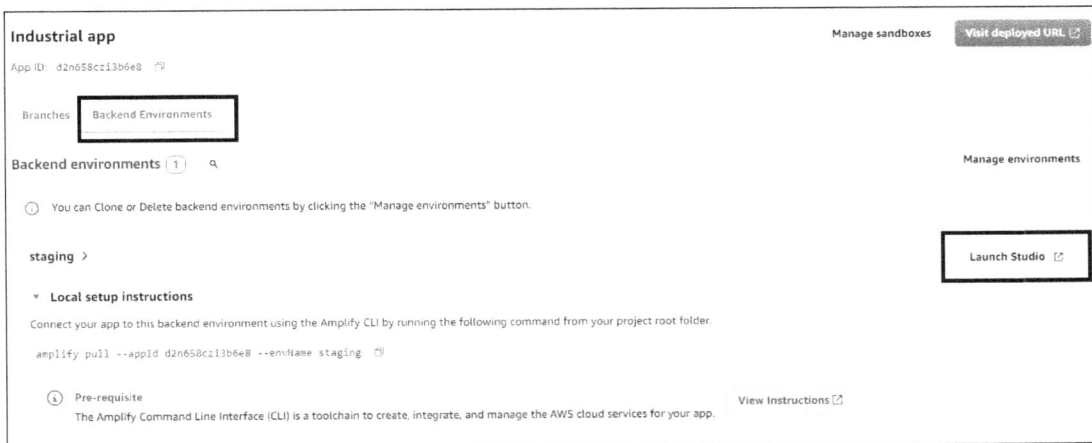

Figure 20.1: *Selecting the environment for the studio*

2. Now, we need to enter the **User Management** tab and **Set up authentication** as shown in *Figure 20.2*:

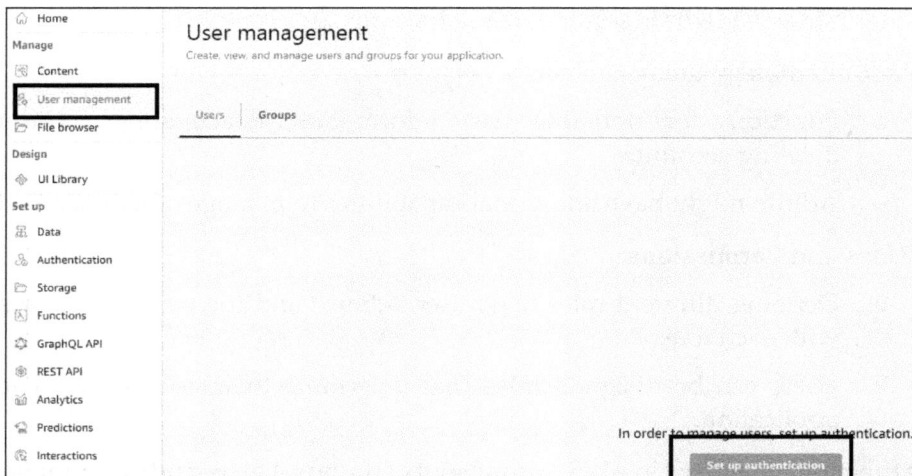

Figure 20.2: Selecting the user management

3. On the next screen, we can customize our authentication by adding login strategies (with Google or Amazon) or customizing password requirements. We will keep everything in the default setting and keep customization for the exercise section. To deploy the user management module, press the **Deploy** button, as shown in *Figure 20.3*:

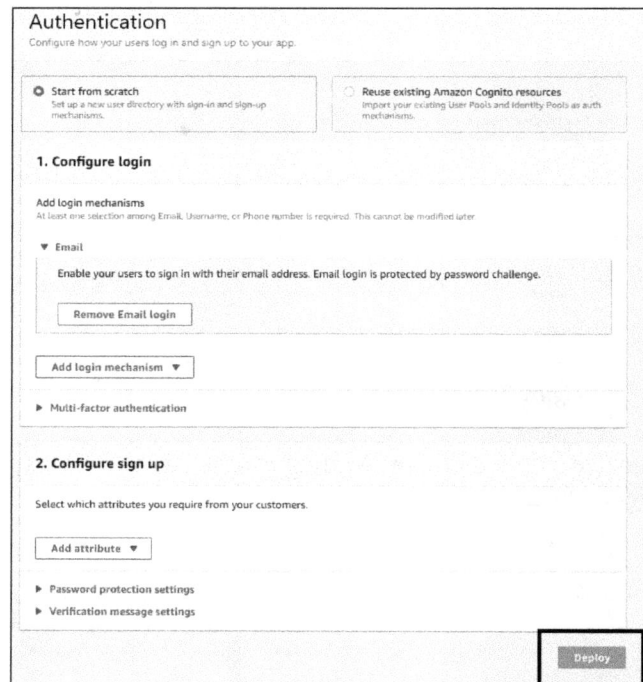

Figure 20.3: Deploy the user management

4. The result will be the same as in *Figure 20.4*. It is important to pull the updates into the project with a command that is highlighted in *Figure 20.4.* The project ID in our case will be different.

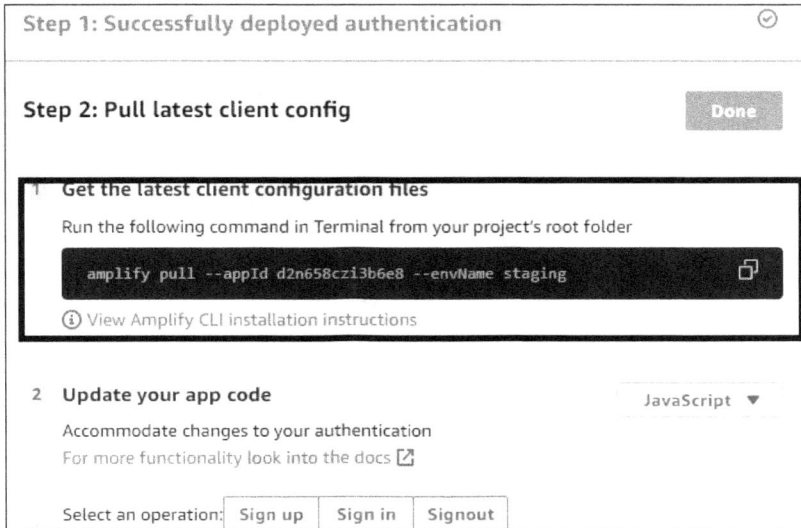

Figure 20.4: *Successfully deployed authentication*

5. If we enter the **User Management** tab again (*Figure 20.5*), we will see the list of users that we have in the system and the possibility to manage them. At this stage, we will have 0 users. We will fix that in the next steps by implementing Auth UI in our project and testing registration.

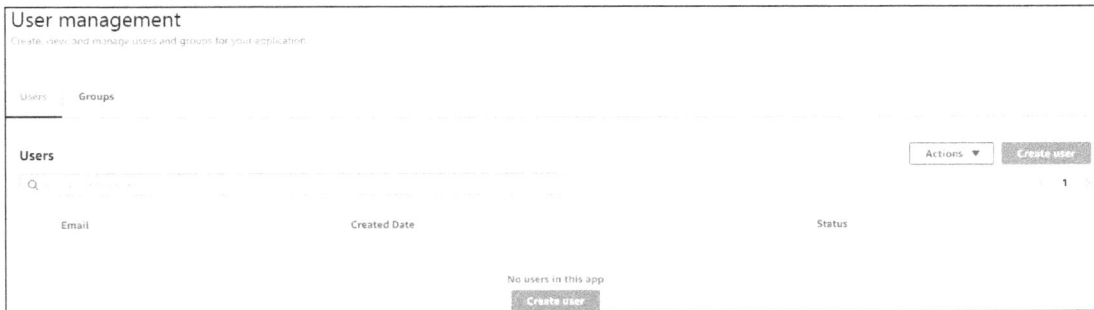

Figure 20.5: *User management after deployment*

Implementation of user sign-in and sign-up

There are two ways to implement sign-up and sign-in with Amplify. The first is to use the API, and the second is to use the more convenient React UI component. To implement the user authorization possibility into the application, we will need to follow these steps:

1. We will need a React UI library and Amplify connected to the project. If not, we use these commands: **npm install @aws-amplify/ui-react aws-amplify** or **yarn add @aws-amplify/ui-react aws-amplify**

2. The next step is to create a private page that will be closed by the sign-in / sign-up process. For this, we create a new folder in the application containing a page file, the same as before. To wrap it with Authorisation, we will create the layout file related to this page. The file structure will be the same as in *Figure 20.6:*

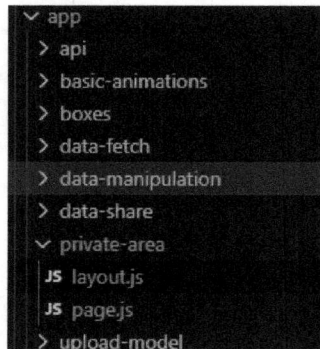

Figure 20.6: *File structure after the update*

3. In the layout file, we need to create the wrapper using the AWS component to hide any content from unauthorized users. We will follow *Code Listing 20.1* to get the code:

```
1.  "use client";
2.  import { Authenticator } from '@aws-amplify/ui-react';
3.  import { Amplify } from 'aws-amplify';
4.  import config from '@/aws-exports';
5.  import '@aws-amplify/ui-react/styles.css';
6.
7.  Amplify.configure(config);
8.
9.  export default function PrivateLayout({ children }) {
10.    return (
11.      <Authenticator>
12.        {({ signOut, user }) => (
13.          <main>
14.            <h1>Hello {user?.username}</h1>
15.            <button onClick={signOut}>Sign out</button>
16.            {children}
17.          </main>
18.        )}
19.      </Authenticator>
20.    );
21. };
```

Code Listing 20.1: *The layout file to wrap all private areas*

The AWS Auth component uses React hooks that do not work with SSR components in Next.js. As we can see in *Code Listing 20.1,* we use the "use client" directive. It leads to all private areas being client or client-rendered applications. It is ok, as it will not be used in SEO. If we need the SSR for some reason for the private area, we will have to use the API way and create the whole authorization flow ourselves.

4. The last step is to create the page that will be visible after login. We collect this code in *Code Listing 20.2:*

```
1. export default function AprivateArea() {
2.   return (
3.     <div>Hello from Private</div>
4.   );
5. };
```

Code Listing 20.2: The page file for the private area

Now that we have both the files, we can open the "private-area" page, and we will see that we already have a fully integrated user management process with the UI, as shown in *Figure 20.7:*

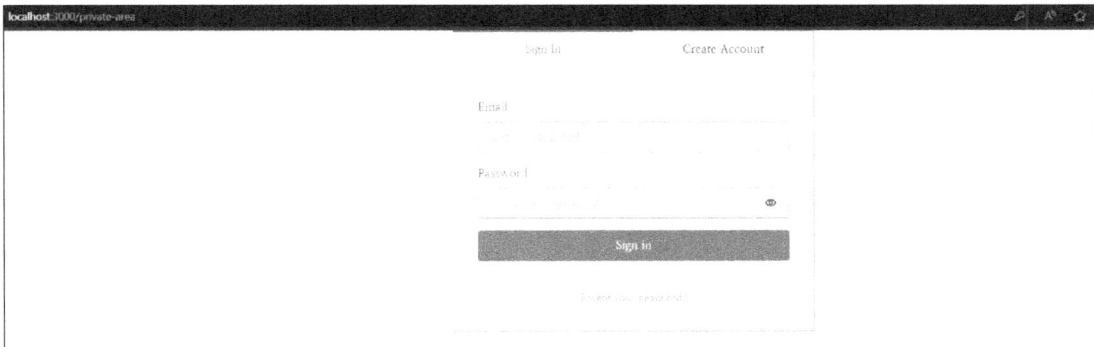

Figure 20.7: User management forms from AWS

Here, we can create an account. The process from AWS will also send the confirmation code to our email, which will be used as the email for the registration. After registration ends, we will be redirected to the private area page with content like in *Figure 20.8:*

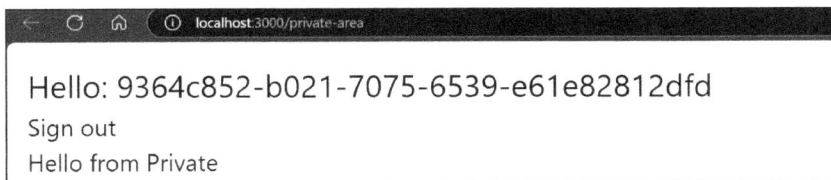

Figure 20.8: Private area content after authorization

Authorization form UI customization

For the UI customization for the Authorisation form, we will have two opportunities:

- Make changes to the UI theme using tokens.

- Add the direct styles for the components in some special cases, like aligning the Auth form in the page middle.

To style the form, we add **ThemeProvider** to our layout, which has a theme object with all changed tokens. We follow *Code Listing 20.3* as an example of changes:

```
1.  "use client";
2.  import { Authenticator, ThemeProvider, useTheme } from
    '@aws-amplify/ui-react';
3.  import { Amplify } from 'aws-amplify';
4.  import config from '@/aws-exports';
5.  import '@aws-amplify/ui-react/styles.css';
6.
7.  Amplify.configure(config);
8.
9.  export default function PrivateLayout({ children }) {
10.   const { tokens } = useTheme();
11.   // Theme object used for styling the Ember Authenticator component.
12.   const theme = {
13.     name: 'Auth Example Theme', // Name of the theme for
    identification purposes.
14.     tokens: {
15.       components: {
16.         authenticator: {
17.           router: { // Styling for the Ember Router component.
18.             boxShadow: `0 0 26px ${tokens.colors.overlay['10']}`,
19.             borderWidth: '2px',
20.           },
21.           form: { // Styling for the authentication form.
22.             padding: `${tokens.space.medium} ${tokens.space.xl}
    ${tokens.space.medium}`,
23.           },
24.         },
25.         button: { // Styling for buttons within the Auth
    Authenticator component.
26.           primary: { // Styling for the primary action button
    (e.g. "Sign In").
27.             backgroundColor: tokens.colors.neutral['100'],
28.           },
29.           link: { // Styling for any links within the Auth
    Authenticator component.
30.             color: tokens.colors.purple['80'],
31.           },
```

```
32.            },
33.          fieldcontrol: { // Styling for the Ember FieldControl component.
34.            _focus: { // Styling for when a form field is focused.
35.              boxShadow: `0 0 0 2px ${tokens.colors.purple['60']}`,
36.            },
37.          },
38.          tabs: { // Styling for the Auth Tabs component.
39.            item: { // Styling for each tab item within the Auth
     Tabs component.
40.              color: tokens.colors.neutral['80'],
41.              _active: { // Styling for the active tab item.
42.                borderColor: tokens.colors.neutral['100'],
43.                color: tokens.colors.purple['100'],
44.              },
45.            },
46.          },
47.        },
48.      },
49.    };
50.
51.    return (
52.      // The ThemeProvider component is used to apply the theme
     object created above.
53.      <ThemeProvider theme={theme}>
54.        <Authenticator>
55.          {({ signOut, user }) => (
56.            <main>
57.              <h1>Hello {user?.username}</h1>
58.              <button onClick={signOut}>Sign out</button>
59.              {children}
60.            </main>
61.          )}
62.        </Authenticator>
63.      </ThemeProvider>
64.    );
65. };
```

Code Listing 20.3: The theme changes for the Auth form

We can also add the CSS changes for the form not included in the tokens. For this, we add *Code Listing 20.4* in the **global.scss** file to add a margin to the form:

```
1. [data-amplify-router] {
2.   margin-top: 50%;
3. }
```

Code Listing 20.4: Adding margins to the form

The result will be the same as in *Figure 20.9* with updated styles for the form:

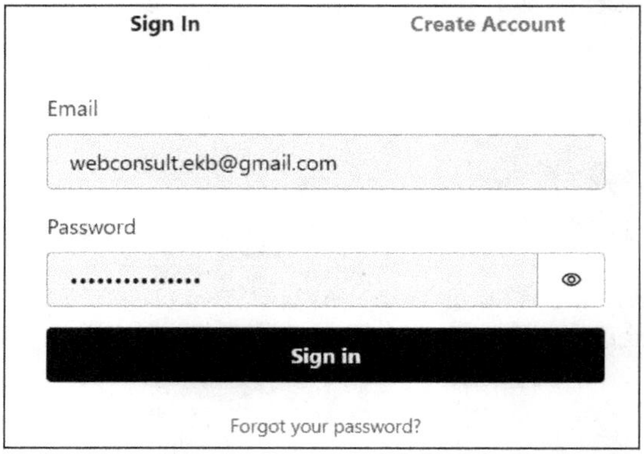

Figure 20.9: *Updated styles for the Auth UI*

Multi-factor authentication

MFA is a security enhancement that requires users to provide two or more verification factors to access a resource, such as an application, online account, or VPN. MFA helps protect users by adding an extra layer of security, making it significantly harder for attackers to gain access even if they have obtained a user's password.

To add the MFA to our project, we select this feature in the Authorisation setup in Amplify Studio and click on **Deploy**. The selections are described in *Figure 20.10*:

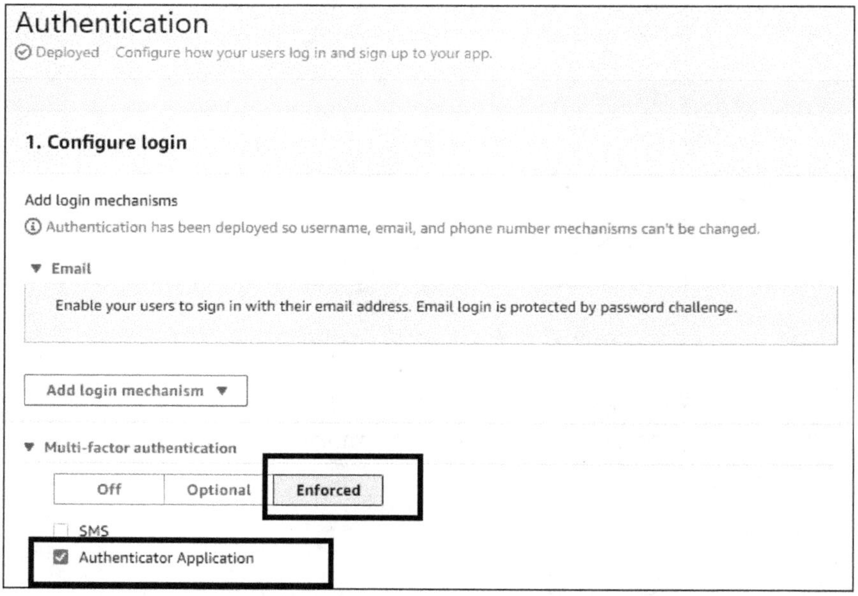

Figure 20.10: *MFA Selections to update the project*

We will use the Authenticator application as it is more secure and saves costs. Users do not need to share their phone numbers to use the applications. For example, we can use the Google Authenticator app for this. To pull your updates, we use a command like this in our root: `amplify pull --appId <YOUR-PROJECT-ID> --envName staging`. Next, if we try to log in, we will see the barcode to initiate the Authenticator app as shown in *Figure 20.11*:

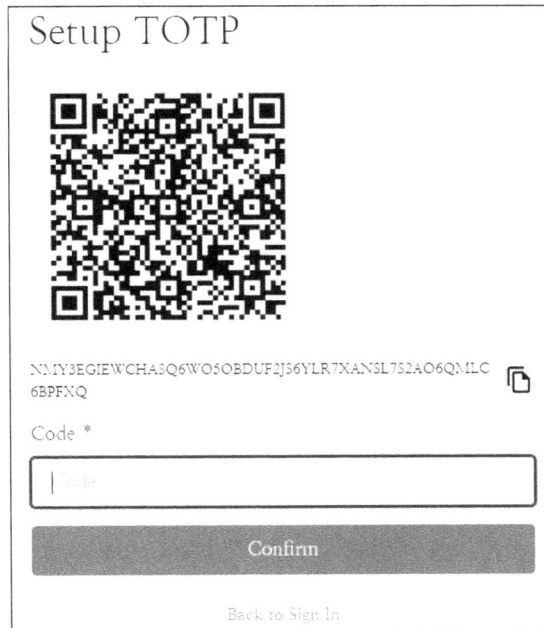

Figure 20.11: *MFA Fronted UI*

As we already mentioned, the whole user management flow is already made for us by AWS Amplify, so there is no need to make anything else. If we use the Google Authenticator app, we add our barcode there and enter the code. After that, we will be signed in to the private page.

Conclusion

In this chapter, we have studied the critical aspects of user management using AWS Amplify, giving us the knowledge to implement robust authentication and authorization systems in our applications. We began with an overview of user management fundamentals, understanding the importance of securing user data and providing a seamless authentication experience. We learned how to implement user sign-in and sign-up features, ensuring users can easily access the application.

We discussed the implementation of MFA, enhancing the security of the application by adding a layer of protection.

This knowledge is a significant step towards building secure, scalable, and user-friendly applications that meet the highest standards of modern web development.

In the next chapter, we will explore the essential aspects of data storage and management in the context of 3D applications. We'll begin by introducing the fundamentals of data storage, focusing on how to efficiently structure and organize data for seamless management. From there, we'll dive into model schema design, demonstrating how to create well-defined schemas tailored for 3D object data. Next, we'll walk through implementing **Create, Read, Update, Delete (CRUD)** operations, providing practical techniques for managing 3D objects dynamically. We'll also cover strategies for file storage, ensuring efficient and scalable handling of 3D object files in your applications. By the end of the chapter, you'll have a solid foundation to manage complex data workflows, enabling your 3D applications to perform efficiently and reliably.

Points to remember

- We do not need to create the UI for the user management process if we use AWS Amplify. Everything is out of the box.

- There are limited social providers to use. On the other hand, we do not need a lot of them.

Exercises

1. Complete the private area described in this chapter. Additionally, please add the social authorization with Facebook. You need to select Add login mechanism in the Authentication configuration and choose Facebook.

2. Update styles for your form with different colors and paddings.

Join our Discord space

Join our Discord workspace for latest updates, offers, tech happenings around the world, new releases, and sessions with the authors:

https://discord.bpbonline.com

CHAPTER 21

Data Storage and Management in AWS Amplify

Introduction

In the previous chapters, we studied the essentials of setting up AWS Amplify services and managing user authentication. We will now return to our core focus: 3D development. This chapter is dedicated to mastering data storage and management, specifically for handling 3D objects within a Next.js and Three.js application.

We will start by exploring how to design and implement model schemas that effectively structure our 3D data. We will learn to leverage various AWS services to **create, read, update, and delete (CRUD)** 3D objects seamlessly. Additionally, we will study the intricacies of file storage using AWS S3, ensuring the 3D model files are securely stored and easily accessible.

Structure

In this chapter, we will discuss the following topics:

- Introducing data storage and management
- Model schemas and design
- CRUD operations for 3D objects
- File storage for 3D objects

Objectives

By the end of this chapter, you will have a solid understanding of designing and implementing model schemas for 3D objects, ensuring efficient data structuring within your application. You will learn how to leverage AWS services to perform essential CRUD operations on 3D objects, enabling dynamic and flexible data management. Additionally, we will explore the integration of AWS S3 for secure and scalable file storage, allowing for seamless handling of 3D model files. Finally, we will walk through the development of a comprehensive CRUD interface, empowering you to interact with 3D objects and their associated data effortlessly. This knowledge will provide a strong foundation for building and managing 3D applications with Next.js and AWS Amplify.

Introducing data storage and management

Data storage and management are fundamental aspects of any software development process. Effective data management ensures that information is efficiently stored, retrieved, and updated, providing the backbone for dynamic and interactive applications. The importance of robust data storage cannot be overstated in the context of web applications, particularly those utilizing Three.js for 3D graphics.

In a scenario where our web application allows users to create and manipulate 3D models. We need a reliable data storage solution to save users' models, track changes, and manage different versions to achieve this. AWS Amplify offers a comprehensive tool suite that makes this process seamless and scalable.

Data storage and management provide several critical benefits:

- **Data persistence**: Ensures data is stored securely and available even after a session ends. For example, user-created 3D models can be saved and accessed later.

- **Data integrity**: Helps maintain the accuracy and consistency of data. This is crucial when dealing with complex 3D objects where precision is key.

- **Scalability**: Allows the application to handle growing amounts of data efficiently. As more users interact with our 3D modeling application, a scalable storage solution can manage the increased load.

- **Security**: Protects sensitive data from unauthorized access and breaches. AWS services provide robust security features to safeguard user data.

In this and the next chapter, we will research these topics:

- **User-generated content**: In a 3D modeling application, users can create and save their 3D designs. AWS Amplify's storage capabilities can be used to save these models, while APIs can provide endpoints for CRUD operations on these models.

- **Version control**: Implementing version control for 3D models allows users to save different versions of their work. This can be managed by storing metadata about each model version in a database and using AWS S3 to store the actual model files.

- **Real-time collaboration**: Enabling multiple users to collaborate on a 3D project in real time requires effective data synchronization. Using AWS Amplify's API and subscription features, we can implement real-time data updates.

Model schemas and design

Data modeling and schema design are critical components of developing robust and efficient applications. In AWS Amplify, these processes are streamlined to help developers create well-structured, scalable, and maintainable applications. AWS Amplify provides tools and services to define, manage, and interact with our application's data models effectively.

Data modeling is the process of creating a data model for the data to be stored in a database. It involves defining how data is structured, including the relationships between different data entities. A well-designed data model ensures that data is organized logically and efficiently, which helps in maintaining data integrity and improving query performance.

Schemas define the structure of the data stored in a database. They describe the types of data that can be stored, how data entities are related, and any constraints on the data. In the context of AWS Amplify, schemas are defined using the GraphQL **schema definition language (SDL),** which provides a clear and concise way to specify the data structure and relationships.

AWS Amplify uses GraphQL to define data models and schemas. Amplify provides a GraphQL transformer that converts a GraphQL schema into a set of AWS resources (such as DynamoDB tables and Elasticsearch indices) that are deployed and managed by AWS CloudFormation.

In the Amplify Studio, we have a graphical interface to easily start with data modeling. Data modeling in AWS Amplify Studio provides a visual interface to easily define, structure, and manage application data without extensive backend coding. To use it, follow these steps:

1. First, we need to open the studio using the link to it shown in *Figure 21.1*:

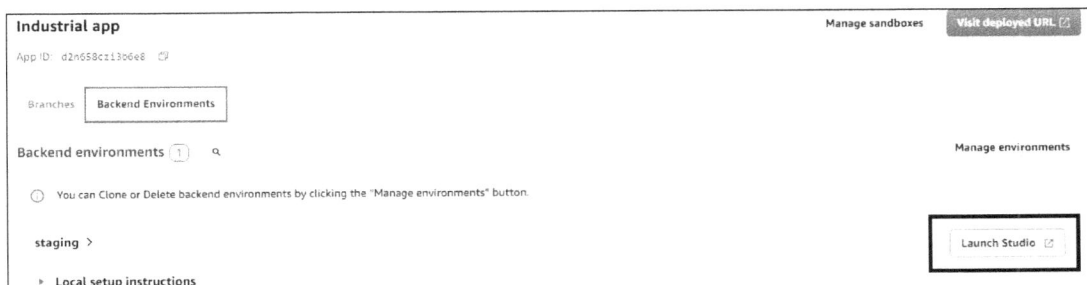

Figure 21.1: Launching Studio Link

2. Next, we need to open the **Data** tab and click on **Add Model** to create our first model, shown in *Figure 21.2*:

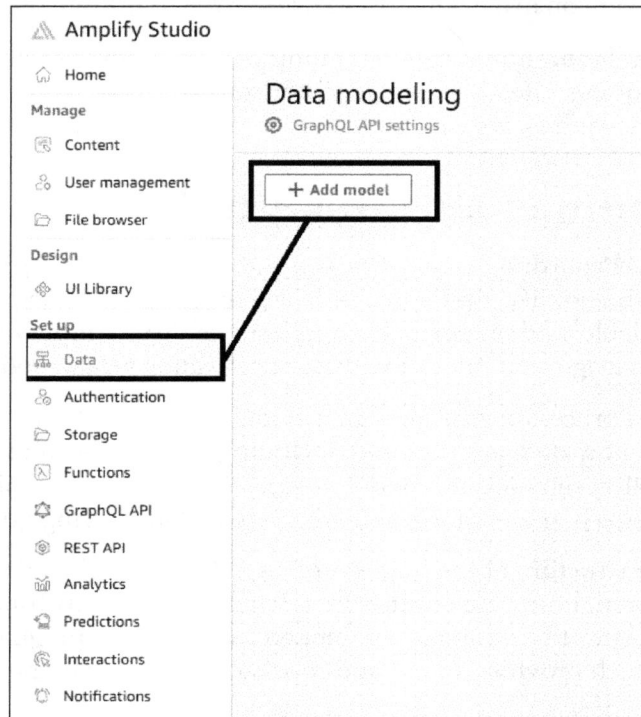

Figure 21.2: Data modeling in Amplify Studio

3. We will start with user-generated items. This item will contain properties that will be linked to the chosen model. We will use basic parameters like colors and some visibility elements. As an example, we will take the model that contains walls with several models inside. The data model will contain the visibility of these objects and material colors.

4. Our first model will have the type described in *Code Listing 21.1*:

```
1.  type BoxProps {
2.    position: number[];
3.    size: number[];
4.    color: Color;
5.    visible: boolean;
6.    id: string;
7.    name: string
8.  }
```

Code Listing 21.1: Element data model type

5. To create this model in Amplify, follow *Figure 21.3* and press the **Save and Deploy** button:

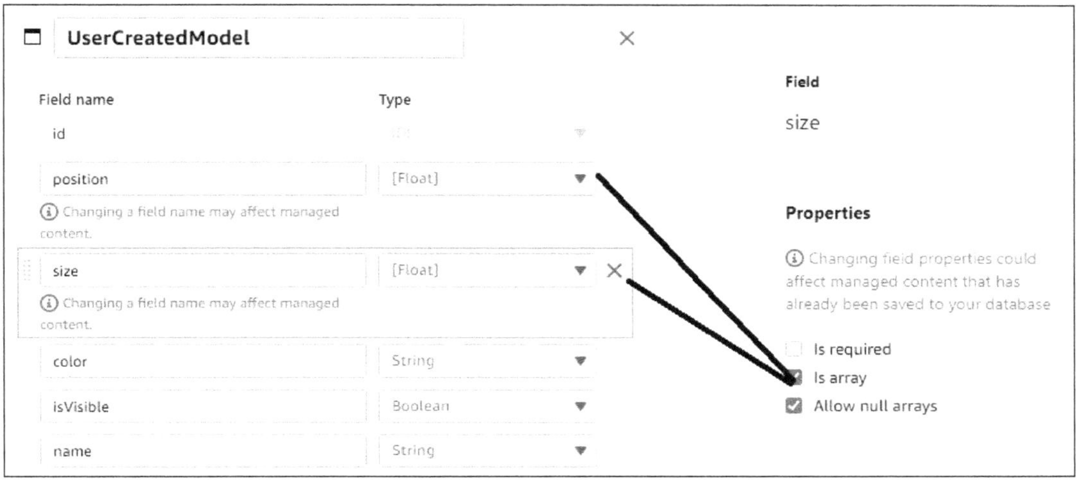

Figure 21.3: Our first model

6. Remember to pull changes to the project on each model update using the command: `amplify pull --appId <YOUR-APP-ID> --envName staging`

7. Now add the model to the application.

However, before that, we need to have an application to add something. Let us see the requirements that we need for the application:

- The application should have a split-screen

   o The left side should have the 3D model view

   o The right side should have controls to manipulate the model

- In the control area block, there should be three tabs

   o Scene configuration

   o Version control

   o Collaboration area to render real-time proposals

- Scene configuration should contain a list of element properties

   o Object name

   o Object visibility

   o Object color

- In the scene configuration tab, there should be a save button. On click, we should create the version that will be shown on the versions tab

- This tab should be a plus button to create a new object on the scene. This object should have random data

- The collaboration area should contain a button to choose one of the versions. After choosing the version, we should have the possibility to make changes to the properties and leave a comment without affecting the current version itself

We have used an Amplify UI earlier to enable the authorization form. This collection contains all the required controls, so there is no reason to create controls from scratch. The *Code Listing 21.2* gives us the initial code that we will use to connect data:

As the code base is too long for the book, consider picking it up from the GitHub repository of this book:

```
1.  // Import packages and set up Amplify
2.  // Box component to render a 3D box in the scene
3.  const Box = ({ position, size, color, isVisible }) => {
4.      // Box component will be here
5.  };
6.
7.  function DataModel() {
8.      const [boxes, setBoxes] = useState([]);
    // State to hold the array of boxes
9.
10.     // Function to generate a random number within a specified range
11.     const getRandomNumberInRange = (min, max) => {
12.         // Inclusive of both min and max
13.     }
14.
15.     // Function to update the properties of a specific box
16.     const setUpdates = (index, propertyName, value) => {/**/};
17.
18.     // Function to add a new box with a random position
19.     const addModel = () => {/**/};
20.
21.     // useEffect hook to initialize the box state with default
    values when the component mounts
22.     useEffect(() => {/**/}, []);
23.
24.     return (
25.         <main className="w-full h-svh m-auto»>
26.             <div className="grid grid-cols-1 md:grid-cols-[1fr_600px]
    gap-8 p-4 md:p-8">
27.                 {/* 3D canvas area */}
```

```
28.                    <div className="bg-gray-100 rounded-lg overflow-hidden">
29.                       <div className="aspect-[4/3] relative">
30.                          <div className="w-full h-full">
31.                             <Canvas
32.                                style={{
33.                                   height: '100vh',
34.                                }}
35.                             >
36.                                // Ambient light for general
    illumination
37.                                <ambientLight intensity={1}/>
38.                             // Point light source
39.                             <pointLight position={[10, 10, 10]}/>
40.                              <directionalLight
41.                                    /* light parameters here*/
42.                                 />
43.                       {/* Floor */}
44.                          <mesh rotation={[-Math.PI / 2, 0, 0]}
    position={[0, 0, 0]}>
45.                                   <planeGeometry args={[10, 10]}/>
46.                                   <meshStandardMaterial
color="#FFDDD2"/>
47.                          </mesh>
48.                       {/* Wall 1 */}
49.                             <mesh position={[0, 2, -5]}>
50.                                <boxGeometry args={[10, 4, 0.2]}/>
51.                                <meshStandardMaterial
    color="#83C5BE"/>
52.                                </mesh>
53.                       {/* Wall 2 */}
54.                          <mesh position={[5, 2, 0]} rotation={[0,
    -Math.PI / 2, 0]}>
55.                             <boxGeometry args={[10, 4, 0.2]}/>
56.                             <meshStandardMaterial color="#83C5BE"/>
57.                       </mesh>
58.                             {/* Render boxes from state */}
59.                             {
60.                                boxes.length > 0 &&
    boxes.map((box) =>
61.                                <Box
62.                                   key={box.id} // Unique key
    for each box
63.                                      position={box.position}
```

```
64.                                          size={box.size}
65.                                          color={box.color}
66.                                       isVisible={box.isVisible} />
67.                                     )
68.                                   }
69.                               <OrbitControls/>
70.                            </Canvas>
71.                          </div>
72.                       </div>
73.                    </div>
74.                    {/* Control panel */}
75.                    <div className="bg-white rounded-lg p-6 shadow-lg">
76.                       <Tabs.Container defaultValue="1">
77.                          <Tabs.List spacing="equal">
78.                             <Tabs.Item value="1">Scene</Tabs.Item>
79.                             <Tabs.Item value="2">Versions</Tabs.Item>
80.                             <Tabs.Item value="3">Collaboration</
    Tabs.Item>
81.                          </Tabs.List>
82.
83.                          {/* Scene Properties Panel */}
84.                          <Tabs.Panel value="1">
85.                             <Heading level={1}>Scene Properties</
Heading>
86.                             <div className="grid gap-6">
87.
88.                                {/* Form to edit properties of
    each box */}
89.                                {
90.                                  boxes.length > 0 && boxes.map(
    (box, index) =>(
91.                                   /* Boxes array here */
92.                                   ))
93.                                }
94.
95.                                {/* Button to add a new box */}
96.                                <Button>/* Button parameters here *
    /</Button>
97.                                {/* Button to save changes */}
98.                                <Button>/* Button parameters here
    */</Button></div>
99.                          </Tabs.Panel>
100.
```

```
101.                                {/* Placeholder content for other
    tabs */}
102.                                <Tabs.Panel value="2">Content of the
    second tab</Tabs.Panel>
103.                                <Tabs.Panel value="3">Content of the
third tab</Tabs.Panel>
104.                            </Tabs.Container>
105.                        </div>
106.                    </div>
107.                </main>
108.            );
109.        }
110.        export default DataModel;
111.
```

Code Listing 21.2: Initial code that contains all the required UI to start

8. When we start the project, we will see the same result as in *Figure 21.4*. We must keep in mind that this code should be on a separate page:

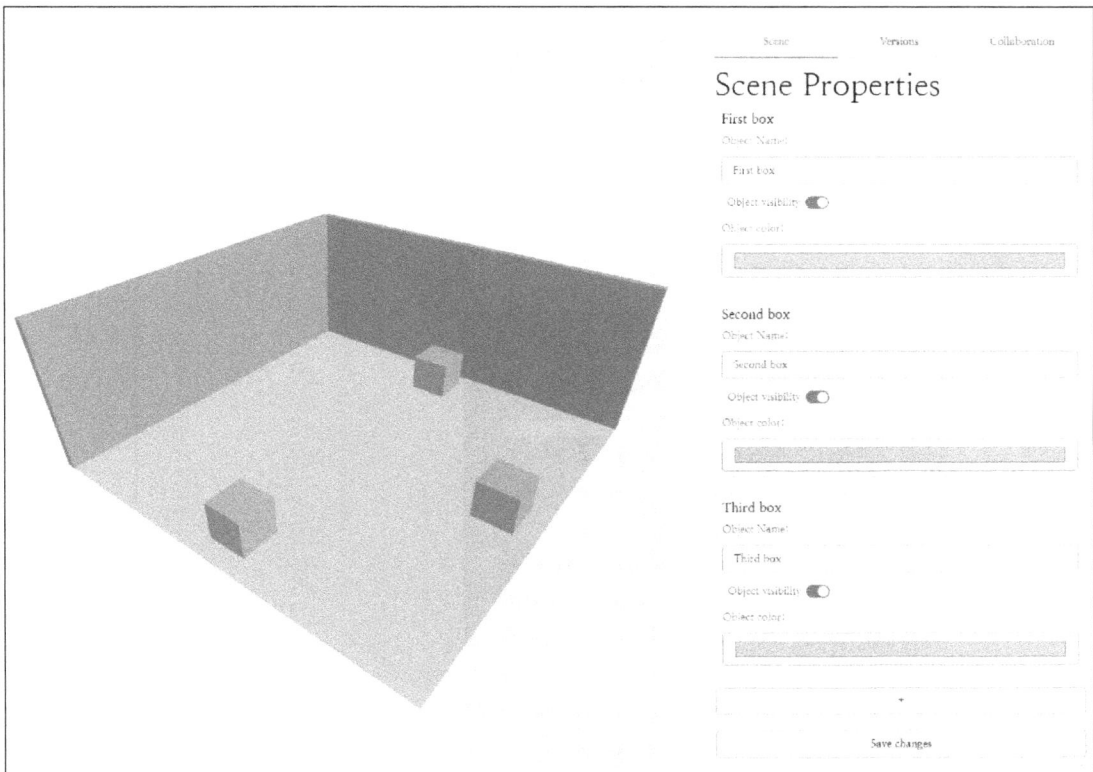

Figure 21.4: 3D object management screen for the initial code

Our first goal is to get data from AWS. As the database is empty, we add something using Amplify Studio. To add data, select the **Content** link in the Studio menu and select the required model. Click on **Create <YOUR-MODEL-NAME>** and fill out the form. Follow *Figure 21.5* to find all the required buttons:

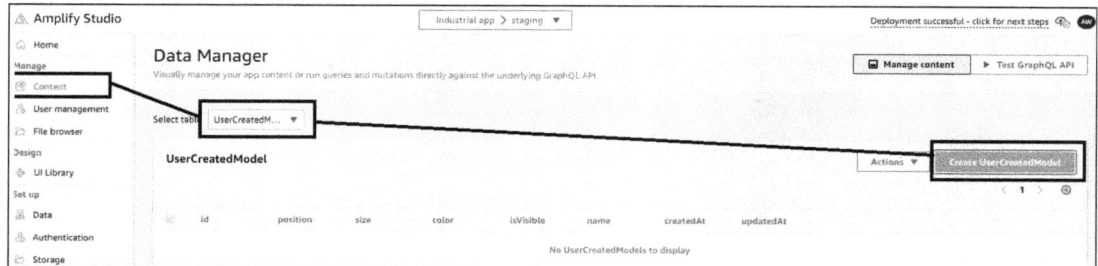

Figure 21.5: Creating the default value that will be shown in the list

We need to get the SDK script to connect Amplify with the Frontend. There is a special helper on how we can get it. In *Figure 21.6*, we can see that if we click on the **Local setup instructions** button, there will be instructions on how to get the data:

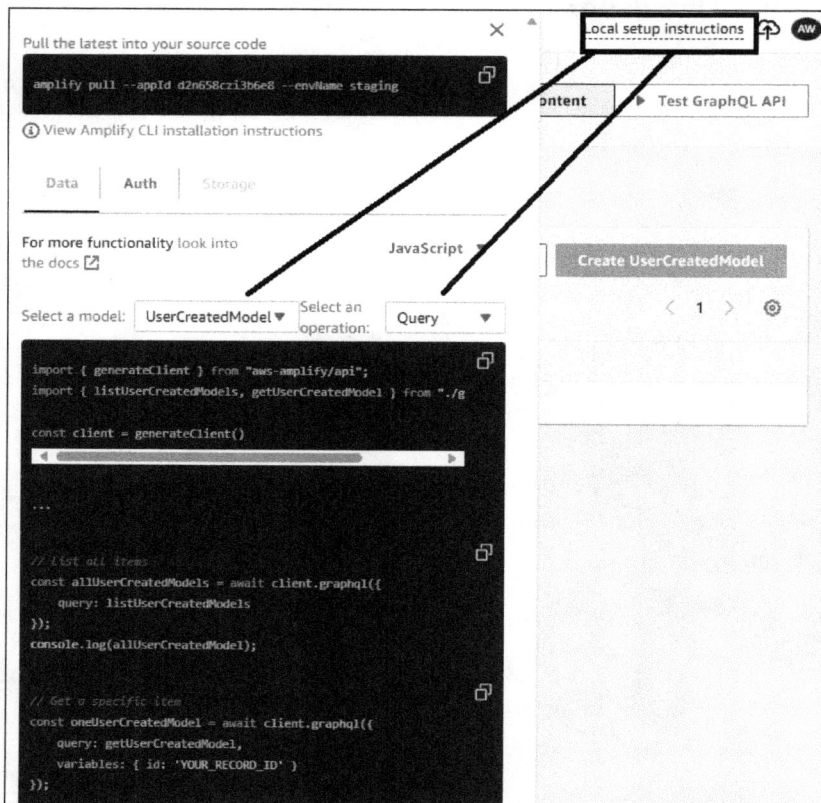

Figure 21.6: Commands to get data from the Amplify

We will use the example code on this page. As a practice, we would have a separate class to work with all API calls. In the end, we will check the optimized structure.

To get the data, we need to sync our code with Amplify and enter this command in the root folder: **amplify update codegen**. This command will generate all required GraphQL files for the project.

The next step is to retrieve data from the GraphQL by updating the **useEffect** code like in *Code Listing 21.3*:

```
1.  useEffect(() => {
2.        const fetchData = async () => {
3.            const allUserCreatedModels = await client.graphql({
4.                query: listUserCreatedModels
5.            });
6.            if (allUserCreatedModels.data.
7.                    listUserCreatedModels.items.length > 0) {
8.                setBoxes(allUserCreatedModels.data.
9.                        listUserCreatedModels.items);
10.           }
11.       }
12.       fetchData();
13. }, []);
```

Code Listing 21.3: Update for the useEffect code

Running the code from *Code Listing 21.3* will initiate retrieving data from the database using GraphQL and provide this data for the page rendering:

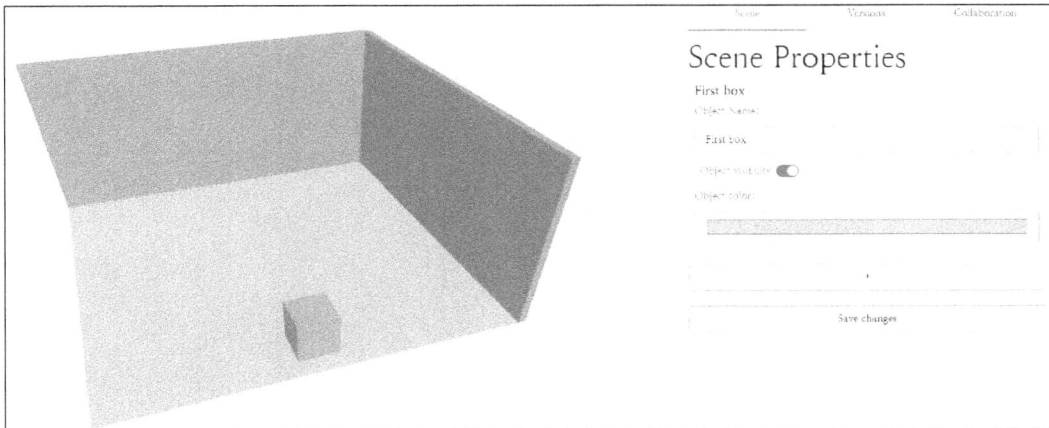

Figure 21.7: Result after the code update

In *Figure 21.7*, we can see the result of how data came from GraphQL. The element data is the same as we created before in the data model.

CRUD operations for 3D objects

Since the **Read** operation is already done in *Code Listing 21.3*, in this section, we will check the **Update** operation. Delete will be for the exercise at the end of this chapter.

In *Figure 21.6*, we saw where to collect the code we need. We just select **Update** instead of **Query** in the dropdown list. As we have the list of elements that are required to be saved, we need to create a function that will iterate through the internal state and save this data in GraphQL. We follow *Code Listing 21.4* to see the code to save updates:

```
1.  const saveData = () => {          boxes.forEach(async (box) => {
2.              console.log(box);
3.              await client.graphql({
4.                  query: updateUserCreatedModel,
5.                  variables: {
6.                      input: {
7.                          id: box.id,
8.                          name: box.name,
9.                          isVisible: box.isVisible,
10.                         color: box.color,
11.                         _version: box._
    version // this is important field
12.                     }
13.                 }
14.             });
15.         })
16.     };
```

Code Listing 21.4: Save data to update it in Amplify

In the comment area, we added a **_version** field, and it is important, since Amplify regulates versions to manage conflicts in case we save from several devices at the same time. Since we added a field, we also need to update the mutation. Follow *Code Listing 21.5* to update the mutation code file:

```
1.  export const updateUserCreatedModel = /* GraphQL */ `
2.    mutation UpdateUserCreatedModel(
3.      $input: UpdateUserCreatedModelInput!
4.      $condition: ModelUserCreatedModelConditionInput
5.    ) {
6.      updateUserCreatedModel(input: $input, condition: $condition) {
7.        id
8.        position
9.        size
10.       color
11.       isVisible
```

```
12.        name
13.        createdAt
14.        updatedAt
15.        _version //Here you can see a new field
16.     }
17.   }
18. `;
```

Code Listing 21.5: Mutation update

We will now add a newly created function to the click action for the **Save** button. After clicking on it at the next page load (for example, we close the web application and open it again, or leave the page and come back) data will arrive from the API.

File storage for 3D objects

Our application now allows us to create the objects from the admin area and update them in the front end. Next, we need to create and save versions of the 3D image. The main requirement will be to save the scene to a file and put it into the AWS storage.

To add the file storage, where we will put our uploaded files, please follow these steps:

1. To add the storage to the project, we follow *Figure 21.8* and put all required checkboxes as shown in the figure. We can manage it according to our needs. In this example, we will select all functions in this list:

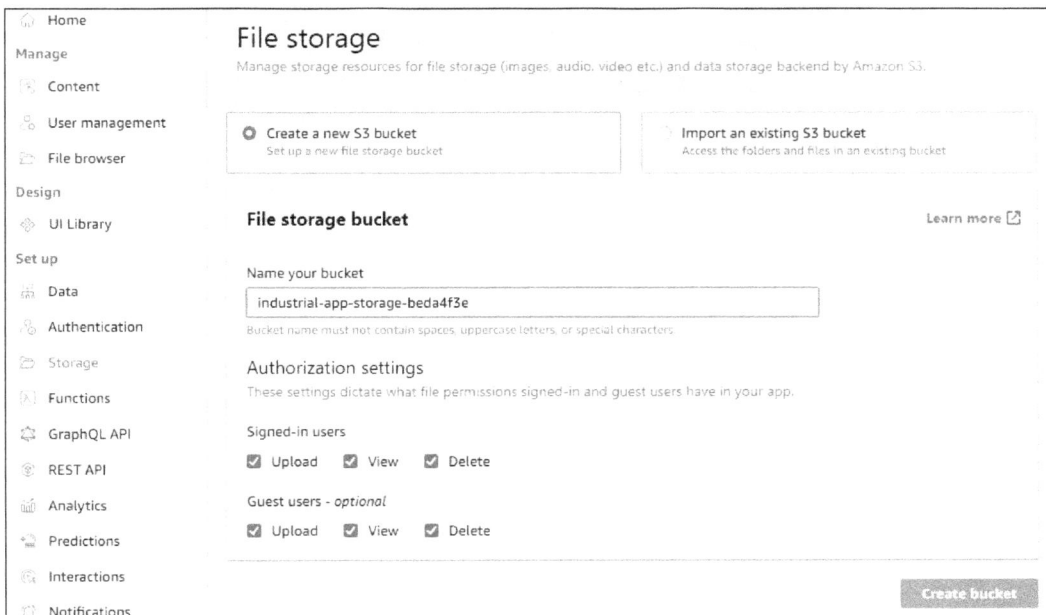

Figure 21.8: Creating the new storage for the application

In *Figure 21.9,* you can see that we need to pull updates:

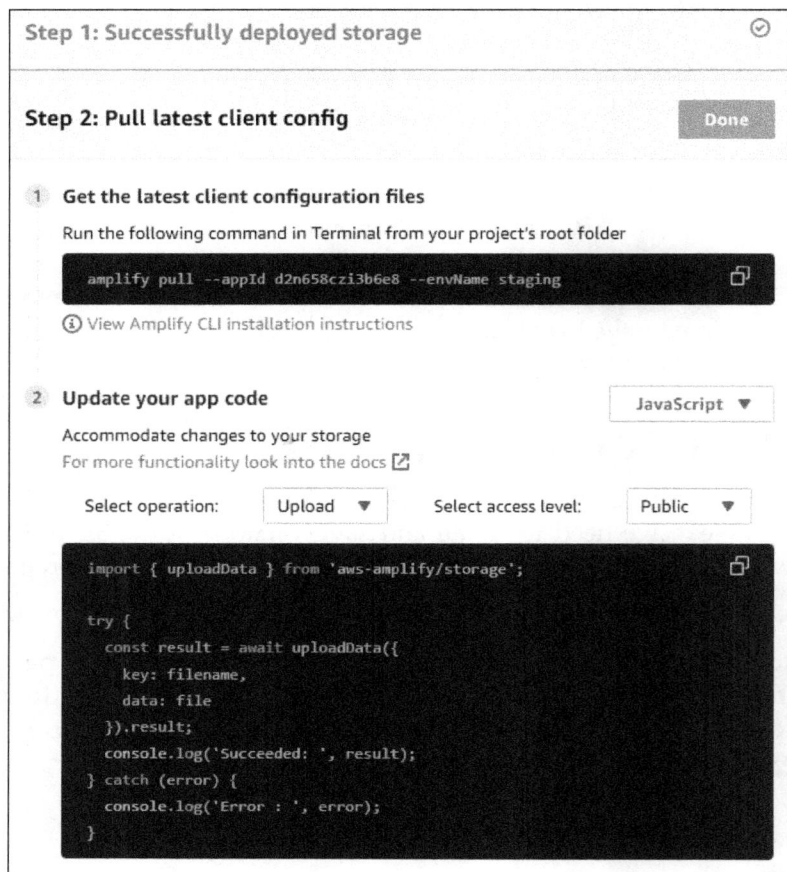

Step 1: Successfully deployed storage ⊘

Step 2: Pull latest client config   Done

1 **Get the latest client configuration files**

Run the following command in Terminal from your project's root folder

```
amplify pull --appId d2n658czi3b6e8 --envName staging
```

ⓘ View Amplify CLI installation instructions

2 **Update your app code**   JavaScript ▼

Accommodate changes to your storage
For more functionality look into the docs ⧉

Select operation: Upload ▼   Select access level: Public ▼

```
import { uploadData } from 'aws-amplify/storage';

try {
  const result = await uploadData({
    key: filename,
    data: file
  }).result;
  console.log('Succeded: ', result);
} catch (error) {
  console.log('Error : ', error);
}
```

Figure 21.9: Creating the new storage for the application

2. The next step is to add new functionality to each click on the save button. As a filename, we will take the version from the previous block and add some strings to it. Let us take the **R3F screenshot** and the current timestamp as an initial string for the filename.

3. We also need to make the folder public for now (as we do not use any authorization here and need to have access to all files). To open the folder as public, we use the link from *Figure 21.10* to enter the S3 console:

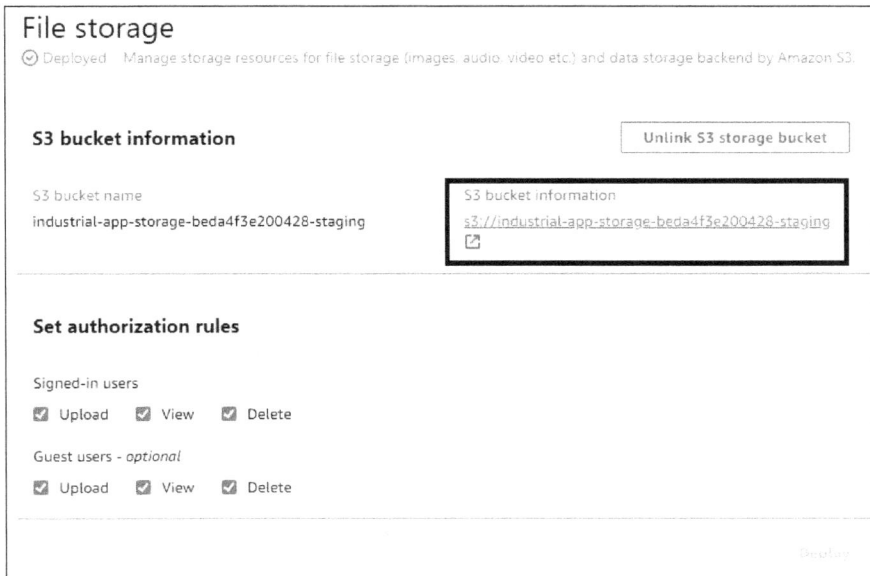

Figure 21.10: Link to S3 console

Note: Be careful with access configuration in the production mode, as it can be critical for application security.

4. Next, we choose the folder in *Figure 21.11* and grant access. In the next screen, we choose **Make public using ACL**. It is not safe for the production mode (important). We need it to not get deep into AWS configuration, as it is not in the scope:

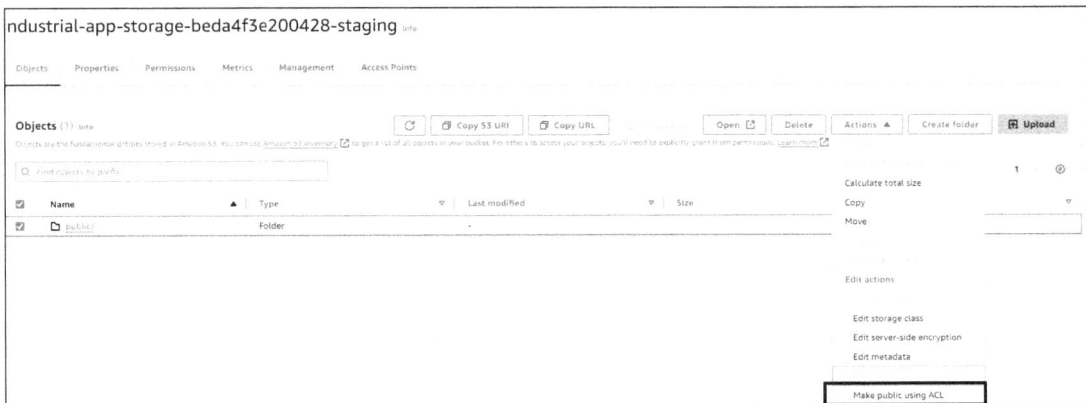

Figure 21.11: Making the folder visible for any user

5. The last step is to update the code and add the function that will upload files into storage that will be visible by the link. We follow *Code Listing 21.6* to get the function:

```javascript
1.  const saveFile = async (file, version) => {
2.      // Generate a unique file name using the current timestamp
    and version
3.      const fileName = `R3F-screenshot-${Date.now()}-${version}.png`;
4.
5.      // Decode the base64 string into a binary string
6.      const byteCharacters = atob(file.split(',')[1]);
7.
8.      // Convert the binary string to an array of bytes
9.      const byteNumbers = new Array(byteCharacters.length);
10.     for (let i = 0; i < byteCharacters.length; i++) {
11.         byteNumbers[i] = byteCharacters.charCodeAt(i);
12.     }
13.
14.     // Convert the array of bytes to a Uint8Array
15.     const byteArray = new Uint8Array(byteNumbers);
16.
17.     // Create a Blob object from the Uint8Array with the MIME
    type 'image/png'
18.     const blob = new Blob([byteArray], { type: 'image/png' });
19.
20.     try {
21.         // Upload the Blob to the server using the
    uploadData function
22.         const result = await uploadData({
23.             key: fileName,
24.             data: blob
25.         }).result;
26.
27.         // Log the result of the upload if successful
28.         console.log('Succeeded: ', result);
29.     } catch (error) {
30.         // Log an error message if the upload fails
31.         console.log('Error : ', error);
32.     }
33. }
34.
35. // Capture a screenshot from a canvas element (ref.current)
    and save it as a PNG file
36. saveFile(ref.current.toDataURL('image/png'), boxes[0]._version);
```

Code Listing 21.6: Save the file and upload it to S3

On save, we will see a new file in the S3 bucket, like in *Figure 21.12*:

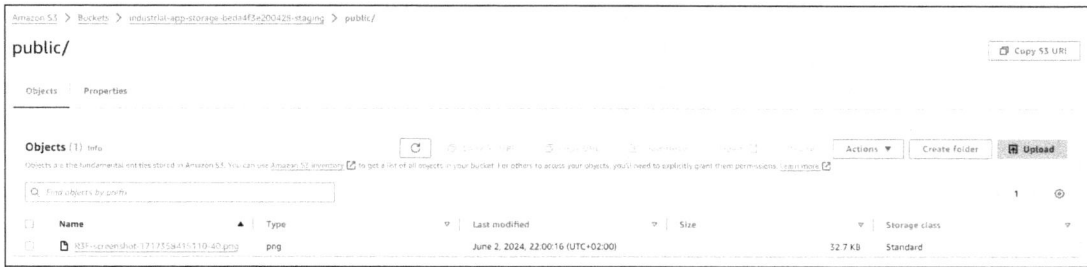

Figure 21.12: AWS S3 Bucket files list

The resulting code can be seen in *Code Listing 21.7 (As the code is too long, please take the result code from the GitHub link)*:

```
1.  'use client'; // Required for Next.js to indicate that this is
    a client-side component
2.  // Import the packages and configure the Amplify
3.
4.  // Box component to render a 3D box in the scene
5.  const Box = ({ position, size, color, isVisible }) => {
6.      if (!isVisible) return ''; // If the box is not visible,
    return an empty string
7.      return (
8.      <mesh position={position}> // Mesh representing the box
9.        <boxGeometry args={size} /> // Geometry of the box with
    specified size
10.       <meshStandardMaterial color={color} />
    // Material of the box with specified color
11.     </mesh>
12.     );
13. };
14.
15. function DataModel() {
16.     const [boxes, setBoxes] = useState([]); // State to hold the
    array of boxes
17.
18.     // Function to generate a random number within a specified range
19.     const getRandomNumberInRange = (min, max) =>
    {/*Function body is here*/}
20.
21.     // Function to update the properties of a specific box
22.     const setUpdates = (index, propertyName, value) =>
    {/*Function body is here*/}
```

```
23.
24.     // Function to add a new box with a random position
25.     const addModel = () => {/*Function body is here*/};
26.
27.     // useEffect hook to initialize the box state with default
    values when the component mounts
28.     useEffect(() => {/*Function body is here*/};}, []);
29.
30.     return (
31.         <main className="w-full h-svh m-auto»>
32.             <div className="grid grid-cols-1 md:grid-cols-[1fr_600px]
    gap-8 p-4 md:p-8">
33.                 {/* 3D canvas area */}
34.                 <div className="bg-gray-100 rounded-lg overflow-hidden">
35.                     <div className="aspect-[4/3] relative">
36.                         <div className="w-full h-full">
37.                             <Canvas
38.                                 style={{
39.                                     height: <100vh',
40.                                 }}
41.                             >
42.                                 // Ambient light for general
    illumination
43.                                 <ambientLight intensity={1}/>
44.                             // Point light source
45.                                 <pointLight position={[10, 10, 10]}/>
46.                                 <directionalLight /*Light params are here*/ />
47.                                 {/* Floor */}
48.                                 <mesh rotation={[-Math.PI / 2, 0, 0]}
    position={[0, 0, 0]}>
49.                                     <planeGeometry args={[10, 10]}/>
50.                                     <meshStandardMaterial
    color="#FFDDD2"/>
51.                                 </mesh>
52.                                 {/* Wall 1 */}
53.                                 {/* Wall 2 */}
54.                                 <mesh position={[5, 2, 0]} rotation={[0,
    -Math.PI / 2, 0]}>
55.                                     <boxGeometry args={[10, 4, 0.2]}/>
56.                                     <meshStandardMaterial color="#83C5BE"/>
57.                                 </mesh>
58.                                 {/* Render boxes from state */}
59.                                 {
```

```
60.                                boxes.length > 0 &&
   boxes.map((box) =>
61.                                    <Box
62.                                      key={box.id}
   // Unique key for each box
63.                                        position={box.position}
64.                                        size={box.size}
65.                                        color={box.color}
66.                                      isVisible={box.isVisible} />
67.                                  )
68.                                }
69.                            <OrbitControls/>
70.                          </Canvas>
71.                      </div>
72.                    </div>
73.                </div>
74.
75.                {/* Control panel */}
76.                <div className="bg-white rounded-lg p-6 shadow-lg">
77.                    <Tabs.Container defaultValue="1">
78.                        /*Tabs are here*/
79.                    </Tabs.Container>
80.                </div>
81.            </div>
82.        </main>
83.    );
84. }
85.
86. export default DataModel;
```

***Code listing 21.7**: Result code for the Data Modeling example (please take it from GitHub)*

Conclusion

In this chapter, we studied the vital components of data storage and management in 3D application development. We started with an introduction to the importance of data storage and management, emphasizing how crucial these elements are for any robust software development project.

We moved on to model schemas and design, where we learned how to structure data efficiently for 3D objects. This foundational knowledge ensures the application can handle complex 3D data with ease and scalability. Next, we studied CRUD operations for 3D objects, utilizing AWS services that enable dynamic interaction with 3D data. We also covered file storage for 3D objects using AWS S3, leveraging the scalability and reliability of AWS S3 for storage needs.

These skills form a robust foundation for 3D development projects, allowing us to manage and manipulate 3D data effectively. With this knowledge, we are well-equipped to tackle more advanced 3D application development challenges, ensuring our projects are both functional and scalable.

In the next chapter, we will learn how to add real-time functionality to our application.

Points to remember

- Consult with the DevOps team about access configuration before going live.
- Cover CRUD interfaces with the authorization form.
- Practice with data modeling to improve your knowledge.

Exercises

As an exercise, we will take two issues with different complexities:

1. Add the delete mechanism for the boxes. For this, you will need to create the button for it and add the delete query function from Amplify Studio.

2. Create a new model to collect versions. Each version will be the screenshot file that we created. This model should contain the filename and status. This status will have 3 options: pending, approved, and declined. This status will be used in the next chapter.

   a. On clicking the Save button, we need to not only save the file but also create the instance in the new model that will contain this filename.

   b. On the Versions tab, we need to have a list of these versions, the same as we have a list of the boxes.

Join our Discord space

Join our Discord workspace for latest updates, offers, tech happenings around the world, new releases, and sessions with the authors:

https://discord.bpbonline.com

Real-time Functionality with AWS Amplify

Introduction

In this chapter, we will study real-time functionality with AWS Amplify. Real-time data exchange has become important in modern applications, providing users with dynamic, interactive experiences. AWS Amplify simplifies adding real-time capabilities to applications, making it easier to keep the data synchronized across different clients instantaneously.

We will enhance our previous 3D application example by adding a collaboration system. Users will vote and comment in real time, transforming our static application into a lively, interactive platform. This chapter will guide us through the setup and implementation of real-time features, ensuring the application is responsive and engaging.

Structure

In this chapter, we will discuss the following topics:

- Introduction to real-time functionality
- Setting up real-time functionality
- Implementing a real-time voting system
- Implementing a real-time comments system

Objectives

By the end of this chapter, you will understand the importance of real-time data exchange in modern applications and how it enhances user experience. You will learn how to configure AWS Amplify for real-time communication using GraphQL subscriptions and apply this knowledge to build interactive features. We will walk through creating a real-time voting system and a live comments feature, covering schema design and data updates. Additionally, we will explore techniques to integrate real-time functionality into a 3D application, ensuring seamless interaction and display of dynamic data. Finally, we will discuss best practices for testing and debugging real-time features, ensuring a smooth and reliable user experience.

Introduction to real-time functionality

Real-time data exchange is crucial for providing users with dynamic and interactive experiences. Whether it is live chat, collaborative editing, social media updates, or live data feeds, real-time functionality ensures that users receive the most up-to-date information without needing to refresh their pages. This immediate data synchronization enhances user engagement and satisfaction by making interactions more fluid and responsive.

Real-time data exchange is important in applications where timely information is critical. For example, in financial trading platforms, social networks, or multiplayer gaming environments, the ability to push updates to users instantly can be the difference between success and failure. By incorporating real-time features, developers can build more competitive and attractive applications that meet the high expectations of modern users.

AWS Amplify offers a comprehensive suite of tools and services that simplify adding real-time functionality to applications. Leveraging **AWS AppSync**, Amplify provides robust support for GraphQL subscriptions, enabling real-time data synchronization between clients and the backend. This allows for seamless updates and interactions across different parts of the application.

Amplify's real-time capabilities include:

- **GraphQL subscriptions:** Automatically push updates to clients when data changes in the backend. This is ideal for implementing features like live chat, notifications, and collaborative editing.

- **API integration:** Easily connect and integrate with other AWS services. This ensures that the real-time functionality is scalable and reliable.

With these tools, AWS Amplify simplifies the development process, allowing us to focus on building the application while it handles the complexities of real-time data management. Whether adding real-time features to an existing application or building a new one from scratch, Amplify provides the infrastructure and support needed to deliver a high-quality user experience.

Setting up real-time functionality

To set up the real-time functionality, we do not need any special configuration. As Amplify uses GraphQL by default, it already has the subscription functionality. For our example, we need to add new data models as we did in the previous example, and pull the changes. The model we will need will contain comments placed in a 3D model layout with drag-and-drop functionality. There will also be a voting system that we will reduce to one user for now. The model schema is shown in *Figure 22.1*.

The schema for the comments should look like the following:

- **User**: This is a string currently, as we are not connected to the Auth system.
- **Comment**: This will be a comment text
- **Position**: An XY coordinate where the comment is located on the screen

For the votes, it will be the following:

- **User**: A string for now
- **Vote**: A number from 0 to 5

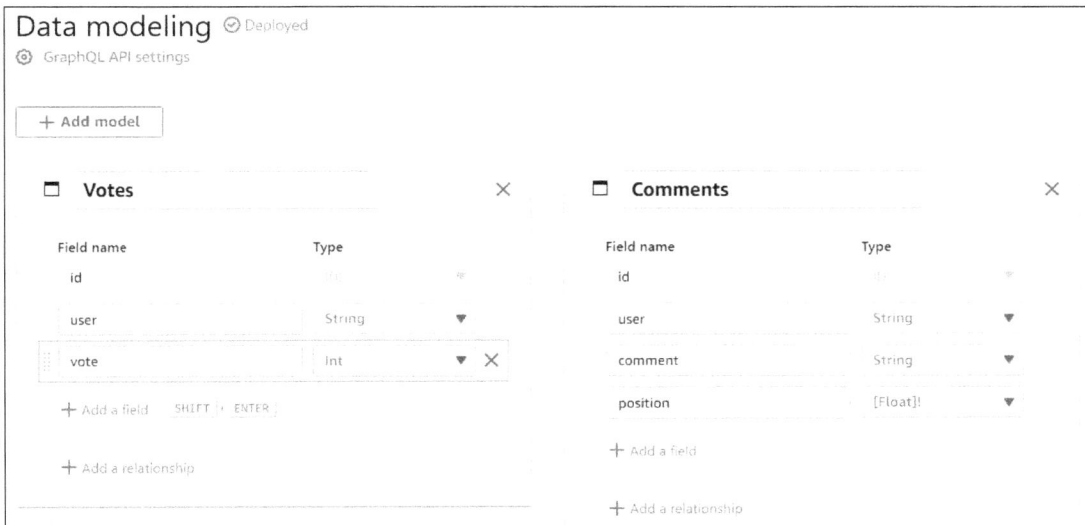

Figure 22.1: New data models for the comments and votes

Next, we need to run a command series in the CLI to update Amplify and GraphQL scripts:

- **amplify pull**: To get updates from Studio
- **amplify push**: To sync updates
- **amplify codegen**: To update GraphQL scripts

As a result, we will have set up the system and be ready for future implementations.

Implementing a real-time voting system

In the previous chapter, we created three tabs to store functionality:

- To create and manage the scene
- To store and show screenshots of variants
- **For collaboration**

In the **for collaboration** tab, that we will code in this section, we will show the voting that will be updated in real-time. Each time the user makes a vote, it will be immediately updated in all open windows.

To proceed with the implementation, we need to create the new component in the component folder. Let us name it **CollaborationTab** and then inject this component into the tab space from the previous chapter. The updated code on the page should look as shown in *Code Listing 22.1:*

```
1.  {/* Old code here */}
2.     return (
3.         <main className="w-full h-svh m-auto»>
4.             {/* Old code here */}
5.             <div className="bg-white rounded-lg p-6 shadow-lg">
6.                 <Tabs.Container defaultValue="1">
7.                     {/* Old code here */}
8.                     <Tabs.Panel value="3">
9.                         <CollaborationTab />
10.                    </Tabs.Panel>
11.                    {/* Use this tab layout for the new component */}
12.                </Tabs.Container>
13.
14.            </div>
15.          </div>
16.        </main>
17.    );
18. }
```

Code Listing 22.1: Collaboration component injection

Let us create the requirements for this component that we will develop in this chapter:

- The component should have 5 buttons with numbers that will represent the vote value
- On button press, we should save data in the API and reload this information in all devices that are currently open, the page, and the current tab

- For simplicity, we will use the Rating component from the Amplify UI kit to show the current rating

In *Code Listing 22.2,* we can grab the initial code for the component that we will update with real-time data functionality:

```
1.  import { Button, Rating } from "@aws-amplify/ui-react";
2.  import { useState } from "react";
3.
4.  export default function CollaborationTab() {
5.      const [rating, setRating] = useState(0);
6.
7.      return (
8.          <section>
9.              <div className="flex gap-2 items-center w-full mb-4">
10.                 <h2>Current rating:</h2>
11.                 <Rating
12.                     value={rating}
13.                     maxValue={5}
14.                 />
15.             </div>
16.             <div className="flex justify-between items-center">
17.                 <h2>Rate this scene:</h2>
18.                 {
19.                     [1,2,3,4,5].map(vote => <Button key={`vote-
    ${vote}`} onClick={() => {setRating(vote)}}>{vote}</Button>)
20.                 }
21.             </div>
22.         </section>
23.     );
24. }
```

Code Listing 22.2: Initial code for the voting component

Having simplified examples with only one scene and no scene ID in the models, we will manually create the data content for the current scene in the Studio. Follow the previous chapter for instructions.

After creating the data in the content area, we need an ID for the item. We can find it in the content list, like in *Figure 22.2:*

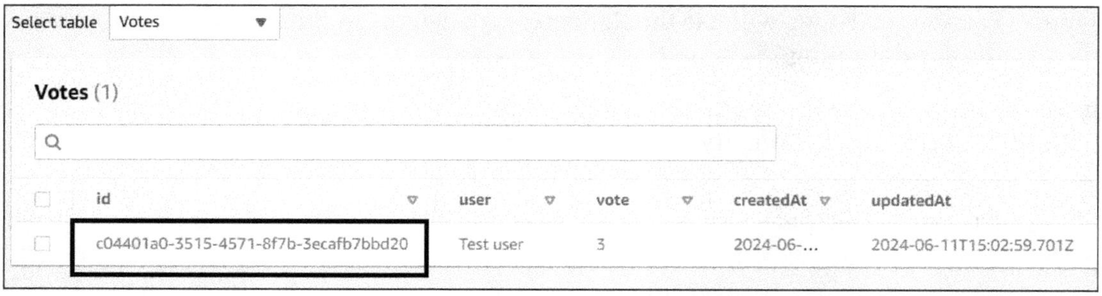

Figure 22.2: ID of required item in the content list

This ID will be required to get and sync the information with the database. In *Code Listing 22.3*, we can see how to connect our front end to the database. In this code, we will get the votes for the current scene:

```
1.  // Import necessary components from AWS Amplify UI library and
    React library
2.  import { Button, Rating } from "@aws-amplify/ui-react";
3.  import { useEffect, useState } from "react";
4.
5.  // Import GraphQL queries and mutations
6.  import { getVotes } from "@/graphql/queries";
7.  import { generateClient } from "aws-amplify/api";
8.  import { updateVotes } from "@/graphql/mutations";
9.
10. // Define the default vote ID and create an instance of the Amplify
    GraphQL client
11. const defaultVoteID = "c04401a0-3515-4571-8f7b-3ecafb7bbd20";
12. const client = generateClient();
13.
14. export default function CollaborationTab() {
15.     // Define state variables for the current rating and version of
    the vote data
16.     const [rating, setRating] = useState(0);
17.     const [version, setVersion] = useState(0);
18.
19.     // Use an effect hook to fetch initial vote data when the
    component mounts
20.     useEffect(() => {
21.         const fetchData = async () => {
22.             // Execute a GraphQL query using the Amplify client to
    get the vote data for the default ID
23.             const voteForTheScene = await client.graphql({
```

```
24.                    query: getVotes,
25.                    variables: {
26.                        id: defaultVoteID
27.                    }
28.                });
29.
30.                // Update the state variables with fetched data
31.                setRating(voteForTheScene.data.getVotes.vote);
32.                setVersion(voteForTheScene.data.getVotes._version);
33.            }
34.        fetchData();
35.    }, []);
36.
37.    // Define a function to update the vote in the database using
       GraphQL mutation
38.    const updateVote = async (newVote) => {
39.        await client.graphql({
40.            query: updateVotes,
41.            variables: {
42.                input: {
43.                    id: defaultVoteID,
44.                    vote: newVote,
45.                    _version: version
46.                }
47.            }
48.        });
49.    }
50.
51.    // Define a function to set and update the rating with the new
       vote value
52.    const setNewVote = async (newVote) => {
53.        setRating(newVote); // Update the local state variable with
       new vote value
54.        await updateVote(newVote); // Call `updateVote` function to
       update the vote in the database
55.    }
56.
57.    // Render the JSX for the CollaborationTab component, including
       a rating display and buttons for user input
58.    return (
59.        <section>
```

```
60.              {/* Display current rating with a title */}
61.              <div className="flex gap-2 items-center w-full mb-4">
62.                  <h2>Current rating:</h2>
63.                  <Rating
64.                      value={rating} // Use the state variable as the
     current value of the rating component
65.                      maxValue={5} // Set maximum possible rating to
     5 stars
66.                  />
67.              </div>
68.
69.              {/* Display title for user input and generate buttons
     for each star */}
70.              <div className="flex justify-between items-center">
71.                  <h2>Rate this scene:</h2>
72.                  {[1,2,3,4,5].map(vote => <Button key={`vote-${vote}
     `} onClick={() => setNewVote(vote) }>{vote}</Button>)}
73.              </div>
74.          </section>
75.      );
76. }
```

Code Listing 22.3: Code update to connect UI with database

Now, we can save the changes in the database. However, we need to add a possibility to sync all the devices at any time. For this, we will need to use subscription functionality. This functionality will allow us to get updates from the database in real time. To add this possibility, we need to update the initial general **useEffect** function that triggers on component init with code from *Code Listing 22.4*:

```
1.  useEffect(() => {
2.      const fetchData = async () => {
3.          const voteForTheScene = await client.graphql({
4.              query: getVotes,
5.              variables: {
6.                  id: defaultVoteID
7.              }
8.          });
9.          setRating(voteForTheScene.data.getVotes.vote);
10.         setVersion(voteForTheScene.data.getVotes._version);
11.         // Set up a subscription to Listen for updates on votes
12.         const subscription = client
13.             .graphql({ query: onUpdateVotes })
```

```
14.              .subscribe({
15.                  next: ({ data }) => {
16.                      setRating(data.onUpdateVotes.vote);
17.                      setVersion(data.onUpdateVotes._version);
18.                  },
19.                  error: (error) => console.warn(error)
20.              });
21.              // Return a cleanup function to unsubscribe when
     the component is unmounted
22.              return () => subscription.unsubscribe();
23.          }
24.      fetchData();
25.  }, []);
```

Code Listing 22.4: Update to code that will create real-time communication

If we open two browsers, we will see that the data is synchronized, and if we change the vote in one browser, it will immediately change the data in the other one, as shown in *Figure 22.3*:

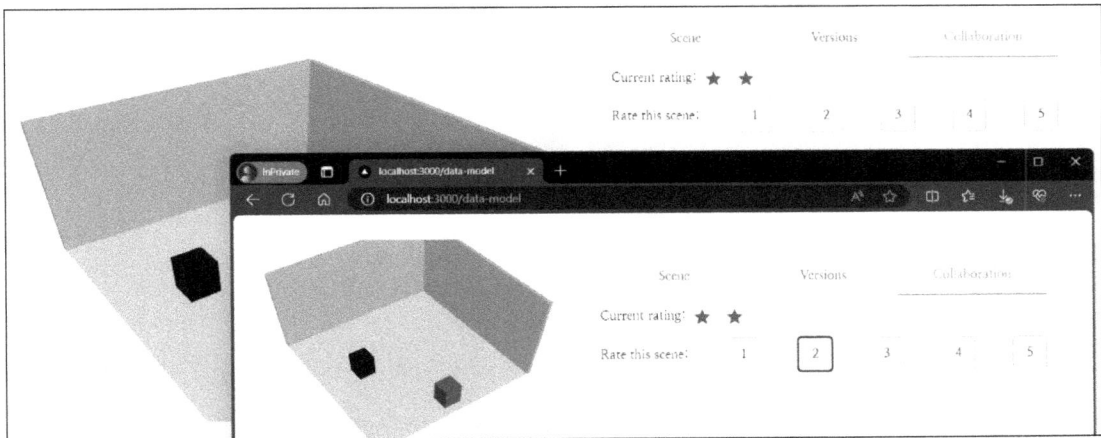

Figure 22.3: Result of our first real-time component realization

Implementing a real-time comments system

In the next example, we will create a possibility to put the comment at any part of the scene. To achieve it, we will need the comment field and also save the coordinates where this comment will be located.

Let us align the requirements for the comment system we will create in the current block:

- Users should be able to point and click on any area in the 3D scene layout.

- We need to create a comment field for the selected area.

- We need a save button to save the comment in the specific area.

- Each comment should appear in real-time on any device, the same as we did with the rating system in the previous section.

- In the user field, we will have the TestUser string instead of real user data.

We have a requirement; let us create the initial component now. This will be a functionality to create the layout with the form. On the save button, we need to show only the comment itself. In the *Code Listings 22.5, 22.6,* and *22.7,* we will find updates and all the required code to start. In *Code Listing 22.5,* we will find updates for the page. Here, we will add the layout with comments on the 3D model using mouse coordinates. In *Code Listing 22.6,* we will use the hook to get the mouse coordinates. *Code Listing 22.7* will contain the comment component with form and functionality to show the comment after clicking:

```
1.  {/*old code*/}
2.  function DataModel() {
3.      const [boxes, setBoxes] = useState([]);
4.      const [tab, setTab] = useState('1');
5.      const [commentsList, setCommentsList] = useState([]);
6.      const { x, y } = useMousePosition();
7.      {/*old code*/}
8.
9.      const createComment = (currentX, currentY) => {
10.         if (tab !== '3') return false;
11.
12.         const divRect = document.getElementById('commentWrapper').
    getBoundingClientRect();
13.         const divX = divRect.left; // X position of the div
14.         const divY = divRect.top; // Y position of the div
15.         {/* we need to collect coordinates that align with the
    wrapper */}
16.         {/* to get them we use the getBoundingClientRect function  */}
17.
18.         setCommentsList([...commentsList,
19.             { x: currentX - divX, y: currentY - divY, id:
    Date.now() }]);
20.     }
21.
22. {/*old code*/}
23.
24.     return (
25.         <main className="w-full h-svh m-auto»>
26.             <div className=
```

```
     "grid grid-cols-1 md:grid-cols-[1fr_600px] gap-8 p-4 md:p-8">
27.                 <div id="commentWrapper" className=
     "bg-gray-100 rounded-lg overflow-hidden relative">
28.                 {/*wrapper to place the comments*/}
29.                     {tab === ‹3› &&
30.                         <div className="absolute w-full h-full z-40">
31.                             <div className="relative w-full h-full"
32.                                 onClick={() => createComment(x, y)}
33.                             >
34.                                 {
35.                         commentsList && commentsList.map(
     (commentItem) => {
36.                                     return <div
37.             className="bg-white shadow absolute border-2 z-50
     rounded-md"
38.                                         key={commentItem.id}
39.                                         style={{
40.                                         top: commentItem.y,
41.                                         left: commentItem.x
42.                                         }}
43.                         onClick={(event) => event.stopPropagation()}
44.                                         ><CommentArea /></div>
45.                                     })
46.                                 }
47.                             </div>
48.                         </div>
49.                     }
50.                     {/*old code*/}
51.                 </div>
52.                 {/*old code*/}
53.                     <Tabs.Container
54.                         value={tab}
55.                         onValueChange={(tab) => setTab(tab)}
56.         {/*collect the tab ID to chow comments only in the last one*/}
57.                         ></Tabs.Container>
58.                 {/*old code*/}
59.         </main>
60.     );
61. }
62.
63. export default DataModel;
```

Code Listing 22.5: *Page update to create and show the comments with tab ID check*

```
1.  import { useEffect, useState } from "react";
2.
3.  const useMousePosition = () => {
4.      const [
5.          mousePosition,
6.          setMousePosition
7.      ] = useState({ x: null, y: null });
8.      useEffect(() => {
9.          const updateMousePosition = ev => {
10.             setMousePosition({ x: ev.clientX, y: ev.clientY });
11.         };
12.         window.addEventListener('mousemove', updateMousePosition);
13.         return () => {
14.             window.removeEventListener('mousemove', updateMousePosition);
15.         };
16.     }, []);
17.     return mousePosition;
18. };
19. export default useMousePosition;
```

Code Listing 22.6: Hook to catch mouse position coordinates

```
1.  'use client';
2.  import { Button, TextAreaField } from "@aws-amplify/ui-react";
3.  import { useState } from "react";
4.
5.  export default function CommentArea({initialComment}) {
6.      const [comment, setComment] = useState('');
7.      const [closed, setClosed] = useState(false);
8.
9.      const saveComment = () => {
10.         setClosed(true);
11.     }
12.     return (
13.         <section className="p-2 flex flex-col gap-2">
14.             {!closed &&
15.             <>
16.                 <TextAreaField
17.                     descriptiveText="Enter a new comment"
18.                     label="New comment"
19.                     name="new_comment"
20.                     placeholder="New comment"
```

```
21.                      value={comment}
22.                      onChange={(e) => {setComment(e.target.value)}}
23.                      rows={3} />
24.                <Button onClick={saveComment}>Save</Button>
25.            </>
26.            }{
27.                closed &&
28.                <div>{comment}</div>
29.            }
30.        </section>
31.    )
32.}
```

Code Listing 22.7: Comment component to show the form before we save the comment

Figure 22.4 represents the UI interface of the **Collaborations** tab with ratings and comments on the screen:

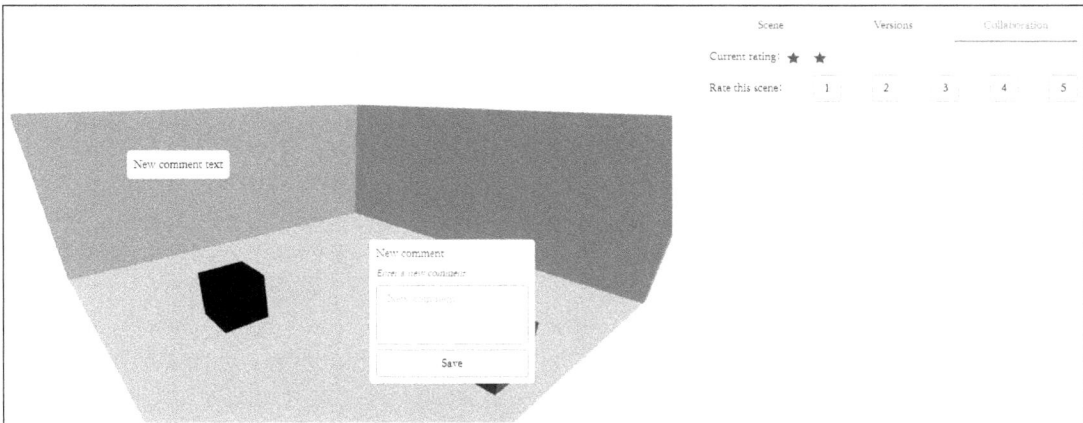

Figure 22.4: Result of initial updates

Now, we need to create the function to create the data on the API side. We also need to get them back from the API on page load. We will follow the Votes example to implement functionality.

Communication with the API will require the following steps:

1. To save the data, we will create a function as in *Code Listing 22.8* to send the new comment to the API.

```
1. const saveComment = async (comment, position) => {
2.        await client.graphql({
3.            query: createComments,
4.            variables: {
```

```
5.                      input: {
6.                          user: "Test user",
7.                          comment: comment,
8.                          position: position
9.                      }
10.                  }
11.          })
12.      }
```

Code Listing 22.8: Function to save the data for the comment

2. Next, we need to update the rendering of the comments list with default comments and send the **saveComment** function to the **Comment** component. The code for the update is in *Code Listing 22.9*:

```
1.  {
2.          commentsList && commentsList.map((commentItem) => {
3.          return <div
4.                  className="bg-
    white shadow absolute border-2 z-50 rounded-md"
5.                      key={commentItem.id}
6.                      style={{
7.                              top: commentItem.y,
8.                              left: commentItem.x
9.                      }}
10.                     onClick={(event) => event.stopPropagation()}
11.                 >
12.                     <CommentArea
13.                         initialComment={commentItem.comment}
14.                         position={{x: commentItem.x, y:
    commentItem.y}}
15.                         saveMethod={saveComment} />
16.                 </div>
17.         })
18. }
```

Code Listing 22.9: Implementing the default comments and save function in the rendering part

3. The next step will be to get the default comments from the API. We will use the same fetching mechanism as before. As we have already implemented real-time synchronization before, we will do it in this step too. This code is in *Code Listing 22.10*; we will put it in the **useEffect** part:

```
1.  const fetchCommentsData = async () => {
2.          const allComments = await client.graphql({
```

```
3.                    query: listComments,
4.                    variables: {
5.                        filter: {_deleted: {ne: true}}
6.                    }
7.                });
8.                if (allComments.data.listComments.items.length > 0) {
9.                    const normalizedCommentsData = allComments.
   data.listComments.items.map(item => {
10.                        return {
11.                            x: item.position[0],
12.                            y: item.position[1],
13.                            comment: item.comment,
14.                            id: item.id
15.                        };
16.                    });
17.                    setCommentsList(normalizedCommentsData);
18.                }
19. }
20. fetchCommentsData();
21.
22. const subscription = client
23.                .graphql({ query: onCreateComments })
24.                .subscribe({
25.                    next: ({ data }) => {
26.                        setCommentsList((state) => [...state, {
27.                            id: data.onCreateComments.id,
28.                            x: data.onCreateComments.position[0],
29.                            y: data.onCreateComments.position[1],
30.                            comment: data.onCreateComments.comment
31.                        }])
32.                    },
33.                    error: (error) => console.warn(error)
34.                });
35. // Return a cleanup function to unsubscribe when the component
   is unmounted
36. return () => subscription.unsubscribe();
```

Code Listing 22.10: Code to get comments and subscribe

4. You can see the interesting part in the query section (*Code Listing 22.11*). AWS will return all values, even if it is deleted from the system. This is why we need to add the filter flag:

```
1.  variables: {
2.                  filter: {_deleted: {ne: true}}
3.  }
```

Code Listing 22.11: Query filter to show only not deleted values

We can use this filter for any request for safe data rendering. This is required because AWS Amplify will return the data even if it was deleted. Deleted values will come with the flag **"_deleted"**.

5. The last step is to update the **Comment** component. The code for the update is in *Code Listing 22.12*:

```
1.  const saveComment = () => {
2.          setClosed(true);
3.          saveMethod(comment, [position.x, position.y]);
4.      }
5.
6.      useEffect(() => {
7.          if(initialComment) {
8.              setClosed(true);
9.              setComment(initialComment);
10.         }
11. }, [initialComment]);
12.
```

Code Listing 22.12: Code for the comment component

As a result, we will see a familiar functionality; every time we create a comment in the **Collaboration** tab, it will be immediately added to any device where we open the same page and tab, as shown in *Figure 22.5*:

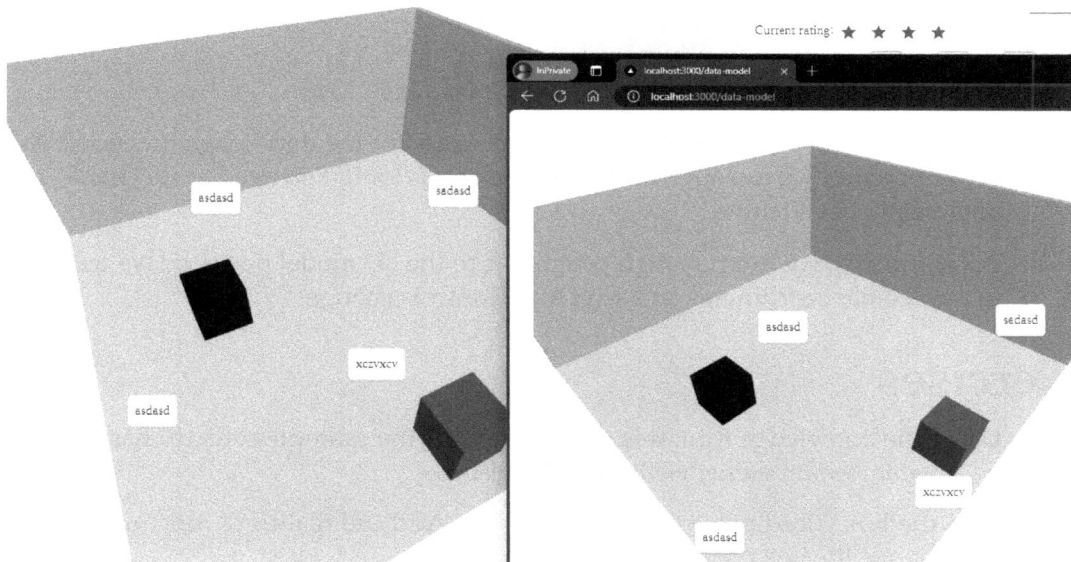

Figure 22.5: Real-time comments functionality in the browser

Conclusion

In this chapter, we studied the real-time capabilities provided by AWS Amplify. We began by understanding the importance of real-time data exchange and how it can significantly enhance user interactions in modern applications.

We then walked through the setup process for real-time functionality, including configuring AWS Amplify and setting up GraphQL subscriptions. We learned how to implement a real-time voting system and a real-time comments system, providing practical examples to apply these concepts.

Finally, we integrated these real-time features into our application, making it more interactive and dynamic. Learning to test and debug these real-time functionalities, we ensured the application remained responsive and reliable.

This chapter has equipped us to add real-time features to our applications, creating more engaging and interactive user experiences.

In the next chapter, we will explore the fundamentals of UI design systems within the React Three Fiber ecosystem, focusing on how to build structured and reusable 3D components. We will introduce Storybook as a powerful tool for developing and documenting React Three Fiber components, providing an efficient workflow for visualization and testing. Additionally, we will dive into Storybook add-ons, enhancing our development experience with tools tailored for 3D interfaces. By the end of the chapter, you will have a solid understanding of how to organize and create reusable 3D UI components in Storybook, streamlining the design and development of interactive 3D applications.

Points to remember

- Real-time data exchange can be expensive on a high load.

- For educational purposes, we made a code copy for the data usage functions. As a better practice, we can align abstracted functions for it. You need to check the votes and comments fetching.

- For simplicity, we did not align comments to the 3D model position. We will need to recalculate coordinates on each Orbit Controls change.

Exercises

1. Using the knowledge from this chapter, update the example code to change object parameters (color, name, visibility) in real-time.

2. Add the box coordinates to each box block. Add the real-time functionality that will change the box coordinates.

Join our Discord space

Join our Discord workspace for latest updates, offers, tech happenings around the world, new releases, and sessions with the authors:

https://discord.bpbonline.com

Creating the UI Design System with Storybook

Introduction

Creating consistent, scalable, and maintainable user interfaces is paramount in modern web development. This is where UI design systems come into play. They provide a structured approach to UI development, ensuring that components are reusable and visually cohesive across an application. Integrating a design system can significantly enhance workflow when working with 3D graphics using **React Three Fiber (R3F)**.

Storybook is a powerful tool that facilitates the development and documentation of UI components in isolation. Using Storybook, developers can focus on individual elements, verify their behavior, and document their usage without the complexity of the entire application. Combining Storybook with R3F, a React renderer for Three.js, allows for the seamless creation and management of 3D components.

In this chapter, we will study how to set up and leverage Storybook for developing 3D UI components with R3F. We will learn the benefits of UI design systems, explore various Storybook add-ons, and create and organize reusable 3D components. By the end of the chapter, we will have a robust understanding of enhancing 3D development projects with Storybook.

Structure

In this chapter, we will discuss the following topics:

- Introduction to UI design systems
- Overview of Storybook for React Three Fiber
- Storybook add-ons for React Three Fiber
- Organizing 3D UI components in Storybook
- Reusable 3D UI components in Storybook

Objectives

By the end of this chapter, you will understand the fundamental concepts and advantages of UI design systems, particularly in the context of 3D UI development. You will learn how to set up Storybook for Next.js and R3F projects, integrating it seamlessly into your workflow. You will explore various Storybook add-ons, such as controls, backgrounds, and accessibility tools, to enhance the development process. Additionally, you will gain insights into organizing and structuring 3D UI components within Storybook for better maintainability and navigation. Through practical techniques, you will learn to create reusable and modular 3D UI components using Storybook's composition capabilities. Finally, we will cover how to leverage Storybook for documentation and testing, ensuring that 3D components align with design specifications and function as intended.

Introduction to UI design systems

The UI design system is a comprehensive collection of reusable components, guided by clear standards, that can be assembled to build any number of applications. The core idea behind a design system is to provide a consistent look and feel across different parts of an application while ensuring that the components are scalable, maintainable, and reusable.

In traditional web development, design systems help with visual and functional consistency. They allow developers to build interfaces efficiently without reinventing common UI elements like buttons, forms, and navigation bars. This consistency is crucial for user experience, as it reduces cognitive load and creates a familiar environment for the users.

Benefits of UI design systems in 3D applications

A well-defined design system is just as crucial for 3D applications as traditional 2D interfaces. By establishing a structured approach to 3D UI development, we can ensure consistency, scalability, reusability, and maintainability across projects. This not only enhances the user experience but also streamlines development, making it easier to expand, refine, and manage 3D components efficiently.

- **Consistency:** As with 2D components, 3D components benefit from a unified design language. Consistent lighting, materials, and interactions help create a cohesive user experience.

- **Scalability:** A well-structured design system allows us to scale 3D applications more efficiently. New components can be added with minimal disruption to the existing system, ensuring the application grows organically.

- **Reusability:** Reusable components are key to efficient development. By creating a library of 3D components (like models, animations, and interactions), we can save time and effort in future projects, as these components can be easily reused and repurposed.

- **Maintainability:** With a clear structure and standard in place, maintaining and updating our 3D components becomes simpler. Changes can be made in one place and propagated throughout the application, reducing the risk of inconsistencies.

Building scalable and consistent user interfaces

The following is the importance of building scalable and consistent user interfaces:

- **3D complexity:** 3D applications introduce additional complexity with aspects like spatial positioning, lighting, and user interactions in three dimensions. A design system helps manage this complexity by providing a standardized approach.

- **Performance optimization:** 3D applications are often more resource-intensive than their 2D counterparts. A design system can include performance-optimized components and best practices, ensuring the application runs smoothly even as it scales.

- **User experience:** In 3D applications, user experience is paramount. Consistent interactions and visual elements help users understand and navigate the 3D environment more effectively. A design system ensures these elements are applied uniformly.

R3F allows developers to leverage the React component model to manage Three.js scenes. It helps the seamless integration of 3D elements into web applications.

Combining React Three Fiber with a UI design system

Incorporating R3F into a design system brings structure and efficiency to 3D UI development. By creating modular components, ensuring consistent interactivity, and streamlining workflows, developers can build scalable and reusable 3D elements with ease. A well-defined system not only enhances maintainability but also fosters a more predictable and cohesive user experience. This combination provides the following advantages:

- **Modular 3D components:** Just like React components for 2D UIs, we can create modular and reusable 3D components with R3F. These components can be standardized and documented within the design system.

- **Interactive and dynamic UIs:** R3F enables the creation of interactive 3D components that can respond to user inputs and state changes. Integrating these into a design system ensures that interactions are consistent and predictable.

- **Efficient development workflow:** A design system with R3F streamlines the development process. Developers can focus on building and refining components in isolation, confident that they will integrate smoothly into the larger application.

Overview of Storybook for React Three Fiber

Using Storybook with R3F for 3D UI components will allow us to solve several problems:

- **Isolated development:** We can develop each 3D component independently, focusing on its behavior, appearance, and interactions without being distracted by the complexities of the entire application.

- **Variations and states:** Storybook allows us to create different stories (variations) for each 3D component. This includes props, states, and interaction variations, enabling comprehensive testing and documentation.

- **Visual testing:** By visualizing 3D components in different scenarios (e.g., different viewport sizes and lighting conditions), we can ensure that they meet design specifications and perform optimally across various environments.

- **Collaboration:** Storybook facilitates collaboration among team members by providing a centralized platform where developers, designers, and stakeholders can review and provide feedback on 3D UI components.

Storybook add-ons for React Three Fiber

Storybook add-ons extend the functionality of Storybook, providing additional tools and capabilities to enhance the development and documentation of UI components. When working with R3F for 3D UI development, certain add-ons can be particularly beneficial. These add-ons help manipulate 3D controls, set backgrounds, and ensure accessibility, addressing the unique needs of 3D components.

In this section, we will introduce all required addons, and in the next one, get into practice using all of them in real examples:

Addon: @storybook/addon-controls

The **Controls** add-on helps dynamically edit component properties through a user interface. This is incredibly useful for 3D components, where we might want to adjust properties such as size, color, position, and rotation.

Example use case: Adjust the position of a 3D object in real-time to see how it behaves within different parts of the scene. The code is shown in *Code Listing 23.1*:

```
1.  import { withControls } from '@storybook/addon-controls';
2.
3.  export const My3DComponentStory = {
4.    component: My3DComponent,
5.    decorators: [withControls],
6.    args: {
7.      position: [0, 0, 0],
8.      color: 'blue',
9.    },
10. };
11.
12. const Template = (args) => <My3DComponent {...args} />;
```

Code Listing 23.1: Controls story example

Addon: @storybook/addon-backgrounds

The **Backgrounds** add-on allows us to change the background color or image of the Storybook canvas. This is especially useful for 3D components, where the background can significantly affect the visual appearance and testing environment.

Example use case: Testing how a 3D object looks against different backgrounds to ensure it is visually distinct and meets design requirements. The code is shown in *Code Listing 23.2*:

```
1.  import { withBackgrounds } from '@storybook/addon-backgrounds';
2.
3.  export const My3DComponentStory = {
4.    component: My3DComponent,
5.    decorators: [
6.      withBackgrounds({
7.        default: 'default background',
8.        values: [
9.          { name: 'light', value: '#ffffff' },
10.         { name: 'dark', value: '#000000' },
11.       ],
12.     }),
13.   ],
14. };
15.
16. const Template = (args) => <My3DComponent {...args} />;
```

Code Listing 23.2: Change background story example

Addon: @storybook/addon-a11y

The **Accessibility** add-on helps test and ensure that the components comply with accessibility standards. For 3D components, ensuring accessibility can involve making sure that interactive elements are navigable and usable by all users, including those relying on assistive technologies.

Example use case: Checking that all interactive 3D elements can be accessed via keyboard navigation and have appropriate ARIA labels. The code is shown in *Code Listing 23.3*:

```
1.  import { withA11y } from '@storybook/addon-a11y';
2.
3.  export const My3DComponentStory = {
4.    component: My3DComponent,
5.    decorators: [withA11y],
6.  };
7.
8.  const Template = (args) => <My3DComponent {...args} />;
```

Code Listing 23.3: Accessibility check story example

Addon: @storybook/addon-storysource

This add-on shows the source code of the stories, which can be particularly useful for educational purposes and for ensuring transparency in how components are configured and used.

Example use case: Getting the source code of the story to understand the usage or find errors in the early stage. To use it, we need to enable it in the storybook configuration. No additional code work is required.

Organizing 3D UI components in Storybook

Organizing 3D UI components effectively in Storybook is important for a streamlined development process. Proper organization ensures that developers can easily navigate, understand, and maintain the codebase, which is especially important in complex 3D applications built with R3F. This section discusses best practices for structuring the Storybook stories and components to facilitate a smooth workflow.

Without a clear structure, managing and finding components can become a daunting task. The following are the benefits of an effective organization:

- **Enhances readability:** Well-organized components and stories are easier to read and understand.

- **Improves maintainability:** A clear structure simplifies updates and modifications.

- **Facilitates collaboration:** Other developers can quickly get up to speed with a logically organized project.

- • **Speeds up development:** Quick access to components and stories accelerates the development process.

Best practices for organizing 3D UI components

Effectively organizing 3D UI components ensures maintainability, scalability, and a seamless development workflow. Following best practices helps create a structured, reusable, and efficient component library.

Component hierarchy

We hierarchically structure our components together so that they reflect their logical relationship. For example, components representing different parts of a 3D scene should be grouped under a common folder.

In this book, we recommend following domain-driven development patterns in code structure. **Domain-Driven Design (DDD)** is a software development approach that emphasizes creating a rich domain model, where the software's structure and language reflect the business domain. This approach helps manage complexity by organizing code around the business logic and domain concepts, rather than technical details. As we use Next.js and a file-based router, each domain is the page representation. If we need to share the code on the pages, we will put it in a shared folder. The structure example shown in *Code Listing 23.4*:

```
1.  src/
2.    app/
3.      independent-page/
4.        Scene/
5.          Floor.js
6.          Wall.js
7.          Box.js
8.    components/
9.      Scene/
10.       Floor.js
11.       Wall.js
12.       Box.js
13.     UI/
14.       Button.js
15.       Modal.js
```

Code listing 23.4: Folders structure example

Consistent naming conventions

We use consistent and descriptive naming conventions for our components and stories. This practice helps identify the purpose of a component, thus reducing confusion.

Example:

- **Component names:** Box, Sphere, CameraControls
- **Storybook stories:** BasicBoxStory, InteractiveSphereStory

Story organization

We organize our stories in a way that mirrors the component structure. We use nested directories and clear labels to make navigation intuitive. A structure example can be taken from *Code Listing 23.5*:

```
1.  src/
2.    components/
3.      Scene/
4.        Box.stories.js
5.        Sphere.stories.js
6.      UI/
7.        Button.stories.js
8.        Modal.stories.js
```

Code Listing 23.5: Stories organization structure example

Use of meta tags

We utilize Storybook's meta tags to provide additional information and context for each story. This includes descriptions, tags, and parameters. An example is shown in *Code Listing 23.6*:

```
1.  // Box.stories.js
2.  import React from 'react';
3.  import Box from './Box';
4.
5.  export default {
6.    title: 'Scene/Box',
7.    component: Box,
8.    parameters: {
9.      docs: {
10.       description: {
11.         component: 'A 3D box component rendered using React Three Fiber.',
12.       },
13.     },
14.   },
15. };
16.
17. export const BasicBox = () => <Box position={[0, 0, 0]} />;
```

Code Listing 23.6: Using meta tags example

Reusable 3D UI components in Storybook

In this section, we finally get into practice. To proceed with examples, we need to fulfill the requirements first:

- We need to create the page with the scene and components:
    - The scene will contain two components: the box and the sphere
    - We will create 3D components using basic geometries
    - Each component will have a story independently
    - Each component will have the possibility to change its properties
- We will use all described add-ons
- We will create shareable components outside of the page
- Stories should be located in the component folder
- We will document each component to have clear documentation for the project

To add all required plugins, we need to run this command:

```
yarn add @storybook/addon-controls @storybook/addon-backgrounds @storybook/addon-a11y --dev
```

```
or
```

```
npm install @storybook/addon-controls @storybook/addon-backgrounds @storybook/addon-a11y --dev
```

We also need to configure .**storybook/main.js** like in *Code Listing 23.7*:

```
1.  module.exports = {
2.      // Add array data in your file if it's not empty
3.      addons: [
4.          '@storybook/addon-controls',
5.          '@storybook/addon-backgrounds',
6.          '@storybook/addon-a11y',
7.      ],
8.  };
```

Code Listing 23.7: Update for your main.js file in Storybook

Depending on the version of StoryBook we are working with, some of the components are already in the system by default. In the latest version of Storybook, features like controls and background customization come pre-installed and ready to use without requiring additional setup or configuration. If you are using older versions, follow the guide for installation

(**https://storybook.js.org/docs/get-started/install**).

We need to create all the required components, by following these steps:

1. Create the page with the required objects. We can collect the code for it in *Code Listing 23.8*:

```
1.  // This is a client-side component, meaning it will be
    rendered on the client side of your application
2.  "use client";
3.
4.  // import the InternalBox and InternalScene components from
    their respective files
5.  import InternalBox from "./components/InternalBox";
6.  import InternalScene from "./components/InternalScene";
7.
8.  // import the InternalSphere component as it is not being
    used in this code snippet
9.  import InternalSphere from "./components/InternalSphere";
10.
11. // Define a functional React component called StoryBookExample
12. export default function StoryBookExample() {
13.     // return JSX to be rendered by the browser
14.     return (
15.         // Set the height of the div container to 100% of the
        viewport height
16.         <div className="h-[100vh]">
17.             {/* render an InternalScene component and pass it to
        children as arguments */}
18.             <InternalScene>
19.                 {/* render an InternalBox component with
        specific properties */}
20.                 <InternalBox position={[0, 1, 0]} color="green"
        size={[1, 1, 1]}  />
21.                 {/* render an InternalSphere component with
        specific properties */}
22.                 <InternalSphere
23.                   position={[2, 2, 0]}
24.                   color="red"
25.                   radius={1}
26.                   segments={{ x: 10, y: 10 }} />
27.             </InternalScene>
28.         </div>
29.     );
30. }
```

Code Listing 23.8: Page with 3D objects

2. Next, create all the required components: the scene, the box, and the sphere. The code can be seen in *Code Listings 23.9-23.11*:

```
1.  "use client"; // This indicates that this component should
    only be rendered on the client side
2.
3.  // Import necessary components from react-three/drei and
    react-three/fiber libraries
4.  import { OrbitControls } from «@react-three/drei";
5.  import { Canvas } from ‹@react-three/fiber';
6.
7.  export default function InternalScene({ children }) {
8.      return (
9.          <>
10.             <h1>Example scene</h1> {/* render an h1 heading */}
11.             <Canvas > {/* create a Canvas element to render
    3D content */}
12.                 <ambientLight intensity={0.5} /> {/* add an
    ambient light with intensity 0.5 */}
13.                 <directionalLight
14.                     position={[5, 10, 7.5]} // set the
    position of the directional light
15.                     intensity={1} // set the intensity of the light
16.                     castShadow // enable shadow casting for
    this light
17.                     shadow-mapSize-width={1024}
18.                     // Set the width of the shadow map size
    to 1024 pixels
19.                     shadow-mapSize-height={1024}
20.                     // set the height of the shadow map size
    to 1024 pixels
21.                     shadow-camera-far={50}
22.                     // Set the far clipping plane distance
    for the shadow camera
23.                     shadow-camera-left={-10} // set the left
    frustum of the shadow camera
24.                     shadow-camera-
    right={10} // set the right frustum of the shadow camera
25.                     shadow-camera-
    top={10} // set the top frustum of the shadow camera
26.                     shadow-camera-
    bottom={-10} // set the bottom frustum of the shadow camera
27.                     /> {/* render a directional light with specific
    properties */}
28.                 {children} {/* render any children components
    passed as props */}
```

```
29.                    <OrbitControls makeDefault />
30.                    {/* add OrbitControls to the Canvas, allowing
     user control of the camera */}
31.            </Canvas>
32.        </>
33.    );
34. }
```

Code Listing 23.9: Scene component that will receive 3D objects as children

To create the **Box** component, follow the *Code listing 23.10:*

```
1.  // Import necessary hooks and components from react-three-fiber
2.  import { useFrame } from '@react-three/fiber';
3.  import { useRef } from 'react';
4.
5.  // Define the InternalBox component as a function that takes in props
6.  const InternalBox = ({ position, color, size, rotationSpeed }) => {
7.    // Create a reference to the mesh element using the useRef hook
8.    const ref = useRef();
9.
10.   // Define an animation callback using the useFrame hook
11.   useFrame(() => {
12.     // If the ref. The current is defined, and the
    rotationSpeed properties are provided.
13.     // rotate the box continuously along the x, y, and z axes
14.     if (ref.current && rotationSpeed) {
15.       ref.current.rotation.x += rotationSpeed?.x;
16.       ref.current.rotation.y += rotationSpeed?.y;
17.       ref.current.rotation.z += rotationSpeed?.z;
18.     }
19.   });
20.
21.   // Render a mesh with the provided position and other properties
22.   return (
23.     <mesh
24.       ref={ref} // Assign the ref to the mesh element
25.       position={position} // Set the position of the box
26.     >
27.       {/* Define the geometry of the box using a boxGeometry
    component */}
28.       <boxGeometry args={size} />
29.
30.       {/* Define the material for the box using a
    meshStandardMaterial component */}
```

```
31.        <meshStandardMaterial color={color} /> // Set the color of the box
32.     </mesh>
33.   );
34. };
35.
36. // Export the InternalBox component as the default export
37. export default InternalBox;
```

Code Listing 23.10: *Box component with configurable properties*

And for the ***Sphere*** component, please take the code from *Code Listing 23.11*.

```
1.  // Import necessary hooks from @react-three/fiber Library
2.  import { useFrame } from '@react-three/fiber';
3.
4.  // Import React hook useRef to get a reference to the mesh element
    in the scene
5.  import { useRef } from 'react';
6.
7.  const InternalSphere = ({ position, color, radius, rotationSpeed,
    segments }) => {
8.    // Create a ref using the useRef hook to get a reference to the
    mesh element
9.    const ref = useRef();
10.
11.   // Use React's useFrame hook to continuously update the component
    on each frame
12.   useFrame(() => {
13.     if (ref.current && rotationSpeed) {
14.       // Check if there is a valid ref and rotation speed prop available
15.       ref.current.rotation.x += rotationSpeed?.x;
16.       // Increment the x rotation of the sphere by the rotation
    speed value
17.       ref.current.rotation.y += rotationSpeed?.y;
18.       // Increment the y rotation of the sphere by the rotation
    speed value
19.     }
20.   });
21.
22.   // Render a mesh element with the provided props and properties
23.   return (
24.     <mesh ref={ref} position={position} castShadow>
25.       {/* Create a sphere geometry using the provided radius
26.       and segments for both horizontal and vertical axis */}
27.         <sphereGeometry args={[radius, segments?.x || 32,
    segments?.y || 32]} />
```

```
28.
29.       {/* Set standard material properties of the mesh with the
   provided color */}
30.       <meshStandardMaterial color={color} />
31.    </mesh>
32.  );
33. };
34.
35. // Export the InternalSphere component for use in other parts of the app
36. export default InternalSphere;
```

Code Listing 23.11: Sphere component with configurable properties

3. After the project starts, we will see the same picture as in *Figure 23.1*. It should be a scene with a box and sphere:

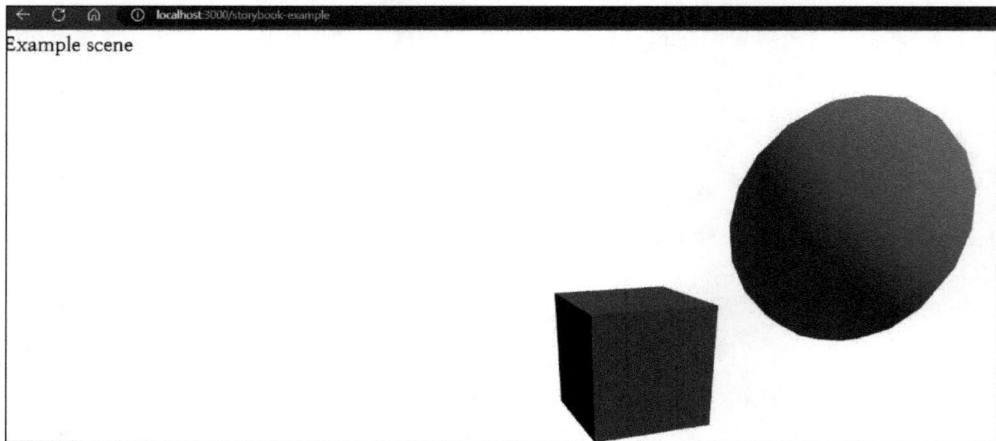

Figure 23.1: Initial scene. Using this scene, we will create the stories for the Storybook.

4. It is now time to prepare our stories. An important point is that 3D objects do not work without canvas objects. This means if we do it the same way as the regular UI component, it will not work properly. Thus, we need to first add a canvas to each story. To add it, we use the Storybook feature called **Decorator**. To add the decorator, we need to put the code from *Code Listing 23.12* in the **.storybook/ preview.js** file:

```
1. /** @type { import('@storybook/react').Preview } */
2.
3. import { Canvas } from '@react-three/fiber';
4.
5. const preview = {
6.   parameters: {
7.     controls: {
```

```
8.        matchers: {
9.          color: /(background|color)$/i,
10.         date: /Date$/i,
11.       },
12.     },
13.   },
14.   // This parameter is required to automatically add
      documentation from the meta tags
15.   tags: ['autodocs']
16. };
17.
18. const withCanvas = (Story) => (
19.   <div style={{
20.     height: «100svh"
21.   }}>
22.     <Canvas shadows>
23.       <ambientLight intensity={0.5} />
24.       <directionalLight
25.           position={[5, 10, 7.5]}
26.           intensity={1}
27.           castShadow
28.           shadow-mapSize-width={1024}
29.           shadow-mapSize-height={1024}
30.           shadow-camera-far={50}
31.           shadow-camera-left={-10}
32.           shadow-camera-right={10}
33.           shadow-camera-top={10}
34.           shadow-camera-bottom={-10}
35.       />
36.       {/* Here we put each story into the decorator */}
37.       <Story />
38.     </Canvas>
39.   </div>
40. );
41.
42. // higher ordered component that will be used for each story
43. export const decorators = [withCanvas];
44. export default preview;
```

Code Listing 23.12: Decorator configuration to add canvas to each story

5. Now, we are ready to create our first story. We will create the file **InternalBox. stories.js** in the components folder. In this file, we will put the code from *Code Listing 23.13*, containing several stories. Since we use the latest Storybook, the format will only have parameters. We will also put metatags with explanations:

```
1. import InternalBox from './InternalBox';
2.
3. export default {
4.    title: '3D/Box',
5.    component: InternalBox,
6.    parameters: {
7.      docs: {
8.        description: {
9.          component: "This is an internal Box component for
   the page ."
10.        }
11.      }
12.    },
13.    // This parameter will disconnect autodocumentation.
14.    // Read the next block for an explanation
15.    tags: ['!autodocs'],
16. };
17.
18. export const DefaultBox = {
19.    args: {},
20. };
21.
22. export const RedLargeBox = {
23.    args: {
24.      color: "red",
25.    }
26. };
27.
28. export const FastRotatingBox = {
29.    args: {
30.      rotationSpeed: { x: 0.1, y:0.1, z: 0.1 }
31.    }
32. };
33.
34. export const ConfigurableBox = {
35.    args: {
36.      color: "green",
37.      position: [0, 0, 0],
38.      size: [2, 2, 2],
39.      rotationSpeed: { x: 0, y:0, z: 0 }
40.    }
41. };
```

Code Listing 23.13: Stories for various Boxes with different parameters

6. The next step is to add some documentation for the component. For this, we will add the file **InternalBox.mdx**. In this file, we will store the custom documentation for the component that contains more than just metadata. The code can be seen in *Code Listing 23.14*:

```
1.  {/* Checkbox.mdx */}
2.
3.  import { Canvas, Meta } from '@storybook/blocks';
4.
5.  import * as InternalBoxStories from './/InternalBox.stories';
6.
7.  <Meta of={InternalBoxStories} />
8.
9.  # Definition
10.
11. You can put some definitions in this block
12.
13. ## Usage
14.
15. Here, you can explain how to use the component and its purpose
16.
17. ## Box
18.
19. <Canvas of={InternalBoxStories.DefaultBox} />
20.
```

Code Listing 23.14: Custom documentation for the Box component

7. After the Storybook starts, we will see the same picture as *Figure 23.2* with the list of stories and documentation:

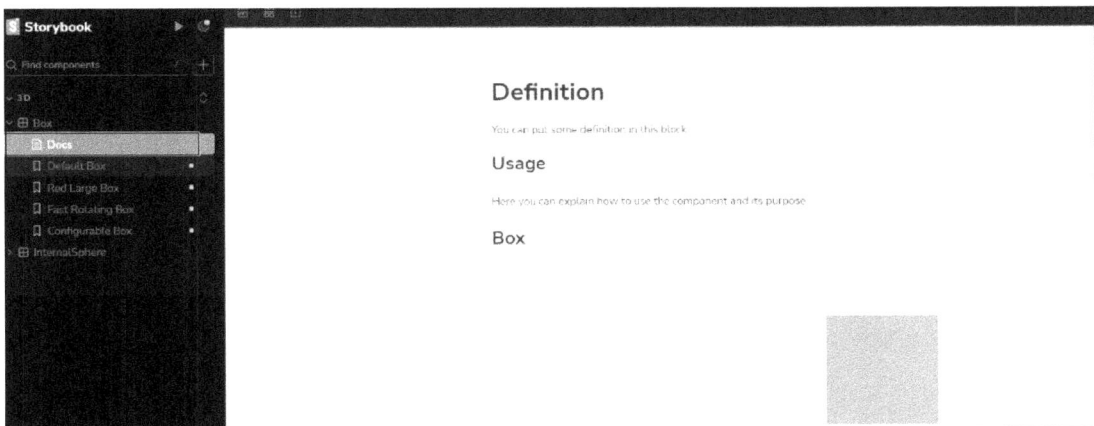

Figure 23.2: Box stories list and documentation

8. If we click on the last story, we will see the possibility of playing around with properties as shown in *Figure 23.3:*

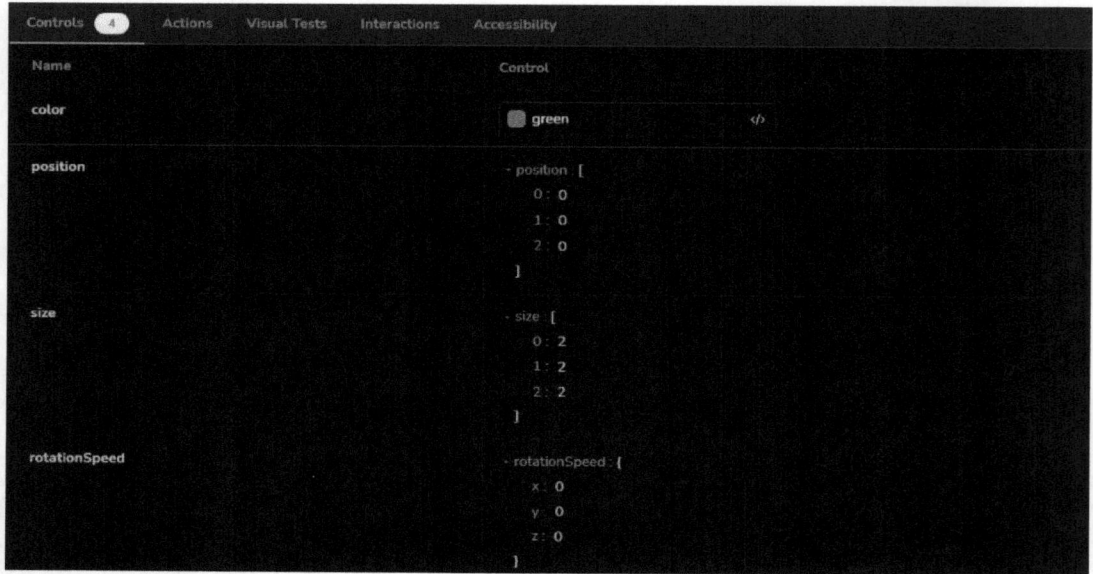

Figure 23.3: Box properties configuration

9. For the sphere, follow *Code Listing 23.15.* It is mostly the same as we used for the box, but here, we will use the auto-documentation feature and put the metatext from the story into the documentation block:

```
1.  import InternalSphere from './InternalSphere';
2.
3.  export default {
4.      title: '3D/InternalSphere',
5.      component: InternalSphere,
6.      parameters: {
7.          docs: {
8.              description: {
9.                  component: "This is an internal Sphere
    component for the page ."
10.             }
11.         }
12.     }
13. };
```

```
14.
15. export const DefaultSphere = {
16.     args: {
17.         position: [0, 1, 0],
18.         color: 'blue',
19.         radius: 1.2,
20.         segments: { x: 10, y: 10 }
21.     },
22. };
23.
24. export const RedLargeSphere = {
25.     args: {
26.         position: [0, 1, 0],
27.         color: 'red',
28.         radius: 3,
29.         segments: { x: 32, y: 32 }
30.     },
31. };
```

Code Listing 23.15: Sphere stories

10. The result for the sphere stories can be seen in *Figure 23.4*:

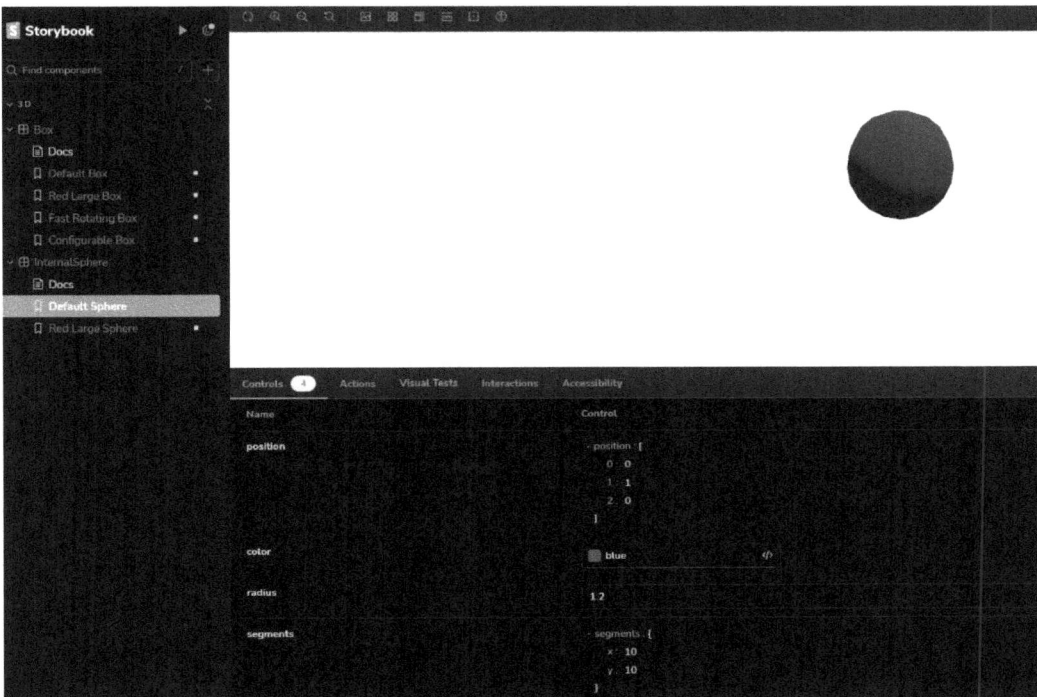

Figure 23.4: Sphere properties configuration

Conclusion

In this chapter, we learned how to integrate Storybook with R3F, aiming to build a more efficient and scalable UI design system for 3D components. We have studied the importance of UI design systems and how they contribute to creating consistent and reusable components. Setting up Storybook and utilizing its add-ons has empowered us to develop, document, and test our 3D UI components in isolation, enhancing our overall development workflow.

By organizing our components systematically and making them reusable, we pave the way for a more maintainable and scalable application architecture. The techniques learned in this chapter streamline the development process and also ensure that our 3D UI components are robust, well-documented, and accessible.

The skills and knowledge gained in this chapter will be invaluable in creating sophisticated and interactive 3D web applications. With Storybook and R3F, we can tackle complex UI challenges and deliver high-quality user experiences in your projects.

In the next chapter, we will outline the final project requirements, ensuring a clear understanding of the essential components needed for completion. We will explore recommended versions and packages to maintain compatibility and stability throughout development. Additionally, we will introduce generative AI features, demonstrating how they can enhance interactivity and automation within the project. Finally, we will discuss the next steps, guiding how to refine, expand, and deploy the project effectively.

Points to remember

- Writing stories will help organize, test, and maintain 3D objects way more easily
- To use the stories for the 3D object, it is a must to create the decorator
- Create as many stories as required to maintain the 3D object

Exercise

1. Create more objects using the knowledge from the previous chapters. Also, you can create the story with configurable parameters.

CHAPTER 24

Final Requirements and Recommendations

Introduction

In this final chapter, we will synthesize all the tools and concepts covered throughout the book to create a comprehensive industrial and multipurpose application using Three.js (and especially React Three Fiber) and Next.js. Throughout the book, we have studied the intricacies of 3D development with Three.js, the seamless integration capabilities of Next.js, the powerful hosting and data management features of AWS Amplify, and the efficiency of building UI design systems with Storybook. We will bring these components together, demonstrating how to build robust, scalable applications with immersive 3D experiences. This chapter aims to provide the knowledge and confidence to integrate these technologies into projects, motivating you to continue learning and expanding your skill set.

Structure

In this chapter, we will discuss the following topics:

- Final project requirements
- Project recommendations, versions, and packages
- Generative AI features
- Next steps

Objectives

By the end of this chapter, you will have a clear understanding of the final project requirements, ensuring that all essential components are well-defined and aligned with best practices. We will explore recommended versions and packages, helping us maintain stability, compatibility, and efficiency in our development workflow. Additionally, you will understand the integration of generative AI features, uncovering how these advanced capabilities can enhance interactivity, automation, and user engagement. Finally, we will outline the next steps, providing a strategic roadmap for refining, expanding, and deploying the project, ensuring a seamless transition from development to a fully functional application.

Final project requirements

In this chapter, we will create a small application that leverages React Three Fiber with Next.js, AWS Amplify, and Storybook. The application will guide users through an authorization process, leading them to a dashboard where they can manage a list of buildings. Each building will have detailed information and a 3D representation based on its build progress. The following are the detailed requirements.

Authorization

- **User sign-in/sign-up**: Implement user authentication using AWS Amplify.
- **Multi-Factor Authentication (MFA)**: Add an extra layer of security with MFA.
- **User session management**: Ensure proper session handling to maintain user state across the application.

After the authorization, the user will be forwarded to the dashboard page.

Dashboard

Managing and displaying building data effectively is crucial for creating an intuitive and functional user interface. This section outlines the structure and functionality of the building management system, including how to list buildings, display key details, and provide interactive options for editing and deleting entries. We will also explore the building detail page, which features additional descriptions and a dynamic 3D representation of build progress using Three.js. Finally, we will cover the essential CRUD operations that enable users to create, read, update, and delete building entries, ensuring seamless data management.

Building list

- Display a list of buildings.
- Each building entry should include:

- o Country
- o City
- o Address
- o Build progress (percentage)
- o Image of the building
- Each list item should have two buttons:
  - o **Edit:** Navigate to the building detail page.
  - o **Delete**: Removes the building from the list.

Building entry structure

Each building entry contains essential details such as location, construction progress, and a visual thumbnail. This structured data ensures clarity and consistency across the application.

- **Country:** Text field displaying the country.
- **City:** Text field displaying the city.
- **Address:** Text field displaying the address.
- **Build progress:** Displayed as a percentage.
- **Image:** A thumbnail image of the building.
- **Buttons:**
  - o **Edit:** Navigate to the building page.
  - o **Delete:** Deletes the building from the list.

Building page

The building detail page provides a comprehensive view of each entry, including additional descriptions and a dynamic 3D representation of build progress using Three.js, enhancing the user experience.

- **Detailed information**:
  - o Display all information from the list (Country, City, Address, Build Progress, Image).
  - o Additional description area: A text field where detailed information about the building can be entered.
- **3D representation:**
  - o Display a 3D box using Three.js.
  - o The box height will represent the build progress (e.g., a 50% build progress will render a box with 50% of the maximum height).

Functionality

The system supports full CRUD operations, allowing users to add, edit, and delete buildings. Interactive buttons enable seamless navigation, while confirmation steps ensure data integrity:

- **Edit building:**
    - o Clicking the **Edit** button on the dashboard navigates to the building detail page.
    - o Allow users to update the building information and save changes.

- **Delete building:**
    - o Clicking the Delete button removes the building from the list after confirmation.

- **CRUD operations:**
    - o **Create:** Add new buildings to the list via a form on the dashboard.
    - o **Read:** Fetch and display the list of buildings.
    - o **Update:** Edit building details on the building page.
    - o **Delete:** Remove buildings from the list.

Project recommendations, versions, and packages

As a base for the project, we will take the following packages:

- **Base Framework:** Next.js v14.2.5

- **UI:** AWS Amplify UI React v6.1.1 and higher

- **Styles:** Tailwind CSS v3.4.7 and higher

- **3D model support:** React Three Fiber v8.16.8 and higher

- **3D helpers:** React Three Drei v9.6.0 (at the moment, please do not upgrade it. We assume that the situation can be changed, but at the moment this book was created, this version is the only stable one to work with Nex.js 14)

- **Project UI collection:** Storybook v8.1.11

To start a project, we will need to follow these steps:

1. Create the UI mockups for each page. We recommend using the v0 service from Vercel. This link **https://v0.dev/** can be used.

2. Some of the UI elements are provided by AWS, like the **Auth form**.

3. Use the storybook to test the components before combining them into pages. It will contain complex components like tables or 3D models. For the atoms, we will use AWS React UI we so we do not need to test it at the atom level.

Generative AI features

In this section, we will experiment with the v0 service mentioned before. In *Figure 24.1,* we can see the prompt field where we can enter the desired explanation of the UI we want to have:

Generate. Refine. Ship.

Generate UI with shadcn/ui from simple text prompts and images.

An ecommerce store for snowboards

🖼 Image   🔓 Public

Product categories ↗   Hero section ↗   Contact form ↗   Ecommerce dashboard ↗

Figure 24.1: V0 service from Vercel generation form

To create the project prototype, we will take part of the description for the list page and use it in the form. The example prompt for the AI will look like the following:

```
I am making a dashboard with a building list.
    • Display a list of buildings.
    • Each building entry should include:
        o   Country
        o   City
        o   Address
    • Build progress (percentage)
    • Image of the building
    • Each list item should have two buttons:
        o   Edit: Navigate to the building detail page.
        o   Delete: Removes the building from the list.
```

We can make it complex or add more explanations and requirements to achieve the result. The results that we got can be seen in *Figure 24.2-3*. We posted only two variants as options; 2 and 3 were similar:

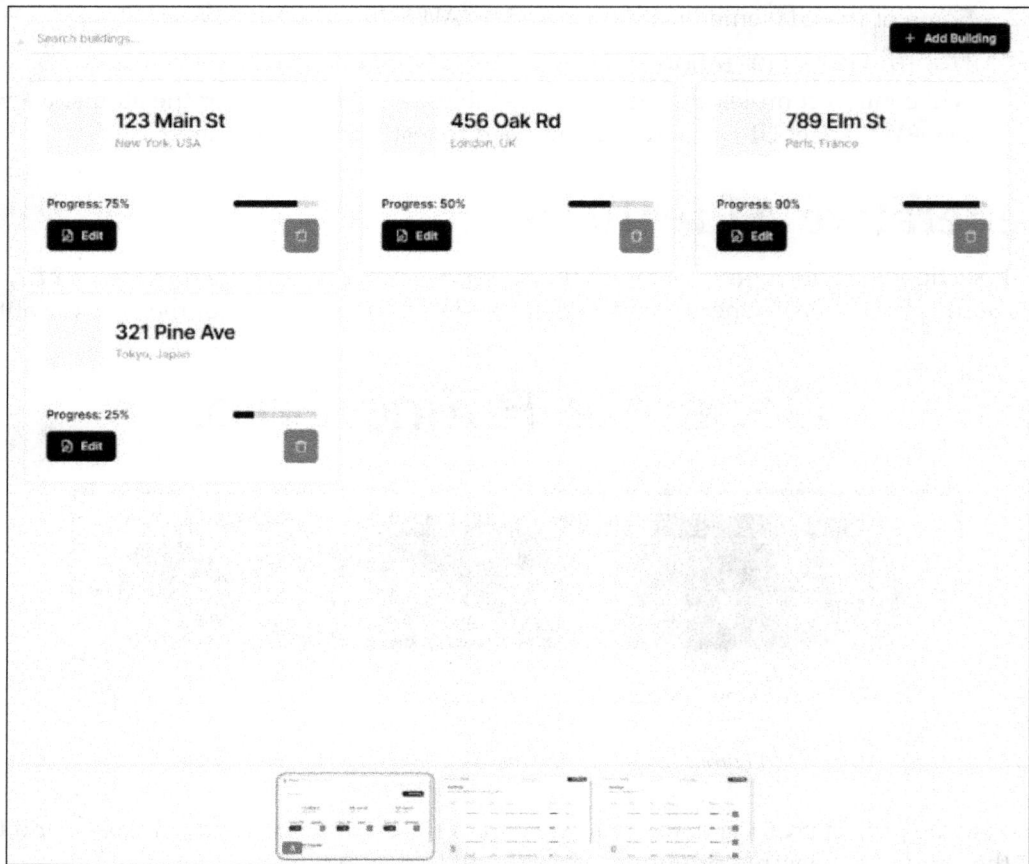

Figure 24.2: First option for the generated page

We can also see more variants like those provided in *Figure 24.3*:

Figure 24.3: Second option for the generated page

We can change the theme with collections of pre-defined themes, like in *Figure 24.4*:

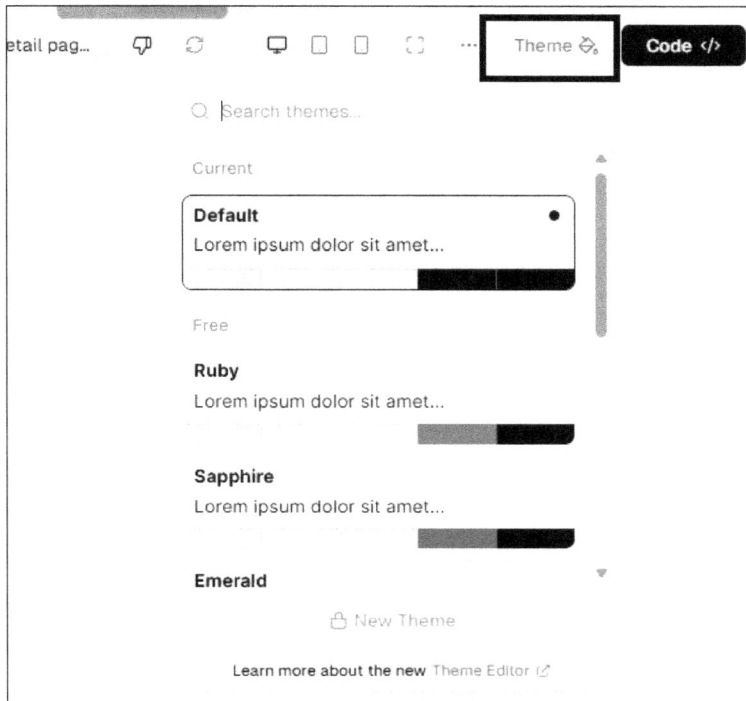

Figure 24.4: Theme selection in the UI interface of V0

In the paid version, we can customize the themes. It is not necessary, as it is a mock process. When we try to change the theme to another one, the result will be like in *Figure 24.5*:

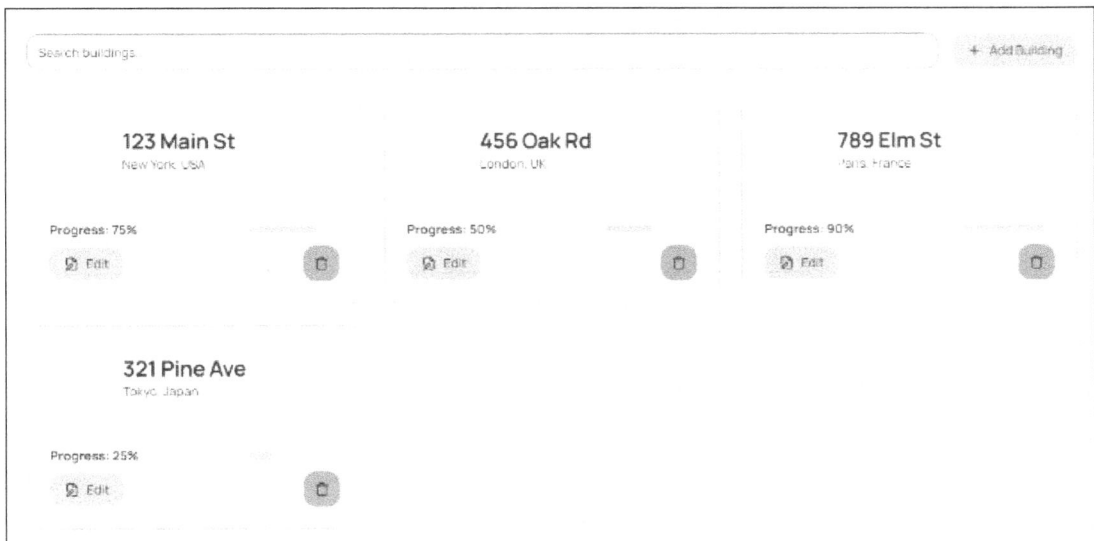

Figure 24.5: Theme change result

We can also check and grab the code by clicking the Code button next to Theme. We will see the same panel as in *Figure 24.6,* with the possibility to directly install this component or take the code. Since we are using our UI library (from AWS), we do not need to install the component, and taking the code will be enough:

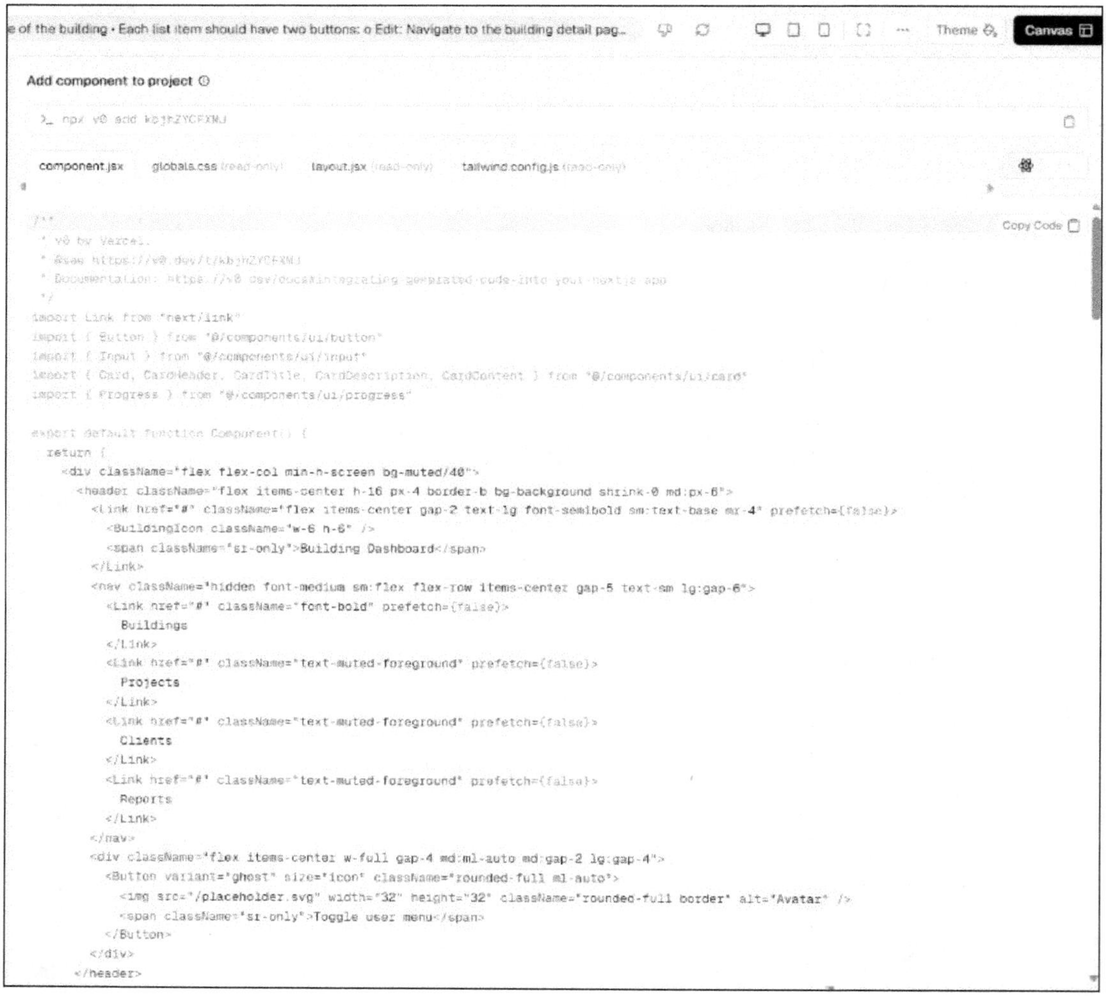

Figure 24.6: The code panel

As we have more requirements for the card we can add them in the AI chat field to update the card.

The prompt will look like this:

```
Add this information to the building card:
    • Country: Text field displaying the country.
    • City: Text field displaying the city.
    • Address: Text field displaying the address.
```

Now, the resulting page that we will use will look like *Figure 24.7:*

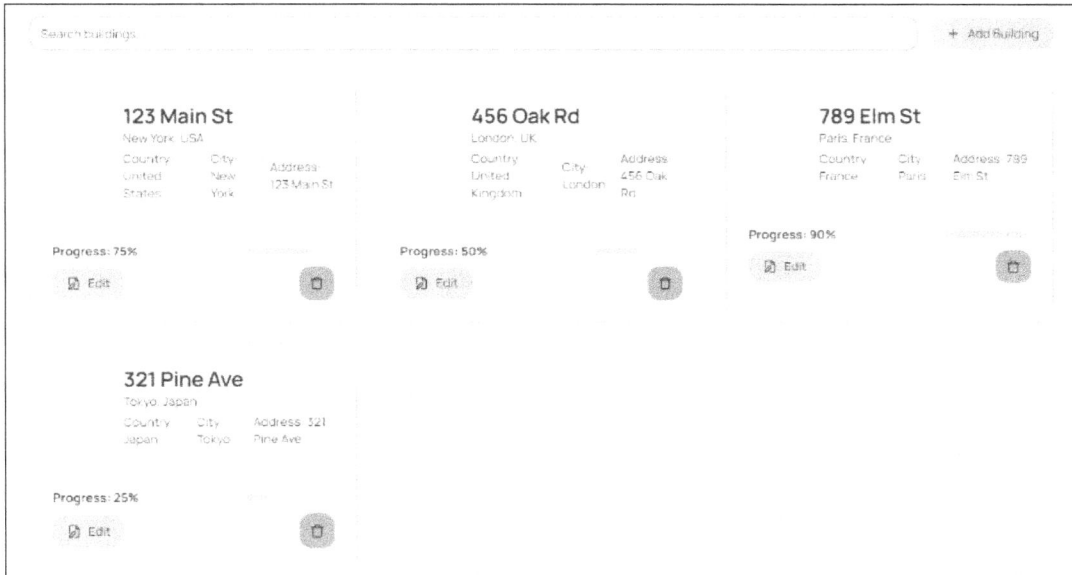

Figure 24.7: The Final result for the list page

The next step is to make the page, which will be opened on the edit button click. We will make the same procedure as before and use the prompt like this:

```
I need a building management page. This page will have 2 parts:
Building Page
Detailed Information:
Display all information from the list (Country, City, Address, Build
Progress, Image).
Additional Description area: A text field where detailed information about
the building can be entered.
3D Representation:
Display a 3D box using Three.js.
The height of the box will represent the build progress (e.g., a 50% build
progress will render a box with 50% of the maximum height).
```

The result will be like in *Figure 24.8:*

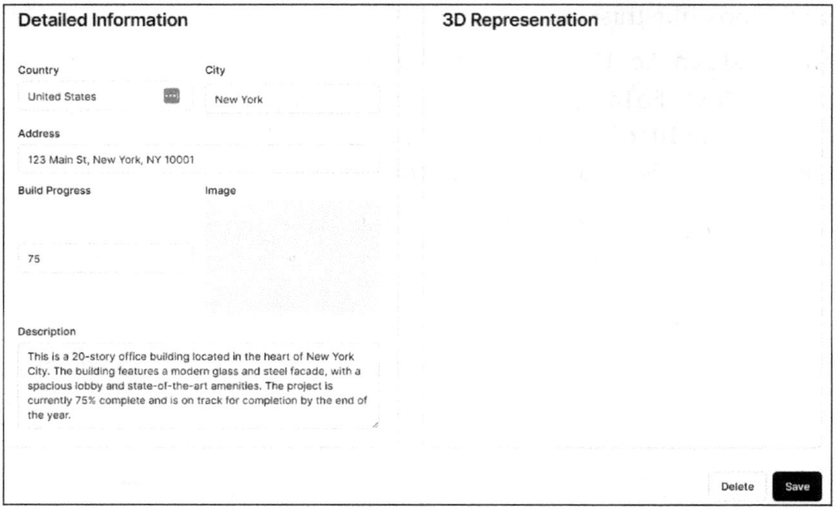

Figure 24.8: Building edit page

Next steps

Now, we have a structured UI to split into components that we can put into the Storybook. From the screens that we have created, we can create these components for the Storybook:

- Header with menu and logo
- Search bar with add building button (by design, adding the building will open the same page as edit, but with empty fields)
- Building Card
- Card list
- Add/edit form that has two parts:
  - Form on the left side
  - 3D model (for simplicity, let us take a box here, or you can play with a real 3d model)

We now have a complete plan and requirements to create our first application that combines the power of Next.js and Three.js. Please proceed with your last exercise. However, if you need help, you can always look at the ready solution in our repository.

Conclusion

Thank you for getting into this part of the book. You now have enough motivation to work with Three.js and especially React Three Fiber in pair with Next.js for scene creation and to bring 3D knowledge into your next startup or ERP.

The world around you needs and is waiting for your great ideas.

Index

www.ingramcontent.com/pod-product-compliance
Lightning Source LLC
Chambersburg PA
CBHW061740210326
41599CB00034B/6738